VALLEY OF THE SHADOW

OSPREY
PUBLISHING

VALLEY OF THE SHADOW

SHADOW

THE SIEGE OF DIEN BIEN PHU

by Kevin Boylan & Luc Olivier

OSPREY PUBLISHING
Bloomsbury Publishing Plc
PO Box 883, Oxford, OX1 9PL, UK
1385 Broadway, 5th Floor, New York, NY 10018, USA
E-mail: info@ospreypublishing.com
www.ospreypublishing.com

OSPREY is a trademark of Osprey Publishing Ltd

First published in Great Britain in 2018

This paperback edition was first published in Great Britain in 2019 by Osprey Publishing.

A catalog record for this book is available from the British Library.

ISBN: HB 9781472824370; PB 9781472824417; eBook 9781472824387; ePDF 9781472824394; XML 9781472824400

19 20 21 22 23   10 9 8 7 6 5 4 3 2 1

Maps by Bounford.com
Index by Zoe Ross
Originated by PDQ Digital Media Solutions, Bungay, UK
Printed and bound in Great Britain by CPI (Group) UK Ltd, Croydon CR0 4YY

Front cover main: Paratroopers of the Foreign Legion landing near Điện Biên Phủ. (ullstein bild via Getty Images)
Top left: Paratroopers make their descent on Novermber 20, 1953. (Photo by: SeM/UIG via Getty Images)

Osprey Publishing supports the Woodland Trust, the UK's leading woodland conservation charity.

To find out more about our authors and books visit **www.ospreypublishing.com**. Here you will find extracts, author interviews, details of forthcoming events and the option to sign up for our newsletter.

The following will help in converting measurements:	
1 kilometer = 0.62 miles	1 metric ton = 1.1 US
1 meter = 3.28 feet	("short") tons
1 centimeter = 0.39 inches	1 kilogram = 2.2 pounds

CONTENTS

ACKNOWLEDGMENTS

This book is dedicated to Lieutenant Colonel Julien Olivier, a French officer of the Foreign Legion who awoke in his son a passionate interest in the siege of Điện Biên Phủ. It's also dedicated to Merle Pribbenow, who translated hundreds of pages of Vietnamese-language publications and online documents, including many that he located himself. Merle's contributions, for which he refused any payment, have immeasurably improved the accuracy and value of this book. We cannot thank him enough.

We also want to express our gratitude to all of the veterans who shared their memories with us. At the top of the list is Michel Chanteux (II/1RCP), secretary of the Điện Biên Phủ veterans' association, who was always ready to help with names and details. General André Mengelle (1RCC) also deserves special thanks for permitting us to reproduce several excellent maps from his book *Diên-Biên-Phu: Des chars et des hommes*. Other veterans who met with Luc Olivier in person or communicated with him by phone are listed below in alphabetic order without ranks.

Jacques Allaire (6BPC), Gaston Amourette (BT2), Jean Bellocq (BT2), Marc Bournazel (III/10RAC), André Boyer (8BPC), Antoine Cerlini (I/13DBLE), Pierre Coquil (II/1RTA), Maurice Courdesses (BT3), Yves Courtille (I/13DBLE), Rémi Dalle (BT3), Jacques Daussy (BT2), Daniel Delalonde (BT2), Roger Delavaux (CTB), Georges de Morbvine (I/13 DBLE), Alain Ducourneau (III/10RAC), Max Durand (BT2), Guy Espèche (1BPC), Pierre Flamen (6BPC), Bernard Forest (III/10RAC), Jean Franchet (BT2), Hans Gawron (1BEP), Jaromir Horniak (I/13DBLE), Jacques Lamarques (1CEPML), Pierre Latanne (5BPVN), Raymond Legoubé (BT3), Yves Lepeltier

(PC Air), Jean Luciani (1BEP), Guy Lunet de la Malène (BT2), Raymond Lutrand (BT2), Pierre Maillet (1BEP), Alfred Martinais (5BPVN), André Mayer (5BPVN), Roger Moro (5BPVN), Guy Ménage (6BPC), Ferdinand Ney (1RCC), Louis Pagès (BT2), Marcel Paygnard (CTB), Robert Peyrol (BT2), Lucien Piers (6BPC), Claude Piquet (I4RTM), Henri Ploskonka (6BPC), Jean-Louis Rondy (1BEP), Michel Savary (BT2), William Schilardi (8BPC), Hermann Schliebach (I/13DBLE), Giacomo Signorini (I/13DBLE), Henri Simon (BT2), Jean Singland (1CEPML), Michel Sleurs (BT2), Georges Suaudeau (5BPVN), Albert Tepass (1BEP), Gérard Thieulin (BT2), Gabriel Touboul (BT2), Aimé Trocmé (8BPC), Roger Ulpat (I/13DBLE), Josef Unterlechner (I/13DBLE), François de Vaugiraud (I/4RTM), and Sauveur Verdaguer (BT3).

We also owe a debt of gratitude to other scholars who have studied the siege of Điện Biên Phủ and generously shared the results of their research with us: Bruno Berteau, the late Roger Bruge (whose research collection at Vincennes proved invaluable), Ivan Cadeau, Laure Cournil, Marie-Daniel Demélas, Marc Isabelle, Pierre Journoud, Guy Leonetti, Philippe de Maleissye, Lars Metzger, Billy Penfold, Sébastien Prost, Hugues Tertrais, and Frédéric Teyzier.

LIST OF ILLUSTRATIONS

Aerial images

Photographs

1. General Võ Nguyên Giáp, commander of the Vietnamese People's Army. (US Army Center of Military History)
2. GONO commander General Jean Gilles, Indochina supreme commander General Henri Navarre, and FTNV commander General René Cogny. (ullstein bild/ullstein bild via Getty)
3. General Giáp and his staff at Điện Biên Phủ Front headquarters. (Collection Jean-Claude LABBE/Gamma-Rapho via Getty)
4. Camouflaged Russian GAZ-51 "Moltava" trucks in VPA service fording a stream. (Collection Jean-Claude LABBE/Gamma-Rapho via Getty Images)

5. *Dân công* pushing a heavily loaded cargo bicycle. (Collection Jean-Claude LABBE/Gamma-Rapho via Getty)

6. VPA troops hauling a 105mm howitzer into position. (Collection Jean-Claude LABBE/Gamma-Rapho via Getty)

7. A VPA flak battery in action. (Collection Jean-Claude LABBE/Gamma-Rapho via Getty Images)

8. Colonel Christian de Castries in his command bunker. (US Information Service)

9. Indochinese paratroops. (US Information Service)

10. M-24 "Chaffee" tank at Điện Biên Phủ. (US Army Center of Military History)

11. M-55 "Quad-50" antiaircraft mount armed with four M-2 heavy barrel .50-caliber (12.7mm) machine guns. (Kevin Boylan)

12. SB2C "Helldiver" dive bombers of Aéronavale Squadron 3F "Ganga." (RDA/Getty)

13. Armée de l'Air B-26 dropping bombs over Điện Biên Phủ. (Bettmann/Getty)

14. Paratroops of 6 BPC jump into the valley on November 20, 1953. (SeM/UIG via Getty)

15. F4U "Corsair" fighter-bomber. The model used at Điện Biên Phủ was the slightly different AU-1, which was optimized for the low-altitude, ground attack role. (Kevin Boylan)

16. Sikorsky H-19 helicopter flying over paratroops at Điện Biên Phủ. (Keystone-France/Gamma-Rapho via Getty)

17. French troops atop one of the Five Hills strongpoints. (Bettmann/Getty)

18. Major Marcel Bigeard, commander of the 6th Colonial Parachute Battalion. (US Information Service)

19. The "Parachute Mafia" at GAP 2 headquarters (left to right): Botella, Bigeard, Tourret, Langlais and Seguin-Pazzis. (Keystone/Hulton Archive/Getty)

20. French troops in action during a sortie on March 27. (US Information Service)

21. VPA flag flying over GONO headquarters. (Apic/Getty)

LIST OF MAPS

LIST OF TABLES

Further tables can be found in the Appendices.

INTRODUCTION

This book is not intended to be a comprehensive study of the siege of Điện Biên Phủ. Other historians have written excellent books that explore every facet of this seminal event in world history, including its significance as a milestone in decolonialization, a turning point in the Cold War, a triumph for Maoist Revolutionary Warfare theory, and a watershed in US foreign policy. But the siege was, first and foremost, a military contest fought on the ground in the valley of Điện Biên Phủ, and an accurate and comprehensive account of that struggle is the indispensable foundation upon which analyses of its larger significance must be built. But although the siege took place over 60 years ago, no such account has yet seen print. This is due in part to historians' commendable desire to explore every facet of the Điện Biên Phủ story, which means that the details of specific engagements are necessarily given short shrift even by authors who present a day-by-day narrative of events.

But for many decades, writing a balanced and comprehensive account of the siege was impossible, since the besiegers generally remained a faceless horde. The books about Điện Biên Phủ published in Vietnam provided little operational or tactical detail, and were overburdened with Marxist cant and propaganda. Indeed, even today, Vietnamese historians must adhere to a "correct line" that stresses the infallibility of the Communist Party's and the Vietnamese People's Army's (VPA's) leadership, the unvarying courage of its troops, and the enthusiastic aid rendered by the hundreds of thousands of civilian laborers who supported them. Yet some Western historians are also wont to mythologize Điện Biên Phủ and depict it as a heroic epic akin to Thermopylae or the Alamo. They tend to highlight the bravery and skill displayed by French troops and commanders, while downplaying their errors and exaggerating the odds they faced. Some also try to shift blame for the debacle onto the shoulders of the non-European troops that provided most of the "French" garrison's manpower.

Many fundamental questions about the siege therefore still remain unanswered. Even something seemingly as straightforward as the battlefield's geography remains obscure, because its topography and the layout and evolution of the French fortifications are poorly understood. And since the two sides used different codenames for individual fortified positions, some of the earliest Western historians of the siege misread what little information could be found in contemporaneous Vietnamese publications about specific engagements. Their errors have been replicated in almost every subsequent book on the topic published in the West. The paucity of Vietnamese data, and French veterans' tendency to exaggerate the odds that confronted them, have also led many Western historians to greatly overestimate the size of the VPA's siege train and supply dumps. The results can be highly misleading. It would be as if an account of the battle of Gettysburg failed to identify Devil's Den as a hill, reported that Pickett's Charge targeted Little Round Top instead of Cemetery Ridge, and claimed that Lee had three times as much artillery as Meade (with ammunition in proportion)!

Other unanswered questions abound. Was defeat inevitable for the French, or could they have made other choices that might have led to victory? Has hagiography prevented us from accurately assessing the quality of both sides' leadership during the siege? Why did some strongpoints hold out against long odds while others quickly succumbed? Why did some French counterattacks fail while others succeeded? Were the garrison's non-European troops really just a liability? How important were civilian porters to the VPA's logistical system? What were its plans for each phase of the siege? Did it win simply by using superior numbers and firepower to swamp the defenders?

This book aims to answer these and other unresolved questions about Điện Biên Phủ by presenting the first account of the siege that accurately depicts both sides' plans and combat operations. It does so by drawing upon novel discoveries in French archives, recent interviews with veterans, and a wealth of new Vietnamese publications and online sources that have become available since the siege's fiftieth anniversary in 2004. We hope that this book will shed light on many aspects of the story that were previously obscure or completely unknown, and allow readers to glimpse the truth behind many of the myths that have been propagated over the decades.

CHAPTER 1

THE ROAD TO ĐIỆN BIÊN PHỦ

Điện Biên Phủ is a remote valley hidden amidst the jagged mountains of northwestern Vietnam which, according to the creation myth of the local Tai mountain peoples, was the legendary land of Muang Thèn ("Heaven"), where the progenitors of humanity descended from heaven and were taught the arts of civilization by Khoun Borôm, son of the king of the gods. The decisive battle of the First Indochina War (1946–54) was fought in this Eden. After a 56-day siege by 50,000 Vietnamese People's Army (VPA) troops, the entire French-led garrison of 15,000 surrendered by May 8, 1954. This defeat toppled the French government, forcing its successor to seek a negotiated end to the conflict at a conference in Geneva, which took up the issue of Indochina on the same day that the last French troops laid down their arms. The Geneva Accords signed on July 21, 1954 placed the northern half of Vietnam under the control of the Communist Democratic Republic of Vietnam (DRVN), while the State of Vietnam government created by France in 1949 governed the southern half. This awkward compromise planted the seeds of a second Indochina War, because 1956 elections that were supposed to establish a single government for the entire nation never took place. One can therefore trace a direct chain of causality linking the French defeat at Điện Biên Phủ to the United States' own disastrous adventure in Vietnam.

Twilight of empire

The origins of the First Indochina War, in turn, can be traced to France's 1940 defeat by Nazi Germany. Denied support from the conquered homeland, the French colonies in Southeast Asia were invaded by Imperial Japan in September 1940. After a brief resistance, the colonial government – which remained loyal to the collaborationist Vichy regime – agreed to allow the Japanese to establish military bases in Vietnam. Over time, the number of Japanese troops and bases expanded, and during the latter half of 1941 all of Vietnam effectively came under Japanese military occupation – though the French colonial administration and army remained in place. This uneasy *modus vivendi* survived until 1945, when the French, realizing that Japan was doomed, conspired to switch sides and throw in their lot with the Allies. The Japanese preempted them by launching a *coup d'état* in March 1945 that overthrew French rule and interned the colonial army. A political vacuum thus emerged when Japan announced its intention to surrender in August 1945. This was filled by the Communist-dominated Việt Nam Độc Lập Đồng Minh Hội (Vietnam Independence League – better known as the "Việt Minh"), which seized power on August 15 while the Japanese stood aside and the French languished in internment camps. On September 2, Việt Minh leader Hồ Chí Minh, who had been agitating for independence since 1919, established the DRVN and launched a bloody purge of non-Communist politicians to ensure that no domestic challenge to his new regime could emerge.

But the French Far Eastern Expeditionary Corps (Corps Expéditionnaire Français en Extrême-Orient – or CEFEO) was already headed to Indochina to restore colonial rule. Fearing the consequences of open warfare, Hồ permitted French troops back into the country and agreed to negotiate Vietnam's autonomy within the French empire. Yet the negotiations stalled on the question of how much power the French would surrender and foundered entirely after the High Commissioner for Indochina, Admiral Georges Thierry d'Argenlieu, established an "Autonomous Republic of Cochin-China" in direct violation of an earlier agreement that had confirmed the unity of Vietnam.[1] Cochin-China, which roughly corresponded to the Mekong River Delta in southern Vietnam, was one of the three colonies into which the French had divided the country. The other two were Tonkin, centered on the Red River Delta in the north, and Annam, which stretched in between. For the Vietnamese, Bắc Bộ (Tonkin), Trung Bộ (Annam), and Nam Bộ (Cochin-China) were merely different regions within a single nation. Tonkin would be the primary theater of operations throughout the war that was now inevitable.

Fighting broke out at the port of Haiphong (in the northeast) in November 1946 and swiftly spread throughout Vietnam. Although the CEFEO possessed superior firepower, training, and strategic mobility, it lacked sufficient troops to occupy the entire country and was stymied by the VPA's guerrilla tactics. The conflict was therefore stalemated until 1949, when the victory of Mao Zedong's Communists in the Chinese Civil War revolutionized the strategic situation. Thanks to weapons and training provided by Mao's new regime, the VPA built an impressive force of regular troops in the wild, mountainous Việt Bắc region just south of the Chinese border. In 1950, these went on the offensive and wiped out 6,000 French troops who were guarding isolated posts along the border.[2] Yet the VPA suffered a series of stinging defeats in early 1951 when it tried to conquer the Red River Delta, which contained Vietnam's capital, Hanoi, and produced most of Tonkin's rice. The firepower of French tanks, artillery, aircraft, and warships (which could navigate many of the Delta's waterways) proved devastating in the wide-open plains.

Thanks to these victories and massive support from the United States, the CEFEO managed to regain its equilibrium. The US government had initially stood aloof from the Indochina War, which it saw as a colonial conflict in which no vital American interests were at stake. That changed after China began supporting the VPA, and by the spring of 1950 the US had come to view Indochina as a vital theater in the Cold War. It became even more important after the Cold War turned "hot" in Korea that June, and China intervened massively in the new war five months later. Now Indochina was seen as a second front where the "Free World" was battling Red Chinese aggression. American weapons and money poured into the region, and by 1954, US taxpayers were shouldering three-quarters of the war's cost.[3] But although American aid staved off defeat, it could not alter the political realities that made it all but impossible for the French to win the war. For Hồ Chí Minh's indigenous DRVN regime unsurprisingly garnered far more support from the Vietnamese people than did the State of Vietnam government – which was unmistakably a mere tool of French imperialism.

The CEFEO's commander, General Jean de Lattre de Tassigny, was determined to guard the vital Red River Delta against another offensive by the VPA or the Chinese – who might intervene directly in Vietnam as they had already done in Korea. He therefore began constructing a fortified line around the Delta's entire periphery. The chain of concrete-and-steel bunkers that sprang up at 1km intervals – and inevitably became known as the "De Lattre

INDOCHINA, JULY 1954

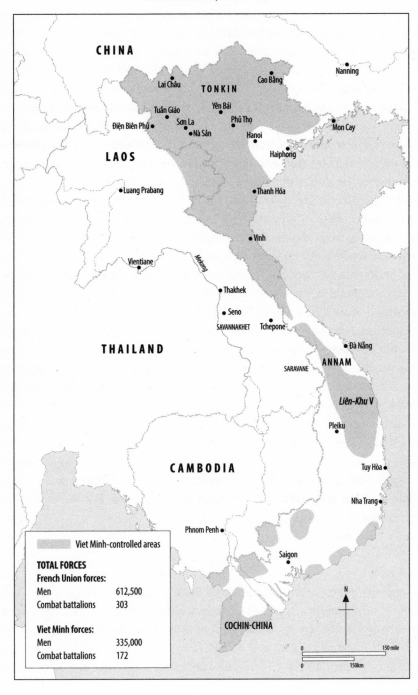

CHINA

Lai Châu
TONKIN
Cao Bằng
Nanning

Tuấn Giáo
Yên Bái
Sơn La
Phủ Thọ
Điện Biên Phủ
Nà Sản
Mon Cay
Hanoi

LAOS

Haiphong

Luang Prabang
Thanh Hóa

Vinh

Vientiane
Mekong

Thakhek

Seno
SAVANNAKHET
Tchepone

THAILAND
Đà Nẵng
ANNAM
SARAVANE

Liên-Khu V

Pleiku

CAMBODIA
Tuy Hòa

Nha Trang

Phnom Penh
Saigon

N

COCHIN-CHINA

Viet Minh-controlled areas

TOTAL FORCES
French Union forces:
Men   612,500
Combat battalions   303

Viet Minh forces:
Men   335,000
Combat battalions   172

0   150 mile
0   150km

Line" – strengthened defense against conventional attack, but proved incapable of preventing infiltration. Supported by regular units that slipped through the fortifications, VPA guerrillas gradually "hollowed out" the Delta from within. By 1953, the French controlled less than a third of the Delta's villages, and regiments of the VPA's 320th Infantry Division were operating inside the De Lattre Line. But as long as the French continued to hold Hanoi and Haiphong, and patrol the principal roads and waterways, the Delta split the VPA forces in Tonkin – and kept them perpetually short of rice.[4] General Võ Nguyên Giáp, a former history teacher who had become the VPA's supreme commander, always dreamed of breaking the French grip on the lowlands.

But having learned just how hard this would be to accomplish, in 1952 Giáp shifted his focus to the jagged mountains of northwest Tonkin, where French tanks, artillery, and aircraft were much less effective. The French had dominated the region for years thanks to the support of the ethnic Tai hill people who comprised the bulk of its population. The Tai country was quickly overrun by the VPA in October–November 1952 except for two *bases aéro-terrestres* ("air-land bases" that could be supplied and reinforced only by air), which the French established at Lai Châu and Nà Sản. The latter base, which blocked a key road toward Laos, was the more important of the two and was defended by 11 hastily flown-in battalions. Giáp took the bait and tried to overrun Nà Sản with six regiments of the VPA's 308th, 312th, and 316th Infantry Divisions. Although their fortifications were incomplete, the French handily repulsed a series of attacks between November 23 and December 2, 1952, and won a major defensive victory. Giáp had over 3,000 killed and wounded, while French casualties were only about 500.[5] Yet this French success did not prevent the VPA from invading northern Laos in April 1953, penetrating to the outskirts of its royal capital, Luang Prabang, and destroying the equivalent of five CEFEO and Laotian battalions. Most of the invaders withdrew when the rainy season began in May.[6]

The Navarre Plan

Though the victory at Nà Sản convinced French commanders that a large *base aéro-terrestre* could resist any attack Giáp might throw at it, by 1953 the French government had given up hope of winning the war outright. General Henri Eugène Navarre, appointed as the CEFEO's seventh commander in May, was therefore instructed merely to secure favorable conditions for achieving a negotiated settlement. But since the United States would not continue its massive support unless the French remained committed to achieving victory, Navarre had to act as if that was his ultimate objective. Thus, while the so-called Navarre Plan (in fact, largely developed by the US Military Assistance Advisory Group – or MAAG) ostensibly aimed to break VPA military resistance in 1955, in fact it merely aimed to improve France's bargaining position. Navarre planned to do so by standing on the defensive in the northern half of Vietnam during the 1953–54 campaign, while using his reserves to go on the offensive in the south and eliminate guerillas operating behind French lines. To free up CEFEO battalions for offensive employment, the State of Vietnam's army would be vastly expanded. American money and equipment would allow 19 new light infantry battalions (Tiểu-đoàn Khinh-quân – or TDKQs) to be formed in 1954, and another 35 during the following fiscal year.[7]

As a first step toward implementing his plan, Navarre ordered the evacuation of Nà Sản. A massive airlift began pulling out the garrison on August 8, and the exodus was completed five days later without any interference from the enemy. The VPA's 88th Infantry Regiment, which had been masking the base, was distracted by French-allied Tai guerrillas who captured its rear base at Sơn La on the night of August 3–4. Other guerrillas ambushing roads delayed the approach of the 312th Division.[8] Giáp may also have been fooled by French radio deception, which hinted that the planes landing at Nà Sản were bringing in reinforcements. Navarre then conducted a series of major anti-guerrilla operations within and raids beyond the perimeter of the Delta in August–October 1953.[9] Having shored up its creaking defenses, his next objective was to eradicate Interzone (Liên-Khu) V, an enemy bastion 800km to the south that embraced four provinces with a total population of 3,000,000. It was to be conquered and "pacified" by Operation *Atlante*, a massive offensive involving 53 battalions (including many new TDKQs) that was to last from January to July 1954.[10]

Giáp was uncertain what to do, since his plan for the 1953–54 dry season had been disrupted by the evacuation of Nà Sản – its intended primary target. Secondary offensives had been planned against Lai Châu and Móng Cái (a coastal town that was the last French outpost on the Chinese border),[11] but neither operation would require more than a fraction of the VPA regulars in Tonkin. Chinese historian Qiang Zhai claims that the Chinese Military Advisory Group (CMAG) had to convince Giáp not to launch another fruitless attack on the Delta and instead adhere to existing plans to take Lai Châu, launch another invasion of Laos, and then turn south to threaten Cambodia and southern Vietnam.[12] Giáp insists that there was no disagreement with the Chinese: "[CMAG commander] Wei Quoquing and I were unanimous that we should open an offensive at battlefields that were important and where the enemy was weak or relatively weak, but which the enemy could not abandon and therefore force the French to disperse their forces. We were also of one mind that we should move toward Lai Châu and toward Central and Southern Laos."[13]

Giáp ordered the 148th Independent Infantry Regiment and the 316th Infantry Division to capture Lai Châu and press on into northern Laos, while elements of the 304th and 325th divisions invaded central and southern Laos. Meanwhile, the two regular regiments in Liên-Khu V would conquer the Central Highlands in Annam. These widely separated offensives would force Navarre to disperse his reserves and possibly enable Giáp to win a major victory somewhere in Tonkin using his own reserves (the 351st "Heavy" Division, and the 304th (-), 308th, and 312th Infantry Divisions). The objective was to "Employ regular troops and appropriate procedures and actions to annihilate the enemy's vital force; perhaps stage a major action in the Delta as training for our soldiers [in large conventional battles]."[14] Giáp had not abandoned the notion of attacking the Delta because the logistical difficulties of operating so far from the Chinese border made it impossible to commit his reserves in either Laos or Annam. The four reserve divisions were like coins "burning a hole" in his pocket. They had to be used someplace – but where?

The Deuxième Bureau (French military intelligence) kept Navarre informed about the enemy's strategic deliberations, and he became worried about the safety of Laos. Although the country had been granted independence in October 1953, it remained a member of the French Union (a supra-national body akin to the British Commonwealth) and Navarre felt obliged to defend it. Even if this connection had not existed, the tiny Lao Army was clearly incapable of defending its national territory – which would open a "back door" to Cambodia and southern Vietnam if it fell into enemy hands. Navarre also knew that Lai Châu was indefensible because the town and its vital airstrip were squeezed into a valley less than 1km wide that was dominated on all sides by towering mountains.[15] Yet it was also the capital of the French-allied Tai Federation, which had supplied thousands of recruits for regular and auxiliary units, and guerrilla bands organized by the French Combined Intervention Groups (Groupes Mixte d'Intervention – or GMI). Like most of the minority hill peoples (*montagnards*), they were antipathetic toward the lowland Vietnamese and generally well disposed toward

22

the French. If Navarre evacuated Lai Châu and abandoned the Tai, he would demoralize other allied minorities, undermine the GMI's thriving guerrilla campaign in northwest Tonkin, and hand the region's valuable opium crop over to the enemy.

Castor and *Pollux*

All these considerations drew Navarre's attention to Điện Biên Phủ, a valley 113km south of Lai Châu that measured 18km long by 8km wide. Apart from those at Lai Châu and Nà Sản, it contained the only "Dakotable" airfield in northwest Tonkin that could handle C-47 "Dakota" transports and other large, multi-engine aircraft. The valley was also the largest rice-producing district in the highlands, sat astride the route to Luang Prabang, and was inhabited by a generally friendly population. Thus, in November 1954, Navarre planned a pair of operations named *Castor* and *Pollux* after the Gemini twins of Greek mythology. Operation *Castor* would capture Điện Biên Phủ by parachute assault and establish a new *base aéro-terrestre* in the valley. Operation *Pollux* would evacuate Lai Châu, with the garrison's regular troops being airlifted out while Tai auxiliary units were to march overland to Điện Biên Phủ – where the Tai Federation's capital would also be relocated.

Navarre expected that the Điện Biên Phủ *base aéro-terrestre* would parry another invasion of upper Laos and act as an offensive launching pad from which mobile columns would radiate throughout northwest Tonkin. But General René Cogny, commander of Forces Terrestres du Nord Vietnam, or FTNV (Land Forces North Vietnam) feared that sending battalions to the northwest would dangerously weaken the Red River Delta's defenses. He envisaged Điện Biên Phủ merely as a lightly garrisoned "mooring point" for the GMI guerrillas and as a means of preserving French political influence in the Tai country. His orders to Operation *Castor*'s commander, General Jean Gilles, therefore precluded the construction of a chain of strongpoints around the airfield. The tension between Navarre's and Cogny's different conceptions of the Điện Biên Phủ base's nature and purpose would cause considerable trouble for its garrison.[16]

Operation *Castor* began on the morning of November 20, when the 6ème Bataillon de Parachutistes Coloniaux – or 6 BPC (6th Colonial Parachute Battalion) – and the 2ème Bataillon du 1er Régiment de Chasseurs Parachutistes – or II/1 RCP (2nd Battalion, 1st Parachute Light Infantry Regiment) – dropped into the valley from 65 Dakotas. 6 BPC jumped onto Drop Zone (DZ) Natasha (which paralleled the runway on the west), and practically landed on top of a company of the VPA 148th Separate Infantry Regiment's 910th Battalion, which was rehearsing countermeasures against an airborne assault! The French prevailed after a hard, close-quarters battle, but even the arrival of 1 BPC and a 75mm recoilless rifle battery of the 35ème Régiment d'Artillerie Parachutiste – or 35 RALP (35th Parachute Artillery Regiment) – that afternoon could not prevent the surviving VPA troops from making their escape. Over the next two days, these three battalions of Groupement Aéroporté 1 – or GAP 1 (Airborne Battlegroup 1) – were joined by another trio belonging to GAP 2. The first Dakotas landed on the roughly repaired main runway on November 25 carrying a pair of 105mm howitzers that were on loan to 35 RALP, and conventional infantry battalions soon began flying in to replace most of the paratroops.[17]

French occupation of Điện Biên Phủ resolved Giáp's quandary about where to commit his reserves, since Cogny publicly announced, "This is not a raid. We've taken the place and we shall stay there."[18] Here was a place where Giáp could hope to destroy a significant fraction of the CEFEO's total strength without having to fight on the Delta's exposed plains. He immediately ordered the 316th Division to accelerate its attack on Lai Châu and then press on to Điện Biên Phủ. A battalion of the 98th Regiment was to be left behind temporarily to secure the supply base at Tuần Giáo against a potential French parachute assault. The 308th Division started marching northwest in the first days of December, and by the end of the month the 312th and 351st Divisions were also on their way to the valley.[19] The 304th Division (less the 66th Regiment operating in Laos) remained behind to guard against a possible CEFEO offensive from the Delta. However, Giáp's greatest worry was that Navarre would order the Điện Biên Phủ garrison to withdraw into Laos after it was joined by the units from Lai Châu.[20]

Operation *Pollux* had begun on December 7, and, within three days, all the regular units and Lieutenant-Colonel André Trancart's Zone Opérationnel Nord-Ouest – or ZONO (Operational Zone Northwest) headquarters had been safely extracted by 183 Dakota sorties.[21] However, the overland withdrawal of the Tai irregulars down the Pavie Track was a disaster. Seven Tai Compagnies de Supplétifs Militaires – or CSMs (auxiliary companies) – left Lai Châu on November 17 to march on Điện Biên Phủ in support of Operation *Castor*. Three of them (CSMs 413, 414, and 415) formed a detachment under Adjutant Clement Cante that separated from the main column and reached the valley intact on November 23 despite having to fight through several ambushes. But of another two-dozen companies that followed in their wake, only a few traumatized survivors staggered into Điện Biên Phủ.[22] Many Tai became demoralized when they realized that the French were abandoning their native villages and deserted en masse. But most were killed or captured by hotly pursuing troops of the 316th Division and 148th Regiment. Excluding Cante's detachment, more than 2,000 Tai and 32 French cadres set out from Lai Châu. Just 278 auxiliaries (22 of them wounded) and ten Europeans (including two wounded) made it to Điện Biên Phủ by December 22 – and only a handful more trickled in over the coming weeks.[23]

Điện Biên Phủ's garrison was unable to help the beleaguered Tai, although the final act of their destruction was played out at the village of Mường Pồn just 18km from the valley. The survivors of many different CSMs were encircled there by the 316th Division's 174th Infantry Regiment. GAP 2 tried to rescue them with three parachute battalions and a pair of 105mm batteries, but was blocked by the VPA 888th and 215th Infantry Battalions, and did not reach Mường Pồn until after the Tai were overrun on December 13. The enemy then turned on GAP 2, which was lucky to make it back to Điện Biên Phủ after several more days of hard fighting.[24] Navarre had expected that troops "radiating" out from the base would be able to maneuver freely in the Tai country, but less than four weeks after Operation *Castor* began, the garrison was already finding it very risky to venture beyond the valley. By late December, the question of whether Điện Biên Phủ still had value as an offensive base was becoming moot, since the rapid approach of Giáp's main *corps de bataille* suggested that it would instead be an embattled fortress.

"The hardest decision of my entire life"

The VPA had developed two methods of attacking fortified bases that can be likened to the antagonists in Aesop's fable about the tortoise and the hare. The risky "Fast Strike–Fast Victory" technique involved launching a massive surprise assault aimed like a dagger thrust at a base's headquarters. Meanwhile, secondary attacks on other parts of the perimeter would confuse and demoralize defending troops who were being threatened from the front and rear simultaneously. If the desired psychological effect was achieved, a base could be overrun quickly with relatively few casualties. The "Steady Attack–Steady

Advance" technique, on the other hand, aimed to destroy a base's garrison methodically, one piece at a time. Although victory was far more certain if these "slow but steady wins the race" tactics were employed, they required a prolonged battle with much higher logistical requirements – and casualties.[25]

Operation *Pollux*'s outcome tempted the VPA's General Staff to use Fast Strike–Fast Victory tactics at Điện Biên Phủ. In late November, it had expected that the 316th Division would take Lai Châu near the end of January, and then need 20 days to reorganize and redeploy. The Steady Attack–Steady Advance assault on Điện Biên Phủ would, accordingly, begin in late February, and was expected to take 45 days to complete. But Lai Châu fell without a fight on December 12, and the 316th Division suffered only modest casualties mopping up the fleeing Tai auxiliaries. This made it possible to attack Điện Biên Phủ much sooner and thereby ensure that the assault ended before the onset of the rainy season in April. But it would also necessitate switching to the Fast Strike–Fast Victory technique, as there would be insufficient time to prepare for a protracted siege. But given the difficulty of sustaining four divisions so far from the VPA's supply bases, a short battle seemed preferable from the logistical standpoint. Striking swiftly would also prevent the French from improving their fortifications, flying in additional troops, or pulling another surprise evacuation like that at Nà Sản.[26]

When Giáp arrived at the Điện Biên Phủ Front's headquarters in mid-January, he learned that, in his absence, the senior officers who had preceded him had agreed that the Fast Strike–Fast Victory technique should be employed. "If we don't fight soon, each one said, the enemy would add forces and consolidate them. Then the key enemy bases would be too strong, the battle would last too long, and maintaining the supply route by road and boat from such a distant rear guard [i.e., base] would be too difficult."[27] The CMAG staff agreed with them, prompting an astounded Giáp to exclaim, "We told Uncle Ho and the Central Committee of the Party that the battle would last 45 days. But, our colleagues planned to settle everything in three nights and two days!"[28] Unwilling at that point to challenge the consensus, he issued orders for an offensive that was to begin on January 20. The elite 308th Division would make the main assault against the base's headquarters area (tucked behind the fortifications known to the French as "Claudine") from the south and west. The attached 888th Battalion of the 176th Infantry Regiment and the 148th Regiment's 910th Battalion were to deal with the isolated southern position "Isabelle." The 312th Division would take "Anne Marie," "Gabrielle," and

"Françoise," and then overrun the main airfield. The 316th Division would seize hill "Eliane-2" and join in the attack on the headquarters area from the east. When that task was completed, it would capture "Eliane-1" and corral the defenders of "Dominique" and "Béatrice."[29] All this was to be accomplished within a mere 72 hours![30]

The breakneck pace of preparations for the assault on Điện Biên Phủ, and the absurdly brief time allotted to complete the operation, suggest that the VPA was determined to finish off the base before a four-power conference (USA, USSR, Britain, and France) opened in Berlin on January 25. This meeting resulted from a brief thaw in the Cold War that followed the death of Soviet premier Josef Stalin in 1953. It was supposed to seek consensus on a broad range of issues, including the status of Germany, Austria, and Korea (where the "hot" war of 1950–53 had given way to an uneasy truce), and the ongoing war in Indochina.[31]

If the assault on Điện Biên Phủ had gone ahead as planned, the French would have won a great victory. The *base aéro-terrestre* was far too large and well defended to be overrun so quickly, and at that time the VPA would have been logistically incapable of switching to a protracted siege. Indeed, its ability even to provide sufficient supplies for an assault lasting just three days is questionable, since a paltry 2,000 105mm shells had been allocated for the entire operation! This unimpressive ammunition stockpile was just one of many factors that caused Giáp to agonize about the wisdom of using the Fast Strike–Fast Victory technique. His anxiety intensified when delays in hauling the artillery into position forced the offensive's start to be pushed back to January 25. And just two days before the new attack date, some guns still were not in place, though the 304th Division's 57th Regiment, which was about to arrive after a punishing, ten-day forced march, would join in the effort. Giáp was also warned that the batteries were poorly fortified and would suffer heavy losses if they were hit by French planes and artillery.[32]

Giáp had other reasons to worry. He had aimed the 308th Division at the *base aéro-terrestre*'s western flank because there was only a single line of fortifications protecting the crucial headquarters area and airfield against attack from that direction. Giáp's intelligence staff had been ordered to keep a close eye on the area and update him daily on developments there. It was a wise precaution, since the French commander, Colonel Christian de Castries, took steps to eliminate this Achilles heel by constructing a massive barbed-wire obstacle known as the "Wavebreaker." On January 21, he reported that it was

VALLEY OF ĐIỆN BIÊN PHỦ[35]

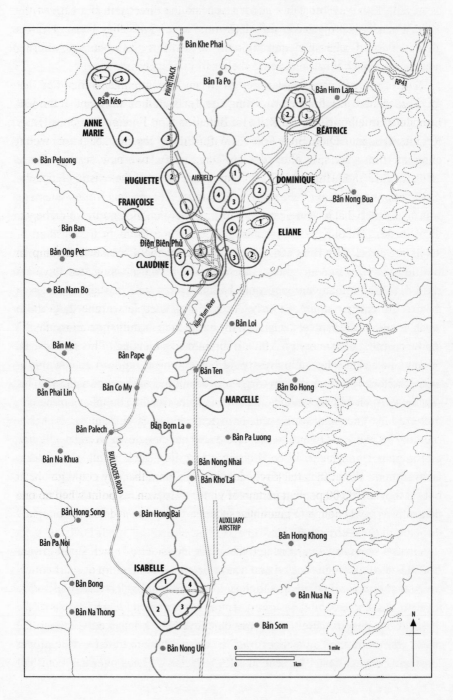

already in place covering Claudine and was being extended to protect Huguette as well.[33] The Wavebreaker's sudden appearance directly in the path of the 308th Division's projected main attack must have given Giáp pause. He was already worried because the terrain in that area was flat as a pancake, offering no cover in which his troops could shelter from French firepower.[34]

More bad news came on January 24, when VPA intelligence reported that the French had just finished airlifting the 1er Bataillon du 2ème Régiment Étranger d'Infanterie – or I/2 REI (1st Battalion, 2nd Foreign Legion Infantry Regiment) – into Điện Biên Phủ.[36] (Within days, the new battalion would eliminate the weak spot altogether by constructing two new strongpoints – "Huguette-4" and "Huguette-5" – 500 meters in front of the existing Huguette fortifications.) Then, on the afternoon of January 24, a French radio message was intercepted that gave the precise date and hour that the assault would begin. Giáp pushed H-hour back 24 hours, but had come to doubt the wisdom of attacking at all. His misgivings were shared by the Chinese leadership in Beijing, which sent several telegrams to the CMAG advising that the VPA should try "to eliminate the enemy one battalion at a time"[37] instead of attacking from all directions simultaneously. After a long, sleepless night, Giáp made what he called "the hardest decision of my entire life as a military commander"[38] on the morning of January 26. Having summoned a meeting of his senior staff, he announced that the offensive would be postponed until arrangements for using the Steady Attack–Steady Advance technique had been completed. This would take many weeks, and Đặng Kim Giang, head of the Supply Department, protested that the delay would greatly increase logistical difficulties. Lê Liêm, head of the Political Department, worried that backing down would deflate the troops' morale – which had been brought to a high pitch by his commissars. Giáp responded that the attack scheduled for 1700hrs that day could go ahead only if they were 100 percent certain of victory. He won his point when no one present was bold enough to guarantee success. This was *the* decisive command decision of the entire campaign.

On that same day, Giáp ordered the 308th Division to launch a raid toward Luang Prabang though the division was to be prepared to return at short notice. This operation was intended to confuse the French, oblige Navarre to disperse his reserves, and aid the invasion of central and southern Laos by troops of the 304th and 325th Divisions. All these objectives were achieved, although the 308th was operating "on a shoestring" because it had no time to make proper logistical preparations. The second VPA invasion of Laos overran about half the country, inflicted heavy losses on CEFEO and Lao troops, and forced Navarre to scatter his reserves. Moreover, the 325th Division reached the Mekong River and cut Indochina in two. In response, the French had to establish several new *bases aéro-terrestres* in Laos that consumed the lion's share of their air transport from late January to late February 1954, forcing Điện Biên Phủ to curtail its ammunition expenditures during a crucial period when Giáp's artillery emplacements were under construction. Over the comings months, VPA troops penetrated into northern Cambodia and linked up with troops from Liên-Khu V to extend DRVN domination over an unbroken stretch of territory extending 1,600km south from the Chinese border.[39]

CHAPTER 2

PEOPLE'S WAR – PEOPLE'S ARMY

Reverting to Steady Attack–Steady Advance tactics meant that Giáp's troops would have to conduct a protracted siege roughly 400km by road from their main supply bases in the Việt Bắc, and 670km from Cao Bằng, where three-quarters of all Chinese aid flowed into Vietnam.[1] Điện Biên Phủ was about 500km from the "Southern Delta Base" in Thanh Hóa Province, which was the VPA's principal source of rice in northern Vietnam. The roads were colonial highways built before World War II that ran along sheer mountainsides, over steep passes, and crossed dozens of waterways and gorges. Many were almost impassable because they had not been maintained for a decade or more. Yet the thinly populated highlands of northwest Tonkin could supply little food – and literally nothing else. Most of the food – and all the fuel, ammunition, and other supplies – would therefore have to be transported over the atrocious roads.

Navarre's staff therefore concluded that it would be a "utopian project" for Giáp to deploy all four of his reserve divisions at Điện Biên Phủ. They were confident that he could sustain only two there and support them with only a modest amount of artillery. His 120mm mortars and 75mm mountain guns could be disassembled for transport over rough terrain, but 105mm howitzers and 37mm antiaircraft guns could not. Even if these multi-ton behemoths were somehow dragged to the valley, French logisticians were confident that they could not be supplied with much ammunition. And if the terrible roads alone did not ensure the accuracy of these predictions, interdiction by the Armée de l'Air (French Air Force) and Aéronavale (French naval air service) surely would. Thus, when Navarre decided on December 3 to accept battle at Điện Biên Phủ, he took it for granted that Giáp would attack quickly. His staff anticipated a movement phase lasting several weeks, an approach and reconnaissance phase of six to ten days, and an attack phase lasting only several days that would end in a VPA defeat. If it had not been for Giáp's "hardest decision," events at Điện Biên Phủ would have played out almost exactly as they predicted.[2]

General mobilization

To sustain a prolonged siege, the VPA had to perform engineering and logistical prodigies. Giáp's staff had estimated the requirements for a Fast Attack–Fast Victory assault at 434 metric tons of ammunition, 7,730 tons of rice, 140 tons of salt, and 465 tons of other foodstuffs – and calculated that those for a Steady Attack–Steady Advance assault would be at least three times greater.[3] More detailed data can be found in *Điện Biên Phủ, Mốc Vàng Thời Đại [Điện Biên Phủ: Landmark of the Golden Era]*, which contains a series of tables that serve as a veritable Rosetta Stone for deciphering the VPA's order of battle and logistics. The following table, adapted from that book, details the planned stockpiles of all major supply items, as well as quantities allocated and consumed. Cases where consumption exceeded allocations probably reflect the use of shells recovered from errant French parachute drops, but these figures are not necessarily complete. For example, Vietnamese historians record that 5,000 misdropped French 105mm shells were captured, raising the total supply of that caliber to 20,000. The lower figure of 16,600 given in *Landmark of the Golden Era* could indicate that many of these shells were used by nearby artillery batteries without passing through the supply chain – and thus were not recorded by VPA logisticians. Another possibility – which is not mutually exclusive – is that not all the shells available were fired. After all, Giáp could not have known that the French defense would collapse on May 7, and was unlikely to have completely emptied his ammo dumps. It should also be noted that the figures in the "weapons" column do not include an additional six 75mm howitzers and four 120mm mortars that reinforced the siege after it was already under way.

VPA LOGISTICAL DATA FOR THE ĐIỆN BIÊN PHỦ CAMPAIGN[4]						
Supply type	Planned	Allocated	Consumed	Weapons	Shells consumed per weapon	Basic loads*
Rice (tons)	20,000	25,056	14,950			
Salt (tons)			268			
Meat (tons)		907	577			
Dried food (tons)		917	565			
Other food (tons)		469	469			
TOTAL (metric tons)		27,349	16,829	Does not include misdropped rations		
Machine gun	1,388,500	1,285,000	950,000			3
Submachine gun	885,000	907,000	840,000		280	
57mm ĐKZ	4,300	4,150	4,000	57	70	2.3
75mm ĐKZ	4,000	4,000	530	12	45	1.5
90mm bazooka	1,720	1,820	1,800	72	25	2.5
60mm mortar	22,700	21,800	23,230	179	130	4.3
81/82mm mortar	34,934	35,993	37,300	162	230	7.6
120mm mortar	4,250	4,360	3,000	16	190	6.3
75mm howitzer	3,750	3,754	4,700	18	260	8.6
105mm howitzer	15,094	15,118	16,600	24	700	14
102mm rocket	4,000	4,000	836	12	70	
37mm AA Gun	46,000	40,600	31,750	33	950	3.5
12.7mm AA machine gun	700,500	706,600	512,000	85	6,000	6
Hand grenade	96,180	96,480	86,080			
Explosive charge launcher	3,000	1,600	1,500	?		
Bangalore torpedo (meters)	6,000	5,300	4,000			
Explosives (tons)	26	27.5	25			
Pick	5,200	4,950	4,700			
Shovel	8,000	8,700	7,800			
Machete	3,000	2,920	2,900			
Lubricating oil (liters)	1,800	1,860				
Grease (kilograms)	280	280				
TOTAL (metric tons)	1,500	1,450	1,200			
TOTAL (shells 57mm+)	94,748	94,995	91,996			
TOTAL (shells 75mm+)	67,748	69,045	64,766			
Medical supplies (tons)	45	55	55			
Military gear (tons)		71	71			
Gasoline (tons)		1,783	1,783	Another 10 tons were captured		
Other items (tons)		51	51			

GRAND TOTAL **(metric tons)**		30,759	19,989	

*Ammunition is typically allocated to units in standardized "basic loads." In the VPA, a basic load was 50 rounds for a 105mm howitzer, 270 rounds for a 37mm AA gun, 1,000 rounds for a 12.7mm AA machine gun, 10 rounds for a bazooka, and 30 rounds for all other heavy weapons.

Transporting these huge tonnages was a daunting task. Since 1952, the DRVN had rehabilitated 4,500km of roads, including 2,000km for motor vehicles. Among these was the stretch of Route Coloniale 13A (RC13A) running from Yên Bái to the Black River, which had been repaired for the siege of Nà Sản. But west of that point, 230km of roads needed to be refurbished, and a series of entirely new roads had to be built to haul artillery into position around Điện Biên Phủ. In the process, innumerable bridges had to be built or reinforced. Over a hundred were required on just the 80km stretch of Route Provinciale 41 (RP41) between Điện Biên Phủ and Tuần Giáo – which had deteriorated into a track suitable only for pack animals. Secondary routes running from China by way of Lao Cai and Thanh Thủy (Hà Giang Province) also had to be improved and waterfalls on the Nậm Na River dynamited to open a water route to the Chinese border.[5]

Yet the VPA had few engineering units and none of the bulldozers, dump trucks, and other heavy equipment that a modern army would have used to execute such an ambitious construction project. It also lacked specialized logistical staffs and units (traffic control, fuel storage, material handling, etc.) to manage the supply lines after they had been upgraded. Giáp thus had to assign responsibility for segments of his supply lines to offices within the DRVN's Ministry of Defense. Each was responsible both for maintaining the roads and managing traffic in its sector, and also carrying out its normal duties. These offices all operated under the orders of the General Logistics Department's deputy director, but his area of responsibility extended back only as far as Sơn La, since for the first time ever the VPA's logistical system distinguished between front and rear.

ĐIỆN BIÊN PHỦ FRONT GENERAL LOGISTICS DEPARTMENT HEADQUARTERS[6]		
Đặng Kim Giang (also Deputy Head of General Logistics Department)		
Sơn La Logistical Sector	RP41 from Sơn La to Tuần Giáo	Đinh Đức Thiện (also Head of Transport Service, General Logistics Department)
Tuần Giáo Logistical Sector	RP41 from Tuần Giáo to Nà Tấu (Kilometer 62)	Vu Van Don (also Deputy Head of Transport Service, General Logistics Department)

Nà Tấu Logistical Sector	RP41 from Nà Tấu (Kilometer 62) to Điện Biên Phủ	Nguyễn Thanh Bình (also Head of Military Supply Department)
Transportation Route Lai Châu–Nậm Cứm	Nậm Na River from China to Lai Châu	Nguyễn Văn Nam (also Head of Military Equipment Department) Bằng Giang (also Commander of Northwest Military Zone)
Transportation Route Mường Luân–Na Sang[7]	This route was used to supply the troops besieging CR Isabelle. It ran from Sơn La to the Nậm Ma River, then along the valley to Mường Luân (about 50km east of Isabelle), and finally over a rudimentary mountain road to Na Sang (about 14km east of Isabelle).	

The campaign rear was managed by the General Logistics Department's director with assistance from other branches of government. For example, the Ministry of Roads and Public Works repaired and maintained the roads from Sơn La to Yên Bái. But this was only one facet of a General Mobilization, declared on December 6, which committed the entire resources of the DRVN regime and civilian population in regions it controlled to support the campaign. A special Council to Supply the Front was created under Deputy Premier Phạm Văn Đồng, and subordinate councils were created at the *Liên-Khu* and provincial levels.[8] The councils alone oversaw the mobilization in areas beyond the jurisdiction of the Điện Biên Phủ Front and the General Logistics Department. Under the slogan "Everything for the Front, Everything for Victory!" a quarter-million civilian laborers (*dân công*) were pressed into service.[9] Those who remained at home had to contribute large quantities of food and transport (including boats, bicycles, and animals).

The northwest provinces alone provided 31,818 *dân công*, 914 workhorses, 2,100 buffalo, 13,000 pigs, 800 tons of vegetables, and an astounding 7,311 tons of rice.[10] These "contributions" must have pushed the population to the brink of starvation, since even their seed for the next harvest was consumed! In addition, 300 tons of rice were purchased in northern Laos and 1,700 more donated by China. But 15,742 tons (63 percent) had to be carried hundreds of kilometers from the Southern Delta Base (mostly from Thanh Hóa).[11] The bulk of it was transported to Hòa Bình on RC12, and then along RC6 to Cò Nòi where it intersected with Giáp's main supply route running from Yên Bái.[12] Thanh Hóa also provided several thousand workers, who were called up for three months at the end of January; when they returned at the end of April, a "general requisition" would produce 4,000 more.[13] Other provinces throughout northern Vietnam were assigned their own quotas for *dân công*, food, and transport. This was a "People's War" with a vengeance, as the entire region became a veritable nation-in-arms.

Many of the *dân công* were teenage "Assault Youth." One of them was Đinh Xuân Bá from Nghệ An Province, who recalled in 2007 that the Assault Youth was a selectively recruited, all-volunteer force. "To join the army, all you had to do was sign up and they took you. But to join the Assault Youth, the people of your hamlet had to come forward to recommend you and to evaluate you to determine if you were worthy. Only then were you allowed to join."[14] This paid off, he says, because it was patriotism and the "romanticism of youth" that sustained him and his comrades through months of back-breaking labor with no pay, no issue of clothing, poor food, poor health (virtually everyone caught malaria), and almost no medical care. Yet even these naïve, enthusiastic young volunteers were ecstatic when they learned in early May that Điện Biên Phủ had fallen, since they had been drafted into the army 15 days earlier and were being marched up from the Việt Bắc to join the fighting, although they had virtually no military training.

Vietnamese authors like to suggest that all the *dân công* served just as enthusiastically. Giáp describes Tai women coming down from the hills and cheerfully joining in the work:

> The ranks of laborers would suddenly break out with one voice in a work chant, but then sometimes you'd hear the soprano voice of a young woman from the Northern Delta or sometimes the bass voice of a young man from Region 4 [i.e., northern Annam]. The singing and the chants were like an answer to the challenge of bombs and shells up ahead. I'd gone on many military campaigns, but I had never witnessed such a joyful atmosphere as this one.[15]

Idealized accounts of "popular enthusiasm" on the supply roads should be taken with a grain of salt. After all, the VPA had found it difficult to recruit porters from among the Tai in October–December 1952;[16] the same problem no doubt arose again in 1954. Yet even many ethnic Vietnamese hailing from provinces that strongly backed the revolution must have balked at the unprecedented sacrifices being demanded of them. And by one account, villagers on DRVN blacklists became "compulsory volunteers" since they would volunteer to serve as laborers in hopes of improving their standing with the authorities – who were certain to choose them anyway.[17]

To make the General Mobilization's sacrifices more bearable, the DRVN's National Assembly passed a "Land-to-the-Tiller" law on December 4, 1953.

The Communists had earlier forced landlords to reduce rents, but, in the interests of national unity, otherwise had not systematically attacked them. But now the entire "landed proprietor class" (including families with only modest landholdings) was to be stripped of its property so that it could be redistributed to their tenants. This was accomplished through mass "denunciation" meetings in which peasants were encouraged to denounce their landlords' alleged crimes against the people. In addition to losing their property, those targeted were subjected to lengthy public humiliation, which was often accompanied by physical abuse and sometimes summary execution by people's courts. Even landlords and relatives who had supported the revolution were denounced, and the land reform campaign caused many middle- and upper-class Vietnamese to flee to areas under French control.[18] But the legislation was popular with the land-poor peasants who provided most of the VPA's troops and *dân công*. It was publicized by a propaganda campaign that included showing a Chinese movie entitled *The White-Haired Girl*, which depicted a poor peasant girl being oppressed by a cruel landlord. Many of the viewers wept as they watched the film, and the importance of such propaganda in sustaining popular commitment should not be discounted.[19]

The labor of a titan

The *dân công* labored alongside thousands of VPA soldiers, including troops of the regular divisions. Four new road-construction engineering battalions were formed and 1,500 recruits from Instruction Center 77 were organized into a new 77th Infantry Regiment and put to work under the direction of engineering officers.[20] French aircraft tried to halt construction, but without much success. Bombing sometimes closed chokepoints for days at a time,[21] but like swarming ants, the *dân công* always repaired the damage. The Điện Biên Phủ Front's supply lines were also threatened by GMI guerrillas. These *phi* ("bandits") proved very troublesome and obliged Giáp to commit substantial forces to keep them at bay. "The enemy strengthened the *phi* troops' activities in Sơn La to sabotage our campaign's rear areas. In mid-March, our Army's General Staff had to transfer its 9th Regiment from Phu Tho to Sơn La and detach our 176th Regiment from the campaign forces and send it to Lai Châu to sweep away the *phi* troops."[22] The diversion of the 176th Infantry Regiment was a major triumph for the GMI, since Giáp would sorely miss the regiment at several key

moments in the siege, which might have ended much sooner had it remained at
Điện Biên Phủ. Giáp also had to guard against a French parachute attack on his
supply lines, and in late March, the 9th Regiment's 323rd Battalion would be
detached to Nà Sản for that purpose.[23]

ĐIỆN BIÊN PHỦ FRONT ENGINEERING ACCOMPLISHMENTS[24]	
Supply roads repaired	308km
Artillery tracks constructed	63km
Bridges built/repaired	1,700m
Soil excavated	35,000m³
Rock excavated	15,000m³
Rapids cleared	2,200m³

Giáp claims that *dân công* contributed a total of 10 million workdays during
the Điện Biên Phủ campaign – though he also says there were 300,000 of them,
whereas other sources put the total 40,000–50,000 lower. But, whatever the
precise figure, their exertions invalidated all the assumptions the French had
made about the force Giáp could deploy and sustain at Điện Biên Phủ. The
crumbling colonial highways were transformed into crude but passable dirt
roads capable of carrying heavy traffic, and remained in operation despite air
interdiction and frequent rains that swelled waterways, triggered landslides,
and clogged the routes with mud. Sufficient supplies to sustain a protracted
siege were stockpiled in and around the valley, and dozens of 105mm howitzers
and 37mm flak guns (and many lighter artillery pieces) were manhandled onto
the surrounding heights over five newly built artillery tracks. This was the job
of the Artillery-Hauling Command headed by the 312th Division's commander,
General Lê Trọng Tấn.[25] The guns were pulled into position in January, hauled
out of their vulnerable emplacements after January 26, and dragged back into
place again in March. It was dangerous, backbreaking work performed by
thousands of troops who hauled the unwieldy weapons up and down steep
ridges. Two heroic soldiers are said to have thrown themselves under the
wheels of wayward guns to prevent them from hurtling downslope.[26]

Giáp was determined that his precious artillery would not be exposed to
destruction as it would have been if the January offensive had taken place. The
Chinese had successfully protected their artillery against vastly superior US
firepower in Korea, and a dozen Chinese engineers who had served there
helped the VPA construct artillery casemates at Điện Biên Phủ that were

virtually invulnerable to bombing and shelling.[27] Giáp describes them in detail:

> The shelters had covers that were more than three meters of wood and earth mixed with bamboo. These could withstand 105mm guns... Each gun position had a sham gun nearby to attract enemy shells. Each gun shelter required digging from 200 to 300 cubic meters of earth and rocks, which were then thrown on the top of the shelter for the roof. Roofing timbers had diameters of about 30 centimeters. Troops hauled all the wood in from sites nine to ten kilometers away in order not to reveal the gun emplacements.[28]

The casemates' only weak points were the embrasures through which the gun barrels protruded, but these were closed off with sandbags between fire missions. Each 105mm battery had four casemates, a rest bunker for the gunners, a command bunker, an ammunition bunker, a supply bunker, and a first aid bunker – all connected by trenches.[29] Each battery position took 10–15 days to build, with approximately 200 men working around the clock.[30] An extensive network of combat and communications trenches were also dug on the heights surrounding Điện Biên Phủ, and in the second week of March these would start pushing down onto the valley floor.

French prisoners of war who saw the VPA's fortifications and supply lines first hand were astounded by what had been accomplished. Colonel Pierre Langlais, who became Điện Biên Phủ's de facto commander (see Chapter 4), described what he saw as "the labor of a titan," and was particularly impressed by how swiftly bomb damage was repaired.

> I saw with my own eyes, while riding to captivity in a Molotova [truck], the efficiency of the system. During a night bombing that the convoy barely escaped, bombs cut the trail at a sensitive point – the Meo Pass between Tuan Giao and Son La... We could distinguish the twisting roads climbing up the pass and the enormous bomb craters. Then, a human anthill carrying shovels and baskets poured out of their holes and the hard work of reconstruction immediately began. Meanwhile, the political commissar was indulgently putting on a little show ... vaunting the efficiency and courage of the laboring masses. This efficiency was not doubted by those who knew the Tonkin delta and its giant dikes – the mechanical marvels of another age; and as for being courageous, one certainly had to be in order to work under threat of delayed-action bombs that were dropped in each attack. Two hours later, the road was repaired and the trucks moved on.[31]

Triumph of the truckers

Many Vietnamese historians like to suggest that an unstoppable mass of civilian workers animated by popular enthusiasm not only repaired the roads, but also transported most of the supplies consumed during the campaign. Most Western historians have accepted the premise that porters, cargo bicycles, and pack animals carried much if not most of Giáp's supplies,[32] and one recent book observed, "the most striking characteristic of the Việt Minh logistical system was the substitution of manpower for mechanization... And, although Việt Minh motor transport capacity grew steadily throughout the war, the Việt Minh remained dependent on the extensive use of porters and animal transport."[33]

Yet the definitive account of VPA logistics in the Điện Biên Phủ campaign states, "motorized transportation became the primary means of transportation. Motorized transportation delivered to the front 94% of the total quantity of supplies, and 85% of the wounded personnel transported to the rear were carried ... on trucks."[34] Trucks accounted for 84.5 percent of all ton-kilometers of cargo transported within the Điện Biên Phủ Front's boundaries, while porters, bicycles, and packhorses combined moved only 8.2 percent. Gaps in the data make it impossible to determine how large a role motor vehicles played elsewhere, but since two-thirds of all the ton-kilometers lifted by truck were tallied outside the Front's boundaries, it must have been great. It may seem odd that the figures for other regions are so high when they had barely half as many trucks, but their better and less frequently bombed roads allowed them to accomplish more with less.

VPA TRANSPORTATION MEANS EMPLOYED[35]			
Transport type	Council to Supply the Front & General Logistics Department	Điện Biên Phủ Front	TOTAL
Trucks	182 (rising to 237)	446	628
Cargo bicycles	18,491	2,500	20,991
Workhorses	0	500	500
Boats	0	11,660	11,660
Large boats, ferries, canoes	140	0	140
Porters	unknown	unknown	unknown

METRIC TON-KILOMETERS OF SUPPLIES TRANSPORTED				
Transport type	Council to Supply the Front	General Logistics Department	Điện Biên Phủ Front	TOTAL
Trucks	1,176,300	1,582,000	1,429,700 (84.5%)	4,188,000
Workhorses, cargo bicycles	unknown	unknown	84,675 (5.0%)	unknown
Watercraft	unknown	unknown	123,900 (7.3%)	unknown
Porters	unknown	unknown	53,980 (3.2%)	unknown

China had given the DRVN hundreds of Russian GAZ-51 "Moltavas" and American 2.5-ton trucks captured in Korea. The more powerful American vehicles were preferred on particularly difficult mountain routes, while the Moltavas were employed in less demanding terrain. In 1953, both types were concentrated in the 16th Motor Transport Regiment, which had nine companies with about 35 trucks apiece. Seven more companies (numbered 93, 95, 96, 97, 209, 210, and 211) with 228 trucks were formed in late 1953 and early 1954. Another 94 trucks borrowed from artillery units brought the total number available to 628, allowing Giáp for the first time to escape the dependence on porters that had hamstrung all his prior campaigns.[36]

A single Moltava could carry 30 60kg sacks of rice, ten 155kg drums of fuel, 80 75mm shells or 240 81mm mortar shells. Porters were much less efficient because they could carry only small loads and added many more mouths that had to be fed.[37] A 12,000-strong VPA division on a 15-day forced march needed 15,000 porters just to transport its food, but each would consume about half of the rice he or she was carrying (assuming a standard load of 25kg and a daily ration of 80g).[38] And this was under optimal conditions; the reality could be much worse. Of 5,250 metric tons of food that porters carried roughly 500km from Thanh Hóa to northwest Tonkin in late 1952, only 410 tons (8 percent) arrived.[39] Cargo bicycles were far more efficient. With its seat removed, a bamboo platform installed on the frame, and sticks attached to the front and rear to facilitate pushing, a cargo bicycle let one worker transport incredibly heavy loads. About 21,000 were employed during the campaign, carrying loads that began at 100kg but were later increased to 200 and even 300kg.[40]

That is not to say that porters played no significant role. Each of the 16th Motor Transport Regiment's companies operated on a specific segment of road between bridges, ferries, passes, road junctions, and other chokepoints that attracted air attacks. This allowed drivers to become so intimately familiar with the route that they could cover it safely at night without using headlights – as their Chinese mentors had in Korea.[41] But it also meant that supplies had to be unloaded and reloaded at the end of each segment. In some cases, cargo also had to be manhandled through the chokepoints or over sections of road that had been damaged by bombing. It was here that porters played a vital role, but even so, the *dân công* contributed to the campaign chiefly by rehabilitating and maintaining the lines of communication rather than by moving supplies.

To reduce pressure on the roads, extensive use was made of water transport. Over 11,000 boats and rafts were mobilized in Phú Thọ and Vĩnh Phúc Provinces at the western extremity of the Red River Delta, and in Thanh Hóa and Ninh Bình Provinces to the south of it. These primitive wooden craft established supply routes running along the Red, Black, and Ma rivers. Since they relied on human muscle-power to move by rowing or poling, their pace when traveling against the current was undoubtedly very slow – and could not have been very impressive even when going with it. Their value must have declined considerably after the rainy season started in April and moving upstream against the swollen rivers' current became even more difficult.[42]

After the campaign was already well under way, a new supply route was opened on the Nậm Na River, which runs from China's Yunnan Province south to Lai Châu. It was used to transport ammunition and 1,700 tons of rice contributed by the Chinese. The watercraft operating there were mostly crewed by skilled female boaters from Thanh Thủy district in Phú Thọ Province, where the Red and Black Rivers merged before flowing into the Red River Delta. Since there were 102 rapids and waterfalls between the border and Lai Châu, the river remained quite dangerous even after the latter were dynamited. Yet the boaters mastered its winding, rocky course so well that by the end of the siege a boat carrying 300kg of cargo needed only a solitary crewmember, while at the outset four had been required to steer one burdened with just 100kg.[43]

Chủ Lực

In addition to 33,300 *dân công*, the Điện Biên Phủ Front included 58,830 VPA soldiers.[44] These were not guerrillas, but uniformed Main Force (Chủ Lực) troops trained and equipped for conventional warfare, and organized into regular divisions. But apart from the 351st, all VPA divisions were light infantry formations that possessed no motor vehicles, few heavy weapons, and had support units (communications, engineer, transportation, etc.) that were company-sized instead of the battalions that were found in the divisions of Western armies. Like the Chinese units on which they were modeled, Chủ Lực infantry formations had a "triangular" structure. That is, a company had three infantry platoons; a battalion three rifle companies; a regiment three infantry battalions; and a division three infantry regiments. In addition:

- Infantry companies had a mortar section with two 60mm mortars.
- Infantry battalions included a support company with four medium machine guns, several bazookas, and two 81/82mm mortars.
- Infantry regiments had a headquarters guard company, a communications-liaison company, an intelligence-reconnaissance (Trinh Sát) company, a 57mm recoilless rifle company, an 81/82mm mortar company, a transport company, and an engineer company.
- Infantry divisions included a headquarters guard company, a commo-liaison company, a Trinh Sát company, a transport company, an engineer company, and a flak battalion armed with antiaircraft machine guns. Their other artillery units are discussed below.

At full strength, a Chủ Lực infantry battalion had only 635 men compared with a CEFEO battalion's 820.[45] But since its troops were recruited locally, the VPA could easily replace losses and generally ensure that its units were at or near full strength at the beginning of a new campaign. French battalions, on the other hand, were chronically understrength and most were no larger than their VPA counterparts. Yet Chủ Lực units possessed only a tiny fraction of the firepower available to their enemies – who were supported by tanks, 105mm and 155mm howitzers, and combat aircraft. In 1954 the VPA had no tanks, aircraft or 155mm howitzers – and a mere two dozen 105s. Lighter artillery pieces were also rare. Some Western historians suggest that each VPA infantry division had an organic artillery battalion armed with 75mm howitzers and 120mm mortars, and that each infantry regiment included four to six 120mm mortars and/or 75mm recoilless rifles.[46] Yet the Deuxième Bureau did not make such claims in 1954 and recent Vietnamese publications suggest that of the four infantry divisions that fought at Điện Biên Phủ only the 304th included a Lilliputian artillery battalion armed with a half-dozen 75mm howitzers, and none had any 120mm mortars or 75mm recoilless rifles.[47] One older book hints that the 308th Division had some 120mm mortars at the siege, but these may have been attached, rather than organic, weapons.

The infantry divisions were supposed to receive 75mm recoilless rifles in 1954 as part of an entire new suite of weaponry that included 90mm bazookas in infantry battalions, and 82mm mortars and 57mm recoilless rifles in infantry regiments.[48] But while the other weaponry arrived before the siege began, the 75s did not start appearing until its final weeks. There are a few Vietnamese sources which hint that the 308th Division had a divisional 57mm recoilless rifle company, and, if so, it is likely that the 312th and 316th did as well.[49] Yet it is also possible that all the VPA's 57mm recoilless rifles belonged to regimental-level companies for which there is plentiful evidence. Until more data becomes available, it will be impossible to say exactly how 57mm recoilless rifles were distributed among the besieging VPA units.

The 75mm recoilless rifles were either American M-20s captured in Korea or virtually identical Chinese Type-51s, while the 57mm recoilless rifles were either American M-18s or Chinese Type-36s. The VPA referred to precision-built, rifled recoilless guns as ĐKZs (Đại-bac Không Ziật – "cannon no shock"). Yet it also used crude, smoothbore SKZs (Súng Không Giật – "gun no shock") built in makeshift arms factories from lengths of pipe in a wide variety of calibers.[50] The VPA had also built other homemade weapons that were not recoilless guns, including mortars, and bazookas and other rocket launchers. The largest were 187mm mortars produced by sawing the tops off oxygen tanks.[51] The homemade weapons were better than nothing before Chinese-supplied heavy weapons became available, but were short-ranged, inaccurate, and their rudimentary warheads were often duds. The French estimated that 80 percent of the VPA's homemade rockets for 2.36in. (66mm) bazookas were defective.[52]

It's unlikely that many SKZs remained in service with the first-line Chủ Lực units which fought at Điện Biên Phủ. But homemade heavy weapons of some kind were present, since bộc phá phóng ("explosive charge launchers") fired 1,500 projectiles during the siege, especially at strongpoints Eliane-1, Eliane-2, and Huguette-1.[53] It is hard to know precisely what these were, since such weapons were more commonly called súng phóng bom ("bomb throwers") and were usually mortars firing over-caliber warheads, which were loaded by inserting a long rod (or "spigot") down the barrel. That is most likely what the *bộc phá phóng* were, and certainly some 120mm shells were fired by 81/82mm mortars at the siege. Yet, SKZ recoilless guns could also hurl oversized warheads.

ĐKZs, SKZs, bomb-throwers, and light and medium mortars were of little consequence, however, compared with howitzers and heavy mortars. The former were relatively short-ranged and/or inaccurate, and even modest fortifications provided substantial protection against their generally small, low-velocity warheads. Only the latter could easily smash the kind of bunkers and pillboxes that would be found in profusion at Điện Biên Phủ. Giáp accordingly brought about 70 percent of all the VPA's howitzers and 80 percent of its 120mm mortars to the siege.[54] Most were concentrated in the 351st "Heavy" Division – which had been formed in 1951 using artillery battalions stripped out of the 308th, 312th, and 316th Infantry Divisions. In March 1954, its 45th Artillery Regiment had four American 105mm howitzers taken from the French and 20 more provided by the Chinese. The 675th Artillery Regiment had 16 120mm mortars and about 18 75mm howitzers. The Deuxième Bureau reported that a dozen of the latter were Type-41 75mm mountain guns seized from Japanese occupation troops in 1945. A propaganda film shot immediately after the battle reveals that there were also some American M-1 pack howitzers present. The new 237th Artillery Regiment included a battalion armed with 81/82mm mortars (variously numbered at 36 or 54 in different Vietnamese sources). The presence of these weapons, which would not have been found above the infantry battalion level in any Western army, shows just how rare "real" artillery was in the VPA.

The VPA could not fully exploit its howitzer's capabilities because their gunners were not very skilled. The 45th Artillery Regiment had spent a year and a half in Chinese training camps, but most of its gun crews had never fired their 105s in combat before Điện Biên Phủ. They could conduct indirect fire (albeit not as skillfully as the French), but the 75mm gunners could only fire over open sights at targets they could acquire by direct observation. These weapons were therefore frequently deployed within a few hundred meters of their targets – leading the French to conclude that they were being hit by 75mm recoilless rifles, since no Western army would have installed howitzers so close to the enemy.

Even the 105mm howitzers were deployed on the forward slope of the ridges around the valley where they could engage targets by direct fire. It would have been safer to place them on the reverse slope, but that would have necessitated using the more difficult indirect fire technique. Using direct fire also allowed batteries to "fire for effect" after expending only a handful of shells zeroing in on their targets. It was a "poor man's" technique that made the most of the VPA's limited ammunition stocks. Yet although the bomb- and shell-proof casemates made it possible to use the forward slope without undue risk, they also restricted the guns' firing arcs and often limited their ability to mass fires – especially against targets of opportunity. VPA artillery was thus most efficient against pre-registered targets; it was much less effective at firing defensive barrages.

The most important VPA weapons of all were its brand-new 37mm antiaircraft guns. All of them were concentrated in the 351st Division's 367th Antiaircraft Regiment, which had been formed in Binyang County, Guangzi Province, China, on April 1, 1953 and its six battalions started returning to Vietnam at the end of the year.[55] Each had three companies of four Russian M1939 (61-K) 37mm guns apiece, and a fourth armed with a dozen DShK (Degtyaryova-Shpagina Krupnokaliberny – "Degtyaryov-Shpagin Large-Caliber") 12.7mm (.50-caliber) antiaircraft machine guns. The heavy flak guns had an effective range of 3,500m and could hit targets at altitudes up to 3,000m. The machine guns, however, could engage only targets that were within 1,800m at altitudes of 1,500m or less.[56]

The 385th and 392nd Battalions guarded the VPA's "strategic rear" in the Việt Bắc throughout the siege. The other four battalions were all originally deployed in the valley, but after the January offensive was canceled, Giáp shifted the 381st and 396th onto the lines of communication. The 304th Infantry Division's 533rd Antiaircraft Battalion and the independent 681st Antiaircraft Battalion also defended the supply lines, bringing the number of 12.7mm AA machine guns deployed there to about 60. The 308th, 312th, and 316th Infantry Divisions' organic air defense battalions were deployed in the valley itself, where just under 70 antiaircraft machine guns were present when the siege began.[57]

Although Giáp's ammunition dumps were relatively small they still held more shells than the French had thought possible. Having broken the VPA's logistical code, in the first week of March the Deuxième Bureau estimated that 15,000 105mm shells, 5,000 75mm shells, 3,000 120mm shells, 21,000 81/82mm shells, and 44,000 37mm shells were stockpiled in or near the valley. A retrospective assessment dated April 2 reduced the March 13 stock to 10,400 105mm shells, and the figures for other calibers may also have been overestimated. Yet even if the higher numbers are correct, the French were much better off, since they had 27,000 105mm shells and about 21,000 120mm shells stockpiled on March 13. And many VPA shells proved to be duds since they had been stored for years in Vietnam's often stifling and corrosively humid climate. Of the VPA's 15,000 105mm shells, 11,700 had been captured on the Chinese border in 1950,[58] while many of its 75mm howitzer shells had been taken from the Japanese all the way back in 1945.

Despite these handicaps, the French would be shocked by how effective Giáp's artillery and flak were at Điện Biên Phủ. Some Western historians have suggested that, at a minimum, the 37mm antiaircraft guns had Chinese crews,[59] but there is only evidence for a single Chinese advisor with each weapon.[60] In 1950–51, Chinese advisors had been found in most Chủ Lực units down to the company level, but their numbers declined sharply as VPA infantry commanders became more proficient. By 1953, CMAG advisors were present only in divisions and the VPA's General Staff, and by the following year only the latter appear to have remained.[61] Yet the demand for engineering and artillery experts reversed the trend during the Điện Biên Phủ campaign, and some historians suggest that CMAG advisors actually directed VPA strategy and tactics during the siege's first phase.[62] Giáp ridiculed the allegation and several other VPA officers interviewed by French historian Jules Roy hotly denied it: "It is inconceivable that we should ever take orders from foreign officers, even Chinese ones. We regard your question as deplorable. Nobody in the People's Army ever prepared baths for the Chinese; nobody ever walked beside their horses."[63]

After Điện Biên Phủ fell, unnamed but "particularly well-informed French military leaders" in Hanoi (probably including General Cogny) told journalists that the final assault succeeded only due to the participation of a Chinese artillery regiment and infantry units.[64] There were certainly no Chinese infantry present, and this claim may be dismissed as mere French excuse-making. However, Dr Sherman Xiaogan Lai of the Royal Military College of Canada, who formerly served as a Lieutenant Colonel in the Chinese People's Liberation Army (PLA) and as a researcher at the PLA's Academy of Military Science, gives credence to the claim that Chinese artillery fought at Điện Biên Phủ. For several of his PLA colleagues asserted that the PLA 14th Corps' heavy artillery regiment (equipped with an unknown number of American 155mm and/or 105mm howitzers) was present in the siege's final days.[65] However, until documentary evidence comes to light, this must be treated as speculative at best. It is possible that the 14th Corps' heavy artillery regiment was merely the source of most of the VPA's 105s.

CHAPTER 3

BASE AÉRO-TERRESTRE

Điện Biên Phủ was a remarkably intimate battle in which the contenders often fought toe to toe for weeks across a no man's land only a few meters wide. To follow the siege's ebb and flow, one must therefore have an accurate picture of how the *base aéro-terrestre* was laid out. Unfortunately, the maps found in most books depict its fortifications as vague, amoeba-like blobs that are meaningless since there were no trenches or barbed wire that followed these outlines. Sometimes the amoebas contain symbols that represent individual strongpoints, but these generally do not depict their shapes properly and are often inaccurately placed. The published maps are poor because the French military maps on which they were based exhibit the same shortcomings. The battlefield was so complex that even General Cogny's staff in Hanoi could not always make sense of it. Peripheral positions were easily distinguishable on aerial photos because they stood apart from the rest, but other strongpoints were crammed cheek by jowl with one another and with entrenchments housing artillery, headquarters, transportation, communications, medical, and logistical units. And as the battle progressed, the aerial photos became overlaid by a bewildering spider web of new trenches and blurred by thousands of white dots representing discarded parachute canopies.

The following map is the most accurate ever produced, but it shows all the French fortifications, although many did not exist when the siege began. New ones are generally shown as "outposts" since they were abandoned before construction could be finished (in a few cases, when it had barely begun). Most consisted of nothing more than trenches surrounded by sketchy barbed wire and sparse minefields. But even fortifications that had been completed were unimpressive, since Điện Biên Phủ was never a true fortress at all. That is, it was not a system of permanent steel-and-concrete fortifications like those found in the De Lattre Line. Instead, Điện Biên Phủ's defenses were "field fortifications" made of earth, wood, and sandbags. They also did not form a continuous trench system like those of World War I, which had three parallel combat trenches covering the entire frontage and linked by perpendicular communications trenches. Điện Biên Phủ's fortifications were built to an entirely different plan, comprising about three dozen separate "strongpoints" (*points d'appui* or "support points") constructed for all-round defense, which generally were not linked by communications trenches when the siege began.

Each strongpoint was usually defended by a company of infantry or paratroops (100–150 men), though some positions had several. Each platoon of 23–35 men occupied three to five bunkers linked by trenches, though if a company had four platoons, one was generally held in reserve near the command post. Otherwise, company headquarters and heavy weapons personnel acted as the reserve. Most strongpoints were grouped into clusters, each of which was typically defended by an infantry battalion numbering 550–800 men. The clusters were given female names and individual strongpoints within them were identified by number (e.g., Anne Marie-1, Anne Marie-2, etc.). The French called these clusters *centres de résistance* ("resistance centers"), but authors writing in English have often confusingly referred to them as "strongpoints" as well. Moreover, *centres de résistance* Françoise, Junon, and Marcelle contained only one *point d'appui* apiece. For the sake of clarity, this book will use the abbreviation "CR" to designate strongpoint clusters.

The CRs were grouped into three subsectors: Northern (Anne Marie, Gabrielle), Central (Béatrice, Claudine, Dominique, Eliane, Françoise, Huguette), and Southern (Isabelle, Marcelle). But it is useful to think of Claudine, Dominique, Eliane, Françoise, and Huguette (and parts of Anne Marie) as a single entity that will be referred to hereafter as the "Main Position." This was the heart of the base since it contained GONO's reserves, the main airfield, hospital, supply and ammunition dumps, and most of the artillery, tanks, headquarters, and support units. Several new CRs (Épervier, Junon and Lily) would be added to the main position after the siege began.

ĐIỆN BIÊN PHỦ MAIN POSITION (FRENCH CODENAMES)

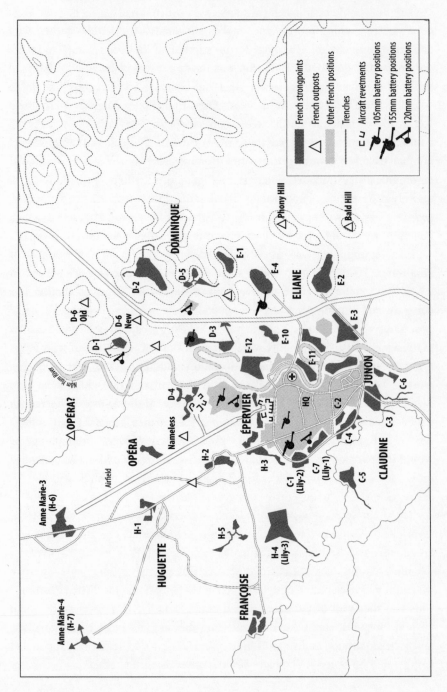

ĐIỆN BIÊN PHỦ MAIN POSITION (VIETNAMESE CODENAMES)

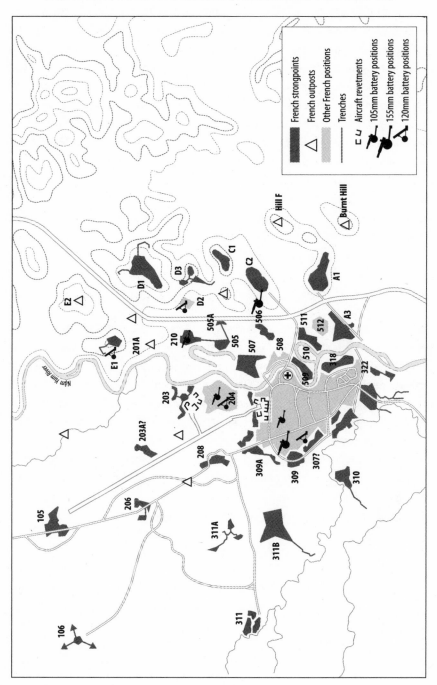

It is unlikely that CR Marcelle was still occupied when the siege began. Built in mid-December 1953 to guard the road to Isabelle, it was also called "Strongpoint Cante" after Adjutant Clément Cante, commander of the Tai auxiliaries who garrisoned it. The Deuxième Bureau warned that Marcelle was going to be attacked by the 312th Division on the night of January 11–12, and III/3 REI had to reoccupy it the next morning.[1] This could mean that Marcelle was overrun, but it seems more likely that the weak, isolated position was evacuated. How long it was held after being reoccupied remains a mystery. Since the French knew that Giáp planned an offensive for January 25, it seems likely that Marcelle was abandoned before that date. On February 9, Moroccan troops reported passing "near the ancient strongpoint Cante,"[2] which suggests that it was indeed vacant. Some historians say that Marcelle was garrisoned until late February or even mid-March, but the preponderance of evidence suggests that it was abandoned in January.[3]

Fortress or offensive base?

As we've seen, General Navarre envisioned Điện Biên Phủ as an offensive base from which the CEFEO would launch attacks throughout northwest Tonkin. Indeed, this role was implicit in the base's official name – Groupement Opérationnel Nord-Ouest – or GONO (Operational Group Northwest). When Navarre learned at the start of December that Giáp planned to eradicate the new base aéro-terrestre, he decided to convert it into a fortified hedgehog on which the VPA regiments would impale themselves.[4] Yet he expected the garrison to conduct an "active defense," responding to each enemy attack with a rapid counterthrust, and launching attacks of its own to seize the initiative and keep the enemy off balance. That is why Navarre chose Colonel de Castries – a dashing cavalryman renowned for his fast-moving operations in the Delta – as GONO's commander.[5] Navarre also went to considerable trouble to provide de Castries with a company of tanks that were expected to keep the valley floor swept clear of VPA troops – at least by day.

Although Navarre had decided to fight a defensive battle at Điện Biên Phủ, the notion of using the valley as an offensive base was not immediately abandoned. On November 30, General Cogny had ordered that half the garrison be employed offensively at any given time, and these instructions were followed much longer than one might expect.[6] Instead of focusing on digging in, GONO continued to launch deep-penetration operations (including a linkup with French troops in Laos) until Christmas. And throughout early 1954, the defenders were constantly launching sallies into the surrounding mountains. Starting in February, many were intended chiefly to determine what VPA units remained at Điện Biên Phủ, since the 308th Division's departure raised the possibility that Giáp had abandoned the notion of attacking GONO altogether. If that was true, then the garrison could safely be reduced to nine or even six battalions before the onset of the wet monsoon season. Losses in these operations were heavy, including 90 killed on February 6 alone. To reduce casualties, on February 17 General Cogny ordered that future sorties be limited to reconnaissance patrols. But as enemy troops and trenches drew ever closer to the outlying strongpoints, de Castries felt obliged to dislodge them, and large sorties were still being conducted as late as March 11. They were costly not only in terms of lives and ammunition, but also time. So many troops were so often engaged in sorties that they had little time left to build fortifications.[7]

Since Điện Biên Phủ was originally an offensive base, its fortifications were not laid out according to an engineering master plan, and were instead developed haphazardly by Cogny, Gilles, and de Castries. Consequently, several significant errors were made. The hospital and the GONO, Mobile Group 9, and GAP 2 headquarters were all located within a hundred meters of each other, presenting a concentrated target for enemy artillery.[8] In addition, the headquarters, hospital, motor pool, and supply dumps were all built on low ground that would be flooded when the rainy season began. Not until February 5 was Major André Sudrat, GONO's senior engineering officer, ordered to move them to higher ground behind the Five Hills. This required building an extensive network of roads, bunkers, and revetments, but all this effort was wasted, since the siege began before these new facilities could be occupied – and none of them ever was.[9] More worrisome from the tactical perspective was the fact that the trench lines on some of the hill strongpoints were poorly sited because their garrisons did not have enough troops to hold more extensive perimeters that would have offered better fields of fire.[10] Efforts were made to remedy this weakness by digging isolated trenches that branched off from the strongpoints, but these could become liabilities since, if lost, they would provide VPA troops with covered routes of approach. Moreover, some strongpoints' layouts violated basic tactical principles. For example, Dominique-3's machine-gun bunkers were sited to fire out perpendicularly to the surrounding barbed wire fences rather than enfilading them from the flanks.[11]

An even more glaring error left two key hills east of Eliane undefended. One was called Mont Chauve ("Bald Hill") due to its bare top. The other was known as Mont Fictif ("Phony Hill"), because I/4 RTM tried to give the impression that it was a proper strongpoint by occupying it with a squad or platoon by daylight, and ambush patrols at night.[12] This deception was aided by the fact that 5 BPVN had constructed a lightly fortified position (originally known as "Strongpoint 21") on the hill in the weeks immediately following Operation *Castor*. Both heights should have been permanently occupied, but Phony was by far the more important of the two. In French hands, it guarded the southern flanks of Eliane-1 and Eliane-4, and the northern flank of Eliane-2. But if VPA troops occupied it, they would have a base for attacks on Eliane-2, and direct-fire heavy weapons emplaced on its crest and mortars dug into its rear slope could enfilade all Eliane's hill strongpoints at close range. De Castries declined to defend the hills because troops and construction materials were scarce, and he believed that his artillery alone could keep them clear of enemy troops. The garrison's breezily confident artillery commander, Colonel Charles Piroth, encouraged this fateful miscalculation.[13]

There were also several dangerous gaps in the main airport's defenses. The runway at Nà Sản had been surrounded by a tight circle of strongpoints, with a loose outer ring of strongpoints on the key heights overlooking it.[14] At Điện Biên Phủ, however, the main runway was completely undefended for fully three-quarters of its length on the eastern side – where an immense gap loomed between Huguette-6 and Dominique-4. The western side, though better protected, still had gaps hundreds of meters wide between Huguette-6 and Huguette-1, and between the latter and Huguette-2. These weak spots would prove to be of critical importance, and should never have been allowed to exist in the first place.

The garrison also neglected to build strongpoints on the heights overlooking the airstrip, but that defect was unavoidable because they were too remote and much too extensive to be defended. Apart from Béatrice, which was situated in the eastern foothills, all the strongpoints were constructed in the valley itself rather than on the surrounding ridges, which loomed 500m higher. The siege has therefore been aptly described as taking place in a stadium, with the French on the field and the VPA in the bleachers. Every move the garrison made was visible to enemy observers except at night and in the early morning, when the valley floor was generally obscured by ground fog that "burned off" as the day progressed. The endless menace posed by the mountains looming overhead had a corrosive effect on the garrison's morale, and must have played a significant role in causing morale to collapse in several defending units.

House of cards

Building a strongpoint was no easy matter. Trenches and mortar firing pits had to be dug; pillboxes for machine guns and protective bunkers for troops, command posts, ammunition storage, etc. constructed; and minefields and barbed-wire fences installed. And since the French knew that the enemy would have 105mm howitzers, their fortifications had to be capable of resisting shells of that caliber. An infantry battalion needed to spend two months doing nothing but digging in to protect itself against 105mm shells, but de Castries' interminable offensive sallies meant that many units did not have time to do the job properly. Local villagers were "mobilized to serve as coolies to help dig fortifications,"[15] but even if they were paid (as seems likely), they lacked the skill and motivation to do the work as well as the troops themselves.

Engineers could not take up the slack because the 31ère Bataillon du Génie – or BG31 (31st Engineer Battalion) – had only two companies with a combined strength of just 326 men.[16] Though supplemented by POW laborers known as PIMs (Prisonniers Internés Militaires), they had more than enough to do building the base's infrastructure and the new headquarters area behind the Five Hills. This included three bridges capable of bearing heavy trucks and tanks, one at Isabelle and two in the Main Position. The northernmost of the three was a prefabricated steel Bailey bridge, which proved so durable that it's still in use at Điện Biên Phủ today.

But the truly insurmountable hurdle to building adequate fortifications was a shortage of construction materials. Major Sudrat calculated that each battalion needed 3,000 metric tons of engineering supplies – that is, 30 tons each for 55 protective bunkers; a dozen tons apiece for 75 pillboxes; and 500 tons of barbed wire, mounting stakes, and mines. Overall, 36,000 tons were required, but the French airlifted in just 4,000 tons of engineering materials, leaving them almost entirely dependent upon locally acquired materials.[17] Protection against 105mm shells required two layers of logs at least 15cm in diameter covered by 1 meter of hard-packed earth. Over this there had to be a rock, metal or concrete "bursting layer" that would detonate the fuses of incoming shells before they penetrated the roof.[18]

ENGINEERING MATERIALS FLOWN INTO ĐIỆN BIÊN PHỦ[19]			
Category	**Type**	**Quantity**	**Metric tons**
Wood	Beams	12,850 meters	130
	Angle supports	4,250 meters	
	Planks	600 meters^3	
	Posts	60	
	Logs	240 meters	
Concrete culverts	60cm diameter	20	5
Cai-Phen	Bamboo matting	21,000 meters^3	12
Cramps	Metal brackets for linking pieces of wood	9,400	10
Barbed wire	Barbed wire, concertina wire, stakes		3,000
Steel I-beams	IPN 180 – 260 girders	118 meters	4.5
Machinery	D4 & R4 bulldozers	5	70
	Accessories and spare parts		8
	P.P.K. two-man chainsaws	21	3
Electrical gear	Generators	15	17
	Battery chargers	5	
	Miscellaneous, including electrical wire	14,700 meters	
Water purifiers	5,300 milliliter (Main Position)	1	16
	3,200 milliliter (Isabelle)	1	
Explosives	TNT sticks	?	23
	Slow fuse	3,200 meters	
	Detonator cord	5,300 meters	
	Primers	2,400	
	Bangalore torpedoes	290	
Bailey bridge			44
Miscellaneous tools			30
Hardware	Screws, nails, bolts, lag bolts		4
Runway materials	Pierced steel plates	22,800	510
	Anchor rods	15,450	
Sandbags		555,000	160
Sheet metal	Corrugated "elephant tusks"		20
TOTAL			4,066.5

Even sandbags were in short supply and often had to be replaced with bamboo matting baskets that were prone to slide off each other when stacked – particularly after the rainy season began. But the most urgent shortage was of lumber. The French flew in just 130 tons of timber – much of which was used to construct bridges – so everything depended on finding wood locally. Since the valley was surrounded by jungle, one might imagine that it would have been an easy matter, but such was not the case. Only CRs Anne Marie, Béatrice, and Gabrielle were wooded and thus provided a ready supply of timber for the units that fortified them. Otherwise, the closest forests were over 2km from the strongpoints, and although the French began felling trees in December, they found it difficult to transport the timber because few trucks were available. Woodcutting had to be suspended in early January when it became too risky. All in all, just 2,200 tons of wood were acquired by felling trees and dismantling villages situated within the defensive perimeter (their inhabitants were relocated elsewhere in the valley). Worse yet, the local timber was badly twisted and gnarled. When these misshapen logs were laid side by side, gaps up to 10cm yawned wide between them. Troops closed the fissures with sandbags or bamboo matting, but the integrity of the roof was badly compromised.[20]

It was also nearly impossible to construct bursting layers, as there was almost no stone in the valley. Concrete was also ruled out because crushed stone would still have to be mixed with cement. Metal was prohibitively heavy to transport by air. Twenty tons of curved, corrugated steel sheets known as "elephant tusks" were used to roof de Castries' command post – but only after the siege had begun, since these had been intended for the new headquarters east of the Nậm Yum.[21] Otherwise, bursting layers had to be improvised. Some units pilfered pierced steel plates from the airstrip, but this practice cannot have been widespread until after it was permanently closed in late March. Scavenged bricks were also used, but there were few brick structures apart from a colonial-era military post on Eliane-2 and the ruins of the Tai prefect's mansion on Eliane-4. In many cases, troops could do nothing more than heap branches atop their bunkers. After the siege began, the garrison tried to strengthen its overhead cover using whatever materials it could "scrounge," including metal ammunition boxes, artillery shell cases, and the iron containers in which 155mm powder charges were delivered.[22] But only so much could be done at that late date. An officer parachuted in on April 21 was appalled to find that his bunker was roofed with fragile bamboo covered by *cai-phen* matting and a mere 25 cm of loose soil.[23]

Yet of all GONO's senior commanders, only Colonel André Lalande expressed concerns about the base's fortifications. De Castries did not prioritize engineering requirements, and on one occasion reallocated a mere pair of C-47s that had been promised to fly in desperately needed construction materials.[24] Indeed, he seems to have been infected with a supreme overconfidence that made digging in properly seem unnecessary. After all, the

French considered a set-piece battle "their" kind of war, and they had been victorious whenever the VPA had risked fighting one in years past. Lieutenant Colonel Langlais admitted as much in his memoirs. "We knew full well that a meter of earth and logs covering a hole 2 meters in depth gave complete protection. Now, nowhere had this been done. The fault lies squarely on the shoulders of Command, and if there is self-criticism, it is on that specific point that it must be borne..."[25]

But then Điện Biên Phủ was the first and only battle of the entire war in which VPA artillery posed a major threat. In most battles, the heaviest VPA weapons were medium mortars and recoilless rifles. The VPA's arsenal also included some 75mm mountain guns and 70mm close-support howitzers seized from the Japanese at the end of World War II, but the only large-caliber weapons employed before Điện Biên Phủ were 120mm mortars and a mere four 105mm howitzers.[26] French commanders had therefore become accustomed to thinking that even sketchy fortifications provided adequate protection. This complacency contributed to Điện Biên Phủ's flimsy fortifications, since even allowing for manpower, materiel, and time constraints, the garrison could have done better than it did. At a minimum, proper communications trenches (which required almost no construction materials) could have been dug. Instead, they were too few and shallow to allow circulation between strongpoints in daylight.[27]

French commanders could also have ensured that strongpoints were all built to the best standard possible, but instead it was left up to each battalion to decide how well it entrenched. The Foreign Legionnaires and Gabrielle's Algerian defenders did a decent job, and Colonel Lalande ensured that Isabelle was fortified as well as circumstances permitted – but other commanders did not. The parachute battalions had little time to spend digging in because they were constantly engaged in offensive sorties. The two Tai battalions did worst of all, since they had no prior experience in positional warfare, and tended to dig trenches deep enough only to suit their small stature. And since units were frequently shifted between strongpoints, troops did not always do their best to dig in a second time after seeing positions which they had already constructed handed over to other units.[28]

Although barbed wire accounted for fully three-quarters of the engineering materials flown in, even this was in short supply. In February, de Castries complained that he did not have enough barbed wire either to build "internal enclosures" or to do more than start sketching out interval strongpoints such as Dominique-5 in the Five Hills.[29] One of the continuing mysteries of Điện Biên

Phủ is the fate of the "Wavebreaker." On January 21, de Castries reported that it was already half completed.[30] But it is visible neither in aerial photos nor on a diorama in the Điện Biên Phủ military museum. Perhaps the Wavebreaker simply does not stand out on photographs, but some portion of it should be discernible. Another possibility is that it was never finished, owing to a lack of materials, and was then "cannibalized" to find barbed wire for the new strongpoints built after January 21 (Huguettes-4 and -5, Eliane-4, Dominiques-5 and -6, etc.).

Mines were also in short supply. The 7,300 flown in before the siege allowed for an average of just 200 to protect each of the roughly three-dozen strongpoints.[31] Most were probably positioned around outlying strongpoints, leaving many second-line positions with few or none. Moreover, with so few engineers available, the job of emplacing mines fell upon infantry units that lacked specialized training for the task. Minefields therefore were not laid out in keeping with an overall plan except on Eliane, where the presence of 2/BG31 ensured that a better job was done. Elsewhere, the engineers became involved in laying minefields only after the siege began. More than 23,000 additional mines were parachuted in after March 13 (not all of which were recovered), but there were never enough to meet the defenders' needs.

The original stockpile included 1,213 American M-2 and M-3 mines (no breakdown data is available) and another 6,260 were dropped in during the siege.[32] Although the M-3 was supposed to be concealed at ground level or only partially buried, most of its shock wave and fragments went upwards instead of radiating out horizontally.[33] The M-2, on the other hand, was a "bouncing" mine which fired a modified 60mm mortar shell upwards. This detonated several meters above the ground, spraying fragments outwards over an area about 20 meters in diameter.[34] The M-2s seem to have been deployed principally around peripheral strongpoints. Before the siege, the garrison also received 5,814 French Model-1948 antitank mines derived from the German "Tellermine" of World War II, but modified for antipersonnel use. The fact that antitank mines had to be used in this way reveals the kind of improvisations that were necessary for France to sustain a war on the far side of the planet. It is also notable that Model-1948s were still being used, although experience at Nà Sản had shown that most of them would not detonate after several days of heavy rainfall. This flaw probably manifested itself at Điện Biên Phủ as well – particularly after the rainy season began in late April.[35]

GONO was also supplied with 290 10kg antitank "plate charge" mines – most likely Model-1948/55s – and ten remote detonators. These were camouflaged above ground so they pointed in the direction from which attack was expected, and would be command-detonated in the face of an assaulting infantry wave. Modified for antipersonnel use, the plate charges sprayed hundreds of fragments up to 200 meters, but often proved useless because the detonating wires were cut by shell fragments. Some hill strongpoints also had command-detonated munitions, improvised from fuel drums, which were intended to illuminate their perimeters or spray fountains of napalm downslope. But these too were frequently put out of action by breaks in their wires. On January 22, there were 131 napalm and 101 illuminating drums on hand, with the delivery of 50 more of each expected.[36]

Finally, 17,190 American M-14 antipersonnel mines were dropped in after the siege began.[37] This was a small, minimum-metal mine made almost entirely from plastic so it would be nearly invisible to electromagnetic mine detectors. Just 5.6cm in diameter and weighing only 100g, the M-14 was known as the "toe-popper" because it had only 29g of Tetryl explosive and was intended to maim rather than kill. A dead enemy merely reduced the foe's combat strength, whereas a permanently incapacitated one had to be evacuated and would remain a burden for some time thereafter.[38]

Infantry

Since the French government had decided for political reasons that conscripts would not be sent to Indochina, no combat units of the French regular army fought at Điện Biên Phủ except for the all-professional II/1 RCP. Otherwise, only troops of the Colonial Army (or "Marines"), the Army of Africa (including Algerian, Moroccan and Foreign Legion units), and the Armée Nationale Vietnamienne – or ANV (State of Vietnam's army) served there. In mid-March, the garrison comprised one Moroccan, two Tai, three Algerian, and four Legion infantry battalions; plus a battalion each of colonial and Legion paratroops. Half of the troops in the 8e Bataillon de Parachutistes de Choc – or 8 BPC (8th Assault Parachute Battalion) – were French, but only 10–15 percent in the Algerian, Moroccan, and Tai battalions (nearly all officers or NCOs), and only a handful served in Legion units.

ĐIỆN BIÊN PHỦ GARRISON (MARCH 10, 1954)[39]					
French	Foreign Legion	Africans	Indochinese regulars	Indochinese auxiliaries	TOTAL
1,412	2,969	2,854	2,150	1,428	10,813
13%	27%	26%	20%	13%	

Indochinese troops (Vietnamese, Tai, etc.) accounted for a third of GONO's manpower and could be found in nearly all the garrison's units. Legion parachute battalions had one "Indochinese" company seconded from the ANV, while colonial parachute battalions had two. Yet even ostensibly "European" parachute companies often had many Indochinese troops. In January 1954, 6 BPC's two Indochinese companies had about 50 Europeans and 125 Indochinese apiece, while the two European companies each included about 90 Europeans and 60–80 indigenous troops.[40] Moreover, most infantry battalions possessed an auxiliary company manned by Indochinese recruits, and several brought them to Điện Biên Phủ (others were left at their battalions' rear bases). There was also the Compagnie de Thaïs Blancs – or CTB (White Tai Company), which was formed at Lai Châu just a week before the town was evacuated. Its troops were stripped out of the three Tai regular infantry battalions that had been established by the French and were manned predominantly by Black Tai. The White and Black Tai – distinguished by the apparel of their women – had been feuding for some years. Most of the CTB's personnel came from the 2nd Tai Battalion, and its leader was the former commander of that unit's 5th Company, Captain Michel Duluat – known to his men as "Tonton Carabine" ("Uncle Carbine").[41]

The garrison also included 11 auxiliary companies that were recruited by the Tai Federation and led by Tai officers, but operated in groups commanded by French officers and NCOs. A Franco-Tai protocol of June 1953 stipulated that each 110-man company would be armed with a 60mm and an 81mm mortar, four automatic rifles, 30 MAT-49 submachine guns and 66 bolt-action MAS-36 rifles.[42] CSMs 413, 414, and 415 survived the retreat from Lai Châu intact, while CSMs 416, 417, and 418 were reconstituted from the survivors of Operation *Pollux*. But CSMs 431, 432, 433, and 434 were raised at Điện Biên Phủ itself in November 1953. Some of their Black Tai personnel had served in other auxiliary units before the valley was lost a year earlier. CSM 454 was also formed at Điện Biên Phủ in mid-January 1954, but it was an administrative unit that had only an ephemeral existence. CSMs 418 and 433 were specially trained to act as "reconnaissance commandos" and guides for French units operating outside the valley.[43]

Indochinese troops featured so prominently in GONO's order of battle because for years the CEFEO had been starved of reinforcements and replacements by a succession of weak French governments that had to contend with mounting public opposition to the endless, unpopular war in Indochina. Since infantry and parachute battalions were always in short supply, they were constantly engaged in back-to-back combat operations (one battalion went nine months without a rest) that caused a steady stream of casualties and kept them perpetually understrength.[44] Since what few replacements were available had to come halfway around the world, CEFEO battalions tried to cover their personnel shortfalls through local recruiting.

The French government's miserly policies also ensured that the CEFEO was perpetually short of officers. Like the units they commanded, officers in Indochina were overworked and suffered disproportionately high casualties because they were expected to lead from the front. They also had to serve multiple combat tours; at the start of 1954, half of all junior officers and NCOs were on their second tour, and many were exhibiting signs of physical and psychological fatigue. Many were also too old to serve in the torrid jungles, pestilential swamps, and jagged mountains of Southeast Asia. In the first quarter of 1954, the average age of second lieutenants was 31; lieutenants, 35; captains, 38; and battalion commanders, 43. And since infantry leaders were in short supply, many officers from other branches (armor, artillery, etc.) were assigned to infantry units although they lacked suitable training and experience. A battalion should optimally have had at least 18 French officers and 60–80 French NCOs, but in practice, most battalions had to make do with 10–12 officers and about 40 NCOs.[45]

Conditions in Indochina were such that a CEFEO infantry or parachute battalion generally had to keep a company in reserve to guard its base camp or rear area in the field. The traditional "triangular" battalion with three rifle companies had therefore been transformed into a "square" unit with four of them. In theory, a "square" CEFEO battalion had 820 troops, while a "triangular" VPA one had only 635, but owing to personnel shortages the two were usually of about equal size. Many CEFEO battalions had also converted their "triangular" companies with three rifle platoons into "square" units, but this was done without any increase in personnel. Instead of having three platoons of three squads each, a company had four platoons of two squads each. This compensated for the officer shortage by simplifying a platoon commander's responsibilities to the point where they could be performed by an NCO, and eliminating the need for skilled squad leaders. In the past, squads had been trained to have one element lay down suppressive fire while another assaulted. After the reorganization, these fire-and-maneuver tactics were generally employed only by platoons, which now consisted of an assault squad that included a sniper and a rifle grenade launcher, and a fire-support squad with a pair of automatic rifles. Although tactical flexibility suffered, this structure trimmed the number of officers and NCOs needed per company from 18 to just eight. It also made it easier to use Indochinese troops who often were not as well trained as their European and African comrades.[46]

In 1954, a CEFEO infantry or parachute battalion had two machine guns, four 81mm mortars and four 57mm recoilless rifles in its weapons company, and two machine guns and a pair of 60mm mortars in each rifle company's weapons platoon (which was often reinforced with one of the recoilless rifles).[47] In addition, each combat parachute platoon was supposed to have a 50mm Modèle 1937 grenade launcher (mortar). But the parachute battalions that jumped into the valley after the siege began evidently left their grenade launchers, 60mm mortars, and recoilless rifles behind (probably for fear that they might be misdropped to the enemy), since just 36 Modèle 1937s, 113 light mortars, and 56 57mm recoilless rifles were lost at Điện Biên Phủ.[48] Some of the armament shortages were resolved by giving the paras heavy weapons that became surplus when demoralized Tai and African units were disbanded during the siege.

Owing to manpower shortages, CEFEO battalions rarely brought along all their mortars and machine guns when engaged in mobile operations, and often carried only modest quantities of ammunition for them.[49] This was not a problem for VPA units that were usually closer to full strength and could use civilian porters to transport their heavy weaponry and ammunition. VPA units also had more submachine guns, and the belt-fed light machine guns they employed at platoon level had a much higher sustained rate of fire than the box-magazine automatic rifles the French used. And since VPA units retained a "triangular" structure, they had a higher ratio of supporting weapons to maneuver units. Given their deficiencies in personnel, leadership, and organic firepower, CEFEO infantry units generally had to rely upon supporting artillery and aircraft to prevail in combat. General Navarre admitted, "If we sent our infantry, given its present quality, outside the radius within which it enjoyed artillery support, then if it encountered Việt Minh infantry, it would be beaten."[50] The parachute battalions were exceptions owing to their superior morale and leadership, and higher allocation of submachine guns.

Firepower

The French therefore pinned their hopes for victory at Điện Biên Phủ on superior firepower. The Nà Sản *base aéro-terrestre* had triumphed, although it had no tanks or aircraft, and its artillery totaled just a dozen 105mm howitzers and four 120mm mortars.[51] Điện Biên Phủ's garrison included just one more infantry battalion, but many times more artillery, plus tanks, fighter-bombers, and spotter planes. But since Giáp was certain to attack at night, the planes would be limited to supporting daylight counterattacks and bombing fixed targets. The tanks could operate at night, but after dark, the artillery would be the backbone of the defense. Colonel Piroth was certain that his gunners were up to the job. They were past masters at shooting under the direction of forward observers and spotter aircraft, swiftly massing fires, engaging fleeting targets of opportunity, and dropping shells just in front of friendly troops. No VPA artillerymen came close to matching their skill.

Two colonial artillery battalions manned primarily by Central African (2e Group du 4e Régiment d'Artillerie Coloniale – or II/4 RAC) and Moroccan (III/10 RAC) gunners and equipped with a dozen 105mm howitzers apiece formed the heart of the garrison's artillery park.[52] Western authors agree that both units were equipped with American M-2 howitzers that had a maximum range of 11.7km. Yet a Vietnamese official history records that four of the 15 105s captured at the end of the siege were M-3 howitzers, and at least one French document indicates that some were present.[53] The M-3, which married a shortened M-2 barrel to the carriage of the 75mm pack howitzer, was much easier to airlift because it weighed just half as much as an M-2, and was issued to US airborne divisions for that reason. But it could not handle the same barrel pressures and recoil forces as its bigger cousin and accordingly had a maximum range of just 7.6km.[54]

If there were M-3s present, they may have arrived with the Batterie Autonome d'Artillerie Laotienne – or BAAL (Laotian Autonomous Artillery Battery) – when it was flown in on November 28, 1953. According to Bernard Fall, this poorly trained unit was armed with worn-out, hand-me-down howitzers that had an effective range of just 1,500 meters. He goes on to say that the whole garrison heaved a sigh of relief when this substandard outfit was replaced by higher-quality artillery units with new howitzers and veteran gunners. But in fact, the BAAL's eight 105s remained in the valley and were used to equip II/4 RAC's 5th and 6th Batteries. Since this would hardly have been done if the howitzers were old and worn out, it seems more likely that if these weapons were indeed short-ranged it was because they were M-3s. We can dismiss the notion that they could not accurately fire beyond 1,500 meters, since if that was true, II/4 RAC could not possibly have accomplished all that it did during the siege.

The 105mm howitzers were supplemented by three Foreign Legion mortar companies armed with French Brandt AM50 120mm heavy mortars with a maximum range of 6.5km. Two of them were "composite" units established in 1952–53 with personnel drawn from the 3rd and 5th Foreign Legion Infantry Regiments. Each Compagnie Mixte de Mortiers de la Légion Étrangère – or CMMLE (Foreign Legion Composite Mortar Company) – had eight heavy mortars. These companies also possessed 81mm mortar platoons, but they were not sent to Điện Biên Phủ. The 1er Compagnie Étrangère Parachutiste de Mortiers Lourds – or 1 CEPML (1st Foreign Legion Airborne Heavy Mortar Company) – created by similar means in September 1953, also normally had eight 120mm mortars. But after being deployed to Điện Biên Phủ, it secured four additional tubes from GONO's "sector" reserves. The Legion mortar companies were divided into two firing platoons that were often deployed on different CRs.[55]

There was also a battery equipped with four American M-1 towed 155mm howitzers that was intended to be the mainstay of the French counterbattery effort. On March 13, three of its guns had just been towed from the headquarters area to a new, defiladed position at the foot of the hill that would become strongpoint Eliane-4. The fourth gun did not join them until after the siege began.[56] The garrison also included a battery equipped with four American M-55 antiaircraft weapons. Each was armed with four M-2 .50-caliber (12.7mm) machine guns that were mounted in a lightly armored, open-topped, power turret that swiveled atop a two-wheeled trailer. The "Quad-50s" were used as indirect fire weapons against ground targets, spraying dense, arcing streams of tracer bullets that proved highly effective against exposed infantry.[57]

Last, but not least, there were ten American M-24 "Chaffee" light tanks that had been disassembled, airlifted into the valley, and laboriously rebuilt there. Carrying each tank's parts required five sorties by C-47s and two by a civilian Bristol 170 "Freighter" that could uniquely fit the tank hull through the large clamshell doors at the front of its fuselage.[58] They were heavily armed with a 75mm gun, a coaxial .30-caliber machine gun, and a pintle-mounted .50-caliber machine gun, but lacked external telephones that would have let infantrymen communicate with the "buttoned-up" crews without having to climb onto the exposed turrets. In keeping with French Army tradition, individual tanks were named after famous battles, but they were collectively known as "Bisons" since that was the tank company's radio call sign. The three tank platoons were likewise commonly identified by their radio call signs – Blue, Red, and Green. The Blue Platoon's personnel were supplied by the Régiment d'Infanterie Coloniale du Maroc – or RICM (Moroccan Colonial Infantry Regiment), which despite its name was an armored reconnaissance unit, while the rest came from the 1er Régiment de Chasseurs à Cheval – or 1 RCC (1st Light Cavalry Regiment).

GONO did not have any 75mm recoilless rifles, although they would have been useful against VPA artillery casemates on the ridges east of the Main Position. These fortifications were virtually impervious to bombs and shells, and so well camouflaged that they could be detected only at the instant that they fired. Captain Guy Hourcabie of III/10 RAC believed the only way to destroy them was to score a direct hit on their open embrasures with a high-velocity, flat-trajectory shell. Tanks could do this, but were rarely present at the instant when an enemy gun fired. By the time a Bison could climb atop one of the Five Hills, the casemate would again be invisible and its embrasure sealed with sandbags. In February, Hourcabie requested a pair of 75mm recoilless rifles so these fleeting targets could be engaged immediately. However, the only ones available belonged to 35 RALP, and it was fully committed to operations in Laos following a brief stay at Điện Biên Phủ after it jumped in during Operation *Castor*.[59] Four guns would eventually be parachuted into the valley in early April.

CR Isabelle was built for the sole purpose of enhancing GONO's defensive artillery barrages. The terms "artillery bombardment" and "artillery barrage" are often treated as synonyms, but in fact have very different meanings. A "bombardment" is meant to destroy, whereas a "barrage" is a barrier of exploding shells that protects friendly troops. When an artillery piece fires multiple shells at the same target, they land in an elliptical "beaten zone" whose long axis follows the direction of fire, because left–right deviation is much less than forward–backward deviation. Thus, a defensive barrage is most effective if the guns are firing at the flank of the attacking troops. Guns shooting at their front are less efficient because their beaten zone lies along, rather than across, the axis of attack. Moreover, to avoid hitting the defenders, relatively few shells will land in the critical area just in front of their trenches. Isabelle's guns were therefore much better placed to fire defensive barrages on the Main

ARTILLERY BARRAGE
COMPARISON

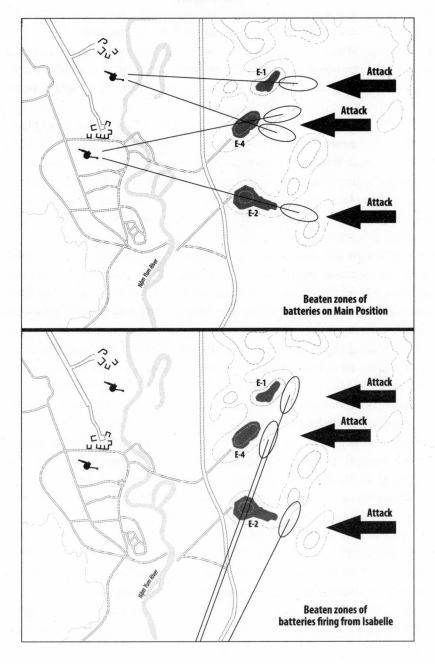

Beaten zones of
batteries on Main Position

Beaten zones of
batteries firing from Isabelle

Position's eastern and western faces – the directions from which attack was most likely – than batteries in the HQ Area and Dominique. And the reverse was true with respect to defensive barrages fired in support of Isabelle. Indeed, most of the garrison's batteries had the primary mission of supporting a subsector other than that in which they themselves were located.

Group	Unit	Deployment	Primary mission	Secondary mission
GONO ARTILLERY ORGANIZATION (MARCH 13)[60]				
A	2 batteries III/10 RAC	Isabelle	Direct Support Central	Direct Support South
	Battery III/10 RAC	HQ Area	Direct Support South	Direct Support Central
	1 CEPML	HQ Area, behind Dominique	Direct Support South	Direct Support Central
	2 CMMLE	Anne Marie, Gabrielle	Direct Support Central	Direct Support North
B	2 batteries II/4 RAC	Dominique-4	Direct Support North	Reinforce A
	Battery II/4 RAC	Dominique-3	General Support	Reinforce A
	155mm battery	HQ Area, Eliane-10	Counterbattery	Reinforce A
	1 CMMLE	Dominique-1	Direct Support Central	Direct Support North
	Quad-50s	Épervier	Direct Support Central	Direct Support North

To ensure that GONO's firepower could be used freely, it was amply provided with ammunition and other supplies. On March 13, its dumps held eight days' worth of gasoline; nine days' worth of 80-octane aviation fuel; seven days' worth of 100-octane aviation fuel; six units of fire for its infantry weapons; 6.5 for the 105mm howitzers, seven for the 155mm howitzers; 7.9 for the 120mm mortars; and nine for the tanks' 75mm guns.[61] A unit of fire is the amount of ammunition a unit is expected to consume in 12 hours (one day) of heavy combat, and is calculated on the basis of shells fired per weapon. This varied by type and caliber: a 105mm howitzer unit of fire equaled 175 rounds per gun (RPG), but only 110 RPG for 120mm mortars and 100 RPG for 155mm howitzers.[62] These estimates proved far too low, since during periods of intense fighting, French batteries could expend several units of fire in a single night!

The superiority of their tanks, aircraft, and artillery caused French commanders to see firepower as a magic talisman that would solve all the daunting challenges facing them at Điện Biên Phủ. It would allow shoddily built strongpoints defended by mere companies to resist assaults by entire regiments; ensure the success of outnumbered counterattacks; prevent the enemy from occupying Phony and Bald Hills; sweep the valley floor clear of VPA troops in daylight; guarantee that the airfield remained open; and silence any hostile guns that had the temerity to open fire. Colonel Piroth was convinced that Giáp could not move his big guns over the sheer mountain ridges around the valley or keep them supplied with ammunition so far from his logistical bases. Indeed, Piroth made this into a mantra that he recited to high-ranking visitors: "Firstly, the Viet-Minh won't succeed in getting their artillery through to here. Secondly, if they do get here, we'll smash them. Thirdly, even if they manage to keep on shooting, they will be unable to supply their pieces with enough ammunition to do us any real harm."[63] This overconfidence was rooted in the assumption that the VPA could never prevail in a conventional battle where all of the accoutrements of modern warfare would be brought into play. It is hard not to suspect that racism played a role in leading the French to make this fatal miscalculation.

By late February, however, Piroth was becoming worried. Giáp *had* gotten his artillery into position and built up a sizeable stockpile of shells for it. And this had been done without the French locating any but a handful of the guns or destroying the few casemates that had been detected. GONO's own artillery, on the other hand, was deployed in open gun pits and its every move was visible to VPA observers on the surrounding ridges. Though he still radiated confidence in public, Piroth privately expressed doubts to Hourcabie: "How can our batteries maintain their fire when the men have no cover? Only our artillery can save Điện Biên Phủ, but we're in the open, firing blind, while the Viets have observers in forward positions. The situation may be irreversible. Not even God can help our cannoneers." But instead of sounding an alarm that might have made his superiors change course, Piroth insisted that Hourcabie keep quiet, saying, "Swear you won't breathe a word of this. It would be terrible for morale."[64] He was still clinging to the hope that Giáp's guns would be destroyed once they revealed their positions by firing long bombardments instead of the brief flurries of shells they had been content with thus far.

GONO's inability to destroy or even detect Giáp's artillery also worried General Navarre. While visiting GONO on March 4, he suggested reinforcing it to compel Giáp to delay his assault closer to the rainy season. He later told a commission of inquiry that the enemy "never launch an attack without the most careful study of the objective. I thought that by putting another two or three battalions in – perhaps creating a new defended locality on each flank – I could delay the opening of his attack by two or three weeks."[65] But Cogny opposed sending any more battalions to Điện Biên Phủ and de Castries knew that it would be difficult to supply them and impossible to find the engineering materials necessary to build additional strongpoints. In any case, most of

GONO's leadership remained confident that they were about to inflict a severe defeat upon Giáp. The last thing they wanted to do was dissuade him from attacking.

Airbase 195

One of the key factors that had drawn General Navarre's attention to Điện Biên Phủ in the first place was its "Dakotable" airfield. During the year in which the valley was under VPA occupation, the runway had been sabotaged by thousands of holes dug in its surface. Since the airfield was the foundation upon which the entire *base aéro-terrestre* would be built, restoring it was the garrison's top priority. And because an all-weather runway was required, merely filling in the holes would not suffice. It also had to be sheathed in Pierced Steel Plate (PSP). Each 30kg plate was 3 meters long by 38cm wide, and had three rows of circular perforations running its length. Integral hooks on the front edge fit into corresponding slots in the rear edge of the adjoining plate. They were laid in a staggered, brick-like pattern to ensure structural integrity and stakes were driven through the holes at regular intervals to keep the assembled matting solidly anchored to the ground. Covering Điện Biên Phủ's 1,156m main runway required over 22,000 plates, and the task was not completed until January 13, 1954.[66]

Although it would have been impossible to provide Điện Biên Phủ with an all-weather airstrip by any other means, the PSP matting had significant shortcomings. Delay-fused artillery shells that penetrated it would detonate underneath, forming craters whose jagged, upward-jutting edges punctured the tires of aircraft passing over them. And because of the way in which they slotted together, it was impossible to remove and replace individual plates. Instead, each damaged section had to be cut out with an acetylene torch, and a new piece trimmed to fit and welded in place. The airfield also suffered from the same lack of stone that inhibited construction of bursting layers. To prevent flooding, drains had to be cut beneath the runway. These would normally have been filled with crushed rock, but since none was available logs had to be used instead. These compressed over time, creating dangerous hollows in the runway surface.[67]

There was also a dirt airstrip near CR Isabelle that was intended to supplement the main airfield and act as a substitute if it was closed by enemy action. However, this runway was completely undefended except at its southern tip and was overshadowed by the eastern foothills just a kilometer away. Dominated by VPA artillery and wide open to infiltration even before the siege began, the auxiliary airstrip was never used. On March 19, a makeshift landing strip for single-engine aircraft was laid out in a less exposed position on the supply drop zone west of Isabelle. It's unclear whether this was ever used either.[68] But even the main runway proved too dangerous to use in daylight, since VPA artillery on the ridges to the east could hit any part of it with observed, direct fire. The effort invested in building revetments to protect GONO's aircraft against artillery fire was completely wasted. VPA gunners had little difficulty "walking" their shells into such obvious (and fragile) targets, which, unlike the French artillery in its gun pits, stuck out above ground like the proverbial sore thumb. Airbase 195 would accordingly be closed for routine operations from the very first day of the siege.

This totally upset French planning, which had taken for granted that one or both runways would remain open. GONO's hospital had just 44 beds because it was assumed that the wounded would be evacuated by air. The Armée de l'Air began the siege without an adequate supply of cargo parachutes[69] because it expected that supplies would be delivered by a steady stream of Dakotas landing on the runway. Cogny and de Castries likewise anticipated that reinforcements and replacements would be flown in as necessary. These faulty assumptions were rooted in the perceived lessons of the 1952 siege of Nà Sản. Its airfield *had* remained in operation throughout the VPA assaults of November–December 1952, and played a decisive role in the French victory.[70] But at Nà Sản, VPA artillery had comprised only a few 75mm howitzers and 120mm mortars; included no heavy flak weapons; and French strongpoints on all the key heights prevented VPA guns from being emplaced in positions overlooking the runway.

In retrospect, it should have been obvious that Điện Biên Phủ would be different because Giáp now had far more artillery, including 105mm howitzers and 37mm flak guns, and was free to deploy it wherever he pleased atop the undefended ridges surrounding the valley. It should also have come as no surprise that heavy howitzers and antiaircraft guns with even a modest supply of ammunition would close the airfield by day and reduce nighttime landings to a trickle. But since Piroth was keeping his fears to himself, most French commanders were confident that their superior firepower and enemy ammunition shortages would prevent VPA artillery and antiaircraft weapons from choking off their aerial lifeline.

The French also erred by assuming that the Armée de l'Air and Aéronavale could do all that was expected of them. When the siege began, Groupement Aérien Tactique Nord – or GATAC Nord (Tactical Air Group North), which controlled all combat air operations in northern Indochina, possessed just 107 bombers and fighter-bombers. And that was a theoretical maximum that was never achieved in practice. For example, only 34 of 45 B26s were operational on March 13 and there were just 33 crews available to fly them.[71] On average, only 75 combat planes were operational on any given day, and that was a pathetically small force with which to interdict Giáp's lines of communication, fly bombing and strafing missions at Điện Biên Phủ itself, and meet urgent demands for air support throughout Tonkin and northern Laos. And most of GATAC Nord's aircraft were single-engine types that could carry only small bombloads and would have little "loiter time" over the valley because it was near the limit of their range – 295km from airbases around Hanoi and roughly 400km from the aircraft carrier *Arromanches* cruising in the Gulf of Tonkin. The carrier-based aircraft later redeployed to Bach Mai airbase near Hanoi so they would be closer to the valley.

GATAC NORD (MARCH 13)[72]			
Combat units	**Service**	**Aircraft type**	**Quantity**
Groupes de Chasse 1/22 "Saintonge," 2/22 "Languedoc"	Armée de l'Air	F8F Bearcat	32
Groupes de Bombardement 1/19 "Gascogne," 1/25 "Tunisie"	Armée de l'Air	B-26	45
Flotille de Chasse Embarquée 11F "Savart"	Aéronavale	F6F Hellcat	12
Flotille d'Assaut Embarquée 3F "Ganga"	Aéronavale	SB2C Helldiver	12
Flotille de Bombardement 28F "Cesar"	Aéronavale	PB4Y Privateer	6
TOTAL			107
Other units	**Service**	**Aircraft type**	**Quantity**
Groupes Aériens d'Observation Artillerie (GAOA) 21 & 22	Armée de l'Air	Morane 500 Cricket	30
Escadrille de Reconnaissance Outremer (EROM) 80 -- based in southern Vietnam, but regularly flew missions in Tonkin.	Armée de l'Air	RF8F Bearcat NC.701 Martinet	12 6
Escadrille de Reconnaissance Photographique II/19 "Armagnac" – based in Tourane (Danang) but regularly flew mission in Tonkin.	Armée de l'Air	RF8F Bearcat ERB-26 Invader	2 4

Escadrilles de Liaisons Aériennes (ELA) 53	Armée de l'Air	NC.701 Martinet Nord 100 Pingouin Morane 500 Cricket	10 15 9
Groupement de Formations d'Hélicopteres de l'Armée de Terre (GFHAT)	Armée de Terre	Sikorsky H-19 and various	42

There were also too few transport planes available to sustain Điện Biên Phủ and the constellation of new *bases aéro-terrestres* that had sprung up in Laos. GONO required 102 tons of airlifted supplies every day, but between January 27 and February 24, deliveries averaged just 64 tons as planes were diverted to help head off the 308th Division's thrust toward Luang Prabang.[73] Indeed, there were never enough transports available even though the US provided another 25 Dakotas and 29 C-119 "Packets" between November 1953 and April 1954. Moreover, the French had neither sufficient pilots to fly nor mechanics to maintain all these extra aircraft. The pilot shortage was partly remedied by Civil Air Transport (CAT), a CIA "front" masquerading as a commercial airline that provided American mercenary crews for a dozen C-119s. But despite the influx of American planes and pilots, in March there were just 112 military air transports (including 24 C-119s) in all of Indochina, and only 94 crews rated to fly them.[74]

FRENCH AIR TRANSPORT UNITS (MARCH 13)[75]			
Unit	Service	Aircraft Type	Quantity
Groupe de Transport 2/62 "Franche-Comté"	Armée de l'Air	Dakota	22
Groupe de Transport 2/63 "Sénégal"	Armée de l'Air	Dakota	22
Groupe de Transport 1/64 "Béarn"	Armée de l'Air	Dakota	22
Groupe de Transport 2/64 "Anjou"	Armée de l'Air	Dakota	22
Detachment "Packet"	Armée de l'Air / CAT	C-119	24
TOTAL			112

Civilian airlines operating in Tonkin also airlifted cargo and personnel to Điện Biên Phủ, but there's no data available on how many missions they flew during the siege, though they undoubtedly played a major role in the safer, pre-battle phase. The smaller aircraft (Austers, Cessnas, Consuls, and Dragon Rapides) would have been of little value in either case.

CIVIL AIRLINES OPERATING IN TONKIN (MAY 7, 1954)[76]	
`Airline`	Aircraft
Aigle Azur ("Blue Eagle") Indochine	5 x Boeing 307 Stratoliner (4-engine) 2 x Bristol 170 Freighter (2-engine) 4 x SO.30 Bretagne (2-engine) 16 x DC-3 Dakota (2-engine) 3 x Curtiss C-46 Commando (2-engine) 2 x Airspeed Consul (2-engine)
Air Outre-Mer ("Air Overseas")	1 x Bristol 170 Freighter (2-engine) 9 x DC-3 Dakota (2-engine) 1 x Auster (1-engine)
Autrex	1 x Douglas DC-4 (4-engine) 1 x Junkers-52 (3-engine) 7 x DC-3 Dakota (2-engine) 6 x DH.89 Dragon Rapide (2-engine)
Compagnie Laotienne de Communication et Transport (CLCT)	3 x DH.89 Dragon Rapide (2-engine) 3 x Noorduyn Norseman (1-engine) 1 x DHC-2 Beaver (1-engine)
Office Commercial d'Approvisionnement (OCA)	2 x Cessna (1-engine) 2 x Auster (1-engine)

To ease the shortage of mechanics, President Dwight Eisenhower covertly deployed 200 US Air Force repairmen at airbases in Da Nang (in Central Annam) and Đồ Sơn (near Haiphong). In addition, a provisional US C-119 squadron went to Cát Bi airbase near Haiphong to ferry aircraft to and from maintenance facilities at Clark Field in the Philippines, and train French and CAT pilots to fly their new planes. Some of its pilots also made runs to Điện Biên Phủ, and as the siege intensified they and other USAF pilots and aircraft would fly in thousands of tons of desperately needed supplies and equipment (including tens of thousands of parachutes) from US depots in Japan and the Philippines. Finally, 44 parachute packers from the US Army's 8081st Air Service Unit were also based on Cát Bi.[77]

These Americans found themselves in the middle of a firefight before dawn on March 7, when VPA sappers who had crept in through the sewers penetrated Cát Bi's perimeter and destroyed four B-26s and six "Crickets." This was part of a coordinated offensive against airbases that Giáp hoped would put a dent in French air strength just before his assault on Điện Biên Phủ began. Two nights earlier, sappers had slipped into Gia Lám airbase near Hanoi, burned the repair shop, and destroyed or damaged two Stratoliners, five Dakotas, one Bristol Freighter, and two Beavers. Đồ Sơn had already been hit on January 31, when four Dakotas were damaged or destroyed. It would be targeted a second time on the night of March 17–18, but although sappers again penetrated its perimeter, they do not appear to have reached the flight line this time. Fortunately, they did not enter through the sector that the American mechanics had been assigned to defend! One historian asserts that 78 aircraft were damaged or destroyed in these raids, but the actual figure was 23 – of which only a dozen were total write-offs.[78]

Another 18 aircraft were destroyed on the ground at Điện Biên Phủ during the first days of the siege, including three Dakotas, one C-119, a C-46, and seven Crickets.[79] Although just eight Bearcats (including two specialized recon variants) were permanently stationed at Điện Biên Phủ, 17 were present on March 12. All but two of the 15 airworthy planes were ordered to leave since the Deuxième Bureau warned that an assault was imminent. Yet one was grounded by a flat tire, two others were unable to lift off because of engine trouble, and four others had to return just after takeoff because their engines started "knocking" violently and losing power. It turned out that water was mixed with their fuel, causing foreign body deposits that prevented the spark plugs from firing properly. The engines were removed for cleaning overnight, but before repairs could be finished, nine Bearcats were damaged by artillery fire on March 13. Two escaped before nightfall and another three hastily repaired planes fled the next morning, but the rest were destroyed. The fuel could have been contaminated by VPA saboteurs or watered down by a crooked supplier.[80]

CHAPTER 4

GIÁP'S FIRST OFFENSIVE

By March 13, 1954 all preparations for the assault were complete. Giáp's artillery had again been laboriously hauled into position, though this time it was nested in solid casemates instead of open gun pits. Antiaircraft units were also ready in their well-camouflaged emplacements. The 394th Battalion's batteries were clustered in rice fields near Bản Nà Hi and Bản Nà Tấu about 1.2km and 4km north of Gabrielle in the Nậm Co Valley. Two of the 383rd Antiaircraft Battalion's 37mm batteries were posted on hills above Bản Quang Tum, about 1.2km northeast of Béatrice, and along RP41 near Bản Na Lời, which was roughly twice as far away in the same direction. The battalion's 817th Battery was deployed on the valley's outer rim and the 818th Battery was split in two. Half of its dozen AA machine guns strengthened the 316th Division's air defenses in the hills east of the Main Position, while the other six were deployed east of Isabelle. Since the 304th Division's flak battalion was absent defending the supply lines, these were the only antiaircraft weapons available in the valley's southern reaches.[1]

Giáp's initial attacks would target Béatrice, Gabrielle, and Anne Marie. It was essential to take these positions because they held VPA troops away from the airfield and denied them access to the valley floor by way of the Pavie Track and RP41. These positions were also attractive targets since they were remote from the Main Position and could be isolated from reinforcement. Béatrice and

Gabrielle were particularly vulnerable because surrounding high ground provided bases from which they could be attacked from several directions simultaneously without the attackers having to cross the exposed valley floor where French tanks and aircraft would be at their most effective.

Béatrice, March 13–14

Giáp insisted "the first strike must be victorious,"[2] since, if it failed, his troops' enthusiasm – which the commissars had brought to a high pitch – would be dampened. Therefore, he aimed his first blow at Béatrice (the VPA called it "Him Lam" after a village just to the east), which was by far the most vulnerable CR. Some historians have suggested that Béatrice's location was so poor that it should never have been constructed in the first place, but there had seemed to be good reasons for siting it in such an exposed position. An attack on Điện Biên Phủ was most likely to come from the northeast, since RP41 was Giáp's main line of supply and the route over which he had to haul his artillery to the siege. The place where the road descended onto the valley floor was invisible from the Main Position because there was an intervening and generally higher line of hills east of the "Five Hills." Between this second hill line and the main mountain ridge was a bowl in the hills where the VPA would be able to move troops, supplies, and artillery without fear of being spotted except from the air.

But if the French could dominate this bowl, Giáp's ability to deploy his forces would be greatly restricted. General Gilles originally proposed to do so by building a strongpoint on Hill 781 or Hill 1066 (located farther up the same ridgeline), but General Cogny vetoed this plan because neither hill could be reached except through a steep, narrow ravine, and he believed any troops posted on them would inevitably be annihilated. The two commanders agreed instead to build a strongpoint on Hill 506, which, though much lower, had the virtue of being accessible by road from the Main Position.[3] Since 506 formed part of the second hill line, it would allow the defiladed "dead ground" behind it – and particularly the spot where RP41 debouched into the bowl – to be brought under the direct fire of French troops and observation by their artillery spotters. The tradeoff was that Béatrice was flanked north and south by jungled hills that allowed enemy troops to infiltrate right up to the edge of its defenses, provided firing positions from which VPA heavy weapons could rake it at point-blank range, and dominated the route over which reinforcements would have to come to its relief.

Yet French commanders believed that Béatrice could weather any attack. This misplaced confidence is easier to understand if one considers that, over the preceding eight years, the VPA had never once captured a fortified position defended by an entire French battalion in a single attack. And it was not just any battalion that held the hill, but the 3rd Battalion of the Foreign Legion's legendary 13ème Demi Brigade de Légion Étrangère – or 13 DBLE (13th Half-Brigade) – a unit which had never known defeat even in the darkest days of World War II.[4] Moreover, Béatrice comprised three sub-strongpoints, each of which was sited atop one of Hill 506's several distinct ridges, organized for all-round defense, and separated from its neighbors by minefields and barbed wire. III/13 DBLE might lose one or even two strongpoints before reinforcements could arrive, but certainly not all of them.

This might have been true if the battalion was at full strength, but like most CEFEO units it was undermanned. On March 10 its strength was just 596: 13 officers, 53 NCOs, 469 enlisted men, plus 58 Indochinese of the 245ème Compagnie de Supplétifs Militaires – or CSM 245 (245th Auxiliary Company).[5] Of these, only about 520 were actually present on Béatrice since 12 men were in the hospital, several dozen in a Peloton d'élèves grades or PEG (Corporal Training Platoon) that took students from Legion units throughout Mobile Group 9 (its total strength was three officers, 10–12 NCOs, and 80 students), and a 26-man platoon from 10th Company was guarding Colonel de Castries' headquarters.[6] Although the platoon's detached mission ended on March 12, it was unable to return to Béatrice the next day because the strongpoint was too closely invested by VPA trenches.[7] On the other hand, Béatrice had been reinforced by a three-man infrared night vision team detached from I/2 REI.[8]

The garrison had also been worn down by three months of lunges into the surrounding heights, and a steady dribble of casualties in routine patrols and road-opening missions. Lieutenant Étienne Turpin recalled that 11th Company went into battle with just 96 legionnaires, 11 NCOs and one officer (himself).[9] The 10th and 12th Companies likewise had only a single officer apiece, while even the more fortunate 9th had just two.[10] Platoons therefore had to be led by NCOs, and if a company commander was killed or incapacitated, there was usually no one available to take his place. Finally, Lieutenants Turpin and André Carrière (9th Company's commander) had both joined the battalion just days before (replacing officers who had

BÉATRICE AND THE FIVE HILLS

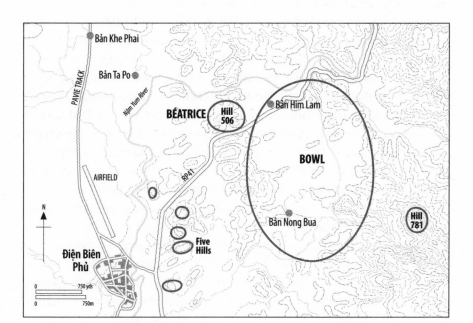

become casualties) and were familiar with neither their troops nor the positions they were defending.

As fate would have it, their companies defended Béatrice's most vulnerable sectors. The 9th Company held Béatrice-1 and 11th Company Béatrice-3. Béatrice-2, which was the least exposed to attack since it faced toward the Main Position, contained the Headquarters, 10th and 12th Companies. By some accounts, 12th Company's northern half of the position constituted a separate strongpoint known as Béatrice-4, but the three companies all shared a single defensive perimeter. CSM 245 had been split up among the four combat companies, with a platoon deployed on each strongpoint.[11] Since the III/13 DBLE did not have enough men to occupy every crest in the jumbled hill mass, each strongpoint had a decoy pillbox built on an outlying hillock to confuse the VPA about the extent of its defenses.

The 312th Division finished digging assault trenches around Béatrice on the night of March 11, but they were filled in the next morning by a bulldozer escorted by infantry and tanks. Mines planted in the trenches before they were filled in greatly slowed VPA troops, who re-excavated them that night.[12] But opening the 2km of road from the Main Position on March 13 still required a major combat operation involving troops of III/3 RTA and BT2 supported by tanks and napalm-dropping fighter-bombers.[13] Fearing that his assault trenches would be filled in again, the 312th Division's commander, General Lê Trọng Tấn, got permission to have the 806th Howitzer Battery fire 20 rounds at Béatrice. This was the first time Giáp's 105s had revealed themselves, and the road-clearing force quickly fell back to the Main Position.[14]

But this demonstration of VPA firepower paled in comparison to the bombardment that began at 1705hrs, when five 105mm batteries, and the 756th and 757th Mountain Gun and 113th Mortar Batteries opened fire on the Main Position's headquarters, artillery positions, and aircraft parking areas, while the 805th Howitzer and 112th Mortar Batteries targeted Isabelle.[15] Lieutenant Erwan Bergot's platoon of 1 CEPML suffered severely. Dug in behind Dominique-5, it lost three of its six 120mm mortars to direct hits, and a fourth when a dump containing 5,000 mortar shells exploded. A dozen of its 35 men were killed and another three wounded.[16] In addition, II/4 RAC had at least one 105mm howitzer destroyed that night, and several more were put out of action by damage to their recoil cylinders.[17] After half an hour French forward observers using sound-and-muzzle flash ranging techniques thought they had pinpointed the VPA batteries, and Colonel Piroth's howitzers began firing counterbattery missions. However, the enemy's casemates, camouflage, and dummy positions (including small explosions to simulate muzzle flashes) ensured that there was no discernable decline in the volume of incoming shells. After several hours of futile counterbattery work, even the 155s switched to firing defensive barrages.

The failure to silence Giáp's artillery doomed Béatrice, since its flimsily built fortifications could not resist the torrent of incoming shells. After 15 minutes of targeting the Main Position, the 804th and 806th Howitzer Batteries shifted fire to Béatrices-2 and -3 respectively. These batteries were located 3km away and forward observers directed their fire. The 752nd Mountain Battery engaged Béatrice-1 over open sights from a range of just 300 meters, while the 753rd, likewise firing at point-blank range, destroyed four bunkers on Béatrice-2 in just ten minutes. The 114th and 115th Mortar Batteries added to the devastation; four 120mm mortars blasted Béatrice-2, while a pair targeted each of the other strongpoints. In addition, there were 17 57mm ĐKZs, the 202nd Mortar Company's 82mm mortars, and other 60mm and 81/82mm mortars that belonged to the infantry units.[18] Sergeant Simon Kubiak of the 9th Company recalled, "We are all surprised and ask ourselves how the Viets have been able to find so many guns capable of producing an artillery fire of such power. Shells rained down on us without stopping like a hailstorm on a fall evening. Bunker after bunker, trench after trench collapses, burying under them men and weapons."[19]

The bombardment devastated Béatrice's leadership. Lieutenant Carrière was killed, Lieutenant Turpin was seriously wounded, and 12th Company's commander, Captain André Lemoine, was knocked unconscious for a time (he would be killed later that night). Worst of all, at about 1830hrs a shell penetrated the battalion command post, killing its commanding officer, Major Paul Pégot, and his executive officer, Captain Vincent Pardi, and putting all the radios out of action.[20] This disaster occurred at a critical moment, since just as the VPA ground assault was starting, the defenders could not adjust barrages being fired by French batteries in the Main Position. The lack of communications also delayed restoration of the chain of command. Although the command bunker was nearby, 10th Company's Captain Philippe Nicolas did not learn of its destruction until he was ordered to take command of the battalion half an hour later.[21]

The 209th Regiment attacked Béatrice-3 from the south with its 130th Battalion, while the 154th Battalion (less a company detached to the 11/141) blocked RP41, and the 166th was in divisional reserve.[22] The peak was surrounded by plate charges and napalm barrels, but they could not be used because the detonators were buried in the destroyed command bunker.[23] The 336th Company quickly breached the wire and overran half the strongpoint, but was halted by machine-gun fire from an intact bunker.[24] Yet although Lieutenant Turpin had resumed command, the defenders were so devastated by the bombardment that they could not exploit this respite. After the troublesome bunker was destroyed with a satchel charge, VPA troops captured the summit at 1930hrs. Turpin clung to the fringes of the position for another hour, when he was forced to retreat across the gully to Béatrice-2 with his last 25 men.[25] But the 130th Battalion's commander was convinced that Legionnaires were still holding out in underground bunkers and requested reinforcement by the 166th Battalion. Its needless commitment merely created a target-rich environment for French artillery, which was pounding the lost position.[26]

The 141st Regiment attacked Béatrices-1 and -2 from the north with its 428th and 11th Battalions (respectively), while the 16th Battalion remained in reserve. To reach their start lines, the regiment's troops had to cross the Nậm Yum River. French artillery took the crossing point under fire, destroying two pre-constructed fords, and almost wiped out the 428th Battalion's weapons company, which lost both its commander and executive officer. Supported by the 752nd Mountain Battery, the battalion's 58th Company nonetheless swiftly breached Béatrice-1's wire and blew up the "Six Submachine gun Bunker" (which may have been the decoy). But the 428th halted at that point because its assault was supposed to be coordinated with the 11th Battalion's attack on Béatrice-2 – which was not going well. Several sections of the 11/141st's trenches had been flattened by shelling, forcing its troops to cross open ground. Pioneers who tried to breach the barbed wire with Bangalore torpedoes (lengths of bamboo packed with explosives) were mown down by several previously undetected machine-gun bunkers on Béatrice-2 itself, and a heavy machine gun on Béatrice-1 that enfiladed their left flank.[27] They were also targeted by a flamethrower – a terrifying weapon that the vanguard 243rd Company had never encountered before.[28] The French machine guns could not be silenced by infantry heavy weapons since all their ammunition had been expended, and the embrasures of the 752nd Mountain Battery's casemates faced the wrong way. The deadly crossfire was eliminated only after the 75mm howitzers were laboriously hauled out of their emplacements.[29]

Since the 11th Battalion was delayed, the 428th Battalion was authorized to attack on its own and overran most of Béatrice-1 within two hours. Led by its executive officer, Lieutenant Georges Jego, 9th Company was driven back into the strongpoint's northwestern corner. Yet the pursuing 670th Company stopped short because, having encountered a barbed-wire barrier in the dark, it wrongly assumed that it had captured the entire position. Left unmolested, the remaining Legionnaires continued to pour a murderous flanking fire onto the VPA troops attacking Béatrice-2. The 428th Battalion's commander spotted the error, but having no communications with his troops on the hill, had to order a reserve platoon forward to eliminate the pocket of resistance. It took a full hour to arrive, and the remnants of 9th Company were not eliminated until 2230hrs. The few survivors fled into the jungle or across to Béatrice-2.[30]

In addition to the galling fire from Béatrice-1, the 11th Battalion was also being savaged by French artillery and III/13 DBLE's 81mm mortars (dug in on Béatrice-2).[31] The artillery liaison officer, Captain Chrétien Ries of 8/III/10 RAC, had been knocked out when the command post was destroyed. But after coming to, Ries restored communications with the Fire HQ and directed barrages all around Béatrice-2.[32] The 45th Artillery Regiment's commander, Nguyen Huu My, responded by ordering all his batteries except the 805th (which continued to target Isabelle), to fire another counterbattery shoot against the French artillery on Dominique. Since mist and darkness prevented observation, the 20 105s swept their shells back and forth over the area, dropping 200 rounds in ten minutes.[33] The paltry allocation of shells, and the slow, deliberate rate of fire can both be explained by the VPA's modest ammunition stocks.

Worried that Béatrice-2 would hold out long enough to be rescued by a counterattack, Giáp telephoned General Tấn to insist that he finish off the defenders before dawn. Tấn answered that the 11th Battalion still had fight left in it and the 141st Regiment was committing its reserve battalion. They launched a second attack at 2130hrs, which was to have been joined by the units that had conquered the neighboring strongpoints. But the 130th Battalion's commander insisted that his men were incapable of making another assault, and the worn-out 166th and 428th were stymied by the interior minefields and barbed-wire obstacles which – unlike those on the CR's exterior – had neither been reconnoitered nor breached. After this assault failed, Giáp ordered yet another counterbattery shoot on the Main Position's artillery batteries and allocated 40 more 105mm shells against Béatrice-2. Both fire missions began at 2300hrs, and Béatrice-2's perimeter was finally breached shortly thereafter. By 2330hrs, the whole of 11/141 was inside the strongpoint, though it took another two hours to conquer it entirely.[34]

Over a hundred Legionnaires escaped, some by slipping through a "tunnel" (covered trench?) that ran southwest to Béatrice-2's decoy bunker,[35] and straggled into Dominique after dawn.[36] Two officers and 196 enlisted men answered roll call on March 14, but about 80 of them had not been on Béatrice, and another nine were badly wounded men evacuated during a truce that morning (see below).[37] The able-bodied survivors were attached to other Legion units. Seventy-five went to I/2 REI.[38] The PEG was employed as a tactical unit for the next three weeks, while Lieutenant Renault's platoon continued to guard de Castries' headquarters.[39]

The III/13 DBLE had been doomed from the start. Understrength, surrounded, poorly fortified, and short of leadership, the battalion had little chance of resisting an attack by two VPA regiments. Its odds of survival shrank to zero when its senior officers were lost and all communications interrupted at a critical stage in the battle. From that point onward, Béatrice could have been saved only by an immediate counterattack. In the following weeks, many strongpoints would be rescued by night counterattacks, but that was impossible in this case because Béatrice was too far from help and so tightly encircled. With the 154th Battalion waiting in ambush along RP41, it would have been madness for de Castries to dispatch reinforcements before dawn.

He could have launched a counterattack at daybreak, however. The French had always done so at Nà Sản and never left a single strongpoint in enemy hands. It had been their intention to follow the same policy at Điện Biên Phủ, but no serious attempt was made to retake Béatrice. There were several reasons for this, including yet another catastrophic hit on a headquarters. The command post of Mobile Group 9 was destroyed at 1930hrs on March 13, killing Colonel Jules Gaucher, commander of the Central Subsector. He was replaced by Lieutenant Colonel Pierre Langlais, who had almost died himself shortly before when two shells penetrated GAP 2's command bunker, but fortunately for him, neither exploded. Langlais' chief of staff, Major Hubert de Séguin-Pazzis, assumed command of GAP 2, which was responsible for conducting counterattacks. Any attempt to retake Béatrice on March 14 would therefore have been led by a commander who was new to his job – hardly a situation which was likely to yield the kind of bold and resolute action that would be needed.

Sergeant Kubiak, who had slipped through to Dominique shortly after dawn, was ordered to join in a counterattack which was preparing to retake Béatrice. He says that enemy resistance halted the advance almost immediately, and that an order to cease fire was issued before a second assault could be attempted.[40] Aside from Kubiak's own account, the only hint of such an operation is another veteran's recollection that 10/III/3 RTA left Dominique-4 that morning to occupy a hill between Dominique and Béatrice (most likely the one where Dominique-6 was later established), and remained there for 20 hours.[41] This sounds more like an outpost mission than a counterattack, and may have been undertaken in hopes of rescuing more Béatrice survivors. The ceasefire occurred because the badly wounded Lieutenant Turpin had stumbled into Dominique carrying a letter from General Tấn that offered a truce from 0830 to 1200hrs so the French could recover their wounded at Béatrice. General Navarre's chief of staff, General Fernand Gambiez, authorized de Castries to accept the offer – thus ruling out a counterattack that day.[42]

In 1955, de Castries told a commission of inquiry headed by General Georges Catroux that a counterattack was prepared, but not attempted, because poor weather prohibited the use of airpower – which he considered essential. He added that a counterattack became impossible after he was instructed to accept the truce. One of the commission's members, General Joseph Magnan, was dubious. "At the time you received this emissary, it was already too late to launch a counterattack. Your counterattack, if you could do it, was going to be done at daybreak. But the truce came later, so there was no direct relationship between the two things." De Castries finally admitted that he was deterred from counterattacking by the realization that "I was not strong enough to it." This was the plain truth, since regarrisoning Béatrice would have needed an entire battalion, which the garrison did not have to spare. The 5e Bataillon de Parachutistes Vietnamiens – or 5 BPVN (5th Vietnamese Parachute Battalion) – was dropped into the valley that day, but it could not have reached Béatrice before nightfall. [43]

Yet a counterattack by the entire 8 BPC or the 1er Bataillon Étranger de Parachutistes (1st Foreign Legion Parachute Battalion) – 1 BEP – would likely have succeeded. Kubiak, who visited Béatrice during the truce, found only a few VPA troops who warned that its fortifications were about to be blown up.[44] Giáp had no intention of tying his troops down defending the strongpoint, and probably would have welcomed the opportunity to assail another French battalion under even more advantageous circumstances. For even after a successful counterattack, the new defenders would have found Béatrice's obstacles breached in a dozen places, many of its bunkers and trenches collapsed, and have had only a few hours in which to make repairs. But demoralization also contributed to the decision not to attempt a counterattack. The fall of Béatrice stunned the entire garrison, particularly since the assault had come as no surprise. Not only had the III/13 DBLE had several months to prepare, but the Deuxième Bureau had identified where Giáp would aim his first blow, and learned the precise day and hour when it would occur.

The French estimated that 500 VPA troops died at Béatrice, but the Military History Institute of Vietnam put the figure at 193 dead plus 137 wounded.[45] The 11th Battalion lost half its troops, though the other battalions suffered less since their attacks were more successful. The 428th and 130th Battalions were both awarded the Medal of Military Merit, 3rd Class, for the Béatrice assault, while the 11th Battalion received no battle honor.[46] An investigation concluded that its trenches had not been deep enough, and this is confirmed by Phạm Văn Nham, who recalled that digging went slowly because the soil was full of pebbles, and pickaxes could not be used for fear of alerting Béatrice's defenders. The trench he helped excavate was only 30 cm deep on the morning of March 13.[47]

Gabrielle, March 14–15

Giáp selected Gabrielle (which his troops called "Độc Lập" (Independent) Hill owing to its isolation) as his next target. It barred the way down the Pavie Track just as Béatrice had blocked access to the valley along RP41. But that was the end of the similarities between the two positions. There were no hills abutting directly on Gabrielle that could be used as bases of attack and artillery emplacements, nor any blocking the route over which reinforcements would come from the Main Position. And unlike the jumble of ridges that comprised Béatrice, Gabrielle was a single hill measuring 457m by 183m, which rose about 60m above the surrounding paddies.[48] The defenders also manned a daytime observation post on Piton Sonnette ("Outpost Peak") – 500m northwest of Gabrielle – which afforded a lengthwise view up portions of the Nậm Co Valley which were invisible from the CR itself. It was abandoned on March 11.[49]

Gabrielle was defended by the 5ème Bataillon du 7e Régiment de Tirailleurs Algériens – V/7 RTA (5th Battalion of the 7th Algerian Rifle Regiment), which had served in Indochina with distinction since 1951. On March 10 its strength was 626 men, of whom 80 were French (including all but one of the 16 officers and 36 of the 77 NCOs).[50] Like the III/13 DBLE, the V/7 RTA lacked officers and many platoons were commanded by NCOs. But it enjoyed the unique advantage of having two battalion commanders present. Major Roland de Mecquenem's tour had ended on March 2, but he remained to familiarize his replacement, Major Edouard Kah, with the battalion's troops and defenses. And to ensure that a single hit on the CP would not leave the battalion leaderless, a secondary command post was established in the officers' mess some distance away.[51] Finally, Gabrielle was the only strongpoint that had a complete second line of defense and won a garrison-wide fortification contest organized by Colonel de Castries.[52] It had good fields of fire, barbed-wire obstacles that were 80m wide, and had been given the best overhead cover possible. To seal off enemy penetrations, *chevaux de frise* of wood and barbed wire were poised to be dropped into all major junctions in the trench system.[53] And since

THE NORTHERN SUBSECTOR

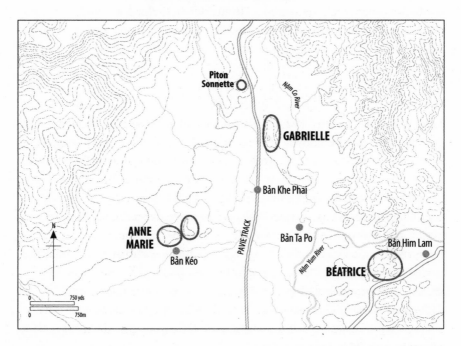

Gabrielle comprised a single position defended by an entire battalion, reserves were close at hand and could quickly move about using the covered interior lines provided by the second line of defense.

Although Gabrielle was formally divided into five strongpoints, these were merely different sectors within a single defensive perimeter. The 1st Company held the northwest, the 2nd the southwest, the 3rd the southeast, and the 4th the northeast.[54] The center of the perimeter was occupied by the Headquarters Company, the 416th Tai Auxiliary Company (CSM 416), and Lieutenant Gilbert Clerget's platoon of 2 CMMLE (2nd Foreign Legion Composite Mortar Company). This normally had four 120mm mortars, but one had been destroyed by shelling on March 13, and another by an accident on March 14.[55] In addition, this area contained a special counterattack platoon led by the battalion's intelligence officer, Lieutenant Pierre Sanselme. By one account, it was created by detaching a squad from each platoon in 2nd Company – which was least likely to be attacked – but that unit's commander, Lieutenant Antoine Botella, insists that a squad was taken from each company in the battalion. Whichever was true, the reserve platoon included a flamethrower-equipped pioneer squad from the Headquarters Company.[56] Finally, Gabrielle's firepower had been reinforced by a dozen machine guns from GONO's reserves.[57]

Giáp originally intended to take Béatrice and Gabrielle on the same night to force the French to split their artillery and reserves, but there were not enough 75mm mountain guns to support two simultaneous assaults.[58] The attack on Gabrielle was therefore rescheduled for the night of March 14–15. The 308th Division's 88th Infantry Regiment would launch a secondary attack, while the 312th Division's 165th Infantry Regiment delivered the main blow.[59] Yet although the 165th Regiment was to bear the brunt of the assault, the 308th Division's General Vương Thừa Vũ was in overall command, with the 312th's Deputy Commander, Đàm Quang Trung, present at his headquarters to facilitate liaison.[60] This arrangement seems needlessly cumbersome, since it would have been simpler to make the assault with two regiments of the 308th Division. But it had just returned from six weeks of hard campaigning in Laos, and was weakened by losses and fatigue. Nguyễn Mạnh Quân, a company commander in the 322/88, recalled, "We returned from Laos just the day before the offensive started. We are tired, and our troops are depleted and disorganized."[61] The 316th Division had likewise been worn down by its operations against the Tai auxiliaries retreating from Lai Châu and the GMI guerrillas that continued to infest the highlands. Giáp explained:

> All regiments of our 308th and 316th Divisions had fought in battles of pursuit spread out over hundreds of kilometers; the numbers had been more or less thinned down. The 312th had built the road, hauled in the artillery, and prepared the battlefield; its soldiers were tired from hard work, though the division's numbers were near the original level. For these reasons, the Front Command chose the 312th as the lead unit to open the battle.[62]

The 165th Regiment was therefore earmarked to deliver the main attack because it was at full strength, but the 312th Division's other two regiments were in no condition to fight again so soon after taking Béatrice. And since the divisional staff could not efficiently plan and direct two major assaults on consecutive days, the 308th Division was given command of the Gabrielle operation.

The mountain and 120mm mortar batteries that had been used against Béatrice had to be hastily repositioned to support the attack on Gabrielle, and the 394th Antiaircraft Battalion's 828th and 829th Batteries also had to be towed from Bản Nà Tấu (about 4km north of Gabrielle) to new emplacements half that distance from the CR near Bản Nà Hi. This bold, daylight move through the open Nậm Co Valley was detected by GONO's last "Cricket" spotter plane, which was circling gingerly under the low cloud cover, and the 155s and Gabrielle's 120s began shelling the convoy. The 829th Battery ran the gauntlet without damage, but the 828th had three trucks set afire – including one loaded with ammunition. Yet the stranded 37mm flak guns remained intact, and all of them were towed into their new emplacements by a gallant truck driver who repeatedly forayed back out into the shell-swept valley to recover them.[63] Despite this high drama, the entire 394th AA Battalion was in position on schedule, but the same could not be said of the artillery. Giáp writes, "Because of the rain and mud, we had not been able to move our 75mm and mountain artillery and 120mm mortars from Béatrice over to Gabrielle on time. For that reason, we could not begin the attack on Gabrielle as planned."[64]

A diversionary attack on Eliane-2 by the 255/174 began on schedule at 1645hrs, and two 120mm mortar batteries, two 75mm mountain batteries, and four 105mm howitzer batteries started bombarding French headquarters, artillery positions, and the airport at 1700hrs.[65] But when it became clear that the artillery redeploying from Béatrice was not going to be ready to open fire at 1800hrs as planned, the feint was called off. Generals Vũ and Trung decided to delay the assault on Gabrielle while destroying its fortifications with those weapons that were already in place.[66] The infantry units' ĐKZs and mortars did most of the work, though the 803rd Howitzer Battery fired some ranging shots at the strongpoint. The shelling started about 20 minutes before nightfall so that VPA artillerymen could zero in on their targets. After dark, ĐKZ gunner Đặng Mạnh Hùng could not even see his weapon's sights, and had to aim by peering through the barrel and shooting when the defenders' fire illuminated a bunker's gun slit.[67]

The shelling intensified around 2000hrs, but slackened half an hour later as VPA troops approached the northern part of Gabrielle. The 564/165 came from the northwest, while the 88th Regiment advanced from the northeast with its 29th Battalion in front and the 322nd in the second echelon.[68] Bernard Fall wrote: "This was no human-wave assault. The Viet-Minh were apparently unwilling to pay the heavy price they had paid the night before at Béatrice."[69] Vietnamese historians insist that no assault was made until hours later; though in the meantime VPA pioneers began breaching the barbed wire and minefields.

But the defenders believed they were under attack, and by midnight Lieutenant Sanselme's reserve platoon and CSM 416 had gone forward several times to shore up the 1st and 4th Companies' sectors.[70]

These forays were prompted by lapses in communication that occurred when a platoon in 1st Company had its radio damaged and 4th Company's command post was destroyed (its commander, Lieutenant André Moreau, survived – for the moment).[71] Overall, Gabrielle's command structure remained intact, and the artillery observer, Lieutenant Georges Collin of II/4 RAC, was in constant communication with the batteries on the Main Position and Isabelle.[72] They rained 105mm shells along the strongpoint's northern and eastern faces, and on enemy assembly areas farther back, while the Quad-50s sprayed tracers over the southern slopes, and machine guns on Anne Marie swept the ridge's western flank. Lieutenant Clerget's 120s and V/7 RTA's own 81mm mortars also fired steadily, but were destroyed one by one. VPA counterbattery fire also took a toll on the Main Position's artillery, knocking out one of 5/II/4 RAC's guns and temporarily disabling another in 9/III/10 RAC.[73] By most accounts, French artillery fire was accurate and deadly, but Company Commander Nguyễn Mạnh Quân in the 322/88 claimed that by the time it reached full force, his troops were too close to Gabrielle to be targeted effectively.[74]

All the while, the tardy mountain guns and heavy mortars – broken down into pieces – were slowly being carried toward Gabrielle on shoulder poles. Since the defenders reported no activity in the 165th Regiment's main attack sector in front of 3rd Company, it's likely that the VPA infantrymen were helping to move the artillery. Maneuvering the disassembled weapons over steep, muddy mountain trails in pitch darkness was exhausting and dangerous work that was made even riskier by French artillery fire that periodically raked the area. At 2400hrs, when the 752nd Mountain Battery was just 700m from its destination, a flurry of airbursts killed and wounded many of its personnel and shattered most of the carrying poles.[75] It took another two hours to get the guns into position, and at 0230hrs an eerie quiet fell over the battlefield. It ended an hour later when the newly arrived batteries (which Western historians misidentify as 105mm) opened fire.[76] A shell killed the 1st Company's commander, Captain Jean Narbey, and wounded its executive officer, Lieutenant Bernard Roux, and this decapitating blow contributed to the success of an enemy thrust that penetrated between 1st and 4th Companies, and reached the second line of defense at 0400hrs. The breach was sealed by Lieutenant

Sanselme's reserve platoon and CSM 416, and Major de Mecquenem sent his executive officer, Captain Daniel Carré, to restore command in the northern sectors. The situation was still serious enough, however, that Lieutenant Collin requested that proximity-fused 105mm shells be airbursted over the first line of trenches even though some Algerians were still holding out in them.[77]

This penetration was probably made by the 564/165, since the 88th Regiment's assault was stalled. Its troops had suffered heavy casualties because their approach trenches were poorly constructed and French shells had destroyed several sections. Then its pioneers had become disoriented in the dark and began slanting across the hillside rather than moving directly up it. When a gap over 100m long had been cleared without penetrating the barbed wire, Squad Leader Nguyễn Văn Tuy spotted the error, and, using a prominent bunker as a guidepost, got his men back on course.[78] But a shortage of Bangalores forced Tuy to adopt the dangerous expedient of using grenades to detonate explosives shoved in amidst the barbed wire. The job was not finished until after 0430hrs when the 322nd Battalion's pioneer platoon came up to assist. Down in 3rd Company's sector, the 542/165 had swiftly opened a breach and assaulted into the trenches with the 115/165 following behind.[79]

Meanwhile, disaster had struck the defenders. At about 0430hrs, a shell penetrated the main command bunker, seriously wounding de Mecquenem and Collin, tearing off one of Major Kah's legs, and destroying all the radios. Lieutenant Sanselme, who had just left, was wounded in both legs, and command of his dwindling reserve platoon fell upon Sergeant-Chief Rouzic, who had joined the army to escape prosecution as a gangster.[80] Like Béatrice the night before, Gabrielle was now leaderless and unable to communicate with the artillery. It was a stroke of incredibly bad luck, since 0430hrs was the first time in hours that all of V/7 RTA's leaders had been together in one place. The only officer whom Langlais could raise by radio, 3rd Company's Captain Henri Gendre, was assured that reinforcements would arrive shortly after dawn. Meanwhile, Lieutenant Clerget, whose last 120s had been knocked out, capably took on the role of artillery observer.[81]

The situation on Gabrielle continued to deteriorate. Captain Carré was second in command, but without functioning communications there was little he could do to restore the situation. He tried to bring up reinforcements from the still unengaged 2nd Company, but Lieutenant Botella reported that he had lost a third of his men to shelling and had none to spare.[82] Meanwhile, the battalion lost yet another key officer when 4th Company's commander

Lieutenant Moreau was killed. Its sector was overrun by 0630hrs and VPA troops penetrated to the heart of Gabrielle. They slowly pushed 4th Company's remnants and Rouzic's reserve platoon (which had been reduced to just seven Algerians) back down the spine of the ridge. By 0730hrs, most of 1st Company's remaining troops, leaderless and exposed to the fire of *bộ đội* ("soldiers") occupying the crest behind them, had been forced to surrender. Meanwhile, the 2nd and 3rd Companies were standing back to back waiting for reinforcements to arrive. But at 0715hrs, 3rd Company had buckled under mounting pressure from the 165th Regiment and been forced to retire to its second defense line. Yet even at this point, it was still not too late for Gabrielle to be saved.[83]

The Gabrielle counterattack, March 15

A counterattack had been launched, as promised, but it was hamstrung from the start by a series of dubious command decisions. De Castries told the Catroux Commission that on March 14 he had allocated two companies each from 1 BEP and 8 BPC (presumably the dual-tasked ones that garrisoned various strongpoints) to the Central Subsector.[84] This questionable decision dissipated the garrison's reserves and left it without a battalion capable of counterattacking at full strength. At least in theory, the problem was solved when 5 BPVN parachuted in that same afternoon. But it was tired after making a combat jump, marching several kilometers under artillery harassment, and then digging in on newly established Eliane-4 (where some sketchy fortifications already existed).[85] Moreover, Langlais did not rate 5 BPVN, whose personnel were all Vietnamese except for its senior officers and NCOs, as highly as the mixed Vietnamese-European colonial and Foreign Legion parachute battalions, and tactlessly told its commander, Captain André Botella, as much after he arrived.[86]

Throughout the night of March 14–15, it seemed that V/7 RTA would repulse the attack on its own, but by 0500hrs it clearly needed help. De Castries testified that, earlier that night, the two 8 BPC companies that remained in reserve had been sent to counter "a number of infiltrations between Dominique and Gabrielle, i.e., north of the airfield."[87] This left only 5 BPVN and two companies of 1 BEP available for a counterattack. Since the enemy was known to be assaulting Gabrielle with two regiments, at least a full battalion would be needed for the counterattack to succeed (by one account, contingency plans called for two entire battalions). Yet Langlais chose to commit only the two Legion parachute companies. Counterattacking with just half a battalion was a half-hearted gesture, which suggests that he was not committed to rescuing Gabrielle. This impression is reinforced by the instructions he gave to Major Séguin-Pazzis, who was going to command the operation. His orders were "to try to retake Gabrielle or at least to recover the survivors."[88]

The counterattack set out at 0515hrs with 1 BEP's 3rd and 4th Companies supported by all seven of the Main Position's tanks, II/4 RAC, and a company of 120s.[89] Within half an hour, Langlais belatedly realized this would not be sufficient, but he did not commit the rest of 1 BEP. Instead, he sent 5 BPVN, which was supposed to replace the decimated V/7 RTA on Gabrielle. This was yet another questionable decision since, although speed was of the essence, the battalion was dead-tired and located east of the Nậm Yum – much farther from the objective than 1 BEP. It was also unfamiliar with the camp's minefields and barbed-wire obstacles, which slowed it far more than the Foreign Legion paratroops, who were well acquainted with them. It took 5 BPVN an hour just to reach the airfield, and it then had to crawl the length of the runway single file through a drainage ditch that paralleled it on the eastern side because sunrise had exposed the troops to VPA artillery observers. While it straggled far behind, the counterattack reached a *radier* (artificial ford) across a stream 1,500m south of Gabrielle around 0630hrs. A small patrol of BT3 had crept over to the crossing half an hour earlier without meeting any resistance, but when Séguin-Pazzis' force arrived it was engaged by what he thought was a full VPA battalion in ambush near the ford and ensconced in a trench that curved around the hamlet of Bản Khe Phai about halfway to Gabrielle.[90] In fact, only two VPA companies were present (the 213th of the 23/88 and the 964th of the 542/165), though they were supported by a 75mm battery firing over open sights.[91]

Enemy fire was heavy enough that Séguin-Pazzis decided to await 5 BPVN before pressing on. This holdup would not have occurred if an entire battalion had been committed to the counterattack from the start, and its consequences were grave. For while the decision to pause was understandable, the delay greatly reduced the odds of reaching Gabrielle in time to save it. Indeed, while the tanks and paratroops were marking time, the situation deteriorated so rapidly that around 0700hrs Langlais radioed a new set of orders instructing Séguin-Pazzis merely to rescue the CR's survivors. Captain Gendre also heard the message, and he naturally began thinking in terms of retreat rather than clinging stubbornly to the hilltop.[92]

Upon receiving this second set of orders, Séguin-Pazzis renewed his attack even though 5 BPVN still had not come up. Resistance at the ford was quickly overcome and most of 4/1 BEP was left to mask Bản Khe Phai while the rest of the force pressed on. The Bisons led the way and knocked out a 75mm howitzer posted on a hillock southeast of Gabrielle.[93] Luckily for the French, the enemy 75s had no antitank rounds and soon ran out of ammunition.[94] The attack was aided by the Tai on Anne Marie-2 who used their machine guns and 57mm recoilless rifles against *bộ đội* who were threatening Séguin-Pazzis' western flank. It was not an easy fight, however, and in addition to heavy losses in 1 BEP, Douaumont was seriously damaged and Sergeant Pierre Guntz, the Red Platoon's commander, was killed when Ettlingen took a direct 120mm mortar hit. Both tanks retreated to the Main Position carrying badly wounded Legionnaires whose blood was splattered on their turrets and rear decks.[95]

Langlais was nonetheless encouraged enough that he altered Séguin-Pazzis' orders yet again. Now he was to decide for himself whether to evacuate Gabrielle's garrison or retake the CR.[96] However, the decision was soon taken out of his hands. 5 BPVN had finally arrived at the ford shortly before the two damaged tanks raced by carrying their gory cargoes. Only 3rd Company and part of 2nd crossed the ford, which was still under fire by enemy artillery. Lieutenant Ty of 2nd Company lost his nerve and went to ground, forcing the following 1st and 4th Companies to halt as well.[97] Without the entire 5 BPVN, Séguin-Pazzis did not have sufficient strength to retake Gabrielle in the face of two VPA regiments.

It's easy to blame 5 BPVN for the counterattack's failure, but this is unfair and obscures other important causes. What ultimately decided the battle was the fact that Gabrielle's battered garrison abandoned its positions just as 3/1 BEP reached the foot of the hill. The defenders' flight was a direct consequence of the contradictory orders that had been emanating from Langlais' headquarters for the preceding two hours. Captain Gendre's failing radio had caught the second set of orders, but not the third. Believing that Séguin-Pazzis had come to evacuate the garrison, 3rd Company's remnants retreated off the hill at 0745hrs, prompting 2nd Company to follow suit at 0800hrs.[98] If Séguin-Pazzis had any thoughts of trying to retake Gabrielle with the force remaining to him, V/7 RTA's retreat forced him to abandon them. Instead, he had to make a hellish march back to the Main Position under constant enemy fire in broad daylight.

Western historians all agree that the key decisions about the Gabrielle counterattack were made by Langlais,[99] but generally fail to note just how irregular this was. After all, he commanded neither the Northern Subsector

GABRIELLE COUNTERATTACK

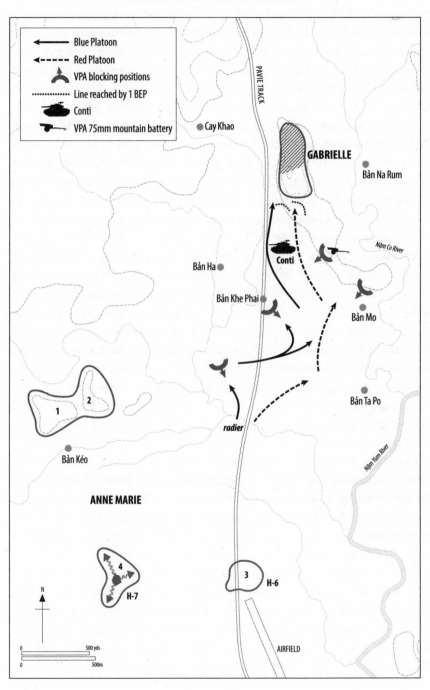

where Gabrielle was situated, nor GAP 2, which conducted the counterattack. All the key decisions should have been made by de Castries himself in consultation with Major Séguin-Pazzis and Colonel Trancart. Yet de Castries delegated operational responsibility for the counterattack to Langlais, who issued orders to Séguin-Pazzis without even consulting with Trancart.[100] In his memoirs, Langlais wrote:

> … on March 18th, on the fifth day battle, in the Northern sector of Điện Biên Phủ the strongpoints Béatrice, Gabrielle and Anne-Marie were overrun. In view of the situation, Colonel de Castries confirmed the mission I received on the first night and now put all the airborne units under my command. From one night to another I passed from commanding 2 to now 3 battalions, all the while still commanding the main resistance centers, meaning all the strongpoints minus Isabelle.[101]

Langlais' meaning is not entirely clear, particularly as there were actually four parachute battalions on hand by March 18. However, he seems to be saying that he retained control of GAP 2's original two battalions, even after assuming command of the Central Subsector. This is not entirely in agreement with de Castries' testimony that he assigned only half of the parachute reserves to the Central Subsector, but such distinctions were becoming meaningless. On the very first night of the siege, de Castries had surrendered most of his authority as garrison commander to Langlais by making him responsible both for defending the Main Position and managing the reserves. This remarkable abdication of authority was symptomatic of a crisis in command that arose because de Castries, stunned by the shocks and reverses of the siege's first hours, had sunk into pessimism and inertia. The bold cavalryman and master of maneuver was plainly out of his depth fighting a positional infantry battle in a beleaguered outpost nearly 320km behind enemy lines. He willingly passed the reins of command to Langlais, who as a paratrooper, was perfectly suited to lead that kind of battle.[102]

That being said, Langlais' own performance was uneven – and instead of admitting his mistakes, he frequently blamed his subordinates. Bison commander Captain Yves Hervouët did not dare breathe a word of his disapproval about how the Gabrielle counterattack had been conducted because he knew that Langlais would take it as a personal affront and explode in one of his infamous towering rages.[103] But it must be admitted that Langlais was in the difficult position of "wearing two hats." On one hand, he had to protect the Central Subsector, which housed GONO's main headquarters, airfield and supply dumps, as well as the bulk of its infantry, armor, and artillery. On the other, he was supposed to use the reserves to launch counterattacks in all three subsectors. These two missions – the one essentially defensive and the other offensive – were at odds with each other and should never have been assigned to the same officer since he would necessarily favor one over the other. Langlais decided that preserving "his" reserves so they could ensure the safety of "his" Central Subsector took precedence over rescuing the northern hill strongpoints (which he clearly thought were indefensible in the long run). If he had still merely been commander of GAP 2, the forceful Langlais would have demanded at least a full battalion for the Gabrielle counterattack and – given his distrust of 5 BPVN – would undoubtedly have insisted that it be 1 BEP or 8 BPC.

As commander of the Central Subsector, however, Langlais was painfully aware that the reserves were manning some of its strongpoints and that only they could garrison the new ones that would be needed to plug gaps in its defenses. It has also been suggested that Langlais and de Castries were reluctant to commit the reserves because enemy troops were feinting against the Main Position while the battle for Gabrielle was raging.[104] Yet by 0500hrs on March 15, when dawn was just over an hour away, it must have been obvious that Giáp was not going to assault another strongpoint that night. It is true that both commanders mentioned the infiltrations in their testimony before the Catroux Commission, but then they brought up every possible excuse why the Gabrielle counterattack was mishandled – including some that were demonstrably specious. Langlais went so far as to tell an outright lie, saying, "Gabrielle fell at about 0500hrs and the counterattack could only collect what remained of the garrison."[105]

This casts doubt on Langlais' testimony that GAP 2 had rehearsed counterattacks in support of Béatrice, Anne Marie, and Gabrielle. Colonel Trancart also testified that infantry and tanks had practiced passing through the camp's minefields and barbed-wire obstacles at night to reach the CRs in his subsector, but he too could have been misrepresenting the facts.[106] 1 BEP's commander, Major Maurice Guiraud, claimed that no rehearsals had taken place, and said that he reminded Langlais of this on March 14.[107] Yet, Lieutenant Jean Luciani, commander of 1/1 BEP, recalled that his battalion and 8 BPC had walked the entire route to Gabrielle so that they would be familiar with the intervening terrain. But whatever the truth was concerning GAP 2's other battalions, 5 BPVN had had no opportunity to acquaint itself with the route, making Langlais' decision to use it even more difficult to defend. Luciani wondered why his own company was not involved, since it was truly in reserve (i.e., not garrisoning one of the Main Position's strongpoints).[108]

If Langlais had committed the entire 1 BEP, and given Séguin-Pazzis unambiguous orders to retake Gabrielle, the odds of success were good. There would have been no need to delay at the ford and V/7 RTA would have clung stubbornly to its remaining positions. With the sun up, an elite para battalion and seven tanks on hand, and improving weather raising the possibility of air support later in the day,[109] Séguin-Pazzis could probably have retaken Gabrielle and installed 5 BPVN as its new garrison. The decimated 88th and 165th Regiments would have been in no condition to launch another attack, and Giáp would have needed at least several days to prepare an assault with the 308th Division's other two regiments. Gabrielle would eventually have had to have been evacuated, but the setback would have denied Giáp the psychological momentum he so greatly desired, and done much to restore the garrison's morale. It would almost certainly have prevented the desertion of the 3rd Tai Battalion just two days later (see below).

In retrospect, Giáp was wrong to have assaulted Béatrice and Gabrielle on consecutive nights, as it was impossible to redeploy the artillery fast enough. He then compounded the error by going ahead with the Gabrielle attack even after learning that the artillery would not arrive on schedule. The delay made a shambles of General Vũ's attack plan and guaranteed that Gabrielle would not be conquered by sunrise, giving the French good odds of saving it with a daytime counterattack. In concrete terms, Giáp would have lost nothing had he postponed the attack by 24 hours, but he seems to have been hell-bent on building psychological momentum by taking two strongpoints on successive nights and was under pressure from CMAG to move quickly since the Chinese did not believe that the VPA could sustain a prolonged siege. Giáp escaped the full consequences of this rash decision only because French commanders vacillated at the crucial moment. He was lucky to have avoided what could have been a stinging and demoralizing defeat.

VPA casualties at Gabrielle were severe – especially in the 88th Regiment. Đình Văn Định, a field training cadre in its 29th Battalion, recalled seeing a cook weeping because there was no one left to eat in his mess. Testimony from other VPA veterans reveals that two-thirds of the 100 men which the 322nd Battalion's 225th Company sent into battle became casualties, while the

115/165 lost about 100 dead.[110] Yet Western historians who estimate VPA fatalities in the battle at between 1,000 and 2,000 are mistaken. Bernard Fall believed the entire 102nd Regiment was involved, making the odds against the V/7 RTA "at least eight to one."[111] But in fact, no unit of the 102nd Regiment was engaged that night, and it seems that only a single company of the 23/88 saw action (at Bản Khe Phai). At most, six VPA battalions were involved in the battle and if we assume an average strength of 500 (which is probably too generous), their total manpower would have been roughly 3,000. If one assumes that 1,000 VPA troops were killed and applies the rule of thumb which predicts that for each fatality there will be two wounded, the attacking battalions suffered 100-percent casualties! This is most unlikely.

The battle had also been costly for GONO. 1 BEP had nine killed and 46 wounded (including its commander, Major Maurice Guiraud, and both company commanders), and V/7 RTA lost about three-quarters of its strength, including de Mequenem, Kah, and Collin, who were all taken prisoner (Kah soon died from his wounds). Just 165 able-bodied men (including four officers) escaped from the hill.[112] The depleted 2nd and 3rd Companies were sent to Isabelle so their presence would not further depress morale in the Main Position. Bernard Fall claimed that, in addition, "the newly parachuted 5th Vietnamese Airborne Battalion had for all practical purposes disintegrated"[113] and describes Captain Botella purging his ranks of hundreds of men who had panicked at Bản Khe Phai. Botella says that 2/5 BPVN's commander, Lieutenant Phạm Văn Phú, presented him with a list of men that should be shot for cowardice. Botella chose instead what he considered the "worse punishment" of expelling the culprits from his unit and the paratroops. He was left with about 450 of the 600 men who had jumped in the previous day. Making allowance for casualties suffered in the interim, perhaps 130 Vietnamese paras were expelled. But, according to Botella, "Most of them soon rejoined the battalion and were able to die well."[114]

Anne Marie, March 15–17

Giáp's gamble had paid off. His troops' morale soared to new heights, while in the opposing camp there was growing demoralization that was especially pronounced in de Castries' headquarters. His chief of staff, Lieutenant Colonel René Keller, suffered a nervous breakdown and sat motionless in the command bunker cowering under a steel helmet that he never removed. Colonel Charles Piroth gave way to depression as the futility of French counterbattery fire – and the emptiness of his pre-battle promises – became obvious. After a "chewing out" by Langlais on the morning of March 15, Piroth retreated to a bunker, pulled the pin from a grenade, and held it to his chest. De Castries radioed that Piroth went missing "in the course of a reconnaissance,"[115] but the truth soon came out and was revealed to the garrison by newspapers that were dropped in.[116]

The French expected that Anne Marie – the obvious next target – would be attacked on the night of March 15–16. If Giáp delayed, he risked dissipating the psychological momentum that had been won at such great cost, and everything suggested that he planned to launch another attack in rapid succession. Yet no assault came that night or the next. Why not? Giáp wrote that the need for 105mm shells was so pressing that on March 15 trucks began rushing them to Điện Biên Phủ in broad daylight despite the risk of air attack.[117] A shell shortage may have delayed the assault on Anne Marie, but it seems unlikely that the VPA's painstaking pre-battle planning was so far off the mark that there had to be a three-day hiatus. Another possibility is that the 308th Division's 36th and 102nd Regiments, having just returned from Laos, still were not fully ready to attack. But it is most likely that Giáp, dismayed by the heavy losses at Gabrielle, chose to delay the assault on Anne Marie while his staff pondered how to improve the VPA's tactics.

Anne Marie was a key CR that guarded the northern approaches to the main airstrip. It was actually two distinct pairs of strongpoints. Anne Maries-1 and -2 were built on adjoining 30 meter high hills overlooking the village of Bản Kéo, while Anne Maries-3 and -4 were a kilometer to the south and were effectively outlying bastions of the Main Position. The entire 1 BEP built and defended Anne Maries-1 and -2 in November 1953, but in December it was replaced by 5 BPVN[118] and then the 301st Vietnamese Battalion, and at some point a third hill strongpoint was added. Anne Maries-3 and 4 were built near the end of December by the 2nd Tai Battalion and the White Tai Company.[119] But in January, the CR's garrison was trimmed to just a single battalion – the 3ème Bataillon Thaï – or BT3 (3rd Tai). The reduction in strength was offset, to some extent, by the fact that BT3 was the only battalion in the garrison which was at full strength (it was, after all, stationed in its recruitment area). On March 10 it had 887 men, including 90 French officers and NCOs, and the 90-strong CSM 272.[120]

Lieutenant Rémi Dalle's 11th Company defended Anne Marie-1, while Anne Marie-2 held the battalion's Headquarters Company (which included a recon "Commando" and an "Intervention" (counterattack) Platoon), CSM 272, and Lieutenant Bernard Michel-Levy's 10th Company. Since BT3 did not have enough troops to defend the third hill strongpoint, its bunkers were demolished and trenches filled in so that the enemy could not use them.[121] Far to the southeast, Anne Marie-3 sat atop the tip of the runway like the dot on an "i." It was garrisoned by Captain Henri Guilleminot's 12th Company and Lieutenant Jean-Paul Fetter's four-tube 120mm mortar platoon of 2 CMMLE.[122] About 500m to the west, Anne Marie-4 was held by Captain Michel Désiré's 9th Company.[123]

BT3's morale was shaky even before the siege. It contained many raw troops who had been recruited after the battalion took heavy casualties in Operation *Mouette* ("Seagull"), south of the Red River Delta in October 1953. But even its veteran troops' morale was weak since their native villages were under enemy occupation and their families exposed to Communist reprisals. The battalion had also lost its longtime commander, Captain Jacques Archambault, when his tour ended in February. The new commander, Major Léopold Thimonnier, was unfamiliar with both Tai culture and his subordinates, and some thought him less energetic than his predecessor. Finally, there were only 13 officers (all French) in the battalion. And unlike V/7 RTA, BT3 did not have a cadre of long-service, non-European NCOs who had fought in World War II. None of the Tai NCOs had any experience in "sweating out" artillery barrages, and were therefore less capable of steadying the enlisted men than their counterparts in other battalions. Two French officers who joined BT3 on March 13 were surprised by how unsteady the troops proved to be under harassing shellfire that afternoon.[124] And it took all the authority of French cadres to prevent the ambush patrols and "listening posts" sent out that night from retreating without orders.[125]

BT3's troops were shocked by the fall of Gabrielle just 1,700m away. They had spent the night of March 14–15 watching its death throes and the failure of the counterattack while being harassed by mortar fire. The next day, VPA trenches crept ever closer while the mortar fire resumed, and blaring loudspeakers warned that Anne Marie would be next and enticed the Tai to desert with promises of good treatment. The defenders were also down to just two days' rations since they had been able to recover only some of the supplies parachuted onto nearby Drop Zone Rita the day before. Morale plummeted. What chance did the Tai have of holding their widely scattered strongpoints when the Legionnaires and Algerians had been unable to defend their tight clusters of mutually supporting positions?[126] Thimonnier urgently requested a company or two of Legionnaires as reinforcements, but was told to do the best he could with what he had.[127]

Demoralization was worst in 12th Company since V/7 RTA's battered survivors had retreated down the road which ran right next to Anne Marie-3. During the daylight hours of March 15, harassment by VPA 105s killed two men and wounded 11 more (including three French NCOs). After nightfall over half of 12th Company's troops abandoned their weapons and deserted. To prevent his remaining troops from deserting, Captain Guilleminot decided on his own authority to abandon the strongpoint and fall back to Huguette. A few more Tai also deserted from Anne Marie-2 – which had had the best view of Gabrielle's demise – and French cadres had to be posted at the gates to prevent more from fleeing.[128] Thus, by dawn on March 16, Colonel Trancart knew that BT3 was collapsing but could do nothing to help it since he controlled no reserves. Only de Castries and Langlais could save Anne Marie, and prudence dictated that they replace or at least reinforce BT3 with more reliable troops. But their response was weak and indecisive. The immediate crisis was resolved by sending a company of I/2 REI to reoccupy Anne Marie-3.[129] Yet although Anne Maries-1 and -2 were far more likely to be attacked in the near term, nothing was done for them because Langlais was unwilling to commit his reserves.

Neither 1 BEP nor 5 BPVN was in the best shape, but 8 BPC had thus far seen little action. It could have replaced or reinforced BT3 without depleting the reserves since 6 BPC was going to jump in that same day.[130] Yet Langlais took no action until after the battalion had arrived, when he personally ordered its 1st Company to Anne Marie. 6 BPC's legendary commander, Major Marcel Bigeard, loudly objected to this breach in the chain of command, igniting a violent shouting match with Langlais. It ended amicably when they agreed that 1st Company would return after making a brief, morale-boosting visit to Anne Marie accompanied by the Red Platoon.[131] General André Mengelle, who served with the Bisons at Điện Biên Phủ when he was a mere lieutenant, wrote that this mission was "gratuitous and the effects perverse, the Tais recalling only its brevity, which had not escaped the Viet Minh observers."[132] FTNV was clearly perplexed by this charade, since it would radio in exasperation that night to inquire: "1) if Anne Marie had been reinforced [and if] 2) in the affirmative, by whom?"[133]

VPA mortar harassment intensified during the morning and flak weapons at the foot of Hill 633 north of Gabrielle also strafed Anne Marie.[134] At noon, the

803rd Howitzer Battery dropped 20 105mm shells on it and continued to fire occasional rounds until nightfall.[135] Shortly before dusk, a VPA officer approached Anne Marie-2 under a flag of truce and announced that wounded Gabrielle survivors could be collected the next morning 600m to the north.[136] But although the night was quiet, more Tai seized the opportunity to desert.[137] At sunrise, the barbed wire was festooned with enemy propaganda leaflets and a large painting that depicted the Tai abandoning their positions. Its caption read, "If you return to the Nation and the people, you will be greeted with kindness."[138] Several Tai women approached the gates and spread dismay by warning that Anne Marie was about to be attacked and urging the defenders to flee north into enemy hands. The recovery of 11 bloody Gabrielle survivors did nothing to raise spirits and VPA mortars opened fire the instant that the stretcher-bearers returned to Anne Marie-2 around 0900hrs – inflicting new casualties and making it impossible to evacuate any of the wounded.[139] The enemy also barraged Anne Marie with loudspeakers. Langlais recalled a VPA colonel boasting, "Give me a battalion and I'll overrun Anne-Marie with ease. All the Tais are ready to desert. The battle of annihilation is about to start. It will end with a complete slaughter."[140]

Major Thimonnier requested that his troops be replaced immediately, but although there was plenty of time to carry out a relief, the only answer he got was to "do his best."[141] Langlais had already written off Anne Marie and at 1230hrs de Castries signaled FTNV that a relief of BT3 "cannot be accomplished without compromising the effectiveness of prepared counterattacks."[142] At the same moment, the 803rd Howitzer Battery began pummeling Anne Maries-1 and -2 with flurries of 20 105mm shells at irregular intervals. This was the straw that broke the camel's back. At 1400hrs terrified Tai began to slip out in small groups and French cadres could not halt the armed deserters, whom enemy loudspeakers were urging to kill anyone who tried to stop them. To keep the rest of his troops from fleeing, Thimonnier got Colonel Trancart's permission to evacuate the two strongpoints. Radios, flamethrowers, and other heavy weapons were destroyed, while the mortar and recoilless rifle ammunition was buried. However, the enemy spotted these preparations and intensified their shelling.[143]

Half an hour after the retreat began at 1530hrs, de Castries had a belated change of heart, since he ordered BT3 to hold out until nightfall, and promised to send paras and tanks to its aid. Thimonnier replied that it was too late, since most of his troops were already gone and could hardly be expected to return.

He left Anne Marie-1 with his last dozen Tai at 1630hrs, just as the Red Platoon was nearing the strongpoint. Its appearance attracted intense VPA artillery fire that convinced Langlais to recall the reinforcements.[144] This is generally described as a token operation that involved only a single company of 6 BPC, but in fact it also included two companies of 1 BEP. If this powerful force had been sent earlier, things could have been very different.[145] Instead, Anne Maries-1 and -2 were occupied without a fight by the 308th Division's 36th Infantry Regiment.[146]

According to BT3 veteran Raymond Legoubé, less than a third of the battalion's troops actually deserted. A Vietnamese book states that 232 Tai deserted to the VPA on March 17 alone,[147] but since this is almost precisely the same number that Legoubé says crossed over *in toto* by that date, it seems likely that the Vietnamese figure also tallies overall desertions.

DESERTIONS IN BT3[148]							
Period	9th Company	10th Company	11th Company	12th Company	HQ Company	CSM 272	TOTAL
Night March 15–16				90			90
Night March 16–17		40			20	58	118
March 17		10			5		15
April 7				35			35
TOTAL	0	50	0	125	25	58	258 (of 887)

The fugitives were sent to Isabelle. 10th Company was down to just 80 men and had abandoned its radios and heavy weapons. 11th Company was in better shape, since according to Legoubé it suffered no desertions (though another source reports 40) and retained all its equipment. Headquarters Company was missing its 81mm mortars (and their commander), and the Intervention Platoon and Recon Commando together could muster only the strength of a single platoon. CSM 272 had just 20 auxiliaries left.[149] These units were broken up and their personnel distributed to II/1 RTA, III/3 REI and Groupement Wieme. Colonel Lalande later reported the Tai proved a useful addition to the Legion and Algerian units.[150] 9th Company, which had held firm, redeployed to Isabelle on March 18 and remained intact. The rump of Captain Guilleminot's 12th Company stayed on the Main Position where it defended second-line Huguette-2.[151] Anne Maries-3 and -4 were placed under the command of I/2 REI and renamed Huguettes-6 and -7.

While not denying his unit's failures, Lebougé argued that they do not prove that BT3 had been worthless. Instead, he insisted, "the battalion was unlucky, being in the wrong place at the wrong time."[152] There is some justice in this, since BT3 was confronted with a situation that even elite paratroops would have found daunting. Having witnessed the collapse of the whole battalions garrisoning Béatrice and Gabrielle, the mere pair of companies on Anne Maries-1 and -2 obviously had no chance of surviving if the enemy attacked in strength. The strongpoints could have been defended successfully only if they were reinforced in advance by at least several solid companies, and could count on a counterattack coming to their rescue. But no reinforcements ever arrived, and de Castries' and Langlais' actions revealed that they were unlikely to fight for Anne Marie. They were both fully aware of BT3's fragility, since before the siege began, de Castries had lobbied to have both Tai battalions replaced with more reliable units.[153] Cogny made a crucial mistake by refusing the request, since if the battalions had been replaced, the siege's outcome might have been very different. De Castries and Langlais compounded the error by failing to reinforce or replace BT3 although they could easily have done so. Instead, they did nothing more than to send 1/6 BPC on its brief, morale-building visit. Even if the company had stayed, it's unlikely that such a modest reinforcement could have saved Anne Marie.

De Castries testified before the Catroux Commision: "I never saw Anne-Marie as a key position. From the moment when the Gabrielle center of resistance was established, it had the main mission of covering the north and northwest."[154] Yet he was clearly being disingenuous, since even if Anne Marie had lost its importance when Gabrielle was constructed, it certainly regained it after the other CR fell into enemy hands. This point was made by General Catroux, who also noted that Cogny had always attached great importance to Anne Marie.[155] Indeed, the value of its outlying hill positions is obvious to anyone who can read a topographic map. In friendly hands, they protected the airstrip and main drop zone from encroachment by VPA infantry and flak. If a quality battalion had been deployed on the hills, they could probably have been held for some time because they were close to the Main Position and the intervening terrain was tailor-made for French tanks and aircraft. And every day that the enemy could be kept at arm's length from the airstrip was precious, since it made parachuting supplies and reinforcements – and evacuating the wounded – much safer and easier.

Conclusions

Giáp's first offensive was wildly successful. In just five days, his troops had captured the entire Northern Subsector, opening routes in the valley along RP41 and the Pavie Track, and clearing the way for the VPA to begin encroaching on the airfield. And French casualties had been extremely heavy, totaling 26 officers, 76 NCOs, and 865 men by March 19.[156] There were several factors that made Giáp's triumph possible.

- Béatrice and Gabrielle were both assaulted by a pair of regiments attacking from different directions. Facing odds of potentially six to one (though only four battalions were engaged at Béatrice and perhaps five at Gabrielle), and unable to concentrate their own reserves and supporting fires in a single sector, the defenders could have been saved only by swift and powerful counterattacks from the Main Position. When the counterattacks came late and understrength – or not at all – the two CRs were doomed.
- III/13 DBLE, V/7 RTA, and BT3 all suffered from severe officer shortages, as virtually all their combat platoons were commanded by NCOs, and most rifle companies were lucky to have even two officers. This undermined combat leadership and made the battalions' command structures prone to collapse if even a few key officers became casualties. This is precisely what happened to III/13 DBLE and V/7 RTA, which both lost most of their company officers and their entire battalion command echelon. The Central Subsector likewise lost its commander and most of his staff, and GAP 2 escaped the same fate only by sheer luck.
- Most of the casualties among key officers were a direct consequence of shoddily built fortifications, and losses among the rank and file were likewise unnecessarily high for the same reason. The French had not dug in as well as they could have, because they had convinced themselves that the VPA lacked the technical skill to employ its artillery effectively and the logistical capacity to supply it with enough shells to cause real damage. Here Colonel Piroth was the chief culprit.
- VPA artillery also contributed to Giáp's triumph by closing the airfield, weakening GONO's artillery, and spreading demoralization that helped cause 5 BPVN to become pinned down on March 15 and BT3's mass desertions. All of this was accomplished with remarkably little ammunition. Giáp reports that just 2,000 105mm shells were allocated for

this first offensive.[157] But VPA artillery could accomplish much with only modest ammunition stocks, because French positions presented such concentrated targets that even shells that missed their mark were likely to hit something of value. As the siege progressed and the French perimeter shrank, the target density would steadily rise.

- Giáp's artillery could not have accomplished all it did if French counterbattery fire had been effective. Before the siege, Colonel Piroth had promised that "No Viet Minh gun will be able to fire three rounds before being destroyed by my artillery!" [158] But in practice, his guns proved incapable of silencing the enemy's or even noticeably reducing their volume of fire. Giáp's artillery was so widely dispersed that a French shell that missed its target was unlikely to hit anything but empty jungle – and so well fortified that nothing but a direct hit on a casemate's open embrasure would knock one out. And targets on steep ridges are also notoriously difficult to hit with bombs and indirect artillery fire, since, on account of vertical separation, a projectile that is "short" or "over" will land much farther from the target than it would on level ground. But French counterbattery fire may not have been completely ineffective, since on March 14, two of the 805th Howitzer Company platoon leaders were killed.[159] This could indicate that this battery, at least, had been hard hit, but it's also possible that these officers had been serving as forward observers.

- French airpower had little impact owing to bad weather. The Armée de l'Air and Aéronavale flew just 50 sorties over Điện Biên Phủ on March 14 and 15.[160] Only three planes were shot down in this period (one Hellcat and two Bearcats), but to avoid the same fate, all French aircraft were forced to fly at much higher altitudes and/or with much greater caution than they were accustomed to.[161]

- Demoralization within GONO's leadership contributed decisively to Giáp's victory. By dawn on March 14, de Castries and Langlais had already abandoned the policy of automatically counterattacking in response to each enemy assault. They were wise to refrain from trying to reoccupy Béatrice, but their reaction to the crises on Gabrielle and Anne Marie can only be described as half-hearted and indecisive. If these strongpoints were worth saving, then a full battalion was needed in either case; if they were judged to be indefensible, no reserves at all should have been committed. Langlais vainly tried to split the difference by initially committing just half a battalion to the Gabrielle counterattack and sending only a single token company to pay a brief visit to Anne Marie before it was too late.

- Some historians have characterized the Béatrice and Gabrielle assaults as wasteful "human wave" attacks, and suggest that these tactics were adopted at the urging of Chinese advisors.[162] But Vietnamese accounts of the Béatrice and Gabrielle assaults suggest that there was nothing unusual about the tactics employed, which seem to have been typical of those the VPA had used against fortified positions throughout the war. Aside from the much greater level of artillery support, they were little different from those employed at Nà Sàn. If casualties were excessive, it had more to do with poor preparation (shallow trenches, sloppy barbed-wire clearance, and late-arriving artillery) than reckless tactics. The heavy losses were also attributable to truly massive French ammunition expenditures, which totaled 17,500 105mm shells, 9,600 120mm shells, and 2,220 155mm shells between March 13 and 16.[163]

CHAPTER 5

THE LULL

For all its success, Giáp's first offensive had not gone entirely as planned. One of the earliest Vietnamese accounts of the siege records the events of March 16:

> The Front Military Committee held a conference to draw a balance sheet of the first phase and define new tasks for the second phase: although we had annihilated an important part of the enemy's forces, they were still strong. That is why our motto remained: "steady attack, steady advance." The Committee confirmed that we had fulfilled only partly our task of attacking the enemy outposts. We had to continue consolidating our positions in order to encircle the enemy from all sides, attack enemy outposts, stand ready to break enemy counter-attacks, constantly threaten the airfield, and carry out more and more small-scale harassing operations to wear out the enemy's forces.[1]

There are several notable things about this statement. Firstly, it reveals that senior VPA leaders believed the siege's first phase was over at a time when Anne Marie was still in French hands. Secondly, one is struck by the slow pace set for future operations and the emphasis placed on small-scale, attritional tactics. In contrast to the breakneck pace of the first offensive, two weeks would pass before another strongpoint was attacked. It is inconceivable that Giáp's original plan called for such a prolonged lull, since it risked prolonging the siege into the rainy season, when the supply roads would be knee-deep in mud, and swollen rivers would impede transporting supplies by land and water alike. The hiatus also dismayed Giáp's subordinates, who feared it would allow the French to regain their equilibrium and thus squander the psychological advantage which had been purchased at such great cost.[2] The fact that Giáp ignored these compelling arguments suggests that the casualties at Béatrice and Gabrielle had forced him to alter his plans. An assault on Anne Marie probably was scheduled for March 15 or 16, but scrapped for fear of the losses it would entail. The psychological warfare coup that led to its bloodless conquest was therefore a major stroke of luck for the VPA.

The big dig

The lesson of Giáp's first offensive was that no shortcuts could be taken when attacking strongpoints. Casualties at Béatrice had been excessive because assault trenches were too shallow and barbed wire breaching took too long. The attack on Gabrielle was bedeviled by the same problems and almost ended in disaster when the supporting artillery arrived late. Giáp decided that henceforth he would attack only when success was guaranteed. This meant his troops would have to deploy heavy weapons in secure positions close to their targets and be given better protection against French firepower. The key to success lay in digging a trench network that would extend up to the very edge of the strongpoints, isolate Isabelle, discourage sorties, and impede the flow of parachuted supplies and reinforcements to GONO.

Though reinforced by the 888/176, the 57th Regiment had too few troops to surround Isabelle entirely, so it dug an arc of trenches that cut the roads to the north. The 308th Division enclosed the Main Position on the west with a trench that ran from Bản Co My to Gabrielle, where it linked up with the 312th Division's trench that continued east to Béatrice, and then turned sharply south. Finally, the 316th Division's trench encircled Eliane and linked up with the other divisions' entrenchments. Communications trenches snaked down to this main trench, battery emplacements sprouted from it, and assault trenches stretched forward toward the strongpoints. Most of the work was done after dark, so VPA soldiers had to adapt to a punishing 14- to 18-hour workday, getting a few hours' sleep in the morning so that they could spend afternoons preparing construction materials (timber, bamboo matting, etc.) and nights digging.[3] Meanwhile, new casemates were being built for Giáp's howitzers so they could move closer to their targets. The 804th Battery redeployed near Béatrice, while the 801st and 802nd shifted west of the Nậm Yum to positions directly behind Anne Marie, and the 805th relocated from Pu Hồng Mèo Mountain to a site nearer to Isabelle – whose artillery it was tasked with suppressing throughout the siege.[4] Flak batteries also leapfrogged forward.

The French were taken aback by these tactics. They had anticipated that VPA troops would descend from the hills at night to attack and fall back to them before dawn. These had, after all, been the VPA's standard tactics throughout the entire war. "The VPA had so far confined itself to combats lasting the space of one night, taking advantage of mountainous terrain and the darkness of night to storm enemy positions and wipe them out, take away booty, and swiftly withdraw with its wounded."[5] The French were astounded when their enemies occupied the valley floor in broad daylight using World War I trench warfare tactics. And as parallels and saps multiplied all around them, some suspected that Giáp was consciously applying the principles of classic siegecraft developed by the Marquis de Vauban, the master military engineer of the 17th century. Langlais wrote, "This phase of the battle kicked off with Giáp's new methodical tactics; the step-by-step forward movement codified by Vauban. It seems we had forgotten that Giáp had read his works... The Vietminh infantrymen applied Vauban's principles to the letter."[6]

Giáp also took steps to strengthen his artillery. A new 116th Mortar Company was formed using three 120mm mortars captured at Gabrielle.[7] And the 754th and 755th Mountain Gun Batteries were summoned to Điện Biên Phủ from the Việt Bắc and Phú Thọ Province, where they had been detached to help guard against a French offensive from the Red River Delta aimed at the siege's supply lines. But the likelihood of such an attack had declined dramatically since Navarre had committed his reserves in Operation *Atlante* 800km to the south. The 755th set out on March 19 and arrived near Béatrice nine days later.[8] The 396th Antiaircraft Battalion's 834th Company (12.7mm machine guns) was ordered to shift from the supply lines to the valley, and was installed on Mount Pu Hồng Mèo east of Isabelle.[9]

Plugging holes

The French also adopted a new strategy that de Castries described for the Catroux Commission: "After the loss of Béatrice and Gabrielle, my feeling about the outcome of the battle still was not negative. To hold out, I decided to seal off my defensive organization and plug the holes. I mean shrink the defense to the central perimeter and Isabelle. No attempt to retake Béatrice, Gabrielle or Anne-Marie. This decision was approved by higher command."[10] The first priority was to strengthen GONO's fortifications. Labor alone could accomplish much by deepening existing trenches and digging communications trenches between strongpoints – though de Castries surprisingly did not order the latter done until March 23.[11] Parachuted barrier materials were used to thicken barbed wire and minefields. On March 20 alone, the garrison was supposed to receive 2,000 Model-1948 mines and 2,000 tripwire fuses that converted hand grenades into booby-traps.[12] Yet efforts to strengthen overhead cover were hampered by the lack of construction materials. On March 28, de Castries complained that metal beams requested two days earlier to build casemates on Isabelle had not arrived (it seems they never did).[13] Its 105s could have been protected in this way because they mostly had to fire in just one direction – north toward the Main Position.

"Interval strongpoints" were also needed to plug holes in GONO's defenses. One gap had been closed on March 14 when 5 BPVN began building Eliane-4, but others remained. On March 16, Langlais ordered 2/5 BPVN to start constructing Dominique-6 on a hill 275m north of the gap between D-1 and D-2.[14] But the weakest spot of all was the 1km cavity that yawned between Huguette-6 and Dominique-1. Gabrielle had covered this gap from a distance, but its loss left the area totally undefended. Starting on March 17, BT2's 6th, 7th, and 8th Companies alternated sending a pair of platoons out nightly to guard the gap, and 7th Company left Dominique-4 to establish an outpost in the drainage ditch east of the runway.[15] That same day, troops of V/7 RTA and BT3 began constructing a small "bridge strongpoint" just east of the river between Isabelle-2 and strongpoint Wieme – which was already in place guarding the southern end of the airstrip and was held by Lieutenant Reginald Wieme's Tai auxiliaries.

Finally, on March 19, de Castries ordered that the reserve battalions' bivouac areas be converted into strongpoints. 8 BPC established CR Épervier ("Sparrowhawk") covering the southern end of the airstrip, Dominique-4, and BT2's drainage ditch outpost.[16] This area had long been called Épervier since it was where the airbase facilities were located. Claudine-6 and 1 BEP's cantonments near the ammunition dump became CR Junon, and the White Tai Company was placed under the battalion's command along with a platoon of stranded Armée de l'Air ground crew formed on March 15.[17] But 2/1 BEP was detached to Épervier to fill the gap left when 1/8 BPC relocated to Dominique-4. BT2's bivouac area became Eliane-12.[18]

OPERATIONAL FRENCH HEAVY WEAPONS[19]				
Period	105mm	155mm	120mm	Tanks
March 12	24	4	32	10
March 16	22	3	16	10
March 21 (evening)	25	4	17	10
March 30 (evening)	21	2	17	9
April 9 (evening)	18	3	15	7
April 13 (evening)	17	3	15	4
April 16	18	3	15	7
April 23	19	2	15	5
April 27	19	1	15	7
May 5	18	1	15	6
May 7 (morning)	8	1	6	5

The French also used the lull to restore their artillery strength. The eight 120s lost on the siege's first two nights were replaced by parachuted tubes,[20] and a new 105mm battery was established on Isabelle using three guns (M-3s?) that were airdropped on March 16 and 17.[21] GONO also needed a steady stream of parachuted parts to repair damaged artillery pieces, including tires so the howitzers could traverse in their gun pits. Thanks to the tireless work of the reinforced 2nd Platoon, 5th Foreign Legion Medium Maintenance Company, a surprising number of French heavy weapons would remain in action until the very end of the siege.[22] Its task was complicated by a flaw in the otherwise excellent American M-1 155mm and M-2 105mm howitzers that allowed them to be silenced by minor damage to their oil-filled hydraulic recoil cylinders.

PARACHUTED ARTILLERY PIECES AND REPAIR PARTS (MARCH 13−MAY 7)[23]						
Item	57mm recoilless	75mm recoilless	75mm tank gun	120mm mortar	105mm howitzer	155mm howitzer
Complete weapons	1−2	4		17	3	
Gun cradles					7	

Recoil springs			4	10	
Recoil cylinders				3	1
Tires				39	4

Many 120mm mortars were also damaged and 11 of them were under repair on March 25. But there was also a shortage of trained crews, since on that same date only 18 of the 25 intact mortars could be manned.[24] To limit future losses, most of the heavy mortar units moved to positions that were less familiar to VPA gunners. The 1 CEPML platoon that had been decimated on March 13 shifted its remaining mortars to pits behind Eliane-4 that had been vacated by the 155mm battery (it returned west of the Nậm Yum). In the headquarters area, the company's other platoon moved to a position near Claudine-1 where it was joined by 2 CMMLE's surviving platoon from Anne Marie, and 1 CMMLE relocated across the river from Dominique-1 to Dominique-4.[25]

The French artillery was reorganized on March 23 to reflect the loss of the Northern Subsector. The 155mm battery and Quad-50s were removed from Groupement B and placed directly under control of the "Fire" Command Post.

GONO ARTILLERY ORGANIZATION (MARCH 23)[26]				
Groupement	Unit	Deployment	Primary mission	Secondary mission
A	2 Batteries III/10 RAC 1 Battery III/10 RAC 1 CEPML 2 CMMLE	Isabelle HQ Area Claudine-1, Eliane-4 Claudine-1	Direct Support Central	Reinforce B General Support
B	2 Batteries II/4 RAC 1 Battery II/4 RAC 1 CMMLE	Dominique-4 Dominique-3 Dominique-1	Direct Support South	Reinforce A
155 Battery	11/IV/4 RAC	HQ Area	General Support	Reinforce Direct Support
Quad-50s	1 GAACEO	Épervier, Junon	General Support	Reinforce Direct Support

On March 26, III/10 RAC's 9th Battery joined the 7th and 8th Batteries on Isabelle, but took only a single 105mm howitzer along; a two-gun platoon was left behind on the Main Position.[27] Including the three airdropped pieces, Isabelle now had a dozen 105s. Major Jean Alliou and III/10 RAC's headquarters remained on the Main Position to facilitate rapid liaison with the "Fire" Headquarters. The batteries on Isabelle were commanded by the battalion's executive officer, Captain Joseph Libier.

Additional medical units were sent to Điện Biên Phủ during the lull. Antenne Chirurgical Parachutiste 3 (Airborne Surgical Team 3) – or ACP 3 – arrived on

March 16 and set up shop on Isabelle. ACP 6 jumped the next day and was installed on Eliane-11. Each had a staff of eight, comprising a surgeon, head nurse, surgical assistant, resuscitator, anesthetist, sterilizer, bandager, and instrument specialist.[28] Yet efforts to improve conditions in the overcrowded hospitals by using ambulance planes and helicopters to evacuate wounded were impeded by VPA artillery, which fired on the aircraft despite their Red Cross markings. The French also violated the Geneva Convention by using medical aircraft to fly in senior officers and evacuate able-bodied personnel including Air Force pilots, navigators, and mechanics, 30 of whom were evacuated by helicopter in Operation *Quasimodo* between March 18 and 21.[29]

A way was eventually found to evacuate wounded on C-47s that glided silently into the blacked-out airstrip at night while other planes noisily flew a low-altitude airdrop pattern to distract the enemy's attention. After five Dakotas landed on the night of March 19–20 and carried 95 wounded back to Hanoi, the French also considered – but rejected – using future medevac planes to land reinforcements. The Peloton d'élèves grades supported these hair-raising nocturnal flights by securing the runway between Huguettes-1 and -6. All in all, 326 personnel (wounded and able-bodied) were flown out on fixed-wing aircraft and another 101 by helicopter before landings became impossible.[30] The very last medevac Dakota landed safely at 0345hrs on March 28, but ran off the side of the runway as it was taxiing in the dark and suffered minor damage that caused an oil leak. Repairs were not completed until after dawn, and VPA shells quickly destroyed the aircraft when the engine was started up to ensure it was working properly. Among the crew was a female Air Force flight nurse named Geneviève de Galard, who joined the staff of the main hospital and served there with distinction until the end of the siege.[31]

Active defense

While they were shoring up their defenses, the French were also operating aggressively beyond them. As if to make up for the vacillation it had exhibited during the siege's opening days, the garrison conducted an extremely active defense throughout the rest of March. Every day, troops sallied out to reconnoiter the valley floor, open the road to Isabelle, and "aerate" the peripheral strongpoints (i.e., give them breathing space) by filling in encroaching enemy trenches and seeding them with mines. Indeed, there was no lull at all for the parachute battalions, which maintained an incredibly high operational tempo and saw action almost every day. As the month wore on, these sorties would evolve into major operations involving multiple battalions.

One of the first sorties was made on March 16 by Lieutenant Wieme's Tai auxiliaries to clear the drop zone where 6 BPC would jump later that day. Probing the village of Bản Hua Na a kilometer southeast of strongpoint Wieme, they ran into VPA troops who were taken unawares digging trenches. Reinforced by the Green Platoon, the Tai inflicted substantial losses on them and captured an automatic rifle and a ĐKZ.[32] Things did not go as well on March 20, when 12/III/3 REI reconnoitered Bản Bong, which lay 2km west of Isabelle. The company was pinned down by mortar and automatic weapons fire 100m from the village, and the Green Platoon had to rush to its aid. While two tanks suppressed enemy machine guns and ĐKZs, the third advanced, sheltering legionnaires who followed behind to recover their dead and injured comrades. Among the wounded was Lieutenant Alain Gambiez, son of General Navarre's chief of staff, General Fernand Gambiez.[33] This unfortunate officer, who had been shot in the knee, would burn to death on March 23 when his medevac helicopter was set afire by enemy shells.

At midnight on March 20, the 57th Regiment's "heroes unit" (a composite unit of elite troops) blasted craters in Isabelle's runway. The 304th Division's official history claims that when enemy infantry and tanks escorted a bulldozer out to repair the damage after dawn, they were repulsed by the 265th Battalion's 17th Company. This engagement is not mentioned in French documents, though they do record that troops of III/REI repaired the runway on March 19. During the night of March 21–22, the 17th and 18th Companies drove a pair of trenches across the runway and put it out of operation for good.[34]

VPA trenches were also encroaching on the Main Position, and its defenders fought stubbornly to hold exposed outposts beyond the perimeter. Among these was a *sonnette* on Bald Hill that was garrisoned by a half-squad of Moroccans when the siege began. As enemy pressure mounted, it was gradually reinforced until 2/I/4 RTM's entire 3rd Platoon was deployed there. Beginning on March 20, it fought a localized, ten-day battle for control of the hill. The platoon was driven off the peak several times, but always returned with the help of other units, though it was reduced to just 14 men in the process.[35] De Castries and Langlais toyed with the idea of installing a new strongpoint on Bald Hill, but lacked both the troops and the engineering materials necessary.[36]

Just as the battle for Bald Hill was beginning, 6 BPC launched a reconnaissance-in-force east of Dominique on the night of March 20–21. After advancing 500m, the vanguard company was pinned down by VPA troops defending a line of trenches and bunkers. Supported by the battalion's own 81mm mortars and II/4 RAC's howitzers, the paras extricated themselves with only minor losses, but the enemy held on to their entrenchments.[37] A noose of trenches was also tightening around 2/5 BPVN on the still incomplete Dominique-6. On March 23, Langlais abandoned plans to build a strongpoint on the hilltop and decided to relocate D-6 in the valley directly between Dominiques-1 and -2. The original site became a *sonnette* which was manned by a platoon in daylight and a squad after dark. This outpost was driven off the hill by a VPA attack at dawn on March 24, but was reinstalled later that day after a counterattack by 4/5 BPVN, which advanced behind a massive creeping barrage.[38] Nonetheless, the situation was so worrisome that III/3 RTA's commander, Captain Jean Garandeau, requested a major effort to "aerate" Dominique.[39]

Langlais responded on March 25 by sending 8 BPC against the trenches north of D-1 and east of D-2. The inner flanks of these sallies were guarded by the D-6 *sonnette*, which had been reinforced by 3/5 BPVN. Some undefended trenches were occupied without fighting, but others had to be taken by assault and the VPA responded with violent harassment by mortars and artillery. Fighting intensified during the afternoon as growing numbers of VPA infantry joined in the battle, and 8 BPC began pulling back at 1500hrs. 2nd and 3rd Companies had to run a gauntlet of fire as they retreated through a ravine that separated Dominique-2 from an unnamed hill just to the east they had captured that morning. They took heavy casualties despite being supported by the Blue Platoon, which had helped I/4 RTM open the road to Isabelle earlier that day. 8 BPC had 16 killed (including a lieutenant) and 57 wounded.[40] 1 BEP's 1st and 3rd Companies also operated in the Five Hills on March 25, clearing 200 meters of trenches in the valley between Elianes-2 and -4 with the assistance of flamethrowers and the Red Platoon.[41]

Believing the Five Hills were secure for the moment, Langlais planned to aerate the entire region from RP41 to the eastern foothills between the Main Position and Isabelle on March 26. This scheme had to be abandoned when the "old" D-6 and Bald Hill *sonnettes* were both driven in overnight. The operation of March 25 clearly had not been as successful as hoped. Thus, on the following day, 6 BPC had to aerate Phony Hill, Bald Hill, and the "old" D-6, and protect engineers from 31 BG while they emplaced 1,500 mines to deny the enemy access to the latter two positions.[42] The *sonnettes* were reestablished, and an ambush 6 BPC left behind north of Dominique inflicted heavy casualties on VPA diggers on March 27.[43] But none of this halted the inexorable advance of the trenches that were strangling the Five Hills. Lieutenant Michel Datin deployed his platoon of 3/6 BPC atop Bald Hill one night to halt digging in the vicinity, but a trench nonetheless materialized between the hill and Eliane-2 before dawn![44]

It took longer for VPA trenches to reach the CRs west of the Nậm Yum because they were much farther from the foothills. Thus, although enemy patrols were frequently encountered close to Huguette, Françoise, and Claudine at night, their garrisons initially had considerable freedom of movement by day. On March 22, I/2 REI sent a patrol all the way to Anne Marie-2, which was found to be defended by VPA troops in platoon strength. Other reconnaissance missions fanning out from Claudine that same day encountered hostiles only after they had scouted nearly 2km out.[45] But the tentacles of enemy trenches soon appeared north of CR Huguette, and VPA sappers blasted a gap in the runway in the wee hours of March 21 and again three nights later.[46] By dawn on March 24, there were trenches within 50 meters of Huguette-6's barbed wire. A company of I/2 REI filled in the undefended trenches that morning under artillery harassment while the Blue Platoon's tanks stood guard 200 meters to the north.[47]

Yet the persistent VPA diggers soon threatened to surround Huguette-6 with a pair of trenches. Its environs were cleared again on March 26 by the Blue Platoon, elements of 5 BPVN and 8 BPC, and two companies of 1 BEP. The enemy fell back before this juggernaut and the Legion paras gave pursuit, killing 20 VPA troops and capturing another, along with a 60mm mortar and four automatic rifles – while their own losses were two men killed and eight wounded.[48] An even larger operation was mounted the following day. Backed by the Red Platoon, BT2 "aerated" H-7, while 5 BPVN's 3rd and 4th Companies did the same for H-6, elements of 8 BPC filled in trenches inching toward the airfield's eastern side, and 1 BEP covered the exposed western flank. Although 4/5 BPVN was struck in the flank and suffered significant losses, 3/5 BPVN and 1/8 BPC advanced all the way to the *radier* south of Bản Khe Phai. By temporarily clearing the vicinity of VPA troops, this operation enabled several platoons of BT2 to establish a new strongpoint (named "Opera" in some accounts) in the middle of the gap between H-6 and D-1 on March 28.[49]

"Aeration" was a Sisyphean task. No matter how many times they were filled in (often with the aid of bulldozers), the trenches always grew overnight. These operations also cost the garrison significant casualties that were mostly concentrated in its reserve parachute battalions, but may have delayed Giáp's second offensive and certainly interfered with preparations for it.

The road to Isabelle

The garrison also devoted considerable effort to maintaining liaison with CR Isabelle. This was a vital mission because the Green Platoon based there formed a key part of the garrison's reserves, and could not intervene in the coming battles around the Main Position if it was cut off 5km away. Keeping the road open was also important from the logistical standpoint. Isabelle initially depended on supplies delivered by daily convoys from the Main Position's depots, but as the VPA "flak envelope" around the Central Subsector thickened, the relationship was reversed. Since there were few antiaircraft weapons – and no heavy 37mm flak guns – around Isabelle, large quantities of supplies were parachuted onto drop zones nearby and then transported north. Many reinforcements found their way to the Main Position by the same route during the siege's opening weeks, including parts of 5 BPVN on March 14 and the entire 6 BPC two days later.

Every day, several companies, with tanks in attendance or on call, opened the road to Isabelle. This involved sweeping the route for mines, filling in trenches, and driving any VPA troops encountered back beyond effective small-arms range. This mission reversed the dynamics of the siege, since it required the French to repeatedly assault fortified positions. There were two roads available to them, one on each side of the Nậm Yum. But although RP41 was overshadowed by the valley's eastern foothills, the French generally used it since the old colonial highway was in better condition. The western route ran along a dirt track carved out by BG 31 in late December 1953.[50] This crude "Bulldozer Road" no doubt degenerated into a mere tangle of mud ruts every time it rained – which was often. The garrison nevertheless cleared both routes during the first days of the siege, and the units garrisoning Claudine (I/13 DBLE, CSM 424, and the CTB) reconnoitered the Bulldozer Road as far as Bản Co My almost every day until March 30.[51]

Opening the roads became increasingly difficult as VPA troops and trenches proliferated between Isabelle and the Main Position. CR Marcelle had given some minimal protection to this undefended expanse of territory, but it had been abandoned. On March 15, the daily convoy encountered an ambush several hundred meters from the vacant strongpoint, and three days later the road was cut by a trench that reached the banks of the Nậm Yum 1km south of Eliane.[52] But the worst bottleneck developed where the 57th Regiment's main trench slashed through RP41 at the twin villages of Bản Nong Nhai and Bản Kho Lai. They stood on opposite banks of the Hong Duai Ta stream, which acted as a natural antitank ditch, and its overgrown banks provided a covered route of approach from the foothills a kilometer to the east.

A major battle for RP41 was brewing and Giáp signaled it was about to begin in earnest by announcing on March 19 that all the villages between Isabelle and the Main Position had to be evacuated by nightfall the following day.[53] The warning came too late for the residents of Bản Nong Nhai and Bản Kho Lai, since III/3 REI's 10th and 11th Companies fought a sharp skirmish with troops of the 57th Infantry Regiment defending a trench just east of the villages on March 20. A larger and longer battle occurred on March 21 after the battalion's 9th and 12th Companies were pinned down south of Bản Kho Lai while clearing RP41. Though they were reinforced by the Green Platoon and elements of II/1 RTA from Isabelle, the roadblock was not broken until the Blue Platoon and a 1 BEP company from the Main Position attacked it in the rear. The paras took no casualties, but III/3 REI had two killed, one missing, and five wounded (including an officer). And although 14 enemy troops were killed, one captured, and two ĐKZs and five automatic rifles destroyed, RP41 was not opened until 1630hrs – disturbingly close to nightfall.[54]

A still bigger battle was fought at the twin villages on March 22, when 1 BEP was tasked with opening the road. 2/1 BEP was ambushed just north of Bản Nong Nhai, and its command group and 1st Platoon took heavy casualties. The tanks helped the company break into the village, but it was pinned down there after its commander and several platoon leaders became casualties.[55] Langlais quickly dispatched reinforcements. Lieutenant Wieme's Tai, two companies of II/1 RTA, and the Green Platoon headed north, while all the Main Position's tanks raced south. Though sandwiched between two hostile forces, the entrenched bộ đội fought with remarkable courage. Thanks to the artillery and tanks, both villages were finally cleared by 1400hrs. The attackers had nine killed, 21 wounded (including three officers), and one missing. But two companies of the 57th Regiment were virtually annihilated. The French counted 175 enemy bodies, and captured eight prisoners, two 60mm mortars, three ĐKZs, five automatic rifles, 15 submachine guns, and 16 rifles.[56] It is unclear precisely which VPA units these were, though the 265th Battalion's 17th and 18th Companies, the 346th Battalion's 50th and 53rd Companies, and the 418th Battalion's 54th, 59th, and 60th Companies all fought on RP41 during this period.[57]

The three-day battle of Bản Kho Lai ended in GONO's first victory of the siege and demonstrated the wisdom of basing a tank platoon at Isabelle – which allowed the roadblock to be assaulted from opposite directions and put the enemy at a huge disadvantage. The 57th Regiment's commander, Nguyễn Cận, had been wrong to stand and fight in such an exposed position, and Giáp took steps to ensure that the error was not repeated. The Deuxième Bureau intercepted a VPA radio message ordering the 57th Regiment to desist, for the moment, from resisting further French sorties. The Blue Platoon and 8 BPC thus met no opposition when they opened the road on March 23, though the battalion still had two men killed and 11 wounded by artillery harassment.[58]

It could have been these casualties that prompted Langlais to place Captain Pierre Tourret under arrest for 15 days on March 23. He had been displeased with 8 BPC's commander since March 15, when 1/8 BPC was ordered to Dominique-4 and Tourret became excessively worried (as Langlais saw it) about how this weakened Épervier's defenses. He was loaned a company of 1 BEP to fill the gap while 8 BPC improved its fortifications, but when Langlais paid a visit several days later, he found that the work was not being done properly. This was the first in a series of events which convinced Langlais that Tourret was unfit for command. He later wrote, "Tourret could be a very brilliant officer. He's not anymore. His failures can no doubt be accounted for by having completed three tours and excessive nervousness."[59] De Castries concurred, signaling Cogny: "8 BPC is poorly commanded – its battalion commander is subject to serious punishment."[60] Devastated, Tourret stumbled into the hospital on the evening of March 23 and told Doctor Paul Grauwin that he could not go on living. Fearful that Tourret might follow Piroth's example, Grauwin hastily summoned the garrison's head chaplain, Father Yvan Heinrich, to console the distraught captain.[61] Yet the sentence cannot have been enforced, since Tourret was back in command of 8 BPC no later than March 28.

Langlais and the recently arrived Colonel Guy Vaillant and Lieutenant Colonel Maurice Lemeunier spent the night of March 23–24 on Isabelle conferring with Colonel Lalande.[62] It was probably this meeting that convinced Langlais to plan a major operation to "aerate" the entire region east of RP41 as far as the first foothills. Scheduled for March 26, it was to involve three parachute battalions and two tank platoons under the command of GAP 2, and would undoubtedly have been supported by a sortie from Isabelle.[63] Langlais may also have privately sought Lalande's consent for a shake-up of the garrison's command structure, which he intended to carry out the following day. Troops of 8 BPC that spent the night on Isabelle cleared the road without trouble the next day, though some new trenches were found and filled in.

But if the 57th Regiment had indeed been told to lie low, no such orders had been given to other VPA units. The 308th Division ambushed 6 BPC and the Red Platoon at Bản Co My when they were opening the Bulldozer Road on March 24. Lieutenant Hervé Trapp's 2nd Company became embroiled in a prolonged battle against VPA troops defending a bunker and a 100-meter trench within the village. When the enemy fled after a lengthy engagement, they left 17 bodies behind, while the French had two men killed, three wounded, and Posen was immobilized by a ĐKZ shell that destroyed one of its road wheels.[64] The 316th Division gave I/4 RTM an equally warm reception on RP41 the next day, ambushing it near Bản Loi. But since the 57th Regiment was still licking its wounds, the Green Platoon came to the Moroccans' aid without running into trouble at Bản Kho Lai. Meanwhile, the Blue Platoon sped down from the Main Position. It was a busy day for that unit since it would later be sent to support 8 BPC's trench-filling operation that was under way in front of Dominique. The road was opened at 1315hrs after the Bisons destroyed four bunkers 600 meters east of Bản Loi; 15 VPA troops were killed, while I/4 RTM had two dead (including a lieutenant) and one wounded.[65]

Although Langlais' plan to "aerate" the entire region east of RP41 on March 26 had to be abandoned, the road was opened without difficulty over the next few days, though the number of mines encountered rose.[66] Yet as the starting date for Giáp's second offensive approached, the 57th Regiment "got back in the game" and resumed blocking the Bản Kho Lai bottleneck. When RP41 was cleared for what proved to be the last time on March 30, a *bataillon de marche* (composite battalion) comprising elements of 1 BEP and 6 BPC had to clear the ill-omened village yet again at the cost of two killed and two wounded.[67]

As with "aerations," one gets a strong sense of déjà vu about these road-opening missions. Over and over, the same French units battled the same VPA units to clear the same bottlenecks – and suffered casualties they could ill afford. And again, casualties were concentrated in GAP 2's parachute battalions, which never seemed to rest. Counting both road-opening and aeration operations, 1 BEP fought major battles at Bản Kho Lai on March 21 and 22, in front of Eliane on March 25, and north of Huguette on both of the next two days. Yet enemy casualties were much higher and the French succeeded in reducing pressure on RP41 during the last week of March. VPA troops fighting there faced a difficult tactical challenge because the dreaded tanks and French artillery could strike from their front and rear simultaneously. One must bow to the bravery of the resolute bộ đội who kept going down to block the blood-soaked roadway despite having to fight under these great disadvantages.

Triumph and tragedy

The Armée de l'Air and Aéronavale were very active during the lull. Between March 17 and 19, they made a concerted effort to knock out Giáp's 37mm flak guns, and enjoyed considerable success against these weapons, which of necessity had to be deployed in open emplacements with 360-degree fields of fire. On the first day of the aerial onslaught, waves of fighter-bombers, B-26s and Privateers focused on the 394th Antiaircraft Battalion's positions. The 827th Battery, which had just redeployed to the foot of Gabrielle, had two 37mm guns knocked out, its commander and his deputy killed, and its political officer severely wounded. On March 18, the 829th Battery lost half its personnel, and the 828th Battery's casualties were so high that cooks and ordnance repairmen had to be used to man its guns. The 383rd Battalion also suffered heavily that day. Its 815th Battery was struck by cluster bombs and five of the 818th Battery's 12.7mm antiaircraft machine guns were knocked out. On March 19, it was the turn of the battalion's 816th Battery, though it emerged almost unscathed from a series of dive-bombing attacks.[68]

COMBAT AIR SORTIES IN SECOND HALF OF MARCH[69]						
Period	Direct support	Counterbattery	Flak suppression	Interdiction	Anti-personnel	TOTAL
March 14–15	48	2				50
March 16–31	606	182	33	17	7	845

Having lost seven of his two-dozen precious 37s in just three days, on March 20 Giáp ordered the 383rd and 394th to withdraw most of their remaining weapons and personnel into hiding. Only some 12.7mm machine guns and the "heavy" 829th Battery remained in position, and the latter was permitted to fire only in defense of a few key targets. This represented a major triumph for French airpower, and its effects were felt through the end of the month because Giáp kept the 37s hidden until his new offensive began on March 30. He hoped the French would conclude that these weapons had all been destroyed and start flying at lower altitudes again. Meanwhile, the 367th Regiment used the respite to refurbish its battered sub-units. The 394th Battalion's 827th Battery was so shattered that it could be rebuilt only by absorbing the personnel and weapons of the 396th Antiaircraft Battalion's 833rd Battery, which were rushed forward from the supply lines.[70]

Three lightly damaged 37s were repaired in the valley, but four severely damaged pieces had to be towed back to Kilometer 52 on RP41. There three of them were fixed by ordnance technicians using two massive workshop vehicles that had – with great difficulty – been brought up from the Chinese border. The fourth, which was too far gone to repair, was "written off" and used for spare parts.[71] Many 12.7mm antiaircraft machine guns also needed repair, and not only from battle damage. The machine guns were firing so continuously that their firing pins and bolt locks frequently broke. Since no spare parts were available in the valley, they had to be forged on the spot from steel acquired by melting down pickaxes.[72]

Air attacks on the steadily expanding VPA trench network were less successful since most of the digging occurred at night. Counterbattery sorties were also disappointing, since Giáp's artillery was so well protected by its casemates and camouflage that little damage was done to it. Hoping that area weapons would prove more effective, on March 20 the French began using C-47 transports to drop napalm on VPA trenches and suspected battery positions. If nothing else, the foliage concealing the casemates might be burned off. These missions were rudimentary to say the least. Bundles of 5-gallon "jerrycans" of napalm with delay fuses were simply pushed out through the planes' side cargo doors, while pilots with no bombsights or experience in bombing acquired their targets by dead reckoning – including at night.[73] C-47s flew 35 of these sorties by the end of March, but it proved impossible to concentrate the napalm on targets by such crude means. The French therefore began using C-119s as well. With their capacious rear cargo doors, they could drop much larger, 4-ton loads of 10-gallon napalm containers all at once. C-119s would fly 78 napalm sorties before they ceased on April 2.[74]

The napalm bombings' results were generally disappointing because damp weather prevented the hoped-for conflagrations.[75] Worse yet, one of the C-119 napalm missions accidentally hit Bản Nong Nhai, whose population was swollen by civilians relocated from villages that formerly existed within GONO's perimeters. The Vietnamese claim that 444 civilians died, while a French source reports 644 victims, without distinguishing between those killed and injured.[76] Why there were still civilians present is a mystery. Giáp had ordered the village evacuated, but many residents may not have complied since their relatives were serving in French CSMs. Yet one would still have expected them to flee after the village became an almost daily battleground, though the French victory of March 22 may have persuaded them it was safe to return. Another mystery concerns the date of the tragedy. It is recorded as April 25 on a memorial that has been built on the site, but this is undoubtedly an error. Several French witnesses place the event at the end of March, including Jean Beguin, who served with Lieutenant Wieme's Tai auxiliaries. He says that the tragedy happened on the night of March 30, and prompted CSM 431's commander, Lo Van Pan, to grant 30 men permission to try to rescue their families from the flaming village just 2km away.[77] Yet it's hard to see how they could have left while a battle was raging around strongpoint Wieme that same night, or searched for their families at Bản Nong Nhai in the middle of another battle fought there the next day (see Chapter 6). Other French accounts link the tragedy to Operation *Neptune* – the very first C-119 napalm mission on the night of March 23. And Isabelle's war diary reports that 30 Tai deserted from strongpoint Wieme on that date.[78]

Putsch of the Parachute Mafia

GONO's command structure was fundamentally altered on March 24. Citing unnamed witnesses, Bernard Fall claims that Langlais and the fully armed commanders of the garrison's parachute battalions marched into de Castries' headquarters and informed him that they were seizing command. De Castries would remain in charge as far as the rest of the world was concerned, but in reality his only function would be to transmit the "Parachute Mafia's" messages.[79] Other historians doubt that this scene played out as Fall describes, since de Castries remained on friendly terms with Langlais and would exercise his command authority on several key occasions after this "putsch."[80] But the chief reason why Fall's account seems suspect is that Langlais had no need to seize the reins of command on March 24, since de Castries had effectively handed them to him ten days earlier.

The real aim of the "putsch" was not to seize command, but to keep it. A group of new senior officers had been flown in to replace those who had died or cracked psychologically: Lieutenant Colonel Gaston Ducruix was to become GONO's new chief of staff and Colonel Vaillant its new artillery commander, while Lieutenant Colonel Lemeunier was to take command of GM 9. Lieutenant Colonel Pierre Voinot had also been sent, though his intended post remains unclear.[81] Since several of these officers were superior to Langlais in rank or grade, there was a very real possibility that his wings would be clipped.[82] For example, if Lemeunier took over GM 9, he would control the Central Subsector and Langlais might revert to merely commanding GAP 2. This was unacceptable to the rugged paras, who were determined that no "outsider" would be allowed to interfere with their existing solution to GONO's command crisis.

The new command structure formalized Langlais' status as GONO's deputy commander for operations, with Lemeunier as his executive officer and Bigeard as his deputy for counterattacks (6 BPC's executive officer, Captain Henri Thomas, assumed command of the battalion). The Central Subsector was abolished and divided in two along the course of the Nậm Yum River. Langlais personally controlled operations in the new Eastern Subsector, while the Western Subsector was commanded by Voinot from Lieutenant Colonel Trancart's former ZONO headquarters. Trancart was left without any sector or troops to command, and found himself relegated to acting as GONO's personnel officer. This seems to have been done deliberately because Langlais (unjustly) blamed him for the loss of Gabrielle and Anne Marie. Séguin-Pazzis remained in command of GAP 2, but in practice Bigeard assumed his functions. Later in the siege, he would become GONO's acting chief of staff after Ducruix fell seriously ill.[83]

The flak raid

If de Castries had been stripped of his command, it's hard to explain what happened on March 27, when he ordered Bigeard to attack the flak west of the Main Position the next day. For although the VPA's heavy flak battalions were in hiding, the 308th Division was aggressively pushing its antiaircraft machine guns toward Claudine. De Castries insisted that they be destroyed despite being warned that there was little time to plan the operation and it was sure to be expensive in casualties.[84] Bigeard says that General Cogny had ordered the raid, which could account for de Castries' assertiveness, but it's still impossible

THE FLAK RAID

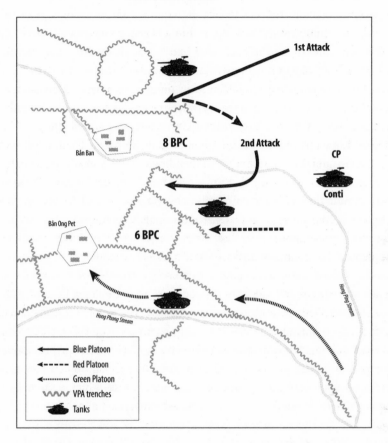

to reconcile his behavior with Langlais' claim that "He [merely] transmitted our messages to Hanoi."[85] Certainly, it was a bold move on his part to give Bigeard *carte blanche* to plan and execute a brigade-size, inter-service, combined-arms operation when by all rights the mission should have been given to GAP 2. The fact that de Castries chose to bypass it could be interpreted as a vote of no confidence in Séguin-Pazzis. He clearly trusted him less than Bigeard, who was renowned throughout Indochina (including in the enemy camp) for his tactical virtuosity.

The plan that Bigeard personally drafted – on a single sheet of paper, he says – called for 8 BPC and 6 BPC to make a dawn attack on suspected flak positions near Bản Ban and Bản Ong Pet (respectively). At 0600hrs, a dozen 105mm howitzers, a dozen 120mm mortars, and two 155mm howitzers would blast Bản

Ban for five minutes, give Bản Ong Pet the same treatment starting at 0605hrs, and then pummel both villages for another five minutes beginning at 0610hrs. After 0615hrs, half the artillery would fire a creeping barrage ahead of each battalion as it advanced. The raid would be supported by all six of the Main Position's operational tanks (the Red Platoon only had two that day), though Captain Hervouët's Conti would remain in the rear with Bigeard's field headquarters. 1 BEP would be in reserve near Françoise (it was never committed) and the Air Force was to make a maximum effort starting at 0630hrs.[86]

Bad weather over the Delta and ground fog in the valley delayed the arrival of air support until 0900hrs, but the mist allowed the attackers to slip silently forward while the tanks idled in the rear. The bombardment began on schedule, but since it was fired "blind" many shells missed the narrow VPA trenches. When the paras jumped off, there was no massed advance, since Bigeard kept his troops dispersed to limit casualties from enemy artillery. 8 BPC crept west, platoon by platoon, through a streambed that led toward Bản Ban. 4th Company, which was in the van, captured the first enemy trench shortly after 0700hrs, but a grenade wounded its commander and two platoon leaders. To maintain momentum, Captain Tourret (back in command despite his earlier arrest) ordered Lieutenant Gabriel Bailly's Indochinese 3rd Company, supported by the Blue Platoon's tanks, to take the lead. It encountered a maze of trenches that had to be conquered one section at a time by small groups of paras that advanced in short rushes, grenading their way from one traverse to the next. As the attack continued, men had to be detailed to block each trench that led into the battalion's rear.[87]

Although the tanks gave 8 BPC a decided advantage, VPA resistance stiffened in Bản Ban, and the 1st and 2nd Companies had to be brought up to flank the village before it was taken. The advance halted at that point because Bigeard ordered the tanks south to aid the hard-pressed 6 BPC. Although 8 BPC was fired upon by 12.7mm AA machine guns, it does not seem to have captured or destroyed any; perhaps they were pulled back during the prolonged battle.[88] Captain Tourret believed his battalion could have done more. "I had the feeling that if they had given me back my tanks, I would have captured the commander of the 308th Division. And with seven tanks I would have grabbed Giáp himself by the scruff of his neck!" [89]

6 BPC, commanded by Captain Thomas, advanced toward Bản Ong Pet through thick vegetation with 1st Company in the lead. Supported by the Red Platoon, the company overran several antiaircraft weapons, though platoon commander Lieutenant Michel Le Vigouroux was killed and VPA troops began

infiltrating into the foliage behind it. The Indochinese 4th Company was committed to the fray, but its commander, Lieutenant Francis de Wilde, lost a hand to a heavy machine-gun bullet and was replaced by his executive officer, Lieutenant Jean Jacobs. As the two companies advanced slowly through the trench system using the same tactics as 8 BPC, several more flak weapons were overrun. Bernard Ladogar of 4th Company recalled destroying one with a phosphorus grenade and then using an entrenching tool in hand-to-hand combat against counterattacking VPA troops.[90]

With the operation taking longer than expected, at midday Captain Hervouët summoned the Green Platoon from Isabelle. Fearing that he would run into a roadblock on RP41, Lieutenant Henry Préaud chose to take the Bulldozer Road and had the good luck to reach the battlefield without encountering any ambushes or wrecked bridges. His tanks arrived shortly after a VPA counterattack threatened 6 BPC's left flank. VPA artillery fire had been light, but 120mm mortar shells suddenly struck 2nd Company's 3rd Platoon, killing and wounding several NCOs. Another volley killed Lieutenant Jacobs, and the now leaderless 4th Company recoiled in disarray, leaving 2nd Company isolated. It was this crisis that prompted Bigeard to order the Blue Platoon south. It buttressed 6 BPC's right flank while Préaud's tanks reinforced the left. With the whole tank company in support, 6 BPC extricated itself from the trap, with 3rd Company acting as the rearguard. Both battalions fell back to the Main Position at 1500hrs.[91]

The raid was initially opposed by the 387th AA Battalion's 78th Company, the 322/88's 229th Company, and elements of the 23/88. They were surprised and effectively out of command since all the battalion and regimental officers had gone to divisional headquarters to receive their orders for the day. The rest of the two infantry battalions, which had been resting in the rear after a night of trench-digging, were soon racing toward the front, but they too were overcome by superior French firepower.[92] Troops of the 387th sent to recover the bodies of their fallen comrades afterwards were appalled by what they saw. "Before us was a scene of desolation. The 78th Company's positions had been completely devastated. All of the defensive works had collapsed. Many of our dead had been mutilated and disfigured after being crushed by enemy tanks."[93]

The French lost 20 killed (including two officers), 85 wounded (including five officers), and had two tanks lightly damaged. The 88th Regiment's official history admits over 100 fatalities,[94] while the French claimed ten captured, 350 killed, and a thousand more probably killed or wounded, plus five flak weapons, 14 automatic rifles, and 100 small arms captured or destroyed.[95] Two 90mm bazookas – the first ever encountered – were also taken.[96] Yet de Castries radioed that 400 enemy bodies were counted and 1,000 more "observed," raised the prisoner tally to 22, and added a pair of machine guns to the captured equipment.[97] Twenty-four hours later the number of flak weapons had mysteriously risen to nine.[98] French historian Henri Le Mire believes that the figures for weapons captured and destroyed were deliberately inflated. Noting that no captured machine gun was ever seen in the Main Position, he concluded that it was "a little publicity stunt that was probably necessary. It was good for morale!"[99]

Exaggeration of the raid's achievements continued after the siege. Upon his release from captivity in September 1954, Bigeard claimed that a dozen .50-caliber machine guns had been captured and identified the five flak guns as 20mm.[100] In his memoir, Langlais lumped these together to arrive at a figure of 17 antiaircraft weapons eliminated.[101] If true, this would mean that the entire 387th Battalion was destroyed, but Vietnamese authors insist that only one of its batteries was overrun. And we know that Bigeard's memory was faulty, since he dated the raid to March 26 instead of the 28th. The initial after-action reports all claimed just five flak weapons destroyed, and since Giáp's 37mm guns were in hiding, they must have been .50-caliber.[102]

Western historians nonetheless make much of the flak raid. It surprised Giáp, boosted French morale, and decimated the 88th Regiment, which had already suffered heavily at Gabrielle. But the raid was not a walkover, since the VPA response had been swifter and resistance stronger than expected, and 6 BPC was in serious trouble for a time. If the tanks had not been on hand, it might have suffered severely. Moreover, the raid conspicuously failed to achieve its paramount objective of rupturing the "flak envelope" around the Main Position. The five antiaircraft guns it destroyed represented less than 6 percent of Giáp's antiaircraft strength. To make the skies over Điện Biên Phủ safe for French planes, a whole series of similar raids would have been required, but GONO did not have enough troops, ammunition – or time.

The last battalion

The French missed a golden opportunity to reinforce the garrison with another battalion during the lull, although Major Jean Bréchignac's II/1 RCP was available, mass daylight jumps were still possible, and there was plenty of time. This was the worst mistake of many made by top French commanders, since it threw away their best chance for victory. De Castries was largely to blame since his pessimism deterred his superiors from sending reinforcements. On March 19 he sent a personal message to Cogny that envisioned the Main Position's collapse in the near term and sought authorization to order Colonel Lalande to break out toward Laos.[103] Cogny, who had never wanted to fight at Điện Biên Phủ in the first place, concluded that it would be futile to sacrifice the additional battalion de Castries had already requested. He radioed, "An Airborne Group is being speedily activated, but its commitment must be reserved to the exploitation of the success. The only immediate possibility is to reinforce you by one battalion in order to compensate your losses suffered during the counterattacks; but even the dropping of that battalion can only be committed on the condition that the integrity of the fortified camp can be guaranteed."[104]

These caveats ensured that no battalion was sent while the window of opportunity was still open. Ironically, the equivalent of another entire GAP would be sent before the siege ended, but each battalion was fed in piecemeal to vainly plug holes in a crumbling dike. If just a single battalion had been sent before the end of March, it might have turned the tide of the battle. Langlais recognized this and forcefully demanded another battalion the day after the putsch. He later wrote, "It is conceivable that if the parachute reinforcements requested on the 25th had jumped in time, the key position D-2, whose peak dominated the entire entrenched camp from less than 2km away, could have been retaken on the evening of the 31st, and that the outcome of the Battle of Điện Biên Phủ could have been something different."[105]

As FTNV's commander, Cogny would have had to have given the order that could have sent II/1 RCP winging west before March 30. He must accordingly bear most of the responsibility for denying Điện Biên Phủ the timely reinforcements that might have been decisive. Yet as commander-in-chief for all Indochina, Navarre could have and should have insisted that the battalion was dispatched. The fact that he did not do so indicates that he too had doubts about Điện Biên Phủ's survival and the wisdom of risking another precious parachute unit. Cogny would no doubt have taken offense had Navarre intruded upon his command prerogatives by insisting that II/1 RCP be sent, but relations between the two men were already toxic anyway. Each was blaming the other for the faulty decisions that had led to the looming disaster and writing self-exculpatory memoranda in anticipation of a future commission of inquiry.

CHAPTER 6

GIÁP'S SECOND OFFENSIVE

The tasks of digging assault trenches and repositioning Giáp's artillery were finished in the last week of March. Bernard Fall claims that another engineering feat was also completed at this time: "As the French artillerymen had predicted, the Communists never succeeded in establishing themselves on top of Phony Mountain. Instead, they burrowed long tunnels right through it. The result was that while nothing changed on the observable surface of the hill, it had become a veritable honeycomb of Communist automatic weapons and recoilless rifles."[1] But there is absolutely no evidence for this in Vietnamese sources and there could hardly have been enough time to dig tunnels by March 30 because 6 BPC had "aerated" Phony Hill just four days previously.

The overall objective of the new offensive was clear in the title of the resolution produced by a campaign command conference held on March 27: "Mass Absolute Numerical and Firepower Superiority to Totally Annihilate the Entire Eastern Portion of Dien Bien Phu In Order to Create Conditions to Enable Us to Shift Over to a General Offensive." On the following day, Giáp assigned his units the following missions for the night of March 30–31.[2]

- The 312th Division would capture Dominiques-1 and -2, overrun the artillery emplacements on Dominique-3, and destroy 5 BPVN and/or

6 BPC. It was reinforced with two 75mm howitzer, one 81mm mortar, and two 120mm mortar batteries.

- The 316th Division would take Elianes-1, -2, and -4, and destroy 6 BPC and/or 5 BPVN. It was reinforced with two batteries each of 75mm howitzers, 81mm mortars, and 120mm mortars.

- The 54/102 was detached from the 308th Division and sent to join in the assault on the Five Hills. Its missions were to destroy BT2's troops on Dominique-5, penetrate deep to wipe out the artillery emplacements on Dominique-3, and assist the 98th Regiment in destroying 6 BPC and/or 5 BPVN.

- The rest of the 308th Division would suppress French artillery in the headquarters area, feint against Huguette-7 and Claudine-5, block the Bulldozer Road to Isabelle, and destroy any paratroops dropped south or west of the Main Position.

- The 304th Division (whose headquarters must have arrived to take command of the 57th Regiment) was tasked with suppressing Isabelle's artillery, destroying any paratroops dropped in the vicinity, and blocking the roads to the Main Position. It was reinforced by the 888/176, one 105mm battery, one 120mm mortar battery, four 82mm mortars, and 18 12.7mm antiaircraft machine guns.

- The 351st Division would bolster the bombardments on the Five Hills, attrite French artillery, and provide antiaircraft cover. It may have retained direct control of several 75mm mountain batteries in addition to most of the 105mm howitzers and all the 37mm flak guns.

The plan was a curious mixture of audacity and caution. Giáp intended to conquer the Five Hills and destroy all the French reserves east of the Nậm Yum in a single night – setting the stage for a General Offensive that would finish off GONO within a few days. His plan also included a three-battalion-strong deep penetration aimed at the Bailey bridge, which suggests that he had hopes that (if all went well) he could rapidly switch to the Fast Strike–Fast Victory technique by mounting a hasty attack on GONO's headquarters area. It was a breathtakingly ambitious plan unlike anything the VPA had ever attempted before. The Béatrice and Gabrielle assaults had been directed at solitary, isolated CRs. The new offensive simultaneously targeted multiple CRs that French reserves could reach without crossing the exposed valley floor. And Langlais and de Castries were sure to fight for the Five Hills and would have no hesitancy about counterattacking. But on the other hand, Giáp's plan exhibited a definite reluctance to leave his troops exposed to French firepower in the full light of day, even if they successfully completed their missions. His orders to the 312th and 316th Divisions stipulated, "After destroying and overrunning these positions, leave behind a small number of troops reinforced by heavy weapons to repair and occupy the fortifications to prevent the enemy from retaking these positions and at the same time immediately establish heavy weapons firing positions to dominate, threaten, and inflict casualties on enemy forces in Mường Thanh."[3] (Mường Thanh – the Vietnamese spelling of the Tai placename "Muang Thèn" – was the village that had formerly existed where the headquarters area was built. The label "Điện Biên Phủ" applied to the valley as a whole; there was no village by that name.)

The eleventh hour

Langlais signaled his determination to hold the Five Hills by making several major redeployments in the last days of March. On March 28, he toured Dominique and Eliane, and found the Algerians and Moroccans fretful and uncertain. Langlais was also shocked to discover that CSM 245 held one entire face of Dominique-2. In his memoirs, Langlais wrote that he redeployed 9/III/3 RTA from Dominique-1 to close this gap.[4] Yet the company actually went to Dominique-3, and the weak spot in Dominique-2's defenses remained. Botella recalled that Langlais ordered him to replace 9th Company with his Vietnamese paras because "I am worried about Dominique-1. I don't like the look of the Algerians."[5]

Although Eliane was lower than Dominique, it was closer to the heart of the base. Eliane-2 was particularly important since no part of the headquarters area was more than a kilometer away. Eliane was, accordingly, the best-defended CR of all. Its garrison included the entire I/4 RTM, two companies of BT2, a company apiece from 8 BPC and 5 BPVN, 2/BG 31 (on Eliane-11), and CSMs 414 and 415 (on Eliane-3). And the entire 6 BPC was in reserve. Its 1st and 4th Companies were on Eliane-4, while 3rd Company was at the foot of the hill and 2nd Company defended a circular hill just to the north that had a series of revetments carved into its western slope that were to have housed the relocated ammunition dump. This plan was overtaken by events, but the revetments' cellular appearance caused the garrison to dub the peak "Honeycomb Hill."[6]

Langlais also redeployed two Quad-50s to Junon so they could support Eliane[7] and planned to have I/4 RTM switch places with I/13 DBLE on Claudine. For while the Moroccans' morale was uncertain, the Legionnaires could be counted on to fight. But Langlais had waited too long. The relief, which would take three days to finish, began only on March 30. I/13 DBLE's 4th Company had replaced 4/I/4 RTM on Eliane-3, and a platoon each from its 1st, 2nd, and 3rd Companies had swapped places with platoons in the corresponding Moroccan companies that remained on Eliane. Caught in mid-stride, Langlais rushed Lieutenant Jean Luciani's 1/1 BEP to Eliane-2 just before the VPA preparatory bombardment began.[8]

Giáp's fire plan called for French batteries and headquarters to be shelled for 15 minutes starting at 1715hrs. Then at 1735hrs an intense, three-minute bombardment would be laid on the Five Hills and Dominique-3. Finally, from 1738 to 1830hrs, VPA gunners would fire creeping barrages to cover pioneers breaching obstacles and infantry units moving into their final assault positions. Another creeping barrage would be fired when reserves were committed against second-line strongpoints, and several more counterbattery shoots would also take place overnight.[9] VPA counterbattery fire would prove highly effective, knocking out one French 155, five 105s, and eight 120s by dawn.[10]

The first and second hills

Many historians claim that the bombardment caught Dominique-1's defenders "with their pants down" because 4/5 BPVN was in the middle of relieving 9/III/3 RTA, and also assert that six 120s of 1 CMMLE were lost on the strongpoint that night.[11] Yet 4th Company's commander, Lieutenant Alfred Martinais, says that the relief actually took place on March 29, when the 1st and 3rd Platoons of III/RTA's 12th Company under Sergeant-Chief Hyacinthe Lopez simultaneously redeployed onto the hill from Dominique-3.[12] And multiple sources agree that the heavy mortars departed Dominique-1 by March 29 at the latest, and redeployed to Dominique-4.[13]

Martinais found that Dominique-1's minefields were poorly laid out, its plate charges and napalm drums were inoperative, and there was no fire plan besides a map tracing of preregistered artillery shoots. He requested engineering help to improve the fortifications, and Bigeard and Captain Botella paid a visit on the morning of March 30 to see the situation first hand. Lieutenant Crépin-

Leblond of BG 31 surveyed the defenses that afternoon, but no improvements could be made before Dominique-1 came under attack just a few hours later. The strongpoint consisted of an all-round defensive position on the summit, and a trench that ran downslope northwest to the bluff overlooking the Nậm Yum. This had been dug to accommodate a pair of .50-caliber machine guns that were intended to support Béatrice and Gabrielle, and to protect 120mm mortars dug in on the reverse slope behind it. But neither the machine guns nor the 120s were present on March 30, and Martinais left the trench undefended because his company had only about 100 men left. He placed the Algerian platoons in reserve.[14]

The newly arrived 755th Mountain Battery and the recently formed 116th Mortar Battery led the bombardment of Dominique-1. The 120s were particularly destructive, though they fired just 50 shells.[15] Martinais asked Captain Garandeau for counterbattery fire on the mortars, but was told that GONO's gunners were answering more urgent requests. He never heard from Garandeau again. When the bombardment lifted, the 141st Regiment's 16th and 428th Infantry Battalions attacked on two axes. One used the northwestern trench to approach the summit, while the other advanced from the northeast.[16] The 312th Division – which was also simultaneously attacking Dominique-2 – had learned its lesson at Béatrice.

On both hills the first People's Army assault companies seemed to spring up out of the ground in the midst of their own shellbursts; they had worked their way right up to the wire unseen, and now began pulling it apart with their bare hands – night-time infiltrators had loosened the pickets so that they could simply be plucked out and thrown down. Others carried long mats filled with earth, which they unrolled over the entanglements as bridges. So quickly did they close with the defenders that the shoots pre-arranged with "Zulu Kilo" [the "Fire" command post] fell well behind them, the forward observers on both hills were soon wounded, and fire correction orders ceased to arrive at the batteries.[17]

4th Company was soon in dire straits. A machine gun covering the northwestern trench fired until its barrel glowed red hot and inflicted heavy casualties, but was eventually overrun. The perimeter was also buckling on the opposite side of the summit. The Algerians were ordered to reinforce the threatened sectors, but instead fled the hill after Sergeant-Chief Lopez was hit. Fuming, Martinais told his men to fire on them and anyone else who retreated without orders.[18] The warning was probably unnecessary insofar as the Vietnamese paras were concerned, since they were excellent troops – many of whom had previously served in 3 BPC. But despite their bravery, the remaining defenders were driven back step by step until Lieutenant Martinais' headquarters was overrun and he was captured. The 141st Regiment claimed that Dominique-1 fell at 1945hrs, but this seems unlikely because GONO did not report its loss until 2150hrs. In any case, 4th Company was wiped out almost to the last man; of the 15 Europeans present, five were killed, six wounded, and nearly all the others captured. The attackers' losses were also heavy.[19]

Dominique-2 fell even more quickly, although its garrison was several times larger. III/3 RTA's 10th Company defended its southeastern face, 11th Company the northeastern, and CSM 425 the northwestern. The Headquarters Company, Captain Garandeau's command post, and a squad of 12th Company detached from Dominique-3 were also present.[20] III/3 RTA was fatigued and understrength after 27 months of almost ceaseless operations, and had only one or two officers per company. There were still some World War II veterans among the Algerian riflemen, but the Vietnamese auxiliaries recruited from Phat Diem – an anti-Communist Catholic bishopric in the Delta – were inexperienced and had never been intended to fight VPA regulars. CSM 425 had also lost its commander, Lieutenant Régis Prost, on March 22, and was understrength although it had been reinforced with a 57mm recoilless rifle and a flamethrower.[21]

Dominique-2 was attacked by the 209th Regiment's 154th and 166th Battalions, supported by a 120mm mortar battery and the 753rd Mountain Battery, which fired from just 300 meters away. The 154th Battalion found that 50 meters of its trench had been filled in by the Algerians, presumably after the bộ đội pulled back to avoid being hit by their own bombardment. Detouring around the blockage, they strayed into a marsh, became pinned down, and took nearly an hour to open a breach. On the other hand, the 166th Battalion's 606th Company needed just five minutes to penetrate three barbed-wire fences and enter the strongpoint.[22] It may have taken advantage of two trenches that curled off the strongpoint like the antennae of a gigantic insect. These allowed the defenders to fire on portions of the lower slopes that were invisible from the summit, but if unoccupied or captured, would have given the attackers covered routes of approach to the main perimeter.

The first VPA attack punched holes in 10th and 11th Companies' sectors. Some Algerians fought well, though a platoon of 11th Company almost gave way in panic. A reserve platoon led by Lieutenant Jean Chatagnier launched a pair of counterattacks that restored the line temporarily. However, a second assault overran CSM 425, whose new commander, Sergeant Joseph Cadiou, may already have been dead. Panic spread quickly as the Algerians were attacked from behind, and many surrendered while others fled toward Dominique-3. Since night had not yet fallen, this rout was visible to much of the garrison. III/3 RTA's French cadres did not run. Two sergeants got a pair of abandoned machine guns back in action and held out for a time near the command post, while others rallied some Algerians in the strongpoint's western tip and launched a hopeless counterattack. They were all killed or captured, and Captain Garandeau was also taken prisoner. GONO lost contact with him by 1925hrs and reported Dominique-2's loss at 2000hrs, though some French veterans claim that pockets of resistance held out until after midnight.[23]

Though Western historians generally believe that Dominique-6 had been evacuated, in fact it was still garrisoned by Lieutenant Phạm Văn Phú's 2/5 BPVN. But the strongpoint's unfinished fortifications were still so sketchy as to be barely distinguishable on aerial photos, and it became untenable after the flanking hills were lost. The defenders had no choice but to retreat when the 141st Regiment's reserve 11th Battalion attacked at 2200hrs.[24] Captain Botella recalled: "The *bộ đội*, without losing their impetus, rush down the southern slopes of Dominique-1 and fall on the flank of Phu's company yelling 'Where is Phu? Find Phu! Capture Phu! Take him alive!' On Dominique-2, it's a stampede. The Algerians tumble towards the Nam Yum and sweep along Phu's company in their flight."[25] No one blamed Phu for falling back, since he was later promoted to captain, and Botella commended him for keeping 2nd Company well in hand. He punished indiscipline by forcing offenders to get on their hands and knees between the first trench and the barbed wire and remain for a period that was determined by the severity of their violation. Phu also forbade the construction of bunkers so his troops would always be ready to respond to enemy attacks instead of huddling underground.

Bisons east

The swift collapse of Dominiques-1 and -2, and Eliane-1 (see below) stunned Langlais, who feared that the whole left bank of the Nậm Yum might be overrun before dawn if something was not done immediately. An urgent request went out to GATAC Nord for air support, but hours would pass before the first planes arrived. And in darkness they would have to use the imprecise "Top" technique in which "Torri Rouge" (GONO's air support control post) assigned to an aircraft a speed, course, and altitude, and told it exactly when to drop its bombs. All 19 B-26s that attacked that night therefore targeted Dominiques-1 and -2, which were now behind enemy lines.[26]

Since airpower could do nothing to stop the *bộ đội* who were assaulting second-line strongpoints, Langlais ordered the Bisons to plug the gaps between positions that were still holding out. From its bivouac area near GAP 2 headquarters, the Red Platoon had seen the Algerians bolting from Dominique-2 and vainly tried to halt their flight by firing machine guns into the ground in front of them. Now its two operational tanks (Ettlingen and Smolensk) took up station between Eliane-4 and Eliane-2, while Blue Platoon, which had already been engaging targets on Bald Hill and Eliane-2 from its bivouac on Junon, arrayed its three tanks along RP41 between Dominique-3 and Honeycomb Hill. Captain Hervouët's Conti guarded the interval between Honeycomb Hill and Eliane-4. Throughout the night, the Bisons functioned as mobile bunkers, shifting ground to find better firing positions and blazing away with every weapon they had. Several were hit, but none seriously damaged, though Hervouët's elbow was broken when the recoil cylinder of Conti's main gun malfunctioned. Recoil failures would become increasingly common since the number of shells fired by each Bison during the siege rose to an average of 1,500 – more than double the figure normally allowed before the entire system had to be replaced.[27]

Two valiant stands

Situated on a lower ridge finger projecting from the Dominique-2 hill mass, Dominique-5 was not attacked on the evening of March 30 – probably because the attackers would have been exposed to enfilading crossfires from Dominique-2 and Eliane-1. The same terrain factors had also hindered digging trenches toward the strongpoint, which was held by 5/BT2. Its troops fired into the flanks of the VPA units attacking Dominique-2 and Eliane-1 – then turned their guns on the Algerians and Moroccans when they fled. No one would have been surprised if the Tai bolted themselves, since BT3's mass desertions had cast doubt on all Tai units' reliability and BT2 had shown signs of unsteadiness even before the siege began. But although the temptation to join the fleeing Africans must have been almost irresistible, the Tai did not budge.[28]

With the flanking hills now in friendly hands, the 54/102 attacked Dominique-5 at 2300hrs. The assault was hampered by the lack of trenches and the strongpoint's intact barbed wire. The attackers also had to attack up a steep slope while being raked by fire from Honeycomb Hill. 5th Company's commander, Lieutenant Guy Lunet de la Malène, massed his men in the threatened sector and gave the attackers a warm reception. The 54th Battalion breached three barbed-wire fences, but its commander was wounded, and the defenders' fire and massive blasts of shrapnel from plate charges prevented any penetration of the perimeter. When it became clear that the assault was hopelessly stalled, the 54th fell back and sent troops of its 273rd Company onto Eliane-1 to find a better axis of attack.[29] The Tai had 20 men killed or wounded, and lost a machine gun, a recoilless rifle, and a 60mm mortar destroyed.

While the attack was under way, Langlais authorized de la Malène to retreat, but he chose to stand and fight. On the following day, de Castries recommended the 27-year-old officer for the Légion d'Honneur and gave the entire 5th Company a unit citation. This collective act of bravery by the much-maligned Tai is completely unknown. Some historians do not mention Dominique-5 in their accounts of that night, while others suggest that its defenders played no part in the battles raging all around them or even ran away. In fact, they significantly interfered with VPA efforts to exploit the victories at Dominique-2 and Eliane-1, and did much to ensure GONO's survival.[30] Giáp clearly expected that 5/BT2 would fold quickly, since the 54/102 was given other offensive tasks to fulfill that same night. A French prisoner of war later heard a rumor that the battalion's commander was sacked for failing to take Dominique-5.[31]

While what happened on Dominique-5 is virtually unknown, the battle for Dominique-3 is one of the most celebrated episodes of the entire siege. This strongpoint comprised three separate positions linked by communications trenches, though these were too shallow to allow rapid circulation under fire. The northern position was held by 12/III/3 RTA's 2nd and 4th Platoons, a platoon of 9th Company, and 4/II/4 RAC. The southern positions were held by 9th Company's other three platoons, plus one 81mm and five 60mm mortars. Some refugees from Dominiques-1 and -2 sought shelter on Dominique-3, but 4th Battery's commander, Lieutenant Paul Brunbrouck, drove out those who were unwilling to fight so their panic would not spread.[32]

Giáp's master plan included a deep penetration that would threaten GONO's headquarters area. The 141st Regiment's 11th Battalion and the 115/165, moving up from the 312th Division's reserves, were to converge on Dominique-3. After it fell, the two battalions would link up with the 54/102, overrun Eliane-10, veer west to seize Eliane-12, and capture the Bailey bridge.[33] But only the 11/141 reached Dominique-3 and it was understrength, because, after storming Béatrice, its 241st Company had been disbanded and merged into the 243rd.[34] The 54/102 was repulsed at Dominique-5, and the 115/165 was pinned down by French artillery barrages after encountering a new minefield, installed north of Dominique-3 just two nights before, whose existence evidently had not been discovered.[35] It may also have been slowed by fire from a disused reserve area (Position 201A) just south of Dominique-1. Since March 14, it had been outposted by a heavy weapons squad of 8/BT2 armed with a light machine gun, and two Reibel medium machine guns borrowed from III/3 RTA. Algerians fleeing Dominique-1 ran through the position, but it was never attacked and the Tai kept their machine guns in action all night.[36]

The failure of two of the three converging thrusts was offset by the 209th Regiment's swift capture of Dominique-2. Its 166th Battalion's 606th and 612th Companies were ordered west to link up with the 115/165 and support its attack on Dominique-3. The linkup never occurred, of course, and the companies' advance was halted by minefields, barbed wire, and artillery barrages. But the reserve 130/209 had no difficulty pushing southwest and attacked Dominique-3's northern position at 2200hrs. However, its pioneers had only enough explosives to clear 25 meters of barbed wire, whereas the strongpoint's obstacles were 40 meters thick.[37] Indeed, Giáp noted that his troops generally did not have sufficient explosives to clear all the interior strongpoints' barbed wire, which suggests that they had not been properly reconnoitered.[38]

The attackers also faced massed artillery fire without the benefit of trenches. Brunbrouck ordered his gunners to *débouchez à zéro* – fire shells with zero delay fuses so they exploded just meters from their howitzers' muzzles – and called in barrages from II/4 RAC's other batteries, though his battalion commander needed some convincing that Dominique-1 and -2 had fallen so quickly. The *bộ đội* were also battered by Dominique-3's mortars and lashed by whips of tracer from Épervier's Quad-50s.[39] Although the 130th Battalion was stopped in its tracks, Langlais still feared that Brunbrouck's guns would be captured, and authorized him to spike them and retreat. But the young lieutenant chose to stand his ground.[40] Bernard Fall credited Brunbrouck with saving GONO from annihilation that night. "Everything now hinged on D3. If it fell, the whole Eliane position would be outflanked and Communist assault troops would cross the Nậm Yum River within hours and overrun the unprotected headquarters area. The battle for Dien Bien Phu would be over."[41] But although Giáp had something very much like that in mind, it was unlikely to occur even if Dominique-3 fell. Before the attackers could break into the headquarters area, they would have to deal with the Blue Platoon's tanks and overrun both Elianes-10 and -12. And even if they reached the Bailey bridge, two companies of 8 BPC were in reserve near the far side.

There was a pause in the assault on Dominique-3 around 0100hrs. When it was renewed, VPA troops assailed the southern positions as well, but were repulsed thanks to support from the Blue Platoon. Brunbrouck again had to *débouchez à zero* after the 11/141 joined in the assault at 0300hrs.[42] Yet even as pressure on the battery slackened at 0400hrs it re-intensified in the south. The lull in the north was disturbed around 0430hrs by the sound of mines being triggered by *bộ đội* who were slipping onto the "island" west of the strongpoint and crawling down a drainage ditch that led into it from the north. 12th Company's commander, Lieutenant Guy Filaudeau, detonated plate charges that had just been installed in the ditch, shredding the densely packed enemy. Yet this did not prevent another assault on Brunbrouck's position and at 0500hrs Langlais again authorized him to spike the 105s and withdraw. Although one of his guns had been knocked out, Brunbrouck again refused and promised to hold out until sunrise.[43] Just after dawn, Langlais radioed Hervouët, "Mount on your Bisons. Gallop up the Him Lam road. Charge, crush all that's left of these bastards!"[44] This drove the surviving VPA troops from the field, though 11/141's 243rd Company grimly clung to a wedge of territory near the river.[45] At 0800hrs 2/8 BPC swept the perimeter and counted over 200 enemy bodies.[46]

The third and fourth hills

Western historians generally depict the VPA as attacking in overwhelming strength, but the 215/98 planned to capture Eliane-1 with its 38th Company, then commit the 35th to seize Eliane-4's eastern crest, and finally use the 34th to take the western one. The 439th Battalion would be in reserve, and if all went well would push on to destroy the rest of 6 BPC.[47] The 938th Battalion was absent in army reserve. Regimental commander Vũ Lăng impetuously promised Giáp that Eliane-1 would fall in just 45 minutes, but worried because the original plan provided no heavy artillery support.[48] Giáp agreed to give him a 120mm mortar battery and the 752nd Mountain Battery (its two guns were on a ridge just 300 meters away), and allocated 30 or 50 (accounts differ) 105mm shells to Eliane-1. These were supplemented by six 57mm ĐKZs, three 12.7mm AA machine guns, and a dozen 81mm mortars (including a 413th Mortar Battalion platoon). Meanwhile, 60mm mortars lobbing huge "torpedo" shells tore gaping holes in all the barbed-wire obstacles except the innermost.[49] These may have been identical to the unexploded 90mm x 500mm shells later found on Eliane-2.

The 38th Company attacked from the east, where an outcropping of the hill shielded it from direct fire until it was close to Eliane-1's perimeter. Pioneers breached the final barbed-wire fence so rapidly that the *bộ đội* needed just seven minutes to enter the strongpoint. Within ten minutes, they had captured a low-walled enclosure surrounding a flagpole (a leftover from the prewar era) on the summit and pushed those defenders who did not flee (mostly Legionnaires from the swapped 2/I/13 DBLE platoon) into the westernmost bunkers. The defenders directed artillery fire onto the summit and launched three small counterattacks that were all repulsed. After a brief pause, the 38th Company finished taking the hill within the promised 45 minutes. It reported just ten casualties while claiming 30 enemy troops killed and 106 captured. Giáp awarded the 215th Battalion a unit citation for this sterling performance.[50]

This version of events is largely supported by French accounts. At 1900hrs, Captain Botella on Eliane-4 reported, "The Moroccans of Eliane 1 are flowing back on me."[51] And at 1925hrs, de Castries radioed that the strongpoint had fallen.[52] Like most non-European CEFEO units, 3/I/4 RTM was prone to panic if its officers became casualties and Captain Camille Girard was the only one remaining in the company after his deputy, Lieutenant Jean de la Haye St Hilaire, was wounded by a mine on the road to Isabelle the day before. The speed with which resistance collapsed suggests that the company disintegrated after Girard was wounded by the bombardment. Other leaders were probably hit at the same time since four of seven French NCOs were also wounded that night.[53]

Preparations for the attack on Eliane-4 began immediately, but there was a delay while the 35th Company moved up through artillery barrages that inflicted heavy casualties on the bunched-up *bộ đội*. Giáp argues that the substitution was unnecessary because the 38th Company had taken few casualties, but another Vietnamese source reports, "it was exhibiting signs of hesitation and wavering, so the battalion commander told it to remain on C1 [Eliane-1] to regroup."[54] Its men must have been dismayed by the volume of incoming artillery fire, which cut all wire communications and wiped out most of the ĐKZ and 81mm mortar crews that the 98th Regiment's deputy commander had just led up onto the hill. The lack of fire support was worrisome, since Eliane-4's obstacles were still intact and there were no assault trenches to provide cover.[55]

Bộ đội called Eliane-4 "Saddleback Hill" because it had two crests separated by a gully.[56] The eastern one was held by 5 BPVN's Headquarters and 3rd Companies, plus 4/6 BPC. The two "Indochinese" companies stood fast as fugitives from Eliane-1 fled through their positions and *bộ đội* materialized in front.[57] Only one VPA medium machine gun and two 81mm mortars remained operational atop Eliane-1, while the defenders had plenty of fire support. Artillery barrages and enfilading fire from Honeycomb Hill pinned the 35th Company down in the saddle between Elianes-1 and -4. After communications were restored at 2040hrs, Lăng sent additional heavy weapons to Eliane-1 and ordered the 439th Battalion's 81st Company to make a diversionary attack from the southeast. The 249/174 was supposed to have joined in the assault from that direction, but was hopelessly bogged down on Eliane-2 (see below). The diversion failed because French fire was so intense that the 81st Company could not advance uphill. And although the 35th Company was reinforced by the 34th, five assaults across the saddle failed between 2100 and 0235hrs. The 35th finally broke into Eliane-4 at 0335hrs, though by then it barely had the strength of a platoon.[58]

The breakthrough could not be exploited as the company had no communications with the rest of the battalion, which was, in any case, pinned down and out of machine-gun and mortar ammunition. Since the assaults on Elianes-2 and -4 were hopelessly bogged down, and Dominique-5 had repulsed the 54/102, it was virtually inevitable that Eliane-1 would be counterattacked after dawn – and the French would be able to hit the hill with crossfires from several directions. Lăng feared that his vulnerable regiment, which lacked a powerful reserve because of the absence of one of its battalions, would be annihilated. So, in keeping with Giáp's guidance that only small bodies of troops should occupy captured strongpoints, Lăng ordered the 215th Battalion to withdraw at 0600hrs, leaving only a platoon and the surviving heavy weapons behind to hold Eliane-1. The 35th Company could not retreat across the fire-swept saddle in broad daylight and was trapped on Eliane-4, assaulted by superior forces and overrun by 0900hrs. After they ran out of grenades, its troops used Bangalores in combat during their last stand. Only 15 wounded survived to be taken prisoner. The 34th and 38th Companies survived, but had both taken severe casualties.[59]

3/5 BPVN had borne the brunt of the defense, and stood fast, although its weapons platoon was wiped out, and its commander, Lieutenant Jean Gaven, and another officer were killed. Overall, 5 BPVN lost 19 killed, 56 wounded, and 65 missing (mostly from 4th Company) that night.[60] The two surviving mortars of 1 CEPML's 2nd Platoon, deployed just behind Eliane-4, were threatened during the night by VPA infantry circling around the hill. Certain that he was about to be overrun, Lieutenant Erwan Bergot had no option but to retreat. Since the 475kg mortars could not be removed under the circumstances, with a heavy heart he destroyed the tubes with phosphorus grenades and fell back. The baseplates, bipods, and sights would be recovered intact the next morning.[61]

The fifth hill

By now a clear pattern has emerged. Assaults on frontline strongpoints succeeded because *bộ đội* attacking from trenches just meters away swiftly breached the wire and got to close quarters before French artillery could intervene. Attacks on interior strongpoints failed because no trenches were available, obstacles were intact, and French artillery laid down effective barrages. But although Eliane-2 was a frontline strongpoint, I/4 RTM's ten-day battle for the Bald Hill *sonnette* had prevented trenches from being driven close to the strongpoint.

> The infantry was to start from the foot of Burnt [Bald] Hill. Our efforts to extend the trenches of approach met with more and more difficulties: the enemy strove to fill up the sections nearest to their lines and had the ground pounded day and night by their artillery and air force. After some hesitation, the Regiment Commander adopted the following solution: instead of trying to push the trenches close to the enemy barbed wire fences he decided to

direct them to the fairly shallow bed of a dried-up stream leading to the foot of Burnt Hill. This negligence later proved a serious mistake.[62]

2/I/4 RTM (minus the platoon on Bald Hill) occupied the lower, eastern half of Eliane-2 known as the "Champs-Élysées," with the swapped I/13 DBLE platoon at the apex. The exterior trenches in this area followed the outlines of the colonial-era military post and probably incorporated portions of its brick perimeter wall into their structure. The western half of the hill was held by 1/I/4 RTM with its swapped Legion platoon. Luciani's paras and I/4 RTM's Headquarters Company with the heavy weapons and a reserve platoon were near the summit. A transverse trench at the western end of the Champs-Élysées could act as a second line of defense. The sides of the hill were protected by obstacle belts 30 to 50 meters thick and two more minefields had been emplaced next to the streambed southwest of Bald Hill.[63]

The 174th Regiment's 249th Infantry Battalion would attack from the east, while the 251st Battalion (minus a company) struck from the southeast. Its detached 674th Company would mount a diversion against Eliane-3 that would be converted into an assault if Eliane-2 fell quickly. After the strongpoint was taken, the 249th would detach a company to join the assault on Eliane-4, or at least support the 98th Regiment with its heavy weapons. The 255th Battalion was held in reserve to reinforce the Eliane-2 assault and/or conduct the follow-up attack on Eliane-3. The 174th Regiment would be supported by 36 artillery pieces, including the 801st Howitzer, 757th Mountain, and 113th Mortar Batteries, five 57mm ĐKZs, a platoon (four tubes) of the 413th Mortar Battalion, and the infantry units' organic 81/82mm mortars.[64]

Things went awry almost immediately. The 249th Battalion had left only a three-man listening post on Bald Hill and this was easily driven off by a sortie from Eliane-2 at 0630hrs. The 653rd Company battled from 0800 to 1600hrs just to retake the hill's lower, eastern crest. Moroccans on the higher, western summit directed artillery fire on the 174th Regiment's assault troops when they reached the foot of Bald Hill at 1700hrs. The streambed gave little protection to the massed bộ đội, who took severe casualties, and the shelling also cut the telephone link to divisional headquarters. The Moroccans were finally eliminated by a 120mm mortar bombardment shortly after 1800hrs.[65]

ĐKZs and machine guns were then installed on Bald Hill's eastern crest, but the emplacements were mere foxholes without overhead cover, and French artillery eliminated nearly all the crews. Shelling forced other weapons which were to have been deployed on Phony Hill to take position on lower ground from which they had to fire upwards at Eliane-2. But the VPA bombardment nevertheless began on schedule with intermittent shelling at 1720hrs that built to a crescendo an hour later. 2/I/4 RTM's executive officer, Paul Brudieu, was killed, its 57mm recoilless rifle and two 60mm mortars knocked out, and the attached Legion platoon decimated.[66] But owing to the cut telephone line, the 174th Regiment did not receive the order to attack when the bombardment lifted. Some time passed before regimental commander Nguyễn Hữu An decided to attack on his own initiative – something which was almost never done in the strictly disciplined VPA.[67]

The attackers had to cross 300 meters of open ground from the streambed on either side of Bald Hill. The 317th and 671st Companies' pioneer platoons accordingly took heavy casualties as they breached the obstacles. The task was completed by 1915hrs, but enfilading fire from Eliane-3, Junon, and a bunker atop "Mannequin Hillock" (so named because shellbursts had twisted a lopped-off banyan tree into a grotesque approximation of the human form) on Eliane-2 caused the 671st to veer east so its gap was only 30 meters from the 317th Company's. This allowed the defenders to concentrate their fire in this small area, delaying the arrival of the assault platoons, which had to slip forward in small groups between volleys of French shells. The assault finally began at 1945hrs – a full hour late – following a second brief artillery preparation. The Eliane-3 diversion never occurred because the 674th Company's commander had been hit, and his troops merely cut a gap into the barbed wire and then waited for the 255th Battalion to appear.[68]

Despite these missteps, both vanguard companies penetrated Eliane-2's perimeter by 2000hrs and were soon reinforced by the 316th Company. I/4 RTM's reserve platoon immediately counterattacked, but in vain. By 2300, 2nd Company's headquarters was in enemy hands,[69] and its 3rd Platoon and the Legionnaires had been wiped out. The survivors formed a new line on the transverse trench, behind which I/4 RTM's headquarters and infirmary were installed in the brick-walled basements and cisterns of the demolished colonial military post.[70] Other underground shelters behind the summit were linked together by deep trenches which had been given thick overhead cover that converted them into tunnels of a sort. These fortifications were so robust that the defenders could safely call down artillery on their own position. When two fresh platoons of the 316th Company (the third had been left behind to hold the eastern breach) assaulted the transverse trench shortly after 2300hrs, the defenders vanished into this subterranean warren.[71]

Realizing that they had to deal with a strong underground fortification, probably the strongest of A-1 and so far unknown to our scouts, our men set to search for its entrances. But they were checked by a new shower of artillery shells which also blocked the way to two reinforcement platoons. Hardly was the thunder of shell explosions over when the enemy emerged again from both flanks of the knoll and counter attacked with submachine guns and grenades. Our two platoons had to withdraw.[72]

The shelling and counterattacks also savaged the 671st Company. Reduced to just seven men, only the timely arrival of two 673rd Company platoons saved it from annihilation.

After communications broke down at 2000hrs, regimental commander An had ordered his chief of staff to take charge of the situation. He was surprised to find that the 249th Battalion's commander, Vũ Đình Hoè, had remained at the start line, leaving his deputy to lead the assault. But although that officer was inside the perimeter, he too was unaware of the real situation and still believed that the rest of Eliane-2 could be taken quickly. He summoned the 316th Company's last platoon forward just as Hoè committed the 315th Company, creating a traffic jam in the eastern breach that resulted in heavy losses. Worse yet, the 315th was virtually wiped out attacking the summit and most of the 249th Battalion's disheartened survivors took refuge in bunkers to escape the incessant artillery fire.[73]

Hoè demanded reinforcements and at midnight An committed the 255th Battalion. Its 924th and 925th Companies took heavy losses passing through the breaches and attacked with little fire support, because regimental heavy weapons had run out of ammunition and the 757th Mountain Battery could not identify targets from 1,300 meters away atop Hill 491 (the excessive distance was another consequence of the failure to take Bald Hill beforehand). The new assault failed because the "enemy repeated the same trick; pounding the assailants with artillery fire, then counter-attacking them with infantry emerging from the underground fortification."[74]

The defenders could counterattack frequently because they had been heavily reinforced. Elements of 2/1 BEP led by Lieutenant Edmond Fournié had been sent up as early as 2050hrs, and were followed at midnight by 3/1 BEP. At about the same time, I/4 RTM's commander, Major Jean Nicholas, decided to shift his command post to one of the rearward shelters.[75] This may have been why Langlais lost radio contact with him (though most accounts place this event at

2300hrs) and jumped to the conclusion that Eliane-2 had fallen. He was about to order a barrage on the summit when Bigeard broke in on the radio to say that Eliane-2 was holding out and promised to send one of his companies to reinforce it.[76] None actually seems to have been sent at this time, but by 0430hrs the attackers had been pushed back down the Champs-Élysées, and the 249th and 251st Battalions each had barely a dozen men still willing and able to fight. An decided to withdraw them, leaving the remnants of the 255th to hold a bridgehead on Eliane-2.[77]

The withdrawal coincided with more French counterattacks. At 0442hrs an ad hoc "march" company led by Lieutenant Pierre Rancoule that was cobbled together from a platoon of 12/BT3 and men "combed out" of I/2 REI's 1st and 2nd Companies had set out from Huguette.[78] At 0500hrs, it was the turn of 4/1 BEP and the Red Platoon. Ettlingen accompanied the counterattacking troops, but withdrew when its ammunition was exhausted, and Smolensk took its place. Though both tanks were hit they took no major damage as their frontal armor was not penetrated.[79] Finally, just after dawn, 3/6 BPC advanced from Eliane-4 to repel *bộ đội* that were thought to be threatening Eliane-2's northern flank. The company returned to Eliane-4 within an hour.[80]

The star strongpoint

Giáp's master plan called for feints against both Huguette-7 and Claudine-5, but GONO reported no attack on the latter that night. It's possible that the 88th Regiment was supposed to have made one, but had suffered so severely in the flak raid that it could not proceed. The "star strongpoint," Huguette-7, was attacked by the 397th Company of the 89/36, supported by regimental heavy weapons and some mortars of the 88th Regiment.[81] The strongpoint was defended by 1/5 BPVN, which had just received a new leader, Captain Alain Bizard, after Lieutenant Marcel Rondeau was wounded leading a sortie on March 28. On the morning of March 30, the garrison sallied out yet again to aerate enemy trenches. The 36th Regiment's mortars began harassing Huguette-7 at 1430hrs to maximize the effect of its diversion.[82] *Bộ đội* were seen approaching at 1600hrs and a bombardment started falling at 1730hrs. Bizard's 60mm mortars were put out of action, and, in the northern bastion, the 2nd Platoon's commander, Lieutenant Jean Claude Thelot, and his deputy, Sergeant Paul Cloâtre, were both killed by a ĐKZ hit on their command post.[83]

The defenders had time to recover from this blow since no assault was made until 2000hrs. And since the trenches filled in that morning had not been re-excavated, the pioneers had to work in the open and many were hit. The *bộ đội* were not deterred, however, and pressure on 2nd Platoon mounted. By midnight, its lines had been penetrated and Bizard requested artillery support and reinforcements. Both were denied by Langlais, whose attention was focused entirely on the Five Hills. The only fire support received was from 1/2 REI's battalion mortars. 2nd Platoon, now led by Sergeant-Chief Jean Tournayre, held on with the aid of two squads detached from the platoons in the other satellite positions. The damaged mortars were repaired by 0530hrs and started shelling the enemy's approach trenches. Some 120mm mortars joined in shortly thereafter and the attackers fell back at 0630hrs, leaving many bodies behind. Taking advantage of the usual morning ground fog, Douaumont escorted a supply convoy to Huguette-7 and helped "cleanse" its perimeter.[84]

Wieme

Off to the south, Isabelle-5 had also come under attack. Nicknamed "Wieme" after its commander – Lieutenant Reginald Wieme – the strongpoint was particularly weak because it was built at a time when almost no engineering materials were available and the Tai auxiliaries were novices at fortification. The trenches were barely a meter deep, the bunkers tiny and roofed with only a layer or two of bamboo, and the obstacles consisted of three simple barbed-wire fences without gates to facilitate sorties. Following a heavy bombardment, VPA troops began breaching the wire in front of the northeastern pillbox shortly after nightfall. They were repelled thanks to an artillery shoot from Claudine and the rapid fire of the strongpoint's four 60mm mortars – which would expend 600 rounds overnight. A second assault from the southeast at 0400hrs was also beaten off though the stubborn *bộ đội* did not give up until dawn. They left 20 dead and several badly wounded comrades littered around the perimeter. One of the latter revealed that the attacks' primary objective had been to enable infiltrators from the 63rd Trinh Sát Company to penetrate the strongpoint and strike a blow at Tai morale by capturing or assassinating Lieutenant Wieme. Since it would have been inexcusable to use elite intel/recon experts as assault troops, the attacks were no doubt carried out by elements of the 57th Regiment.[85]

The counteroffensive

Although GONO's reserves had been depleted in the overnight battles, Langlais planned to retake the lost positions on March 31 with the aid of Major Jean Bréchignac's full-strength II/1 RCP. The battalion was on alert in the Delta and at midnight de Castries had asked that it be dropped in before dawn. No action was taken on his request because General Cogny was enjoying a social engagement and General Navarre was flying up from his headquarters in Saigon. Contrary to protocol, Cogny was not on hand to greet Navarre when he arrived at FTNV's headquarters at 0115hrs. In his absence, Navarre drafted a defeatist message that urged de Castries to continue tying down Giáp's divisions as long as possible and reminded him that the tanks, artillery, and ammunition could not be allowed to fall into enemy hands.[86] The CEFEO commander-in-chief obviously feared that GONO might collapse in short order, and was consequently reluctant to commit another precious parachute battalion.

When Cogny finally appeared at 0745hrs, he and Navarre engaged in a violent shouting match that irrevocably wrecked their professional relationship. Then, at 0845hrs, Cogny received a message from de Castries stating that GONO needed two battalions and a promised 75mm recoilless rifle battery that day.[87] But Navarre and Cogny had reservations enough about sending II/1 RCP alone, and imposed strict conditions that had to be met before it would be committed. GONO wanted the battalion to jump onto Drop Zone Sonia around a kilometer south of Eliane-2 so it could quickly join in the counteroffensive. Cogny insisted that the DZ had to be cleared, and a corridor secure against small arms fire opened between the Main Position and Isabelle. And since the egressing Dakotas would pass directly over Dominiques-1 and -2, they had to be retaken or "at least neutralized." If these conditions were met, 200 replacements for the parachute battalions, another airborne surgical team, and a 75mm recoilless rifle platoon would take off at 1100hrs. A dozen Bearcats based in Laos would protect the drop against VPA flak and infantry. If all went well, II/1 RCP and the rest of the recoilless battery would jump from a second wave of planes that was to depart the Delta at 1500hrs. These provisos gave Navarre and Cogny plenty of excuses to avoid sending the battalion, though they did promise plentiful air support. A dozen B-26s would bomb Dominique-2 and Eliane-1 at 1200hrs, and eight Helldivers, six Hellcats, and eight Bearcats would support the counterattacks starting at 1230hrs. But as there was low overcast that morning, it seems likely that many of these aircraft were delayed or never arrived.[88]

Langlais planned to have III/3 REI (reinforced by elements of BT3) and the Green Platoon open the road from Isabelle, clear DZ Sonia, and then seize Bald Hill. They left Isabelle at 0700hrs, with the bulk of the force following RP41, while 10/III/3 took the Bulldozer Road. At Bản Kho Lai they ran into what the French thought were two entire VPA battalions. In fact, only the 265th Battalion's 19th Company was initially present, though its troops used various ruses to seem more numerous than they were. The Legionnaires broke into its first trench at 0800hrs, were driven out by a counterattack, then made a second assault that cut the company in two and killed its commander and senior commissar. But as the seesaw fighting continued, VPA reinforcements threatened to envelop III/3 REI. A company of the 346th Battalion was battling 10/III/3 REI on the Bulldozer Road, while the 418th Battalion's 59th Company launched a flank attack from the foothills east of RP41. The fifth and final French assault was defeated when the 265th Battalion deliberately left a gap in its lines, then struck the attackers in the flank after they had advanced through it. At 1150hrs, the Legionnaires began falling back to Isabelle with Neumach – which had been immobilized by a bazooka – in tow. The operation had cost them 15 missing and 50 wounded, including three officers.[89] The road to Isabelle would remain closed for the rest of the siege.

Meanwhile, supported by Smolensk, the *mélange* of French troops on Eliane-2 was fighting to retake the Champs-Élysées. They counterattacked constantly from 0430hrs onwards, maintaining heavy pressure on the 255th Battalion's survivors and some *bộ đội* who had inadvertently been left behind when the other battalions withdrew. As the morning wore on, the VPA troops ran short of ammunition and virtually all their platoon- and company-level officers became casualties. Lacking leadership, communications, and a clear chain of command, the disorganized survivors retreated without orders at 1130hrs. Eliane-2's garrison could finally rest after 18 hours of intense combat, though it was harassed throughout the afternoon by enemy artillery.[90]

6 BPC launched the counterattack on Eliane-1 before 1100hrs. It was supported by the fire of 5/BT2 on Dominique-5, and 1/6 BPC and 5 BPVN's 2nd and 3rd Companies on Eliane-4, which targeted enemy positions on Phony Hill as well as Eliane-1.[91] The hill was held by the 215th Battalion's remnants, the 439th Battalion's 82nd Company, and a platoon of the 54/102nd's 273rd Company. If the retreat order issued at dawn had arrived in a timely fashion, Eliane-1 might have been defended by a mere platoon. But it had been delayed in transit by yet another breakdown in communications and did

not arrive until after the counterattack had begun. In a hasty Party Committee meeting, the surviving officers and commissars decided to ignore the order and sent the 215th Battalion's commander, Bùi Hữu Quán, to inform regimental headquarters in person. He was killed by a shell while descending the hill at 1200hrs.[92]

6 BPC attacked on two axes. Lieutenant Trapp's 2/6 BPC advanced from Honeycomb Hill with Lieutenant Roland Corbineau's platoon in the lead. It was repulsed, but Lieutenant André Samalens' platoon leapfrogged through and continued the assault while VPA artillery landed on friend and foe alike. After Samalens was wounded, Sergeant-Chief Flamen took command and captured 25 prisoners.[93] Lieutenant Le Boudec's 3/6 BPC attacked from Eliane-4, with Lieutenant Boulay's platoon on the left and Lieutenant de Fromont's on the right. A platoon of 4/6 BPC eventually joined the attack as well. Progress was slow because Eliane-1's fortifications had been plowed under by shelling and VPA resistance was stiff. De Fromont was badly wounded in the face by shrapnel and Boulay was also hit but continued to lead his troops.[94] The paras managed to capture the "Flagpole Compound" around noon.

By then, Langlais and de Castries knew that the sortie from Isabelle was not going to clear DZ Sonia, but they clung to the slim hope that some tanks could be freed up to protect the drop zone. At 1150hrs they radioed Hanoi, "We will realize to the maximum the security conditions demanded for parachuting but these drops must take place."[95] They were willing to risk severe losses, but Navarre and Cogny were not. At 1250hrs, FTNV radioed that owing to bad weather and the urgency of dropping supplies, the morning mission had been canceled and II/1 RCP might not arrive that day.[96] A supply drop was urgent since GONO was out of grenades and 81mm mortar shells, but de Castries insisted that reinforcements were also desperately needed.[97] In the end, only 25 tons of supplies and no reinforcements arrived that day. Since it was unwilling to drop II/1 RCP on unsecured DZ Sonia, FTNV instead proposed using DZ Opéra – which straddled RP41 a kilometer southeast of Isabelle. GONO rejected this at 1645hrs, presumably because the battalion might not be able to break through to the Main Position. But this debate was arguably moot, since II/1 RCP probably could not have joined in the counteroffensive unless it had jumped in sometime before dawn on March 31.[98]

Meanwhile, the Eliane-1 counterattack had become bogged down. 6 BPC could not advance beyond the summit since the eastern slope was invisible to French artillery observers and swept by crossfires from Dominique-2 and

Phony Hill. In seesaw fighting, the "Flagpole Compound" changed hands many times between 1400 and 1600hrs, though by the end barely a platoon's worth of able-bodied VPA troops remained in the strongpoint.[99] 6 BPC's companies were also ground down and lost another key officer when Lieutenant Le Boudec was wounded at 1600hrs. The paras could also see the 439th Battalion's 81st Company moving up through a newly dug trench. With darkness approaching, no reserves available, half of Eliane-1 still in enemy hands, and no obstacles in front of the recaptured positions, it seemed suicidal to remain on the hill. At 1800hrs Bigeard reluctantly ordered a retreat. The 98th Regiment had paid a high price for Eliane-1 and -4, suffering 496 casualties – the equivalent of an entire battalion – in just 24 hours.[100]

While 6 BPC spent seven hours fighting on Eliane-1, the Dominique-2 counterattack was a curiously half-hearted affair that lasted just two hours. The mission was given to Tourret's 8 BPC, but neither he nor his executive officer, Captain Jean-Marie Lamouliatte, commanded it in person, and just over half the battalion was involved. 4/8 BPC spent the day rescuing one of its platoons that had gone out on ambush toward Anne Marie the night before and been cut off.[101] Only a platoon and a half of 1/8 BPC participated, because the rest of the unit and 8 BPC's Headquarters Company stayed behind to hold Épervier and lay suppressing fire on Dominique-1.[102] Conti did the same from a position just south of the hill, while Smolensk and Posen were deployed near Dominique-6. The strongpoint was also hit by artillery and numerous air attacks.[103]

The authors of 312th Division's official history mingled the events of March 31 with those of April 1. Thus, when they say that a French counterattack retook Hill E (Dominique-1) on the afternoon of April 1, they mean the day before. In keeping with Giáp's orders, Dominique-1 was held only by the 428th Battalion's reinforced 670th Weapons Company. It reportedly repelled several infantry attacks supported by artillery, tanks, and airstrikes, but was forced to retreat after it had suffered nearly 100 casualties. There was no infantry attack, but French firepower alone made the hill untenable, and the fact that its fortifications were so flimsy now worked to their advantage. GONO could have easily reoccupied the position had it been aware of the situation and had any troops to spare.[104]

And if Dominique-1 had been retaken, the siege's outcome could have been very different indeed, especially since the Dominique-2 counterattack came very close to succeeding. It was led by Captain François Pichelin's 2/8 BPC, which passed through vacant Dominique-6 along the way – feeding the enemy's perception that Dominique-1 was under infantry attack. Concealed by a smokescreen and accompanied by III/3 RTA survivors who guided them through the barbed wire and minefields, Pichelin's troops began climbing Dominique-2's western slope at 1330hrs. Since French artillery fire had eliminated the VPA sentries, the company's Assault Platoon was not spotted until it reached close quarters. According to Sergeant (later Colonel) Paul Franceschi, the surprised *bộ đội* fled like a herd of stampeding cattle.[105] 2nd Company was soon joined by Mulhouse and Lieutenant Gabriel Bailly's 3rd Company, which had climbed up behind Dominique-5. Yet VPA artillery kept up a steady bombardment that killed Captain Pichelin and the Assault Platoon's commander, Sergeant Armand Carré (all of 2nd Company's platoons were led by NCOs), and Lieutenant Bailly had to assume command of both companies.[106]

The 209th Regiment's official history admits that the 525th Company lost most of Dominique-2 in just 25 minutes and that the 154th Battalion's executive officer, Lê Xuân Quang, was killed. But it insists that the company's survivors clung to a corner of the strongpoint and were reinforced by the 366th and 520th Companies.[107] This is disputed by French witnesses who insist that the entire position was retaken and could have been held.[108] Lieutenant Bailly did not agree, however, and sought permission to retreat. If he was wrong, one must sympathize with a junior officer who found himself commanding a much larger force than he was accustomed to and fighting for the most crucial terrain on the entire battlefield. It is inexcusable that Tourret did not take charge himself or at least send Lamouliatte. He requested reinforcements, but Bigeard replied that none were available and advised, "If you can't hold it, pull out."[109] Bailly fell back at 1530hrs, covered by Mulhouse. When it was the tank's turn to retreat, it became immobilized by barbed wire that wrapped around its tracks and had to be towed loose by Bazeilles.[110]

De Castries reported that Dominique-2 had been evacuated because it was being struck by powerful VPA counterattacks.[111] This is disputed by Franceschi, who insisted that, apart from shelling, there was no enemy pressure when the withdrawal began. Otherwise, how could he and several other NCOs have had the time to re-climb the hill to retrieve Pichelin's and Carré's bodies, which had been left behind on trapped Mulhouse's rear deck? Franceschi believed that Tourret's heart was never in the operation since he should have commanded it in person and committed the entire battalion, even if it meant abandoning 4th Company's surrounded platoon.[112] Tourret may indeed have deliberately shortchanged the operation, but if his aim was to limit casualties, 8 BPC still had 22 killed, 97 wounded, and three missing on March 31 – though some were lost on Eliane-2 after dark (see below).[113]

Since Dominique-5 was hopelessly exposed to enemy forces occupying higher ground on either flank, Lieutenant de la Malène sought permission to evacuate the strongpoint. It was granted at 1900hrs and his company took over the defense of Eliane-10.[114] Down on Dominique-3, Lieutenant Brunbrouck's three remaining 105s had been towed to Claudine that morning, while all of III/3 RTA's survivors were sent to Junon for reorganization. 6/BT2 replaced them, but after 8 BPC pulled back from Dominique-2, the company was ordered to abandon the northern position as it was too vulnerable to plunging fire from the towering hill just a few hundred meters away.[115]

The second night, March 31 to April 1

Although his regiments had taken very heavy losses, Giáp was determined to remain on the offensive. The key objective was Eliane-2, but the 316th Division had no fresh units available. Major General Hoàng Văn Thái, Deputy Chief of the VPA's General Staff, suggested that the 308th Division's 102nd Infantry Regiment be used to capture the strongpoint and Giáp approved his plan. Tramping through mud and fording the Nậm Yum under constant harassment by French aircraft and artillery, the 18/102 took ten hours to make the 6.5km trip from the western siege lines to Bald Hill. The 54/102 was already east of the river, but was also delayed.[116] Overall, just four companies arrived on schedule and they were merged into a composite unit led by the 18th Battalion's commander.[117] It would attack from the east, while the 251st Battalion's reinforced 674th Company – the only intact unit in the 174th Regiment – struck from the southeast. This was an unimaginative plan that merely duplicated the previous night's failed assault, but there was no time to prepare anything else.

The 801st Howitzer, 757th Mountain, and 113th Mortar Batteries began harassing Eliane-2 at nightfall, but the 102nd Regiment's troops went astray and the assault did not actually begin until 2230hrs. To achieve surprise, there was no final artillery bombardment, only an intense, three-minute burst of fire by regimental heavy weapons.[118] Though the breaches were still open and trenches had been dug into them, troops on the wings of the assault had to cross open ground and clear intact obstacles.[119] The attackers nonetheless quickly overran the Champs-Élysées and captured 15 prisoners from 4/6 BPC, which had arrived on Eliane-2 that afternoon. The defenders again retreated into the bunkers, called down artillery on themselves, and then counterattacked. And once again, VPA troops vainly searched for the entrances while French barrages prevented reinforcements from arriving.[120]

Bigeard claims that at 2200hrs Langlais authorized him to abandon the remnants of Dominique and Eliane if they could not be held. He replied: "Mon colonel, as long as I've got one man left alive I'm not going to let go of Eliane!"[121] Langlais does not mention this incident in his memoirs and the notion of abandoning everything east of the Nậm Yum seems premature since no other strongpoint there was attacked that night (though Eliane-3 would be probed at 0230hrs[122] and Dominique-1 reoccupied by 11/141[123]). And even if Langlais did briefly consider abandoning the left bank, he had already started reinforcements on their way to Eliane-2. 3/6 BPC and elements of 8 BPC's weak 2nd and 3rd Companies were dispatched, and a pair of platoons from 2/I/13 DBLE that carried ammunition onto the hill around 2100hrs also joined the defense. Smolensk and Ettlingen arrived less than an hour later and remained until their ammunition was expended. The Blue Platoon relieved them during a lull between 0300 and 0400hrs, but its crews were dead tired and could not see what was happening around them. This enabled a bazooka team to creep up and fire into the thinner armor on Bazeilles' left side. A hit on the turret stunned the crew, while another set the engine ablaze. The crew abandoned the tank, which was immobilized on Eliane-2 and used as a static bunker for the rest of the siege (it remains there today). Mulhouse also took a hit that wounded the entire crew, but it could still move and withdrew with Douaumont.[124]

A battle was also under way west of the Nậm Yum, where the 308th Division had been ordered to switch from feinting against to annihilating Françoise and Huguette-7.[125] But with the 88th Regiment evidently still *hors de combat* and the 102nd Regiment fighting on Eliane-2, the division only attacked Huguette-7. Bizard had requested reinforcements in the afternoon, but Langlais again had none to spare. He did send the Red Platoon – which had been in action almost without a break for about 18 hours – to shoot up the trenches north of Huguette just before nightfall. Since Bizard did not have enough troops left to defend the whole sprawling strongpoint, he evacuated the northern bastion and central redoubt, and ordered that gaps be opened in the barbed wire to facilitate movement between the various positions.[126]

VPA artillery began bombarding the vacant northern bastion at 2100hrs, followed by a ground assault an hour later (most likely by the 89/36). The attackers seem to have been puzzled by the lack of opposition, since they did not occupy the central redoubt until nearly 0300hrs and made little effort to assault the other two positions. At dawn, Bizard pounded the central redoubt with artillery and led a counterattack by his 1st and 3rd Platoons through the gaps from the eastern and southwestern bastions. The entire strongpoint was retaken by 0700hrs.[127] Within an hour, the paras were relieved by a march company, led by Lieutenant Dante Spozio, that incorporated a platoon each from I/2 REI's 2nd and 4th Companies. Lieutenant François Huguenin, who commanded 2nd Company's platoon, claims the entire force numbered just 40 men including Spozio and himself.[128] Lieutenant Pierre Latanne of 5 BPVN remained behind to familiarize the Legionnaires with the position.

Although no strongpoints fell overnight, GONO's reserves were being rapidly depleted and no reinforcements had arrived. At 2113hrs on March 31, de Castries had requested that II/1 RCP jump onto DZ Opéra at dawn,[129] but at 0114hrs he suggested instead that it use a much closer DZ extending north 1,200 meters from Bản Co My. He promised to use a march battalion to occupy the village and secure the DZ, but the plan came to nothing owing to poor weather.[130] "The morning of April 1st had an acid taste for those at Dien Bien Phu. The sky was foul. Large, migrating clouds swollen with tepid water paraded in front of the sun."[131] And April 1 was also the day that Cogny reneged on his earlier promise to commit another entire GAP, radioing instead that reinforcements would be limited to a single parachute battalion and a 75mm recoilless battery. GONO could not be sure that even these forces would be sent, since Cogny's message also stressed that under no circumstances could surrender be considered and reminded de Castries that no heavy weapons or ammunition should be allowed to fall into enemy hands.[132]

The third night, April 1–2

The French launched three counterattacks on Eliane-2 during the daylight hours of April 1. The 102nd Regiment had only 50 able-bodied men (30 from the 54th Battalion and 20 from the 18th) remaining inside the perimeter, but VPA heavy weapons emplaced on Phony and Bald Hills barred the access to the low-lying Champs-Élysées with a deadly, 90-degree crossfire. Nonetheless, when the third and final counterattack began at 1500hrs, there were just 17 *bộ đội* still fighting (others were hiding in bunkers). The 102nd Regiment's commander, Nguyễn Hùng Sinh, saved the day by personally leading a group of regimental headquarters personnel and the 18th Battalion's late-arriving 259th Company onto the blood-soaked hilltop. After the crisis was overcome, he withdrew the 674th Company, which had just eight troops remaining.[133]

The French had also taken heavy casualties, including Captain Edmond Krumenacker and Lieutenant Pierre-Emile Gerardin of I/13 DBLE, and Lieutenant Luciani of 1 BEP, who were all wounded. Langlais sorted out the hodgepodge of units on Eliane-2 by putting 1 BEP in charge of its defense and redeploying most of the troops that belonged to other battalions. I/4 RTM headed to Claudine, as planned, and the survivors of I/13 DBLE's 1st and 2nd Companies also headed back over the river (though 4/I/13 DBLE remained on Eliane-3). 8 BPC's companies went to Épervier, and Lieutenant Rancoule's march company returned to Huguette with just 16 of the 80 men that he had led to Eliane-2 two nights earlier.[134]

Although five VPA battalions had already been decimated on Eliane-2, Giáp was determined to capture it no matter what the cost. The new assault would be led by two march companies formed from the 18th and 54th Battalion's survivors, plus another assembled from the shattered 174th Regiment. But "their morale was poor and they were generally pessimistic, they now overestimated the enemy's strength, and they said that because of the enemy's underground bunker, his powerful artillery fire support, and his large counterattack forces they no longer believed that they could win victory." Moreover, "Our forces … did nothing to try to circle around to find another route of approach. They simply followed the same routes that had been followed during the attack the previous night."[135]

The 102nd Regiment was to use the eastern breach, while the 174th Regiment's march company entered by the southeastern one. But the latter did not reach its start line until 0500hrs the next morning, and the 102nd Regiment wound up attacking on both axes at 2400hrs. Its assault was stopped cold by the underground bunkers. No Bisons reinforced Eliane-2 that night because the Red Platoon was being given a badly needed rest, and the Blue Platoon had only Douaumont still operational (though it aided the defense from its bivouac on Junon). The flamethrower team of I/2 REI's Headquarters Company, 3/6 BPC, and two companies of 1 BEP counterattacked down the Champs-Élysées at 0300hrs. But although the 102nd Regiment's two march companies had been reduced to the strength of a single platoon, they clung to the hill's eastern tip with the aid of a company from the 79/102 that appeared just in the nick of time.[136]

Huguette-7 was also attacked that night. The 80th Battalion assaulted from the north and the 84th Battalion from the west. The battered 89th Battalion deployed a platoon east of the strongpoint to block French reinforcements, but otherwise remained in reserve. The assault would be supported by regimental heavy weapons and a pair of the 754th Mountain Battery's howitzers atop Anne Marie. But H-hour had to be delayed until 1830 because French airstrikes and artillery fire had decimated the gun crews. The surviving weapons' fire was supplemented by the 803rd Howitzer Battery's 105s, which dropped 35 shells onto Huguette-7. Here again, one is struck by how carefully Giáp had to ration artillery shells.[137]

The attackers easily penetrated the perimeter because Spozio had so few troops that he too chose to defend only the eastern and southwestern bastions. Yet the 36th Regiment's official history reports that the 80th Battalion met resistance in the central redoubt, and killed or captured 33 enemy troops there. The battalion then attacked the eastern bastion, which was held by Huguenin and 20 Legionnaires, and overran it by 0200hrs. Spozio held out longer in the southwest bastion because the 84th Battalion's 41st Company veered off course in the dark and broke into the central redoubt instead. Realizing its error, the company hastily redeployed against the southwest bastion, which was already under attack by the 45th Company. Spozio and a few surviving Legionnaires slipped out of the doomed position before 0400hrs, and stealthily made their way to Huguette-1.[138]

At dawn, Langlais ordered a counterattack by Bizard's depleted 1/5 BPVN, which had the strength of just two platoons. It was accompanied by the Blue Platoon's three tanks (Conti had joined it and Mulhouse had been repaired overnight). Bizard encountered the wounded Spozio at Huguette-1 and learned that Huguette-7 was entirely in enemy hands. After picking up a platoon of Legionnaires as reinforcements, Bizard pressed on to Huguette-6, which had been probed overnight by the 165th Regiment. His troops helped 3/I/2 REI clear its perimeter, then headed west. But when Huguette-7's outskirts were reached at 0800hrs, it proved to be occupied in strength by enemy troops. Since he had just 80 infantrymen on hand, Bizard concluded that he could neither retake Huguette-7 nor hold it if he did. Langlais authorized him to fall back after the Bisons and artillery had given the strongpoint a good pounding.[139]

The loss of Huguette-7 shook the morale of CSMs 413 and 434 on Françoise, which had been harassed overnight. Fearing that they would be assaulted after nightfall, 40 Tai deserted with their weapons at 1400hrs.[140] Leaving the demoralized CSMs to garrison GONO's most exposed strongpoint had obviously been a poor choice, but there were no better troops to spare. The mass desertion on Françoise was not an isolated event. After the defeats of March 30–31 – and the destruction of their families at Bản Nong Nhai – similar incidents had occurred in several other Tai CSMs during the first days of April. Langlais, who had never thought much of the Tai, decided to disband the worst-affected units – CSMs 414, 415, 417, 434, and 454.[141] Since CSM 416 had been destroyed on Gabrielle, GMPT 1 now had less than half its original strength. Some Western historians imply that the Tai were universally worthless and all deserted by the end of the siege. But in fact, five depleted CSMs (413, 418, 431, 432, and 433) fought on to the bitter end.

Fears about the reliability of the Tai on exposed strongpoint Wieme no doubt played a role in Colonel Lalande's decision to reinforce them with 20 Algerians from V/7 RTA on April 2.[142] Otherwise, the day was a relatively quiet one on Isabelle, which continued to play a key role in the battles raging around the Main Position with its flanking artillery barrages. However, counterbattery fire by the 805th Howitzer, 756th Mountain, and the 112th Mortar Batteries ensured that Isabelle's gunners paid a high price. Owing to personnel shortages, only six of Lalande's nine intact 105s were operational on April 2, and Algerian riflemen of II/1 RTA and 5/7 RTA had to be transferred to fill out the understrength gun crews.[143] Gunners were also short in the Main Position, and de Castries, with some slight exaggeration, radioed Hanoi that he could man only a dozen 105s (including four at Isabelle) and demanded that six entire gun crews be sent as soon as possible.[144]

GONO's combat battalions were also melting away at an alarming rate. II/1 RCP was still available, but owing to the density of VPA flak around the Main Position and the closure of the road to Isabelle, it could not be dropped by daylight. Nighttime drops were slow because planes could not fly in formation and had to drop their passengers singly. And since the only drop zone available paralleled the main runway, jumpers who overshot it would land in the enemy trenches north of Huguette. Only half of a 12-man "stick" could jump at a time and each plane had to make several passes. To ensure accurate landings, the Dakotas also had to fly so low and slow that they could not operate while "Luciole" ("Firefly") aircraft were dropping flares. And because even a brief pause in illumination might doom a strongpoint, personnel drops could occur only during lulls in VPA attacks. Thus, although the entire II/1 RCP spent much of the night orbiting overhead, only parts of its Headquarters and 4th Companies landed before dawn on April 2. The rest of the battalion returned to the Delta.[145]

The fourth night, April 2–3

By now Eliane-2 was so choked with corpses that *bộ đội* had to walk on their fallen comrades and were so short of food that they had to eat rice recovered from their comrades' bodies even though it was saturated with congealed blood.[146] Despite being reinforced by 60 men of the 249/174 at 0630hrs, there were only 50 able-bodied VPA troops remaining when the French counterattacked at 0800hrs. Yet regimental commander Sinh had plenty of cadres on hand, including three deputy battalion commanders and a senior political officer, and assigned each of them a trench to hold to the last man and took responsibility for another himself.[147] But the 18th Battalion's commander, Vụ Văn Kha, allegedly abandoned his post and swept along some of his troops as he fled. In truth, the 255th Battalion's commander, Nguyen Don Tu, convinced Kha to withdraw after a nearby shell explosion left him deaf and mute. Tu was appalled when he later learned that Kha had been court-martialed, expelled from the Communist Party, and sentenced to ten years' imprisonment. After the siege, Tu and other officers successfully appealed for Kha's release, but he was never "rehabilitated" and official histories published decades later still made him a scapegoat for the failure to take Eliane-2.[148] In contrast, Major Guiraud left Eliane-2 without any fuss after he was wounded. Captain François Vieules took command of 1 BEP, which lost 13 killed, 23 wounded, and nine missing that day.[149]

A final French counterattack at 1100hrs was halted just short of the Champs-Élysées' eastern tip by the crossfire from Phony and Bald Hills, and an ad hoc platoon of reinforcements from the 174th Regiment. Undeterred by the carnage, Giáp ordered a fourth attack using every able-bodied soldier the 102nd Regiment could still muster. This amounted to barely a company's worth of troops inside the perimeter and another outside. "The soldiers were exhausted and most of the officers were wavering and did not believe that victory was possible. Most of the enlisted men were newly arrived raw recruits who had not received basic infantry training, so their fighting skills were very poor. Although the regiment's heavy weapons had been resupplied, they still had only a small amount of ammunition."[150]

VPA artillery opened fire at 1800hrs, the reinforcements began moving up from Bald Hill an hour and a half later, and the assault started at 2230hrs.[151] When the defenders again withdrew underground, the *bộ đội* detonated eight 10kg explosive bundles against the wall of the hilltop bunker, but it was unscathed, and, after a flurry of shells, the French sallied out to counterattack yet again. The frustrated attackers resumed looking for the bunker's entrances, but still could not find them. At 0400hrs, Sinh decided to halt the attack and withdrew his decimated units, leaving only a single platoon inside Eliane-2.[152]

The 57th Regiment probed strongpoint Wieme with at least two companies at 2130hrs that night,[153] while the 312th Division tested Dominique-3's and Huguette-6's defenses. The latter was held by Lieutenant Jacques Donnadieu's 3/I/2 REI, reinforced by some PEG troops and 25 Béatrice survivors. The strongpoint's water tanks were destroyed during the attack – a seemingly minor incident that would soon prove consequential.[154] At noon on April 3, a *bộ đội* waving a white flag offered a truce so the garrison could recover some wounded survivors of Huguette-7. This was accepted and a party of stretcher-bearers crossed into enemy lines, where they were shocked to find not wounded men, but four brutally mutilated bodies. This psychological warfare gambit served its purpose, since later in the day, a dozen Béatrice survivors cut a gap in the barbed wire and deserted to the enemy. Since this sort of thing simply did not happen in the Foreign Legion, it shocked and dismayed Huguette-6's remaining defenders.[155]

And that was not the only bad news. During the night, more Tai had deserted from Françoise and the rest retreated from it without orders. Legionnaires of I/2 REI's 1st and 2nd Companies sallied out at dawn to rescue the French cadres, and recover abandoned weapons and ammunition. They returned before dark, surrendering Françoise to the enemy.[156] In addition, Mulhouse had been knocked out by an artillery hit on its turret and would not be operational again until April 6.[157] Worst of all, just 106 reinforcements had jumped in overnight (32 artillerymen and the rest of 4/II/1 RCP). Langlais was incensed because he believed that drops could be greatly accelerated if restrictive DZ regulations were discarded and pilots were permitted to drop personnel anywhere inside the Main Position. Colonel Henri Sauvagnac, commander of Troupes

Aéroportées d'Indochine – or TAPI (Airborne Troops – Indochina) – refused to allow this since he was convinced that jump injuries would skyrocket if men had to land amidst trenches, bunkers, barbed wire, minefields, vehicles, artillery pieces, and wrecked aircraft in the dark.[158]

The fifth night, April 3–4

Both sides adjusted their forces on Eliane-2 during April 3. The fresh 4/I/13 DBLE moved up from Eliane-3 to replace a depleted company of 1 BEP, while the 102nd Regiment's tattered remnants were withdrawn to Mường Phăng, 15km northeast of Điện Biên Phủ, to regroup and absorb replacements.[159] It had suffered 890 casualties – the equivalent of two entire battalions.[160] The 255/174 sent one company to hold a bridgehead inside Eliane-2, while the rest of the battalion remained some distance away so it could absorb replacements and reorganize. Yet French documents report that on the night of April 3–4, Eliane-2 repelled another attack with the assistance of the Blue Platoon's tanks firing from Junon. Since Vietnamese historians make no mention of this attack, what most likely occurred was that an exchange of shots between sentries flared up into a prolonged but inconclusive firefight.[161]

In retrospect, Giáp had been wrong to keep beating his head against a brick wall at Eliane-2. For it was not only the best-fortified strongpoint, but also among the easiest to reinforce because it was close to the headquarters area and a trench running from Eliane-3 provided a covered route of approach. By April 4, Giáp had learned his lesson, and shifted his attention to Huguette's flimsily constructed outlying strongpoints, which could be attacked in isolation. Huguette-6 was the next logical target. Its capture would guarantee that the French never used the runway again and deny them access to much of the main drop zone.

The 165th Regiment assaulted Huguette-6 on the night of April 3–4 while the 308th Division feinted against Claudine-4.[162] Following a short bombardment in which the 802nd Howitzer Battery participated,[163] VPA troops struck from the north and east at 1915hrs. Lieutenant Francis Pencreac'h of II/4 RAC directed barrages around the perimeter, including a curtain of tracers from Épervier's Quad-50s that barred access from the south.[164] But owing to the deserters' breach in the wire, the defenses were soon penetrated from the northeast.[165] Langlais ordered a counterattack by 4/8 BPC and the Red Platoon, which advanced up the eastern side of the runway and fell upon the rear of the units attacking Huguette-6. The wide-open terrain was perfectly suited for the tanks, which routed the enemy in just half an hour. French accounts describe surprised *bộ đội* fleeing in panic and being scythed down in windrows by the Bisons' machine guns.[166] The counterattack also benefited from a lucky mortar hit on a VPA headquarters.[167] Langlais must have been glad that the battle ended swiftly since it was imperative to halt "Firefly" operations so a large personnel drop could begin (see below). Huguette's battered garrison was relieved on April 4 by 1/I/2 REI, which was replaced on Huguette-4 by troops of I/4 RTM. The relief took all day. At dusk, the PEG detachment was still in place and Lieutenant Donnadieu's departure was delayed until the next morning because 1st Company's commander, Lieutenant Jean François, had been slow to arrive because he had to familiarize the Moroccans with Huguette-4's defenses.[168]

Over on Eliane-2, the defenders saw at dawn that the Champs-Élysées was empty. Patrols probed down to the hill's eastern tip without meeting resistance, but Captain Vieules followed Bigeard's advice to leave the area undefended because it was too exposed to crossfires from Phony and Bald Hills. Vietnamese accounts insist that 255th Battalion troops always remained inside the perimeter, though the defense of this enclave depended primarily on crossfires from the neighboring hills. These conflicting accounts can be reconciled if one assumes that the battered 255th did indeed withdraw from the Champs-Élysées, but quickly returned when it realized the French were not going to occupy it themselves.[169]

The French thus finally had cause for optimism on the morning of April 4. Giáp had abandoned the assault on Eliane-2, taken a bloody thrashing at Huguette-6, and a day had passed without another strongpoint being lost. Best of all, 390 men had been dropped in overnight, including 85 individual replacements and the bulk of II/1 RCP (its commander, Major Bréchignac, the rest of Headquarters Company, half of 2nd Company, and the entire 3rd Company). For Langlais had won his argument with Colonel Sauvagnac and had the reinforcements dropped directly on the camp itself using the reflection of a flaming gasoline drum on the surface of the Nậm Yum as a marker. He was vindicated when jump casualties remained well within acceptable limits.[170]

The sixth night, April 4–5

On April 4, II/4 RAC's 6th Battery relocated from Épervier to a less exposed position adjacent to 4th Battery's new gunpits in the Headquarters Area. This was most likely accomplished in the early morning hours, when ground fog would have shielded the redeployment from enemy observation. Thus, of all the Main Position's howitzer batteries, only 5/II/4 was still in the same position it had occupied on March 13. Indeed, the battery would remain in place until the end of the siege, allowing its fortifications to be steadily improved. During the second half of April, its gunpits would be converted into casemates with overhead cover. This was possible because 5th Battery was tasked with supporting CR Isabelle, and thus needed only a narrow field of fire.[171]

De Castries claimed that the 165th Regiment lost 450 men killed and 50 captured at Huguette-6 on the night of April 3–4. If even just an equivalent number were wounded, two entire battalions would have been rendered *hors de combat*. Yet, the 165th nonetheless attacked again just 24 hours later. A document captured by the French indicated that all three of its battalions and another from the 141st Regiment made the new assault, but a Vietnamese source implies that only the 115/165 and the 243rd Company of the 11/141 were involved.[172] A protracted bombardment began at 1815hrs, followed by feints against Huguettes-1 and -5. Huguette-6's defenses were also probed between 2200 and 2330hrs, but the assault began in earnest only at 0030hrs with simultaneous thrusts from the north, east, and west. Despite intense French barrages, the eastern attack broke into the perimeter, and the outnumbered defenders (who numbered fewer than 100) were driven back step by step.[173]

At 0040hrs, Langlais ordered Lieutenant Bailly's 3/8 BPC, accompanied by Conti and Douaumont, to rush to Huguette-6's aid. They moved up the eastern side of the airfield, with the paras sheltering behind the tanks as they advanced. Navigating by the fitful light of parachute flares, Conti strayed into a minefield and was immobilized. It was left behind while the rest of the relief force pressed on northward. Two platoons slipped into Huguette-6 at around 0115hrs, but the others became pinned down in the drainage ditch and Bailly was hit twice in the leg. Douaumont also came close to being crippled, and escaped that fate only because the bazooka rocket struck a box that had been attached to its hull as extra protection. Meanwhile, the situation inside the strongpoint was going from bad to worse, and its command post was overrun at 0135hrs.[174]

Undismayed, at 0225hrs Langlais ordered Lieutenant Maurice Viard to lead a march company of I/13 DBLE to Huguette-6. However, feints against Huguettes-2 and -5 blocked the way up the Pavie Track and Viard never made it.[175] The way east of the runway was still open, however, and was taken by the Red Platoon and Captain Marcel Clédic's fresh, but half-strength 2/II/1 RCP, which had jumped in just the night before. Ettlingen was detached to tow Conti back to base, but the immobilized tank detonated another mine and was hauled only as far as Huguette-3 so its consort could rejoin the battle. The damage was so severe that Conti was not repaired and served as a static bunker for the rest of the siege.[176]

Since Bailly's troops clogged the drainage ditch, Clédic led his 60 paras across the runway above Huguette-1 and, supported by Posen and Smolensk, pushed up the Pavie Track. They overcame a VPA blocking force halfway to Huguette-6, and captured a machine gun and two automatic rifles. But they were halted by the enemy's superior numbers, and Clédic had to fall back a short distance when there was a pause in flare-dropping.[177] Realizing there were still not enough troops on hand, at 0500hrs Langlais ordered Bigeard to organize a daylight counterattack. He quickly drafted a plan to commit two companies of 6 BPC that had about 80 effectives apiece, with a company of 1 BEP in reserve.[178] The counterattack repelled a final VPA assault that had begun at 0700hrs, and the tanks and excellent close support by French aircraft turned it into a rout. *Bộ đội* fleeing the strongpoint toward the east had to sprint 180 meters under fire from Douaumont before reaching the first good cover – a pair of bomb craters. The battle became a massacre and by 1030hrs Huguette-6 had been completely retaken.[179] Crippled by a leg wound, the 115th Battalion's commander, Nguyễn Chuông, was captured, but successfully masqueraded as an enlisted man named Vi Hải.

Vietnamese authors have little to say about the assaults on Huguette-6. Giáp merely writes, "On the night of April 4, we attacked the stronghold 105, which protected the Muong Thanh airfield. However, the assault was unsuccessful."[180] Giáp also criticized an unnamed battalion commander for attacking Huguette-6 with three platoons instead of three companies as planned, but does not specify the date.[181] The 312th Division's official history's terse account of the April 4–5 assault puts its losses at 50 killed, 180 wounded, and seven missing – which is certainly too low.[182] The French lost 23 killed (including Donnadieu), 112 wounded (including Bailly), and 86 missing, but de Castries reported that 800 enemy bodies were counted.[183] If one applies the two-to-one rule of thumb, then the VPA casualty rate was 100 percent! De Castries may have deliberately inflated the body count to encourage Cogny and Navarre to send more reinforcements.

It's probably a coincidence, but that very afternoon two of the 75mm recoilless rifles that had been promised on March 31 were finally parachuted in. They were misdropped near Bản Me, more than 2km southwest of Claudine, and de Castries radioed that he would try to destroy them with artillery or air strikes. But in fact, they were recovered intact by a Legion patrol at dawn the next day.[184] VPA troops had not discovered the guns since there were many errant parachute loads for them to collect. The 57th Regiment recovered 50 out of 120 pallets of supplies (weighing between 50 and 200kg each) dropped over Isabelle on March 31, and 85 of 290 dropped there on April 2. The booty included 776 boxes containing two 105mm shells apiece.[185] Strongpoint Wieme's Tais had to be prevented from firing on planes that misdropped their loads!

Misdrops were so frequent because, since March 17, planes had been making daylight supply drops from altitudes much higher than the optimal 200 meters. On March 28, the French began dropping cargo from 1,200 meters with 25-second-delay fuses. These devices reduced drift, but failed to work 15 to 20 percent of the time and as the flak envelope tightened the drop altitude kept increasing. On April 5, it rose to 2,600 meters with a 40-second delay, and in May it was raised to 3,000 meters with a 50-second delay. Dakotas, which had to make multiple passes owing to their small, side-mounted cargo doors, had little choice but to use this technique. But since the C-119s' big rear cargo doors allowed their loads to be dropped in a single pass, they sometimes dove down to lower altitudes even by day.[186]

General Cogny's staff had hatched a plan to evacuate nearly 200 wounded in broad daylight on April 5. After notifying Giáp by radio 24 hours in advance, GONO would cease all fire and halt all other air missions at 1345hrs, and signal that a plane carrying neutral observers and journalists was orbiting overhead. At 1400hrs, a Beaver bearing Red Cross markings would attempt to land. If there was no VPA reaction, it would be followed at short intervals by ten Dakota ambulance planes.[187] The operation was canceled because Giáp did not respond to the radio message and the airstrip was under regular artillery harassment.[188] Any thoughts of making another attempt were dashed on April 6, when a Cricket was hit by flak and its artillery spotter, Lieutenant Bertrand de la Choue de la Mettrie, seriously wounded. The pilot, Sergeant Ribière, managed to land the plane, but VPA gunners immediately destroyed it, gravely wounding him and killing de la Mettrie.[189]

Giáp calls a halt

The debacle at Huguette-6 finally convinced Giáp to end his offensive after six days of massive bloodletting. Most of the eight regiments deployed around the

Main Position had been reduced to battered shells (the same was true of nearly all the defending battalions). The Điện Biên Phủ military cemeteries hold the remains of 765 VPA troops who were killed during March, and 284 more that died in the first five days of April.[190] But even allowing for French exaggeration, the total of just 1,049 fatalities is too low and must exclude many more whose bodies either were never recovered or were reclaimed by their families and interred elsewhere. One *bộ đội* who was tasked with retrieving fallen comrades from Eliane-2 admitted, "There are still others who stayed forever on this hill, for we never succeeded in recovering their bodies."[191]

The following table draws upon French and Vietnamese sources to arrive at rough estimates of the casualties each VPA infantry regiment took between March 13 and April 5, and what its remaining offensive potential was. Five had taken such heavy casualties that they could not attack again until after they had absorbed masses of replacements. Indeed, the 88th Regiment, which seems to have played no role in the offensive, was evidently *hors de combat* before March 30. The other four regiments had all been significantly reduced, and of them only the 36th was still close to its initial strength. Yet, like the rest of the 308th Division, it was already understrength after the campaign in Laos. Thus, while the 249/174 took 500 men into battle on Eliane-2, the 18/102 had just 300. Giáp had no choice but to end the offensive because he had almost no combat-ready units remaining and his troops' morale was likely to crack if the carnage continued.

VPA CASUALTIES (MARCH 13 TO APRIL 5)					
Division	Regiment	Casualties			Offensive potential
		Modest	Heavy	Severe	
304	57	Bản Kho Lai, Wieme	Bản Kho Lai		REDUCED
308 (Laos)	36	H-7			REDUCED
	88			Gabrielle, Flak Raid	WEAK
	102	D-5		Eliane-2	WEAK
312	141	D-6, H-6	Béatrice, D-1, D-3		WEAK
	165		Gabrielle	H-6	WEAK
	209	Béatrice	D-2, D-3		REDUCED
316	98	E-1	E-1, E-4		REDUCED
	174			Eliane-2	WEAK
	888/176				STRONG

Giáp was also running short of ammunition, particularly 105mm howitzer shells. There were only about 15,000 in the VPA's entire arsenal (including 440 captured in Laos) and most of this stockpile had been consumed by April 5. Giáp ordered that the handful of shells in Laos be laboriously hauled over the mountains to Điện Biên Phủ. He also sent an urgent appeal to the Chinese for more, but their own stocks had been almost entirely depleted by the Korean War. The 105mm shell crisis was symptomatic of a general depletion of VPA ammo dumps that applied to all artillery calibers.[192]

Conclusions

GONO could not have survived if its senior commanders had not found their feet. Langlais' leadership during this period was generally excellent, which suggests that his earlier indecisiveness had flowed from doubts about the wisdom of trying to hold the northern hill positions at all. Apart from the arguably premature retreats he considered on March 30–31, Langlais now acted boldly and decisively. He worked well with de Castries, who played an important supporting role in what became an effective partnership. The charismatic and ever-optimistic Bigeard bolstered the entire garrison's morale and essentially acted as deputy commander for the Five Hills. The three leaders employed aggressive defensive tactics that mirrored the "instantaneous counterattacks" launched by the Germans in World War II. They had learned that it was best to strike before the VPA could finish capturing a strongpoint or consolidating its positions on one that had just been taken.

These tactics demanded highly skilled junior officers who would act aggressively on their own initiative and lead from the front to inspire their men to attack even when facing long odds. Given the paucity of platoon- and company-level leadership, this meant that French officers had to accept great personal risks that resulted in a very high casualty rate. VPA officers also led from the front and took heavy losses, but their army's rigid command structure, highly choreographed offensive tactics, and lack of experience in positional warfare discouraged them from acting on their own initiative. And while the bộ đội fought with remarkable bravery and determination, they could not match the Legionnaires' and paras' skill in this unaccustomed form of warfare. Time and again, these asymmetries allowed the French to seize fleeting opportunities more rapidly than their foes and thus secure tactical advantages that decided the outcome of crucial engagements.

Yet qualitative advantages in personnel and leadership by themselves did not suffice to defeat Giáp's second offensive. Superior firepower was also crucial. On March 30 and 31 alone, GONO's artillery fired an astounding 13,000 105mm, 1,200 120mm, and 855 155mm shells.[193] Thus, in little more than 24 hours, the defenders expended almost as many 105mm shells as the VPA's logistical system delivered to Điện Biên Phủ during the entire siege! The same was true of other calibers as well. On February 10, GONO's dumps had held 32,000 81mm shells.[194] Some must have been consumed before March 13, but were undoubtedly replaced by airdrops after the siege began. It is safe to conclude, therefore, that GONO had expended at least 32,000 shells between the start of the siege and March 31 – when it reportedly had none left. Therefore, in little more than two weeks, French 81mm ammo consumption equaled at least 85 percent of the 37,300 shells of that caliber which the VPA fired during the entire siege (see Chapter 2).

Thus, for every incoming shell, there were at least several outgoing ones, ensuring that the VPA suffered disproportionately heavy losses. And since GONO's gunners could sustain barrages all night while their VPA counterparts could not, there was a mobility differential that favored the defenders. French reinforcements could maneuver with considerable freedom at night, while VPA units were slowed to a snail's pace and some never made it into battle at all. These lop-sided ammunition expenditures continued even after GONO's stocks were considerably depleted. On April 6, Colonel Vaillant reported that he had only 300 155mm, 7,000 105mm, and 1,500 120mm shells remaining, and recommended that consumption be limited to 1,000 shells a night until the dumps had been replenished.[195] But although this was a parsimonious quota by French standards, it was still many times more than what Giáp could afford.

The Bisons also contributed decisively to GONO's fire superiority. Langlais' errors had prevented the tanks from fulfilling their promise during Giáp's first offensive. Indecision had plagued the Gabrielle counterattack on March 15; excessive caution prevented the Bisons from accomplishing anything more than the sham reinforcement of Anne Marie on March 16, and procrastination ensured that they arrived too late to save it on March 17. But the Bisons played a key role in defeating Giáp's second offensive. Their intervention may have saved the entire left bank on the night of March 30–31, and Eliane-2 on several different occasions. But the confining terrain of the Five Hills restricted their maneuverability, limited their fields of visibility and fire, and made them vulnerable to skulking bazooka teams like the one that knocked out Bazeilles. They came into their own in the battles for Huguette-6, where the wide-open terrain facilitated maneuver and made it possible for their fire to hold greatly superior enemy forces at bay and inflict severe casualties on them.

AIR COMBAT SORTIES DURING GIÁP'S 1ST AND 2ND OFFENSIVES[196]						
Period	Direct support	Counterbattery	Flak suppression	Interdiction	Vs. Depots & cantonments	TOTAL
March 14–15	48	2				50
April 1–5	173	50	10	78	10	321

French airpower also played a more prominent role during Giáp's second offensive than it had in the first. The weather was not optimal, since the reversal of wind direction that heralded the approach of the rainy season typically laid a blanket of mist over the valley that did not lift until 0900–1000hrs, and returned between 1600 and 1700hrs in the afternoon.[197] Yet French combat aircraft flew, on average, over 60 combat sorties a day in support of GONO during this period, while in mid-March the figure had been just 25. They were particularly active during the Huguette-6 counterattack after dawn on April 5.

Giáp was a great general, but he was fighting his first prolonged, conventional battle – and it showed. By his own account, he also fell ill just as the second offensive was about to begin on March 30: "That day I became fatigued. I was struck down by a fever at exactly the wrong time. I lay in my hut, tossing and turning, reliving my days in the Cao-Bac-Lang war zone, walking through the vast, dense jungle, wading through strong streams."[198] But well in advance of that date, he had approved the overly complex plan for a converging, deep-penetration attack at night which was virtually bound to break down. It reminds one of the mistake that another great revolutionary general, George Washington, made when he attacked with four converging, night-marching columns at the battle of Germantown in 1777.

Giáp also erred by dispersing his regiments around the Main Position so that each could threaten a different sector. This left him without a strong reserve. The decision to shift the 102nd Regiment came too late and delays in transit ensured that it never launched a full-strength assault on Eliane-2. But continuing to attack Eliane-2 was itself a major error. Taking Eliane-4 could also have unhinged what remained of the Five Hills defense line, but it was not attacked between March 31 and April 5. The 312th and 316th Divisions presumably lacked the strength to capture it, but Giáp could have committed the 102nd there instead of at Eliane-2 (particularly as the 54/102 was already nearby). He probably would have done so had he realized the strength of the underground bunkers on Hill A1.

But if VPA commanders were novices at positional warfare, they were also quick learners – and the French committed errors of their own. The decision to leave Phony Hill undefended subjected Eliane-1 and Eliane-2 to enfilading crossfires that made their lower, eastern slopes almost untenable. This was a key reason why the Eliane-1 counterattack failed and the Champs-Élysées was not reoccupied. Tourret's mishandling of the Dominique-2 counterattack was also a grave mistake. This critical operation almost succeeded – and likely would have if the entire 8 BPC had participated in it. Whether the hill could have been held without reserves is uncertain, but the subsequent course of the siege would have been very different if it had been.

Langlais and Bigeard might have persevered with the March 31 counterattacks had even a company or two of II/1 RCP been available. If the entire battalion had been present, one can reasonably predict that both Dominique-2 and Eliane-1 would have been retaken, leaving Giáp with nothing to show for 24 hours of intense combat and massive casualties. Such a stunning setback after such great and unprecedented exertions would have shaken VPA morale and might have forced Giáp to consider breaking off his offensive. The failure to drop in II/1 RCP before March 30, and the vacillation that prevented even a fraction of it from arriving on March 31 thus contributed decisively to GONO's eventual defeat. This critical error must be laid at the feet of Navarre and Cogny, who had given way to defeatism and spent much of their time engaging in mutual recrimination and finger-pointing. Neither was inclined to put his endangered career and reputation at even greater risk by taking bold action on behalf of the embattled garrison.

Some authors lay blame for the loss of Dominique-2 and Eliane-1 squarely on the shoulders of the African troops that were garrisoning them, suggesting that if they had not fled, the hills could have been successfully defended. The case of Dominique-1 suggests otherwise. The Vietnamese paras on the hill did not run, but were annihilated all the same since the odds against them were simply too great. 3/I/4 RTM faced the same stark reality on Eliane-1 and was crippled by the loss of key leaders. And the Algerians on Dominique-2 did not flee without a fight, but repulsed the 209th Regiment's first attack and routed only after a second overran CSM 425. Langlais claims to have identified the weak spot, but inexplicably did nothing about it. The loss of Dominique-2 must therefore be attributed in large part to a leadership failure on his and/or Garandeau's part. Eliane-2 survived because the Bald Hill *sonnette* had kept VPA trenches at a distance, it had the strongest fortifications in the valley, was garrisoned by the three regular companies, and received five more plus two tanks as reinforcements. Any of the other strongpoints would have held out too if it had enjoyed all these advantages.

Giáp's second offensive had failed, but it laid the foundation upon which victory would ultimately be built. Isabelle's permanent isolation was a major accomplishment, since the rest of the garrison was thereby denied the support of the Green Platoon's tanks and access to the safer southern DZs. The capture of Huguette-7 and Françoise brought VPA troops to the very edge of the main drop zone. But most important of all, Dominiques-1 and -2 had been taken. The loss of these lofty observation posts greatly reduced the effectiveness of GONO's artillery, since the hills of Eliane were lower and had much narrower fields of vision, and Cricket artillery spotter planes flying from Mường Sai 120km away could loiter over the valley for an hour at most.[199] Worse yet, the loss of Dominiques-1 and -2 exposed GONO's whole interior to close-range VPA heavy weapons fire. For, in keeping with Vauban's principles of siegecraft, having taken these bastions, Giáp now began installing flak and artillery on them. The 351st Division would soon build casemates on the hills from which 75mm mountain guns could drop shells on the garrison's headquarters, artillery, supply dumps, reserves, and drop zones from less than 2km away. VPA mortars and ĐKZs set to work immediately.

CHAPTER 7

GRIGNOTAGE

On April 8, Giáp presided at a Campaign Cadres' Conference that performed a post-mortem on the recently concluded offensive. It found that VPA units had committed many errors in planning and executing their assaults. The 174th Regiment was reproached for botching the attack on Eliane-2, and especially its failure to push trenches close to the hill. This was a common problem, since "no unit built fighting positions that met the standards and requirements that we laid out."[1] And the response to French counterattacks had been poor since concrete plans had not been developed to deal with them. It seems that, having been lulled into complacency by GONO's indecisive response to their first offensive, VPA commanders were startled by the speed and aggressiveness of French counterattacks – especially at night. Gunners were taken to task for wasteful ammunition expenditures. One divisional flak battalion had fired 12,000 rounds in a single day, while an 82mm mortar unit ran through 2,195 shells in just five. This prodigality not only drained ammunition stocks, but also caused excessive barrel wear and malfunctions.

Communists believe that warfare is a scientific process in which the outcome of battles and campaigns can be predicted with mathematical precision if all relevant factors are "objectively" weighed beforehand. Even psychological factors can be made predictable if the "correct" line is followed in political indoctrination. Unsuccessful operations are therefore attributed to the "subjectivity" and "rightist tendencies" of commanders and units that lacked the proper scientific perspective and/or ideological commitment.[2] It comes as no surprise, therefore, that the conferees found that these were the cause of all the errors they had identified. "When you look for the source of the problem, in the end it is because our cadres do not clearly understand their responsibility to the Party, to the army, and to the people. Their spirit of responsibility is lacking and their ideology is not solid." And since "the formula and battle plan put forward by the General Military Party Committee was very precise and correct,"[3] these ideological shortfalls were solely to blame for the offensive's limited success.

This was disingenuous, since Giáp himself had erred by setting over-ambitious objectives, failing to maintain a powerful reserve, and persisting in fruitless attacks. And it was those errors, as much as anything else, that now obliged him to slow down the pace of operations although the rainy season was fast approaching and each day's delay would increase his logistical difficulties. But bad weather would not be allowed to end the siege prematurely. "If we have not yet annihilated the entire enemy force by the time the rainy season begins, then we must continue the fight into the rainy season in an all-out drive to annihilate all of the enemy's troops."[4]

The conference's guidelines for future operations stressed the importance of economizing manpower and ammunition. "The battle plans must be concrete and meticulous. The goal is to inflict large numbers of casualties on the enemy while suffering few casualties of our own." Trenches would have to be improved to give better protection against the rains and French firepower. And with artillery shells in short supply, more reliance would have to be placed on infantry heavy weapons and even small arms to wear down enemy manpower. For until the ammunition supply crisis was resolved, the besiegers would have to limit major assaults and rely instead upon grinding attrition to erode GONO's defenses. Giáp described the tactics employed during this period as *grignotage* – or "nibbling away" at the French.

Tightening the encirclement would limit the French Air Force and artillery, and reduce our troop losses. Since the campaign's start, the light firepower of our soldiers (who were numerically stronger) had not been very effective because our soldiers were too far from the enemy. If we tightened the encirclement, we could wear down the enemy's ranks with our infantry weapons, including rifles and grenade. Then, our troops could destroy the

The overhead photographs appearing on the following pages were cropped from a series of aerial photos taken by a French reconnaissance plane from altitudes between 2,400m and 4,200m in March after the battle started. Although the VPA had already been assaulting Điện Biên Phủ for about two weeks, the French strongpoints and support positions were still mostly intact, and their trenches had not yet been obscured by encroaching enemy trenches (though some of these are visible) and thousands of discarded parachute canopies. Nevertheless, some strongpoints stand out more clearly than others, and outposts generally are not visible because they were so sketchily built as to be virtually indistinguishable from high altitude.

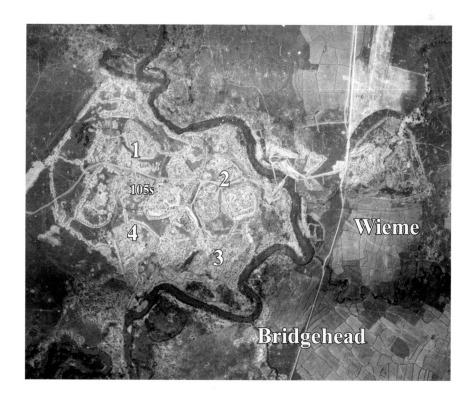

1. CR Isabelle © Service historique de la Défense, CHA Vincennes, cote (SHDAI, AI 75 E 557, HV334, 0004 2)

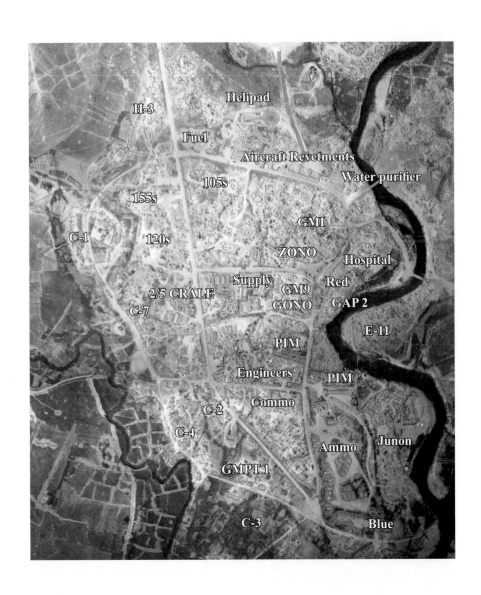

2. GONO headquarters area © Service historique de la Défense, CHA Vincennes, cote (SHDAI, AI 75 E 532, HV278A, 0203 2)

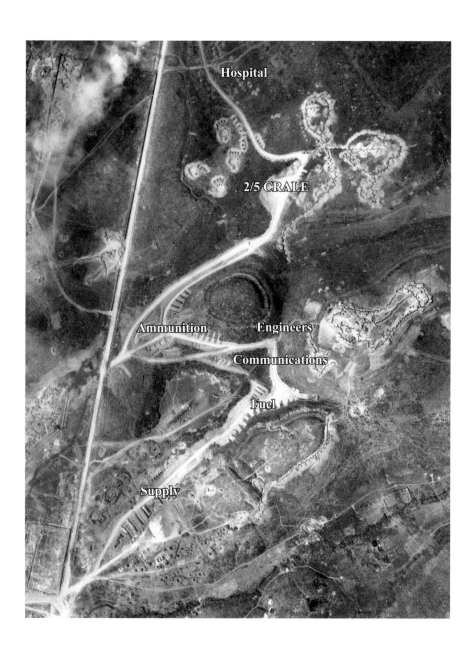

3. Proposed new headquarters area © Service historique de la Défense, CHA Vincennes, cote (SHDAI, AI 75 E 532, HV278B, 0260 2)

4. CR Béatrice © Service historique de la Défense, CHA Vincennes, cote (SHDAI, AI 75 E 532, HV278B, 0318 2)

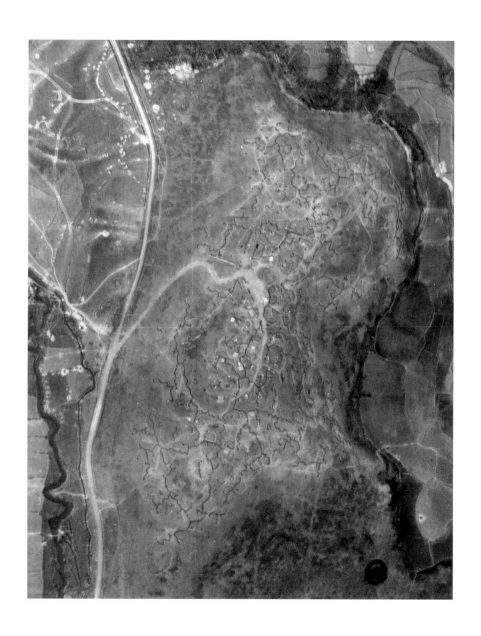

5. CR Gabrielle © Service historique de la Défense, CHA Vincennes, cote (SHDAI, AI 75 E 532, HV278A, 0212 2)

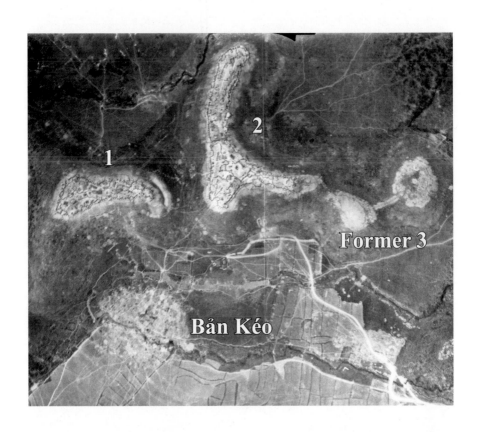

6. Anne Marie hill positions © Service historique de la Défense, CHA Vincennes, cote (SHDAI, AI 75 E 532, HV278A, 0145 2)

7. CR Anne Marie © Service historique de la Défense, CHA Vincennes, cote (SHDAI, AI 75 E 532, HV278A, 0145 2)

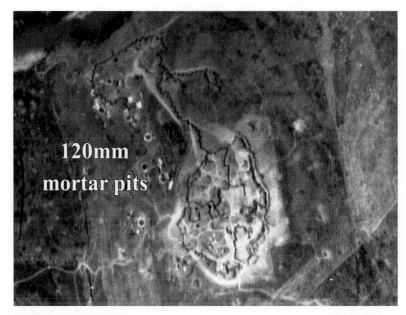

8. Dominique-1 © Service historique de la Défense, CHA Vincennes, cote (SHDAI, AI 75 E 532, HV278B, 0262 2)

9. Dominique-2 © Service historique de la Défense, CHA Vincennes, cote (SHDAI, AI 75 E 532, HV278B, 0262 2)

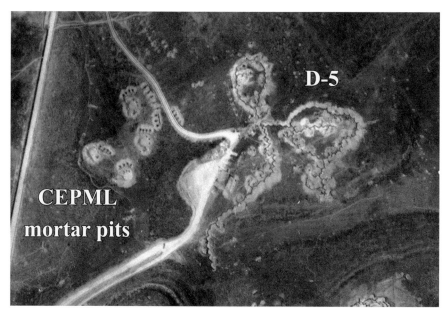

10. Dominique-5 © Service historique de la Défense, CHA Vincennes, cote (SHDAI, AI 75 E 532, HV278B, 0260 2)

11. Dominique-3 © Service historique de la Défense, CHA Vincennes, cote (SHDAI, AI 75 E 557, HV336, 0018 2)

12. Eliane-1, Eliane-4 and Honeycomb Hill © Service historique de la Défense, CHA Vincennes, cote (SHDAI, AI 75 E 532, HV278B, 0260 2)

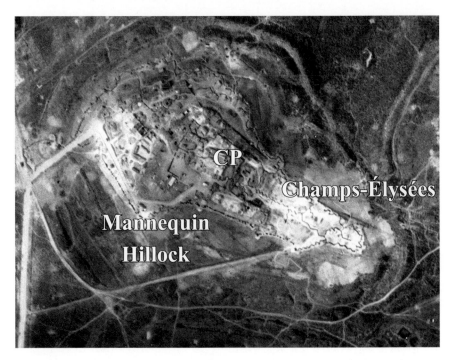

13. Eliane-2 © Service historique de la Défense, CHA Vincennes, cote (SHDAI, AI 75 E 532, HV278B, 0260 2)

14. Huguette-7 © Service historique de la Défense, CHA Vincennes, cote (SHDAI, AI 75 E 532, HV278A, 0145 2)

15. Wieme © Service historique de la Défense, CHA Vincennes, cote (SHDAI, AI 75 E 557, HV334, 0004 2)

16. Huguette-6 © Service historique de la Défense, CHA Vincennes, cote (SHDAI, AI 75 E 532, HV278A, 0145 2)

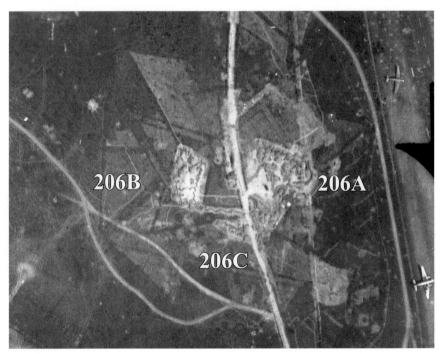

17. Huguette-1 © Service historique de la Défense, CHA Vincennes, cote (SHDAI, AI 75 E 532, HV278A, 0204 2)

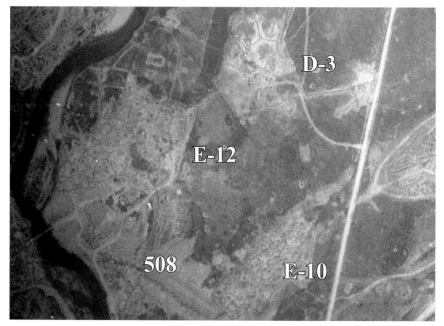

18. The 'Low Elianes' © Service historique de la Défense, CHA Vincennes, cote (SHDAI, AI 75 E 557, HV336, 0018 2)

19. Huguette-5 © Service historique de la Défense, CHA Vincennes, cote (SHDAI, AI 75 E 532, HV278A, 0204 2)

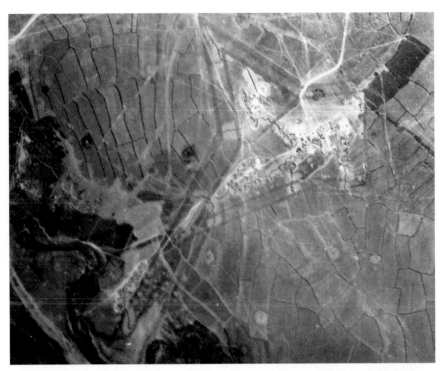

20. Huguette-4/Lily-3 © Service historique de la Défense, CHA Vincennes, cote (SHDAI, AI 75 E 532, HV278A, 0203 2)

21. Claudine-5 © Service historique de la Défense, CHA Vincennes, cote (SHDAI, AI 75 E 532, HV278A, 0203 2)

1. General Võ Nguyên Giáp, commander of the Vietnamese People's Army and victor at the siege of Điện Biên Phủ. (Courtesy of the US Army Center of Military History)

2. Three French generals (left to right facing camera): GONO commander General Jean Gilles, Indochina supreme commander General Henri Navarre, and FTNV commander General René Cogny. (Photo by ullstein bild/ullstein bild via Getty Images)

3. General Giáp and his staff at Điện Biên Phủ Front headquarters. (Photo by Collection Jean-Claude LABBE/Gamma-Rapho via Getty Images)

4. Camouflaged Russian GAZ-51 'Moltava' trucks in VPA service fording a stream. (Photo by Collection Jean-Claude LABBE/Gamma-Rapho via Getty Images)

5. *Dân công* pushing a heavily loaded cargo bicycle. (Photo by Collection Jean-Claude LABBE/Gamma-Rapho via Getty Images)

6. VPA troops hauling a 105mm howitzer into position. The weapon is a captured American HM-2. (Photo by Collection Jean-Claude LABBE/Gamma-Rapho via Getty Images)

7. A VPA flak battery in action. The weapons are Russian DShK 12.7mm (.50-caliber) antiaircraft machine guns. (Photo by Collection Jean-Claude LABBE/Gamma-Rapho via Getty Images)

8. Colonel Christian de Castries in his command bunker. Note cai-phen bamboo matting on the wall behind him. (US Information Service)

9. Indochinese paratroops. The two men closest to the camera are armed with French 7.5mm MAS-36 bolt-action rifles. The third man has an American .30-caliber (7.62mm) carbine, either a semi-automatic M-1 or a selective-fire M-2. (US Information Service)

10. M-24 "Chaffee" tank at Điện Biên Phủ. Note the mixed crew of European and Indochinese troops (which was typical) and the M-2 .50-caliber machine gun mounted at the rear of the turret. (Courtesy of the US Army Center of Military History)

11. M-55 "Quad-50" antiaircraft mount armed with four M-2 heavy barrel .50-caliber (12.7mm) machine guns. (Kevin Boylan)

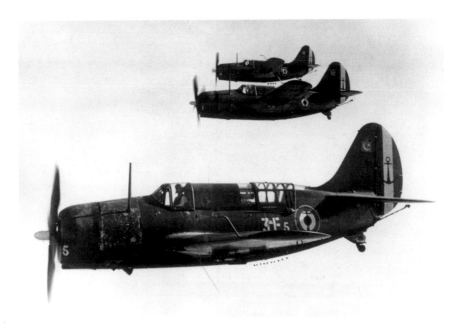

12. SB2C "Helldiver" dive bombers of Aéronavale Squadron 3F "Ganga." (Photo by RDA/Getty Images)

13. Armée de l'Air B-26 dropping bombs over Điện Biên Phủ. (Bettmann/Getty Images)

14. Paratroops of 6 BPC jump into the valley on November 20, 1958. (Photo by SeM/UIG via Getty Images)

15. F4U "Corsair" fighter-bomber. The model used at Điện Biên Phủ was the slightly different AU-1, which was optimized for the low-altitude, ground attack role. (Kevin Boylan)

16. Sikorsky H-19 helicopter flying over paratroops at Điện Biên Phủ.
(Photo by Keystone-France/Gamma-Rapho via Getty Images)

17. French troops atop one of the Five Hills strongpoints. (Bettmann/Getty Images)

18. Major Marcel Bigeard, commander of the 6th Colonial Parachute Battalion. (US Information Service)

19. The "Parachute Mafia" at GAP 2 headquarters (left to right): Botella, Bigeard, Tourret, Langlais and Seguin-Pazzis. (Photo by Keystone/Hulton Archive/Getty Images)

20. French troops in action during a sortie on March 27. The weapon is a French 7.5mm Modèle 1924 M29 automatic rifle with a 25-round box magazine. (US Information Service)

21. VPA flag flying over GONO headquarters. Note the corrugated metal "elephant tusks" covering the bunker's roof. (Photo by Apic/Getty Images)

resistance sites and barbed wire entanglements... The tightening would simultaneously reduce the enemy's area of occupation, lessen our losses, help us capture enemy supplies (especially the ammunition we badly needed), narrow the enemy's air space, and eventually sever the enemy's source of supplies and reinforcements.[5]

The first task was to tighten the flak envelope. The 392nd Battalion's detached 820th Battery shifted its dozen antiaircraft machine guns from Mount Pu Hồng Mèo to Dominiques-1 and -2, while the 316th Division's 536th Battalion sent one of its companies to Eliane-1, another to Bald Hill, and the third to a position near Isabelle. The 37mm batteries also moved closer to the Main Position. The 394th Battalion, which had relocated near Anne Marie in March, now moved to Bản Peluong west of Huguette-7. The 383rd Battalion shifted from near Béatrice to fields surrounding Bản Nong Bua and Bản Thit Moi in the "bowl" east of the Five Hills. The gunners camouflaged their gun pits by covering them with parachutes, thousands of whose discarded canopies now littered the valley floor.[6]

But to sever GONO's aerial lifeline once and for all, the VPA had to capture CR Huguette, whose importance Langlais highlighted in his memoirs: "We simply could not afford to lose Huguette. The position, which still covered the outbound flight path, was crucial for our airdrops."[7] If it was lost, the flow of parachuted supplies and reinforcements would shrink to a trickle. Thus, on April 10 Giáp issued the following orders:[8]

- The 308th Division was to dig trenches toward Claudine-5 and Huguettes-1, -4, and -5, and prepare to attack the last three positions. It would also dig other trenches to block communications between Huguettes-1, -2, and -6, and, in coordination with the 312th Division, to bisect the runway south of Huguette-1.
- The 312th Division would consolidate its defenses on Dominiques-1 and -2; dig trenches toward Huguette-6, Dominique-4, Épervier, and BT2's outpost in the airfield drainage ditch; and prepare to attack those positions. It would also dig a trench to link up with the 308th Division's south of Huguette-1.
- The 316th Division was to consolidate its defenses on Eliane-1; dig assault trenches toward Elianes-2, -3 and Châu Ún Hill[9] (Eliane-4); and prepare to attack those positions.
- The 304th Division would tighten its trench network around Isabelle,

prepare to attack it, curb its artillery, and ensure that the roads to the Main Position remained closed.

- The 351st Division's missions were unchanged except that it was to install 75mm mountain gun batteries in casemates on the captured Dominique hilltops.

All infantry units were to wear down French manpower with their organic weaponry, use machine guns and even rifles to thicken antiaircraft fire, and form special detachments to engage French parachutists and recover supplies that fell into no man's land. All units were to absorb replacements, trim support elements to transfer personnel into combat units, and train their troops in the lessons learned during the recent offensive.[10] To prevent attrition by disease and fatigue, steps were to be taken to improve food, sanitation, and living conditions on the front lines. All these preparations were to be completed by April 13. The attacks on Huguettes-1 and -6 were to be ready for April 15 and the runway was to be cut the same day. The other planned assaults were scheduled to start on April 18. As it turned out, few of these deadlines were met.[11]

Thanks to the General Mobilization, Giáp had little difficulty finding replacements to fill the gaps in his ranks and the French estimated that 25,000 replacements were sent to the valley during the siege.[12] Some had previously served as guerrillas, but many were mere teenagers and had no prior military experience. The 174th Regiment received some who had never fired a rifle and had to be taught such basic skills as aiming and cleaning their weapons. Dương Văn Lâm, a platoon commander in the 439/98, recalled that the replacements suffered disproportionately high casualties owing to their ignorance of basic tactics. They did not know, for example, that it was dangerous to fire in bursts at night because the muzzle flash would reveal the shooter's position to the enemy. Many died before the veterans even learned their names.[13]

"I was still confident in our victory"

The new strongpoint that BT2 had started building southeast of Huguette-6 was abandoned in early April because the loss of Dominique-1 made the sketchy position untenable. As the perimeter contracted, Cogny's staff found it hard to distinguish the interior strongpoints on aerial photographs, and even lost track of which ones GONO still occupied. On April 6, FTNV inquired if Françoise was in friendly hands, and three days later it demanded map coordinates for all the interior strongpoints in Claudine, Dominique, Eliane, Épervier, Junon, and Lily.[14] The confusion about Françoise could have arisen because neither side occupied it on April 6; VPA official histories state that the position was taken on April 7.[15]

At about this time Major Michel Vadot, GM9's former chief of staff, replaced Langlais (who had been juggling too many responsibilities) as commander of the Eastern Subsector.[16] Langlais' chief concern was reorganizing his battered battalions. III/3 RTA's survivors were rallied on Junon and reorganized into a march company comprising a headquarters platoon, a heavy weapons platoon, and five infantry platoons. This unit, commanded by Lieutenant Filaudeau, returned to Dominique-3 on April 2.[17] Meanwhile, I/4 RTM finished redeploying west of the Nâm Yum. 3rd Company, which had routed from Eliane-1, returned to duty after five days of reorganizing on Junon.[18] Since this would have been impossible if it had had 106 men captured on March 30, as Vietnamese histories claim, that figure is likely exaggerated. On April 8, I/4 RTM took charge of a new CR named "Lily" that had been carved out of Claudine and Huguette.[19] Major Nicolas' headquarters was on Lily-1 (C-7), 2nd Company on Lily-2 (C-1), and 1st Company on Lily-3 (H-4).[20]

3rd and 4th Companies remained on Claudines-4 and -5 (respectively), defending these strongpoints alongside troops of I/13 DBLE. The Legion battalion needed the help because its 4th Company was still on Eliane-2, and its 1st Company had been dissolved on April 2 (the survivors went to 2nd Company).[21] The battalion had received a new commander on April 3, when Major Robert Coutant replaced Major Roger de Brinon, who was reassigned to 13 DBLE's Headquarters Company. This may have been a routine matter, since a note at the end of the battalion's war diary for March states that circumstances made it impossible to replace de Brinon when his command tour finished.[22] Yet Coutant had flown into the valley back on March 23 and switching commanders in midstream was risky. A veteran of I/13 DBLE asserted that de Brinon was replaced because he had turned to the bottle as a means of dealing with the stresses of command – though there is no other evidence for this.[23]

Like I/13 DBLE, many other battalions had to disband a company in early April. Sometimes this was merely administrative housecleaning, since the units had already been destroyed (e.g., 4/5 BPVN on Dominique-1 and 1/I/2 REI at Huguette-6). But other companies were broken up largely because they had no officers left. Thus, 4/6 BPC was dissolved on April 8 because its last officer, Lieutenant Héry, had been captured on Eliane-2.[24] The death of Captain Pichelin likewise obliged Tourret to disband 2/8 BPC and reallocate its personnel to his 3rd and 4th Companies.[25] 1/1 BEP also had no officers left and was merged with the 4th Company.[26]

BT3's 12th Company likewise was disbanded after the loss of a key commander. Although the company was defending second-line Huguette-2, its morale began to crack after Captain Guilleminot was wounded on April 3. Three days later as many as 80 men deserted. Langlais disbanded the unit, disarmed its troops, and ordered Bizard's 1/5 BPVN to take over the strongpoint.[27] Forty Tai volunteered to serve with the artillery, while the Europeans (including Guilleminot after he recovered) transferred to 5 BPVN. But 50 disarmed Tai shirked all further duty and went to ground in bunkers along the riverbank west of Dominique-3, joining other demoralized Indochinese and African troops who were already hiding out there.[28]

The ranks of these "Rats of the Nâm Yum" would swell as the siege progressed, and some historians claim that these internal deserters eventually numbered in the thousands and became a law unto themselves, defying GONO's leadership and seizing parachuted supplies that landed in the area. But several French veterans suggest that the number of Rats has been exaggerated, and deny that they presented an armed challenge to the garrison's command structure. Sergeant Chief Robert Salaun, leader of the base's Gendarmerie (military police) detachment, recalled that he was tasked with locating important parachute bundles so that Major Vadot could have the Rats recover them. Some unauthorized looting did occur, he admits, but the culprits could just as easily have been other troops. Salaun also argues that many of the Rats were not truly deserters since they had not abandoned their units, but fallen back with them and then been "left to rot" because Langlais saw no point in putting unreliable troops back into the line.[29] And some Tai had little choice but to join the Rats after their units were disbanded.

GONO acquired another infantry company on April 9 (without any accretion to its strength), when the PEG and several dozen Béatrice survivors were used to reconstitute 10/III/13 DBLE with a strength of 100 so it could carry on the tradition of the defunct battalion.[30] Far more consequential was the fact that the entire II/1 RCP was now on the ground.

Navarre and Cogny had said that it would be the last parachute battalion risked at Điện Biên Phủ, but they were warming to the idea of sending another. For a mood of cautious optimism was emerging as it became clear that GONO had not only weathered the storm of Giáp's second offensive, but also inflicted crippling losses on the attackers. The siege had not been broken, but at least it now seemed possible that it might not end in disaster. Indeed, Langlais intended to seize the initiative and retake the lost ground.

On April 7th, the reserve elements still totaled a dozen companies or three battalions, and I was still confident in our victory. I recall having made a bet with [Air Force] Commandant [Maurice] Blanchet, whose stake was a case of Muscadet (I still owe it to him), on the success of three projects: recapturing Dominique-2, recapturing Eliane-1, and reestablishing liaison with Isabelle... Finally, in agreement with Bigeard, I decided on the recapture of Eliane-1 and received the approval of Colonel de Castries. I was thinking of doing the job with two battalions, one for the attack and the other to relieve it on the conquered position. These units would probably be exhausted by nightfall. So, before making a final decision, a new Battalion was asked for and sent in.[31]

Cogny proposed sending the all-Vietnamese 1 BPVN, but Langlais insisted upon getting Major Hubert Liesenfelt's 676-strong 2 BEP. He radioed that if GONO was "swindled" he would disarm the Vietnamese paras and use them as coolies![32] 2 BEP's 7th and 8th Companies (272 men) and half of its Headquarters Company were dropped on the night of April 9–10. The rest of the battalion would arrive by April 12, followed by Airborne Surgical Team 5 the next night.[33] Many individual replacements were also arriving. The parachute battalions could draw upon jump-qualified personnel from their rear bases and gunners of 35 RALP reinforced GONO's artillery. But since there were few jump-qualified replacements available for other units, Langlais convinced Colonel Sauvagnac to drop in unqualified volunteers after only a few hours of training. The scheme was tried out on the night of April 5–6, and although the volunteers were making their very first jumps into an embattled fortress in darkness, jump casualties were no higher than for fully qualified paratroops. All told, 985 reinforcements were dropped between April 7 and 12, and the vast majority landed safely.[34]

The reconquest of Eliane-1

Assured that his reserves would be reconstituted, Langlais scheduled the Eliane-1 attack for April 10 – seizing the initiative on the very day that Giáp issued his orders for the siege's next phase. Since the assault was a set piece for which Bigeard had the luxury of taking several days to prepare, his planning was meticulous. He had a trench dug from Eliane-4 to provide a covered route of approach and produced an integrated fire plan that combined artillery, airpower, and direct fire weapons to pulverize Eliane-4, "cage" it with barrages, and suppress adjoining VPA positions. Starting at 0600hrs, 20 105s and a dozen 120mm mortars would drop 1,800 shells on the hilltop in just ten minutes. The disparity between French and VPA ammunition consumption was never more pronounced, since no more than 50 105mm shells had been expended before the 98th Regiment's attack of March 30! The assault would also be supported by four Bisons that would race into position on RP41 and Elaine-4 as soon as the bombardment started.[35]

6 BPC, which had been reduced to three companies of just 80 men apiece, would advance behind a creeping barrage at 0610hrs, while the heights to the north and east were blinded by smoke shells and suppressed by air attacks and infantry weapons. 1 BEP would pour fire onto Phony and Bald Hills from Eliane-2, while 8 BPC and the Quad-50s dealt with Dominique-2. From Eliane-4, 5 BPVN and 6 BPC would target Eliane-1 itself. All 40 of the Main Position's 81mm mortars – which normally fired only on behalf of their own battalions – would support the assault. Bigeard would control the operation from a foxhole on Eliane-4 that was crammed with eight radios so he could simultaneously remain in contact with 6 BPC, Langlais, and the reserves, artillery, tanks, and aircraft.[36]

Before dawn, a platoon of 5/BT2 established an artillery observation post on Honeycomb Hill, which had been occupied by VPA pickets since March 31.[37] The assault began late at 0645hrs, when Lieutenant Trapp's 2nd Company advanced in small parties that were ordered to penetrate Eliane-1's perimeter as rapidly as possible, ignoring any bộ đội bypassed along the way. This was intended to reduce casualties by minimizing the number of men under fire at any given moment and denying the enemy opportunities to use artillery without hitting his own troops. The paras "leaned on the barrage," following as close as 40 meters behind exploding 105mm shells and just 20 meters from 81mm shellbursts. However, the 804th Howitzer Battery and VPA 120mm mortars laid a barrage across the saddle between the two hills, while machine-gun fire from an intact bunker on Eliane-1 pinned down Trapp's men. Bigeard committed Lieutenant Le Page's 1/6 BPC, which took heavy casualties as it ran the gauntlet. But a flamethrower team made it through, torched the bunker, and sowed terror among the defenders, who had never encountered this weapon before. By 0800hrs the paras had taken the summit. [38]

Eliane-1 was defended by the 938th Battalion's 70th Company. But sensing that an attack was imminent, the 98th Regiment's commander Vũ Lăng rushed two platoons of the 439th Battalion's 28th (82nd?) Company up as reinforcements and ordered battalion commander Hoàng Vượng to take charge of the defense. He arrived just before the assault began, but the two platoons were delayed by French barrages and did not appear until after the summit had been lost. When they showed up, the defenders pushed the paras back to the Flagpole Compound, where fighting continued for several hours.[39] 6 BPC finally secured the summit for good at 1130hrs, but could advance no farther because the strongpoint's lower eastern part was being raked by plunging fire from Dominique-2. Since there were no aircraft available to neutralize the threat – and the respite would have been only temporary – Bigeard decided to halt the attack there.[40] The situation was almost identical to that which 6 BPC had faced on March 31, but this time GONO had fresh reserves available. At 1400hrs, II/1 RCP's 3rd and 4th Companies relieved the assault units.[41] 6 BPC reported 15 killed, 23 wounded, and ten missing – and six Vietnamese paras deserted immediately afterwards – but GONO claimed 300 *bộ đội* were killed.[42]

There was a surge of optimism among the French. General Cogny hoped that with the rest of 2 BEP on the way, the other lost Five Hills strongpoints would shortly be recovered as well. Indeed, his staff seems to have thought that another already had been, since that afternoon it inquired "if Dominique 5 is occupied or not by us."[43] De Castries felt obliged to sound a note of caution. At 1330hrs he warned Cogny that it would take 48 hours to restock artillery ammunition and that no assault on Dominique-2 could be considered unless its defenses were thoroughly smashed by bombing beforehand. He wanted every available aircraft to target the hill on April 11 and 12.[44] Cogny concurred that Dominique-2 should not be attacked until sufficient ammunition and air support could be ensured, but still anticipated that the operation would occur within a few days.[45] GONO duly responded, "The occupation of Eliane-1 permits the envisaging of action to reoccupy Dominique-2 and -6 in the coming days."[46]

The 316th Division counterattacked Eliane-1 at 0045hrs on April 11, and the absence of obstacles in front of II/1 RCP's positions ensured that the battle quickly degenerated into hand-to-hand fighting. Yet no ground was lost, and GONO reported that the enemy had committed no fresh units and was conclusively repulsed by 0400hrs.[47] II/1 RCP's war diary entry suggests that its losses may have been only nine killed and four missing.[48]

A major realignment of GONO's command structure occurred on April 11, when Langlais established five "districts" whose commanders now all answered directly to him. West of the Nậm Yum, Captain Tourret of 8 BPC remained in charge of Épervier, but Major Guiraud of 1 BEP assumed command of Huguette, and from now on GM9's former chief of staff, Major Vadot, would supervise Lily, Claudine, and Junon. East of the river, Major Bréchignac of II/1 RCP took command of the newly established "Upper Elianes" (Elianes 1 through 4), while Major Chenel of BT2 was assigned the "Low Elianes" (Dominique-3, and Elianes 10 through 12). Since Bréchignac had assumed his (unofficial) role as deputy commander for the Five Hills, Bigeard left Eliane-4 and would henceforth share Langlais' GM9 command post.[49]

Certain that Eliane-1 would be hit by a more robust counterattack that night, Langlais visited the strongpoint that afternoon and ordered Lieutenant Gilles de Fromont's platoon of 3/6 BPC to reinforce it immediately. The platoon arrived just shortly before VPA artillery opened fire on Eliane-1 at 1845hrs.[50] Yet fire support for the ground assault was minimal since the 316th Division's attached 120mm batteries were out of ammunition, the mountain batteries had only a few shells left, and Giáp could allot only 20 105mm shells to the operation. He did, however, order a battalion of the 312th Division (most likely the 130th) to attack alongside the 439/98.[51] Eliane-4 was hit by several diversionary probes, so parts of one battalion must have been engaged there.[52]

Since there were still few obstacles in place, the bộ đội quickly swamped the defenders, who held out in isolated pockets of resistance.[53] Yet although Langlais had several fresh companies of 2 BEP available, he kept them in reserve and sent 1 BEP's battered remnants to the rescue. 2/1 and 3/1 BEP were merged into a march company of about 100 men that set out from Junon at 2200hrs under Lieutenant Louis Martin. To steel their courage, Martin's men sang the marching song "Contre les Viets" ("Against the Vietnamese") as they climbed onto Eliane-1.[54] The Legion paras were followed by Lieutenant Phu's 2/5 BPVN and half of 3/5 BPVN, leaving just 40–45 men behind to defend Eliane-4. Since the State of Vietnam's army did not yet have a marching song of its own, Phu had his French NCOs sing the "Marseillaise" and about a dozen Vietnamese troops knew it well enough to join in.[55]

Thanks to these slim reinforcements, the situation on Eliane-1 was stabilized, though the 98th Regiment continued attacking until 0400hrs (it attempted four attacks in all).[56] The *bộ đội* fell back at 0700hrs, leaving many bodies behind. Regimental Commander Vũ Lăng expected that the enemy would try to capture the rest of Eliane-1 on April 12 and was surprised when no attack came that day or the next. "The enemy only fired scattered shots, and occasionally an individual squad would try to make an assault. Only then did we understand – the constant, extremely ferocious counterattacks that our troops and the troops of the other attached battalion had made had worn the enemy out. All he could do was survive – there was no way he could take another step forward."[57] French casualties had indeed been severe. Lieutenant Fromont was killed and only three men of his platoon came through the battle alive and uninjured.[58] 1 BEP lost about half the troops it sent to Eliane-1,[59] while II/1 RCP had ten men killed, 66 wounded (including both company commanders), and 21 missing. The survivors fell back to Eliane-4, where 4/II/1 RCP's survivors were absorbed into 3rd Company, which was now led by Lieutenant René Leguéré.[60] Martin's depleted march company was relieved by 7/2 BEP later in the day. 5/2 BEP, which had jumped in overnight, was soon sent up as well.[61]

The exhausted *bộ đội* on Eliane-1 were relieved on April 12 by troops of the 888/176, which transferred back to the 316th Division from the siege lines around Isabelle.[62] While most of the battalion went into reserve, its 811th Company was sent up to Eliane-1. Since the shell-churned hilltop's fortifications had been reduced to ruins, the company needed to rebuild the smashed bunkers and trenches, and use scavenged French mines and barbed wire to create obstacles in front of them. Before that could be done, however, hundreds of rapidly decaying corpses had to be removed. The stench was so overpowering that the *bộ đội* wore facemasks in a vain effort to make this gruesome task more bearable.[63] The Legion paras were simultaneously engaged in the same gory work on the other side of the hill.

The costly battle for Eliane-1 obliged both sides to reassess their plans. Casualties had been so high that the French had to abandon any notion of retaking Dominique-2. Similar considerations forced Giáp to leave the French in possession of two-thirds of Eliane-1. The fighting had cost him the better part of two battalions, but if he had persisted in trying to retake the hill, it could have become another meatgrinder like Eliane-2 and consumed entire regiments. The battle for Eliane-1 was also distracting attention from the decisive operations planned west of the river. Unlike the Five Hills, Huguette's outlying strongpoints were not mutually supporting, and could not be reached by defiladed routes that were screened from VPA observation and direct fire.

The battle for Eliane-1 also consumed a great deal of artillery ammunition at a time when it was imperative for the VPA to conserve its depleted stocks. An urgent appeal had gone out to China for another 720 tons of munitions, but the first deliveries would not arrive for several weeks.[64] Until then, ammunition would be so scarce that the 803rd Howitzer and 752nd Mountain Batteries would both have to cease fire for several days, and Giáp had to place strict limits on consumption. Without his personal approval, the head of the Combat Operations Department could authorize firing no more than ten shells and divisional commanders no more than three. Regimental and battalion commanders could not even request artillery support without prior authorization from their superiors.[65] The French were, as usual, much better supplied with ammunition. Nguyễn Hữu Chấp, commander of the 290th Company's mortar platoon on Dominique-1, recalled that "We need only fire one shell for the enemy to reply with dozens of shots including 105mm."[66]

Via dolorosa

Giáp pressed ahead with plans to capture Huguettes-1 and -6, but with his gunners running low on ammunition, he dared not risk a major assault on either until it was hermetically sealed off from reinforcement. There could be no repetition of the earlier bloodbaths! The strongpoints' (and GONO's) fate would therefore be decided by daily battles for the routes leading to them – a replay of the struggle to keep the road to Isabelle open on a smaller scale but with much higher stakes.

Giáp committed nearly half his infantry against Huguette. The 308th Division's 36th and 88th Regiments would sever the Pavie Track by driving trenches into the gaps above and below Huguette-1 (respectively),[67] while the 312th Division's 141st Regiment pushed trenches toward the runway from the east.[68] Still licking its wounds, the 165th Regiment merely tightened its grip on Huguette-6. These four understrength regiments were opposed by only a weak battalion's worth of Legionnaires and paras. The two II/1 RCP companies on Huguette-6 had been withdrawn on April 9–10, and replaced by Bizard's 1/5 BPVN and Lieutenant Jean François' 3/I/2 REI (which had absorbed 1st Company's remnants). Huguettes-1, -3, and -5 were held by the rest of I/2 REI, while the reincarnated 10/III/13 DBLE defended Huguette-2.[69]

The battle for the Huguettes began in earnest on April 11, when Lieutenant Henri Legros' platoon of III/13 DBLE and another of I/2 REI "aerated" trenches northwest of Huguette-1. They were suddenly assailed in the flank by two VPA companies that surged out of Huguette-7 and only rapid intervention by the artillery saved them from annihilation. A counterattack was hastily organized with the rest of 10/III/13 DBLE, a platoon of 2/I/2 REI, and the Blue Platoon. The pinned-down troops were extricated after this force seized a VPA trench 100 meters in front of them, but Legros and two Legionnaires went missing, and there were four killed and ten wounded. Mulhouse survived a glancing bazooka hit without damage, but its recoil system broke down the next morning. It would be out of action for several days while the 75 was replaced with one stripped from immobilized Conti.[70]

As the battle for Eliane-1 was raging on the night of 11–12, VPA troops also probed Claudine-5 and planted "Bakelite" plastic mines that could not be located by metallic mine detectors in the gap between Huguettes-1 and -6.[71] On the following night, 8 BPC deployed a series of ambushes west of the gap that killed or wounded an estimated 30 *bộ đội* and enabled the nightly supply convoy to reach Huguette-6 without trouble. But when Douaumont and Ettlingen reconnoitered the area after dawn, their crews saw that three new trench branches had appeared overnight, one stretching south toward Huguette-1 and two more aimed at the runway. Freshly dug trenches were also observed across the runway near the drainage ditch.[72]

By that evening, GONO had no 60mm or 81mm mortar ammunition left. There were still 12,023 105mm (4,017 at Isabelle), 4,222 120mm, and 496 155mm shells on hand, but during the day, routine fire missions (many of which targeted enemy flak) had consumed 900 105mm shells, while another 800 were destroyed by hostile artillery and friendly aircraft.[73] Just after midday, a fighter-bomber had accidentally hit an ammunition dump, and soon after VPA 105s began harassing the Main Position's batteries using misdropped shells with deadly short-delay fuses. By 1700hrs, Lieutenant Brunbrouck (the hero of Dominique-3) was dead, a 105 had been knocked out, and several hundred more shells destroyed.[74] And to add insult to injury, a C-119 dropped another load of 105mm ammunition into enemy hands north of Dominique-1.[75]

The night of April 13 was a busy one for both sides. 8 BPC again sent out ambush parties to protect the route to Huguette-6 for a column of PIMs that was escorted by a BT2 march company and 8/2 BEP. This was 2 BEP's Indochinese Company and it does not seem to have been rated as highly as the battalion's three European companies, since it remained west of the Nậm Yum and specialized in retrieving parachute drops and protecting supply convoys. But these were now neither safe nor easy tasks, and the escorts had to fight their way to Huguette-6 while it was being probed by the 165th Regiment. BT2 had two men killed by a machine gun that had been installed in the nose of the wrecked Curtiss.[76]

Meanwhile, the 23/88 was rapidly trenching into the gap between Huguettes-1 and -2. The leading platoon lost a third of its strength to French shelling, but overall casualties were modest because recesses dug into the sides of the trench had been quickly roofed with planks and covered with soil. By 0400hrs, the diggers had reached the runway and blasted a trench across it. Since the trench could accommodate only a single platoon, battalion commander Nguyễn Quốc Trị deployed the 209th Company's other two west of the runway in positions from which they could fire obliquely across it.[77]

When French patrols probed northward from Huguettes-2 and -5 after sunup, they were halted by minefields, and heavy mortar and artillery fire.[78] Despite ammunition shortages, VPA artillery was becoming more effective because the 120mm mortars were now dug in just behind the eastern hills, while the 75mm mountain guns had been installed in new casemates built on their forward slopes. The 755th and 753rd Batteries were on Dominiques-1 and -2 (respectively), while the 757th Battery shifted onto Bald Hill.[79] From these eyries the guns could sweep the entire right bank, but the French constantly tried to silence them and inflicted heavy losses on their crews.[80]

The pinned-down patrols from Huguettes-2 and -5 were extracted with the aid of the Red Platoon's tanks. From the tops of their turrets, the tank commanders could see that there were three parallel trenches barring the way to Huguette-1.[81] Farther east, however, there was only the solitary trench bisecting the runway. Supported by the Blue Platoon, 1/8 BPC attacked toward it up the drainage ditch, but was repeatedly halted by shelling and the crossfire from west of the runway. At one point 30 men rushing forward through a cloud of smoke and dust broke into the trench, but were soon driven out with heavy casualties. VPA losses were also high and the 209th Company's commander was among those killed. Battalion commander Trị withdrew the platoon on the runway and the French pounded the empty trench for a time before occupying it. Trị then counterattacked with the 209th's other two platoons, but they were pinned down by the tanks and French artillery inflicted 20 casualties. Then the paras overran 50 meters of trench west of the runway. A counterattack at

0900hrs by the 211th Company retook the lost section of trench, but just minutes later a shell killed its commander, and wounded two platoon leaders and 30 other troops.[82]

8/2 BEP reinforced the assault at 1000hrs, and an hour later Trị sent his 213th Company to relieve the 211th. To limit casualties, he ordered company commander Mai Viết Thiềng to gnaw his way onto the runway instead of counterattacking in the open. Langlais ordered a retreat after Douaumont was immobilized by a bazooka and had to be towed back by Mulhouse. Exultant *bộ đội* quickly reoccupied the runway trench. The 23rd Battalion could be proud of its deeds that day, since it had maintained the blockade of Huguettes-1 and -6 in broad daylight against the full panoply of French heavy weaponry.[83] And if this wasn't enough cause for celebration, VPA gunners harassed the Main Position throughout the afternoon and scored numerous hits on its batteries and food depots.[84]

Langlais doggedly launched another attempt to link up with Huguettes-1 and -6 at 2200hrs. Major Liesenfelt commanded the operation, which involved 4/1 BEP and 8/2 BEP. It took four and a half hours just to break through to Huguette-1, and Huguette-6 was not reached until 0600hrs. Then, after sunrise, the exhausted paras had to fight their way back south, since *bộ đội* had filtered back into the trenches above and below Huguette-1.[85] The first hurdle was overcome with the support of the whole artillery, but the three parallel and interconnected trenches south of Huguette-1 formed a veritable strongpoint protected by minefields and even some barbed wire. And the 23rd Battalion had expanded its runway trench into a circular defensive perimeter.[86] To help Liesenfelt break through this obstacle, Langlais ordered 10/III/13 DBLE to attack from Huguette-5 while 3/8 BPC repeated the previous day's attack. Neither assault went well. The Legionnaires were pinned down almost immediately with heavy casualties, and had to be rescued by 2/I/2 REI.[87] Supported by two Blue Platoon tanks, the paras jumped off at 0700hrs on April 14, but although they gained a foothold in the runway position at 0745, the attack stalled there.[88]

To cover the eastern flank of the paras returning from Huguette-6, the unsupported Bisons drove up the runway until they enfiladed the first enemy trench. They were immediately targeted by bazookas firing from multiple directions. To engage these threats as rapidly as possible, the commanders climbed out to man the exposed .50-caliber machine guns mounted on the rear of their turrets. Douaumont's Sergeant Robert Bousrez was soon knocked unconscious by a bazooka rocket that hit his machine-gun mount, and the tank withdrew after Ettlingen relieved it at 0815hrs. Fifteen minutes later, Mulhouse had to retreat after its commander was also wounded. Finally, at about 0845hrs, a shellburst threw up a cloud of dust that obscured Ettlingen's vision ports. A bazooka gunner seized the opportunity and put a rocket through the turret's left side, killing one crewman and gravely wounding another. Since there was no reserve of tank crews in Tonkin, replacements had to be found among cavalry personnel who were serving at Điện Biên Phủ in other roles. Four NCOs with experience on M-24s were transferred from 8 BPC.[89]

8 BPC's attack dragged on. Although the paras captured two small sections of trench, they could advance no farther, and were pushed back by a counterattack shortly before noon. Fighting continued for much of the afternoon, but efforts to regain a foothold in the trench west of the runway failed. However, 8 BPC did succeed in establishing an outpost in the drainage ditch about 100 meters from the airfield trench that "corked" the gap between it and another trench that was approaching from the east.[90] At 1600hrs, the rest of the battalion fell back, having lost four killed, 26 wounded, and three missing.[91] GONO had again failed to dislodge the enemy from trenches just over a kilometer from de Castries' headquarters in broad daylight. And artillery harassment that day destroyed 5,000 survival rations and another 300 105mm shells.[92]

After dark, 3/6 BPC and 4/1 BEP set out for Huguette-6. Captain Jacques Chevalier's 4/I/13 also participated in the operation, but remained behind to secure the gap between Huguettes-1 and -2. Under its protection, other Legionnaires began digging a trench to link the two strongpoints.[93] The convoy finally reached Huguette-6 at 0200hrs, but much of its supplies had been lost en route since 42 PIMs were killed or wounded. Most worrisome for Captain Bizard, he received just 50 gallons of water out of the 150 the convoy had set out with. Since Huguette-6's water tanks had been destroyed, his troops were suffering from severe dehydration.[94]

Meanwhile, the 36th Regiment had closed the encirclement of Huguette-6 by linking its trench up with a 141st Regiment trench coming from the east. And at 0500hrs, two companies of 16/141 captured 8 BPC's drainage ditch outpost, which bộ đội called the "Airfield Four-Way Intersection."[95] Later that day, de Castries would radio Hanoi, "the enemy prevents the permanent occupation of a strongpoint precariously installed east of the runway. Our elements, dominated by Dominique and lacking the materials necessary for their protection, cannot remain there."[96] These difficulties may also explain GONO's puzzling failure to permanently occupy the VPA strongpoint below Huguette-1 – though having to attack it every night seems like an even worse option![97]

The paras returning south from Huguette-6 broke through the trench above Huguette-1 by taking advantage of the morning ground fog to overrun an outpost held by the 84th Battalion's 43rd Company.[98] And since Chevalier was still holding the bottleneck below Huguette-1 open, the final leg of the trip was made without difficulty. The paras were safe once they reached communications trenches roofed with PSP plates stripped from the runway. The French called this network of virtual tunnels "Le Métro" after the Paris subway, and rumor in the enemy camp exaggerated its character and extent. One Vietnamese account describes it stretching all the way from Dominique-4 to Huguette-6. "The route was a secret, camouflaged communications trench dug deep into the earth through which troops and even jeeps could move to help defend the airfield and the surrounding strong-points."[99]

The daylight hours of April 16 were quiet. Giáp ordered the 308th Division to start shifting the 88th Regiment into the trenches around Huguette-6, leaving only a reinforced company behind to harass Huguette-5. After replacing the decimated 165th Regiment, the 88th was to finish its assault preparations on April 18, double-check them the following day, and capture Huguette-6 on April 20.[100] Confident that this assault would succeed, Giáp was already planning another major offensive. Calculating that he would need 2,000 more replacements by May 5, on April 17 he ordered the 77th Infantry Regiment to send its last 500 recruits up from the supply lines and summoned 1,500 Local Force troops from the Việt Bắc region. These men were to begin marching to the valley on April 18, and another 2,000 troops from Interzone 4 (half from the 44th Infantry Regiment) were to set out two days later. Interzone 4 was also to be prepared to dispatch another 1,000 replacements when ordered.[101]

GONO's morale received a boost on April 16 when word came that most of its leadership had been promoted. De Castries was now a brigadier-general, Langlais and Lalande full colonels, Bigeard a lieutenant-colonel, and many captains and lieutenants were also advanced a grade. Celebrations were brief, however, since another supply convoy headed north just after dark. It was escorted by Lieutenant René Le Page's 1/6 BPC and Lieutenant Charles Galopin's 4/I/4 RTM, which remained behind to guard the way to Huguette-1, while troops of BT2 extended the trench from Huguette-2.[102] Le Page became pinned down north of Huguette-1 at 0300hrs and 4/8 BPC had to be sent to reinforce him. Huguette-6 was finally reached at 0615hrs.[103] East of the Nậm Yum, the 316th Division probed Eliane-1 at 2330hrs to get the defenders to reveal their positions, then attacked in force at 0100hrs following a very brief artillery preparation. 6/2 BEP held its ground, however, and the enemy was repulsed by a II/1 RCP counterattack, leaving 80 corpses behind.[104]

Despite de Castries' pessimistic message of the day before, GAP 2 tried to reestablish the drainage ditch outpost on April 17. Reinforced by elements of 2 BEP, 1/8 BPC once more attacked up the drainage ditch, while 4/1 BEP and a pair of tanks thrust eastward from Huguette-1. Thanks to the Bisons and flamethrowers, 1 BEP carried the first enemy trench but was halted in front of a second by a very effective VPA mortar barrage. The other drive also encountered difficulties because the ditch was so thickly mined that 8 BPC's troops had to advance on the open runway. Just after midday, they were pushed back by a counterattack that had to be broken up by the artillery. The operation remained at a standstill throughout the afternoon, since it was impossible to advance while VPA gunners and artillery observers on Dominique could hit the attackers with pinpoint fire. After dark, 3/8 BPC, 2/5 BPVN, and a platoon of engineers finally took the second trench and began constructing what would become strongpoint Opéra.[105]

Meanwhile, across the runway, 1 BEP's two surviving companies, with Douaumont and Mulhouse in attendance, were trying to link up with Huguette-6. Their objective was to evacuate its garrison since Langlais had decided the strongpoint was serving no purpose worth the prohibitive cost of keeping it supplied. The relief force stalled in front of the trenches surrounding Huguette-6 at 2200hrs. 1/6 BPC and then a company of I/4 RTM reinforced the Legion paras, but still no breakthrough could be achieved and the operation was broken off before dawn. 1 BEP would report 17 killed, 84 wounded (including five officers), and three missing on April 18. In addition, a shellburst damaged one of Douaumont's track rollers.[106]

Breakout from Huguette-6

Huguette-6's commander, Captain Bizard, turned 29 years old that Easter Sunday, but, instead of celebrating his birthday and the holiday, he was facing annihilation. An assault which his isolated garrison could not possibly survive was clearly imminent since *bộ đội* had removed the last vestiges of the barbed wire overnight.[107] Having been authorized by radio either to surrender or attempt a breakout, Bizard opted for the latter and his troops began sabotaging the radios and heavy weapons. All the seriously wounded had to be left behind. One of them was Sergeant Horst Ganzer, a mortar observer from 1 CEPML, who volunteered to man the last intact automatic rifle. He would die covering his comrades' escape.[108]

Hoping to slip out in the fog, Bizard chose to forgo an artillery bombardment in favor of a surprise attack relying upon grenades for firepower. Some men slung sandbags across their backs and chests as protection against grenade fragments. The breakout began at 0800hrs and, thanks to the fog and absent barbed wire, exited the perimeter without being noticed by the enemy. The troops stealthily advanced southward in a skirmish line, but the morning's deceptive calm was shattered when they encountered a trench 200 meters below Huguette-6. Its occupants, who had been expecting another attack from the opposite direction, were taken by surprise, and most of Bizard's men got across the trench after showering it with grenades. Then they fled south while *bộ đội* to the left, right, and rear blazed away at them through the fog. It was every man for himself as they raced down the runway while French 120mm mortars fired overhead to suppress the enemy fire.[109]

3/II/1 RCP, which had spent the night near the wrecked Curtiss, remained in place holding the bottleneck south of Huguette-1 open.[110] The company was joined by a platoon of 1 BEP that returned north to recover wounded who had been left behind overnight. It was accompanied by Mulhouse, which blasted VPA machine guns that were targeting the escapees, and immobilized Conti joined in from Huguette-3 with its machine guns. Bizard later complained that some of his men were cut down by "friendly fire" from the tanks.[111] Since just 60 survivors escaped unhurt, it's generally believed that both 1/5 BPVN and 3/I/2 REI were destroyed in the breakout, but most of their casualties were actually suffered earlier. Bizard reported his garrison's total losses as 106 killed, 49 wounded, and 79 missing, but these figures covered the entire period of April 8–18. 1/5 BPVN's casualties in the breakout were five killed, 16 wounded, and two missing, while I/2 REI's losses for the day were three killed (including Captain François, promoted just the day before) and 19 wounded.[112] This suggests that Huguette-6 had barely 100 able-bodied men left on April 18.

The fall of Huguette-6 deflated the optimism that had prevailed among the French after Eliane-1 was retaken just a week earlier. By choosing not to attack until the strongpoint was totally cut off, Giáp had forced the French into an attritional battle for its supply lines that they could not win – or afford to lose. Indeed, he had reversed the whole equation of the siege by compelling the French to attack fortified positions day after day and night after night. And his tactics had neutralized the potent combination of French armor, artillery, and airpower on wide-open terrain in broad daylight. Last, but not least, Giáp had made considerable progress toward cutting GONO's aerial lifeline, and flak batteries quickly redeployed so they could engage planes just after they dropped their loads, and were winging northward over Huguette on predictable courses.

The fall of Huguette-1

Giáp's next target was Huguette-1, but again he was unwilling to risk a major assault – especially when his ammunition dumps were so low. And the strongpoint was a tough nut to crack because the surrounding terrain provided no cover and was perfectly suited to French tanks and aircraft. It was also protected by four barbed-wire fences, each 4 or 5 meters thick, set 15 meters apart with minefields and trip flares in between. And Huguette-1 was unlikely to fall quickly because it was divided into three sub-positions separated by additional obstacles. One containing the command post and mortar pits was east of the Pavie Track, while another was on the western side, and the third straddled the road south of them. These were known to the VPA as positions 206A, 206B, and 206C.[113]

With the onset of the rainy season, the 36th Regiment's trenches were filling with mud and water, and the French sortied out daily to "aerate" them. Urged on by three young recruits who had previously served as guerrillas and used underground passages to escape French sweeps, the regiment decided to dig tunnels toward Huguette-1. Fears that this would slow progress proved baseless since work could continue around the clock, whereas trenches could be excavated only at night. A line of ĐKZs, bazookas, and mortars was established to deter sorties and knock out bunkers one at a time. It was supplemented by snipers who were assigned specific sectors to ensure that every portion of Huguette-1 was constantly under threat. Private Đoàn Tương Líp was credited with nine kills, but usually aimed for the legs to wound and immobilize, knowing that other enemy troops would come to the injured man's rescue and present additional targets. The deliberate pace of these tactics prompted the 36th Regiment to dub them the "creeping siege attack."[114]

As the VPA tunnels were burrowing unseen toward Huguette-1, Langlais decided to withdraw I/2 REI from Huguette and replace it with the less debilitated I/13 DBLE. On the night of April 18–19, the two battalions' headquarters companies switched places on Huguette-3 while Mulhouse and Douaumont helped relieve Captain Phu's 2/5 BPVN on Opéra.[115] It was replaced by Bizard's 1/5 BPVN, which had been hastily reconstituted with Legionnaires, Chasseurs Parachutistes, Air Force personnel, parachuted replacements, and survivors from various disbanded units. Though still formally part of 5 BPVN, two-thirds of the rebuilt unit's personnel were "European" and French historian Henri le Mire describes it as an "elite company."[116]

Captain Chevalier's 4/I/13 DBLE, supported by a march company of I/4 RTM, did not break through the trenches north of Huguette-2 until dawn, and the relief of 4/I/2 REI on Huguette-1 was not completed until 1000hrs on April 19. It had taken Chevalier 14 hours to make the 1,400-meter journey from Claudine![117] The route to the strongpoint was barred even more solidly that night, when elements of 6 BPC and 4/I/4 RTM vainly tried to open the way for a supply convoy. The effort was finally abandoned because flare-dropping in support of the battle was delaying a desperately needed personnel drop. The Moroccan company's commander, Lieutenant Galopin, and his deputy, Adjutant-Chief Paul Charron, were both killed and another officer wounded. The Moroccan company was accordingly replaced on Lily-2 by 2/I/4 RTM, which deployed one of its platoons in the communications trench running to Lily-3.[118]

Langlais ordered that work be accelerated on the trench from Huguette-2 and an outpost that was being built at the crossroads just to the north. Captain Camille Chounet's 2/I/13 DBLE took over the project on April 20, while, off to the west, Captain Roland Capeyron's 3rd Company replaced 3/I/2 REI on Huguette-5. After nightfall, Chounet's troops tried to open the way to Huguette-1, but failed, despite being reinforced by a pair of Bisons and elements of both 6 BPC and I/4 RTM. Across the river, II/1 RCP launched a brilliantly successful raid on Dominique-6, which had been well behind enemy lines for three solid weeks, and demolished four bunkers, killed 19 *bộ đội*, and captured three more. A narrow supply corridor to Huguette-1 was finally opened late on the morning of April 21 after 2/5 BPVN launched a flank attack from Opéra. The following night was also marked by a successful raid east of the Nậm Yum – where 6 BPC destroyed a bunker on Dominique-5 – and another failure to break through to Huguette-1. It was finally resupplied for what proved to be the last time at 0840hrs on April 22.[119]

The 36th Regiment's siegeworks had advanced on schedule except on the southern side, where the work was interrupted by French breakthrough attempts and because the 89th Battalion's "officers and men were worried and afraid of the intense enemy fire."[120] Regimental Commander Phạm Hồng Sơn took corrective action by organizing each platoon into one digging squad, which was relieved every two hours, and two firepower squads that protected its flanks. He also conceived a psychological warfare gambit to put Huguette-1's defenders off their guard. Sơn arranged to have the 803rd Howitzer Battery fire 20 105mm shells into the strongpoint at dusk on April 20 and then had his troops yell "Assault! Assault!" at the top of their lungs. This performance was repeated at dusk on the following two nights as well.[121]

In fact, Sơn had no intention of launching a conventional assault with waves of infantry advancing through breaches in the wire. Gaps had been cut in the outer fences – though the wire was left lying on the ground to conceal the fact – and the inner fences would be gapped once the assault began. However, Sơn planned to strike stealthily through three tunnels using minimal manpower. A platoon of the 80th Battalion's 61st Company would make the primary attack on 206B from the west, while a squad of the 84th Battalion's 42nd Company hit 206A and a squad of the 89th Battalion's 39th Company assaulted 206C. The bulk of the 89th Battalion's troops would guard against a relief attempt, and most of the spearhead companies' personnel would keep the waterlogged tunnels bailed out.[122]

The attack began at 2356hrs on April 22 with a brief artillery preparation, while the spearhead units began opening their tunnels inside the perimeter. It appears their objective was merely to seize and fortify bridgeheads inside Huguette-1 in preparation for a final assault that would occur after dark on April 23, when 75mm mountain guns would be installed just outside the perimeter.[123] The Legionnaires were thrown into confusion when bộ đội suddenly materialized inside their trenches. Captain Chevalier radioed that although Huguette-1 was not being seriously attacked, "the Viet seems to be getting through all over the place."[124] The northern and western spearheads established bridgeheads and quickly installed heavy weapons in the captured bunkers. The southern attack was delayed because its tunnel was not quite complete. Benefiting from the distraction caused by the other penetrations, it finally broke into 206C shortly after 0100hrs.[125]

Yet the *bộ đội* inside the perimeter were too few to take the strongpoint and the Legionnaires had recovered from their surprise and were offering fierce resistance. The 84th Battalion's commander ordered his water-bailers into 206A and requested reinforcements. Sơn realized that there was an opportunity to finish off Huguette-1 immediately, but he had no reserves ready to exploit it. So, he ordered all three battalions to commit their water-bailers (which would soon render the tunnels impassable) and rush in whatever other reinforcements they could. A platoon each of the 84th Battalion's 43rd Company and the 80th Battalion's 63rd Company were committed, and Huguette-1 fell sometime after 0230hrs. Langlais thought the battle was still undecided because Sơn ordered that captured machine guns continue to be fired outward as a deceptive measure. The 36th Regiment killed 31 defenders (including Chevalier) and captured 117.[126] A handful of men escaped and linked up with a company of 1 BEP that was escorting a supply convoy to Huguette-1. It had predictably failed to break through despite being reinforced by 2/6 BPC (then stationed on Huguette-2), and fell back after learning that Huguette-1 had fallen.[127]

The "creeping siege attack" had been a great success. One of GONO's most crucial positions had been captured with minimal ammunition consumption (just 13 105mm shells were expended in the preparatory bombardment) and only modest loss to the attackers, who reportedly had just four men killed and 21 wounded. These figures seem low, but are not beyond the realm of possibility given the 36th Regiment's novel tactics, which stunned the defenders and negated GONO's most powerful weapon – its artillery. Vietnamese accounts repeatedly mention the silence of the French guns, which could not intervene because the attackers and defenders were thoroughly intermingled.[128] All other VPA units were encouraged to emulate the 36th Regiment's "creeping siege" tactics.

The Huguette-1 counterattack

The loss of Huguette-1 doomed GONO. Opéra would have to be evacuated, giving Giáp control of most of the airfield and main drop zone. The area still in French hands would be too small to receive an adequate flow of parachuted personnel and supplies, and misdrops would increase dramatically. De Castries, who had focused on logistical issues since relinquishing tactical control of the siege, ordered that Huguette-1 be recaptured that same day. Langlais and Bigeard both disagreed, because they feared that the operation would decimate 2 BEP (their strongest reserve battalion though it had only 350 men left) and doubted that Huguette-1 could be held even if it was retaken. Langlais later wrote: "the 2nd B.E.P. was intact and I jealously watched over its employment when the General decided to reoccupy Huguette 1. I have already mentioned that this was my only serious 'falling-out' with my boss and of course I bowed to his judgment."[129] This proves conclusively that de Castries had not been cut out of GONO's chain of command, since here we see him asserting his authority over two very forceful subordinates.

Bigeard insisted that Liesenfelt command the counterattack. This uncharacteristic abdication of authority suggests that he was trying to dodge responsibility for an operation he thought was unwise and likely to fail.[130] But Bigeard drew up the plan with his customary efficiency. The operation would commence at 1345hrs with a massive airstrike on Huguette-1 and surrounding VPA positions. Bigeard's after-action report mentions four B-26s and 12 fighter-bombers, but in fact the air program was much larger. A dozen Bearcats and six Hellcats would blast Huguette-1 itself, while three B-26s targeted Huguette-6, another six B-26s and two Privateers hit Huguette-7, and between three and five B-26s suppressed the batteries on Dominique-1.[131] After the planes were finished, the artillery would pound Huguette-1 with 1,200 shells starting at 1400hrs. Protected by smokescreens to the north and east, the assault would begin halfway through the ten-minute bombardment. Two companies would deliver the main attack from Opéra, a third would strike from Huguette-2, and the fourth would be in reserve. The operation would be supported by Douaumont and Mulhouse – the only Bisons that were fully operational that day.[132]

Since 2 BEP was defending frontline positions on Eliane, shifting it across the river was a complex business that required no fewer than 14 companies to redeploy. This unusual activity was spotted by VPA gunners, who increased their harassing fire.[133] Indeed, VPA commanders were expecting a counterattack and had already taken steps to defeat it. The 88th Regiment had sent its 29th Battalion to reinforce the 23rd in the trenches above Huguette-2, and the 308th Division's commander, Vương Thừa Vũ, had brought up the 79/102 to act as the 88th Regiment's reserve.[134] And several days before, Giáp had ordered the creation of a fire support headquarters that would, for the very first time, allow

HUGUETTE-1 COUNTERATTACK

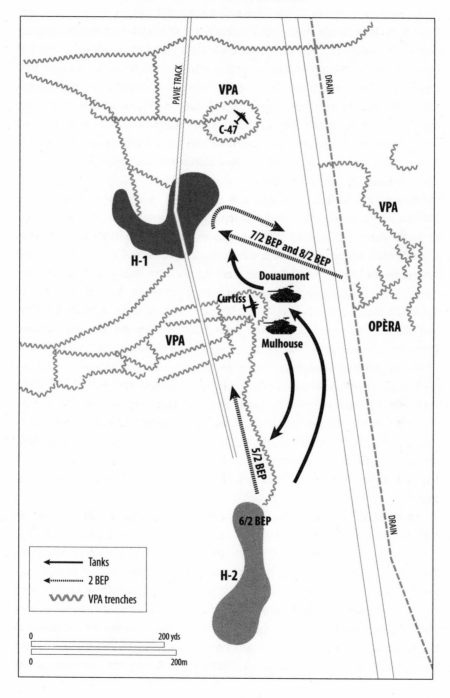

his gunners to mass and shift fire rapidly. Vũ was designated Fire Support Commander, with the 312th Division's deputy commander, Đàm Quang Trung, as his second in command, and the 45th Artillery Regiment's deputy commander as artillery liaison. This headquarters controlled five 105mm batteries (all but the 805th) and all the organic mortars of the two infantry divisions. The artillery battalion and battery commanders had accompanied Trung to an observation post on Mount Hồng Lếch, where they plotted barrages on road junctions, bridges, movement routes, and likely counterattack assembly areas.[135]

8/2 BEP, which was already west of the river, was on its start line at Opéra as scheduled by 1330hrs. However, only part of 7th Company was there, 5th Company was just starting to arrive on Huguette-2, and 6th Company was even farther behind. The redeployment had been slowed by the paras' unfamiliarity with the maze-like Métro as well as artillery harassment and the late arrival of relieving units on Elianes-1 and -2. Liesenfelt accordingly asked that H-Hour be delayed. Langlais replied that while the airstrike could not be put off, the bombardment would be postponed until the infantry was ready. The planes pulverized Huguette-1 with pinpoint dive-bombing in the single most effective air attack of the entire siege – which some Vietnamese authors insist was conducted by American planes! Watching from Douaumont, Lieutenant André Mengelle concluded the attack was going to be "a piece of cake."[136]

But the artillery opened fire as soon as the planes departed, and by the time the bombardment was halted, nearly half of the allocated shells had been expended. By Liesenfelt's account, Bigeard was already present at his headquarters on Huguette-3, having arrived just before the airstrike began. But Bigeard claims that, exhausted by days of inadequate sleep, he napped until 1500hrs, when de Castries asked that he take charge of the operation because it was "lacking punch."[137] Liesenfelt's memory seems more reliable, since it's unlikely that Bigeard would (or could) have slept through more than an hour of such a crucial and noisy operation. With the 5th and 7th Companies finally in place, the bombardment resumed at 1425hrs and the ground assault jumped off at 1430hrs. Things immediately began going wrong. 8th Company's commander, Lieutenant Pétré, had been wounded and only two of its platoons joined 7th Company in the attack from Opéra. Then a machine gun firing from the left – supposedly in the nose of the wrecked Curtiss, although this is unlikely since the position was too exposed – decimated the attackers as they crossed the runway. Worse yet, the 36th Regiment had used the half-hour intermission to rush fresh troops into Huguette-1 and their fire halted the attack 50 meters from the strongpoint. The paras were pinned down in bomb craters and hammered by VPA artillery.[138]

Though supported by the Bisons, 5th Company's attack fared no better. Mengelle thought that the planes and artillery had focused too much on Huguette-1, leaving the VPA "strongpoint" south of it practically untouched. Vietnamese accounts confirm that few bombs landed in that area. And when 5th Company emerged from Huguette-2, it was quickly targeted by the 801st, 802nd, and 806th Howitzer Batteries. Their fire repulsed the first assault, and the company commander, Lieutenant René de Biré, was badly wounded. Captain Leonce Piccato, who was sent to replace him, was killed as soon as he arrived. Undaunted, the paras crawled north through the communications trench and broke into the 23/88's lines near the Curtiss. The Bisons moved up east of the wreck and enfiladed the 213th Company's trenches to great effect, but drew intense counterfire from bazookas, Dominique's mountain guns, and what Mengelle described as "panzerfausts" (Russian RPG-2s?). One of these hit Mulhouse's turret, wounding its gunner and stunning the entire crew.[139]

Mengelle informed 2 BEP's headquarters that 5th Company was bogged down near the Curtiss, but it insisted the company was fighting on the southern edge of Huguette-1. Liesenfelt had placed his command post on Huguette-3, where he had no view of the battle. Thus he had no idea what was happening when communications with 7th and 8th Companies broke down. Bigeard wrote that upon arriving at Huguette-3 around 1500, Liesenfelt told him things had to be going well since he was hearing nothing from those units. Bigeard claims that a quick turn of the dial revealed that the radio was on the wrong frequency. Liesenfelt counters that the runway's metal surface was interfering with the radios (as it often did), Bigeard had been present from the start, and it took him 15–20 minutes to reestablish communications once the problem was recognized.[140]

Both accounts agree that Bigeard now took control of the operation and called off the attack. To cover 7th and 8th Companies' retreat, he had four standby B-26s bomb Huguette-1, laid on another bombardment, and ordered Douaumont to head north. 7th and 8th Companies' survivors emerged from the craters simultaneously to flee across the runway in one desperate leap, but many were still cut down. Among them was 8th Company's acting commander, Lieutenant Jean Garin, who was immobilized by a wound and then killed himself to save the lives of men who were crawling out to rescue him.[141] Some historians put 2 BEP's butcher's bill for the day at over 150 men, but it was actually just under a hundred (19 killed, about 70 wounded, and six missing).[142] It was still enough, however, that on the following day the remnants of the two Legion para battalions would be merged into the Bataillon de Marche Étranger de Parachutistes (BMEP) under Major Guiraud. Liesenfelt was left without a command.

The failure to retake Huguette-1 forced Opéra's evacuation. On April 24, Douaumont and Ettlingen (the only Main Position tanks with working 75mm guns) prepared the way by demolishing nearby enemy bunkers. Bizard's troops booby-trapped the strongpoint and fell back down the drainage ditch to a point about 150 meters from Dominique-4. There they established a new outpost that some French sources refer to as "Opéra bis" but is more commonly known as the "Nameless strongpoint." The rain-swollen drainage ditch and trenches that sprouted from it were perpetually waterlogged – often waist deep.[143]

The garrison's morale was shaken by the defeat at Huguette-1 and its leadership knew that – barring a miracle – GONO's fate was now sealed. There was plenty of blame to go around, starting with de Castries, who had insisted on the counterattack, although it was obvious that Huguette-1 could not be held for long even if it succeeded. Then there was Liesenfelt, who mal-positioned his command post, lost control of the battle, and failed to realize that communications had broken down. And lastly there was Bigeard, whose plan had several major flaws. First of all, since it greatly underestimated the time required to bring 2 BEP across the river, the airstrike was scheduled too early and gave the enemy 30 precious minutes in which to reinforce Huguette-1. Secondly, the bombing left the "strongpoint" largely undamaged – perhaps because the pilots fixated on Huguette-1. And finally, Bigeard's plan sent a solitary company against this enemy bastion, although it had proven almost impossible to penetrate in daylight over a week before.

Vietnamese historians claim the VPA won another important victory on April 23 when gunner Phùng Văn Khẩu of the 755th Mountain Battery destroyed four French 105s that had been towed out of their emplacements. The 755th's three guns were deployed on Dominique-1 in casemates whose embrasures were closed with sandbags between fire missions. Since Khẩu was illiterate, he aimed his 75 by peering down its bore, and had to remove only enough sandbags to let the muzzle protrude. The other two gunners used their sights and consequently had to make larger apertures. During a 20-minute duel with French tanks, both of those guns were knocked out, seven men were killed and 11 wounded. Khẩu's better-protected gun remained intact, though by the end he was the only crewmember still on his feet.[144] French documents record no such incident, but

Dominique's mountain guns were inflicting considerable damage. On April 20, GONO radioed, "We again ask with extreme urgency that D1 be permanently and rapidly matraquée ['clobbered'] by the Air Force or we shall soon find our whole artillery shot to pieces and our depots on fire."[145]

The only French success of April 23 was an early afternoon *coup de main* that seized Honeycomb Hill from VPA pickets. A new *sonnette*, which seems to have been held by a detachment of Captain Phu's redoubtable 2/5 BPVN, was established on the peak to protect CR Elaine against infiltration from the northeast.[146]

Strangulation

In his memoir, Langlais refused to admit defeat in the battle for Huguette: "Twenty-four days of combat, three regiments, fifty guns, to eliminate three little strongpoints, three ridiculous squares of rice paddy whose [individual] garrisons never exceeded a hundred men. The battle of the three Huguettes was lost, but at the price of such a wholesale slaughter that the enemy could not call it victory."[147] But while Giáp paid heavily for Huguette, he had won a decisive victory by getting a chokehold on GONO's aerial lifeline. Antiaircraft machine-gun batteries shifted even closer to the perimeter, sometimes to within a few hundred meters of strongpoints still in French hands. The 37mm batteries also advanced though they remained at a more respectful distance. The 398th Battalion started shifting its guns to Bản Ong Pet and would eventually deploy some near Françoise. East of the river, the 383rd Battalion moved its 37s closer to the Five Hills and deployed one battery just a kilometer from Eliane-2. And as early as April 19, a new tactic had been developed in which two-gun 37mm flak platoons were hauled up near the front after dark and withdrawn before dawn.[148]

GATAC Nord made a considerable effort to suppress VPA flak during April, but without much discernable effect. For example, a flak battery which the French christened "YA" was targeted by a total of 18 B-26s and seven Privateers on April 3, 5, and 10. Although four 2,000lb, 75 1,000lb, and 36 500lb bombs were expended in these attacks, the battery was not silenced. It would finally be destroyed by eight direct bomb hits on May 1.[149] GONO's artillery proved more effective, and sometimes neutralized VPA flak for 2–3 hours at a time.[150]

AIR COMBAT SORTIES DURING THE LAST THREE WEEKS OF APRIL[151]						
Period	Direct support	Counterbattery	Flak suppression	Interdiction	Vs. Depots & cantonments	Total
April 6–30	366	222	250	178	32	1,048

There were several reasons for this ineffective bombing. First and foremost, the B-26 pilots were poorly trained because the Armée de l'Air's role in the recently established NATO alliance was purely defensive and bomber training facilities had been closed to save money. Many pilots were accordingly transferred from transport squadrons with little or no conversion training. Secondly, armorers were unfamiliar with the new American fuses they were receiving, and set their delay too long, causing the bombs to bury themselves deep in the muddy landscape before exploding. Finally, the B-26s never carried more than half their theoretical maximum bombload of 8,000lb – evidently owing to habits acquired years before when Cát Bi Airbase's runway had been 1,200 meters shorter than it was in 1954.[152]

GONO's defenders put greater faith in the fighter-bombers, which made far riskier and more accurate dive-bombing attacks. They were particularly fond of the Aéronavale pilots, who during April flew almost three times as many sorties over Điện Biên Phủ as Air Force Bearcats, and had to be true daredevils to land on the pitching deck of an aircraft carrier. But the cumulative psychological pressure of their daily, death-defying missions began to tell on the navy pilots. On April 30, Squadron 11F's flight surgeon grounded the entire unit for several days because its pilots were suffering from severe combat fatigue. Thus, the arrival of Squadron 14F "Gayal" merely maintained Aéronavale strength rather than increasing it. The squadron was equipped with 25 AU-1 "Corsair" fighter-bombers that had been delivered to Da Nang by the USS *Saipan* on April 22. However, these planes were worn-out survivors of the Korean War and none was judged airworthy upon arrival. Working around the clock, mechanics got many of them flying, but it's doubtful that more than a dozen Corsairs were operational on any given day.[153]

The French air supply effort, already hamstrung by the loss of Huguette-1 on April 23, suffered another crippling blow on each of the next two days. During the night of April 23–24, a CAT C-119 was hit by a 37mm shell that wounded pilot Paul R. Holden. On the morning of the 24th, the American crews refused to fly to Điện Biên Phủ, pointing out that their contracts prohibited them from performing combat missions. They did not resume flying to the valley until April 30, after it was agreed that they would make time-delay drops from 3,000 meters and GATAC Nord would improve flak suppression. Only French C-119 crews continued to fly low-level missions.[154] The "strike" was thus doubly damaging because the C-119s not only had triple the cargo capacity of the Dakotas, but also dropped their loads more accurately. On April 19, GONO reported that 70–75 percent of the cargo dropped by C-119s at low altitude was recovered, while the figure for C-47s making high-altitude drops was just 45–50 percent.[155]

The next blow landed on April 25, when the wet monsoon arrived in full force. Weather conditions at Điện Biên Phủ had been unusually good in the period April 6–16, but thereafter rainfall became an almost daily occurrence. Starting on April 25, the valley began getting heavy downpours under thick cloud cover that might lift in the afternoon, but sometimes lasted throughout the day. Unsafe weather conditions caused air mission aborts to spike, and the rains would soon put most of the headquarters area and virtually all of Isabelle underwater, and cause many trenches and bunkers to collapse.[156]

Finally, deaths, wounds, and combat fatigue were wearing down S/GMMTA's aircrews. Thus, although deliveries from the US and transfers from France raised the number of transport planes to 130 during April (including 29 Packets), at one point there were only 82 crews available – a dozen fewer than when the siege began.[157] The net effect of the aircrew shortage, the tightening flak envelope, the worsening weather, and the CAT strike was catastrophic. Supply drops, which had averaged 142 metric tons per day between April 1 and April 23, fell to an average of just 56 tons in the last week of the month. No supplies at all were dropped on April 28. And these figures tell only half the story, since misdrops rose as the DZ shrank. When C-119s switched to high-altitude drops, as much as two-thirds of their cargo landed outside the perimeter.[158]

AIR SUPPLY OF ĐIỆN BIÊN PHỦ (METRIC TONS)[159]												
Date	Total tons	Inf. ammo	Art. ammo	Food	Other	Date	Total tons	Misdrop tons	Inf. Ammo	Art. ammo	Food	Other
Mar 14	80	31%	30%	33%	6%	Apr 11	181		12%	54%	24%	10%
Mar 15	77	23%	57%	14%	6%	Apr 12	174		5%	58%	25%	12%
Mar 16	55	6%	49%	12%	33%	Apr 13	151		4%	56%	33%	7%
Mar 17	138	10%	35%	32%	22%	Apr 14	217		14%	50%	22%	14%
Mar 18	205	5%	75%	11%	9%	Apr 15	229		16%	50%	26%	9%
Mar 19	107	13%	67%	3%	17%	Apr 16	216	22	21%	42%	23%	15%
Mar 20	108	22%	44%	15%	19%	Apr 17	188	33	13%	55%	23%	9%
Mar 21	125	20%	53%	13%	14%	Apr 18	136	23	12%	32%	28%	28%
Mar 22	115	26%	46%	15%	13%	Apr 19	121	18	12%	48%	19%	21%
Mar 23	108	29%	35%	19%	17%	Apr 20	82	7	40%	16%	28%	15%

Mar 24	113	6%	63%	23%	8%	Apr 21	136	26	18%	22%	47%	14%
Mar 25	110	8%	63%	21%	7%	Apr 22	181	18	26%	24%	36%	14%
Mar 26	101	17%	54%	17%	12%	Apr 23	107		20%	18%	46%	16%
Mar 27	83	12%	61%	25%	2%	Apr 24	118	31	32%	2%	46%	21%
Mar 28	57	22%	41%	31%	6%	Apr 25	63	35	12%	23%	48%	17%
Mar 29	77	9%	50%	35%	7%	Apr 26	92		39%	18%	30%	13%
Mar 30	39	16%	17%	53%	13%	Apr 27	90		43%	17%	31%	9%
Mar 31	22	58%	32%	1%	9%	Apr 28	0		0%	0%	0%	0%
Apr 1	102	34%	56%	5%	4%	Apr 29	31		16%	38%	37%	9%
Apr 2	134	32%	51%	9%	8%	Apr 30	212	64	21%	10%	61%	8%
Apr 3	114	26%	51%	12%	11%	May 1	186		30%	23%	32%	15%
Apr 4	109	26%	58%	9%	6%	May 2	119		56%	32%	11%	2%
Apr 5	144	22%	53%	12%	12%	May 3	54		17%	35%	26%	23%
Apr 6	94	31%	61%	4%	4%	May 4	58	23	45%	17%	21%	16%
Apr 7	83	9%	66%	13%	12%	May 5	67	21	11%	40%	23%	27%
Apr 8	110	0%	54%	40%	6%	May 6	195		32%	28%	25%	14%
Apr 9	171	10%	53%	31%	6%	May 7	85		6%	44%	49%	0%
Apr 10	80	18%	51%	26%	5%	TOTAL	6,409		19%	43%	26%	12%

Misdrops data is listed only on dates for which it's available. Misdropped tonnage is included in the "Total tons" figure. The average misdrop percentage for the period March 30 to April 15 was estimated at between 10% and 15%.

GONO's personnel situation was also bad. Since the last troops of 2 BEP jumped in on April 11–12, reinforcements had been arriving in a trickle that never kept pace with losses. Although some units received what were, in relative terms, substantial infusions of personnel (e.g., 1 BEP got 44 men on April 12,[160] while 13 DBLE received 69 on April 16 and 18[161]), their strength continued to wither away. As the weather worsened and the flak belt tightened, growing numbers of troops who were flown to the valley never got the chance to jump. On the night of April 22, a mere 35 of 100 promised replacements jumped, and just 36 men hit the silk four nights later while another 44 circled vainly overhead. Only a single Dakota managed to penetrate the thick cloud cover and drop its troops on the night of April 27; another 20 returned to Hanoi with their passengers still aboard. Worse yet, no reinforcements at all arrived on April 28.[162] These figures prompted a series of increasingly bitter radio messages to Colonel Sauvaugnac from Langlais, who accused the pilots of playing it safe. It seems that his accusations were generally unwarranted, since the harsh realities of terrain, weather, flak, and GONO's ever-shrinking perimeter simply made it impossible to deliver adequate numbers of personnel or supplies.

PERSONNEL REINFORCEMENTS (MARCH 14–MAY 6)[163]				
Nationality	**Officers**	**NCOs**	**Enlisted**	**TOTAL**
French	92	303	1,003	1,398
Foreign Legion	31	131	800	962
African		1	29	30
Indochinese	10	68	1,823	1,901
TOTAL	133	503	3,655	4,291

Nearly half of all personnel reinforcements (and perhaps a quarter of the 680 unqualified volunteer jumpers!) were Africans and Indochinese, and some had difficulty adapting to the harrowing conditions inside the beleaguered fortress. On April 29, de Castries requested that, henceforth, all reinforcements be Europeans, since he believed only they were capable of rapid acclimatization.[164] What GONO needed most of all, of course, was a fresh, full-strength battalion to reconstitute its reserves. However, there was only one "European" parachute battalion remaining in Indochina – 1 BPC – and Navarre and Cogny were understandably loath to send it to Điện Biên Phủ. This time their reluctance to throw another battalion into the meatgrinder was fully justified, since by the last week of April, the French had undoubtedly lost the battle and GONO's annihilation was just a matter of time.

GONO INFANTRY STRENGTH (APRIL 25)[165]				
CR	**Strongpoints**	**Garrison**	**Reserves**	**TOTAL**
Claudine	C-2, C-3, C-4, C-5	I/2 REI	1 company	400
Low Eliane	D-3, E-10, E-11, E-12	BT2 (550), III/3 RTA (200)	Coy 6 BPC (100)	850
High Eliane	E-1, E-2, E-3	II/1 RCP (400 men), 5 BPVN (200), I/13 DBLE (350)	2 coys 6 BPC (200)	1,150
Épervier	D-4, Épervier	8 BPC (400), 1/5 BPVN (80), 2 platoons BT2 (50)	1 platoon	530
Huguette	H-2, H-3, H-5	BMEP (600)	1 company	600
Junon	C-6, Junon	CTB, Air Force Detachment		180
Lily	L-1, L-2, L-3	I/4 RTM (390)	2 platoons	390
MAIN POSITION TOTAL			5 companies	4,100
Isabelle	All	III/3 REI (400), II/1 RTA (490), BT3 (370), V/7 RTA (140)	1 company	1,400
OVERALL TOTAL			6 companies	5,500

Operation *Vulture*

The January 1954 Berlin Conference had failed to produce a solution to the Indochina conflict – or consensus on the future of divided Germany and Korea. Yet the French, British, American, and Soviet diplomats in attendance had agreed to end the occupation of Austria and reestablish it as an independent (and neutral) nation. They also resolved to meet again at Geneva in late April to resume negotiations on Korea and Indochina. The Indochina discussions were set to begin on May 8 and this became a critical date for the French. If GONO could hold out until then, there was a chance that it might be saved by an 11th-hour ceasefire. But snatching victory from the jaws of defeat at Geneva was a long shot, since the Soviets and Chinese were unlikely to allow it. GONO could readily be saved, however, by the Americans. The US Far Eastern Air Forces (FEAF) dwarfed the puny French air contingents in Indochina, and the valley was within range of B-29 strategic bombers based on Okinawa and the Philippines. The bombers could be supplemented by jet warplanes flying from aircraft carriers of the US Navy's 7th Fleet in the Gulf of Tonkin (as they would do a decade later during the 2nd Vietnamese War).[166]

The possibility of American aerial intervention was first raised at a meeting between French General Paul Ely and Admiral Arthur Radford, Chairman of the US Joint Chiefs of Staff (JCS) in late March. However, General Jean Valluy had already warned the Americans that the Navarre Plan was not (as promised) going to deliver victory in 1955, and that France could continue the war into 1956 only with direct US participation. Thus, airstrikes would merely be the first step in a far larger military intervention. This was an unattractive prospect for President Dwight Eisenhower, who had just ended the conflict in Korea and was reluctant to fight another war in Asia. The French themselves were of two minds about the proposed airstrikes – codenamed Operation *Vautour* (*"Vulture"*) – because they could trigger direct Chinese intervention in the war and/or scuttle any chance of a settlement at Geneva. But as GONO's plight became ever more desperate, they concluded that *Vulture* offered the only hope of avoiding a humiliating and decisive defeat.

Admiral Radford strongly favored Operation *Vulture*, but other JCS members were uncertain and US Army Chief of staff General Matthew Ridgway was strongly opposed. His experience as supreme commander in Korea during 1950–51 made him doubt that airpower alone could decide the war, and a recent US Army study had concluded that at least 275,000 personnel (three air wings, a carrier battle group, and one airborne and six infantry divisions) would be required. Ridgway was also appalled by political, terrain, and infrastructure conditions that would make Indochina an even more challenging theater of operations than Korea. His pessimism was echoed by the Army's Chief of Research and Development, General James Gavin, who recalled, "the more we studied the situation the more we realized that we were, in fact, talking about going to war with China… If we would be, in fact, fighting China, then we were fighting her in the wrong place on terms entirely to her advantage."[167]

But mindful of the political fallout of "losing Indochina" and pressured by his hawkish Secretary of State, John Foster Dulles, Eisenhower was willing to consider intervention if it was authorized by Congress and included active participation by allied nations – most notably Great Britain. But British Prime Minister Winston Churchill rebuffed Dulles' calls for "united action" because he doubted victory was possible and was determined to cut the best deal possible at Geneva. Congressional leaders, including Senator Lyndon Johnson, balked when they learned that no allies had signed on to provide troops and responded unfavorably when Vice President Richard Nixon publicly floated a trial balloon about unilateral action on April 16. All possibility of "united action" vanished on April 24, when British Foreign Minister Anthony Eden ignored Radford's plea for a declaration of support at a NATO Council meeting in Paris. Unilateral action was rejected five days later when Eisenhower met with the JCS and only Radford enthusiastically favored intervention, while Ridgway and Secretary of Defense Charles E. Wilson denounced it.

While the politicians and diplomats were debating, American military commanders had been planning how to execute *Vulture* if it was authorized. General Joseph Caldera, head of FEAF's Bomber Command, produced a plan for a massive raid by 98 B-29s. Displaying the hubris typical of an airpower zealot, he claimed that the operation "could have effectively destroyed the entire enemy force."[168] This is patently absurd, since by late April the combatants at Điện Biên Phủ were entrenched so close together that it would have been impossible to target VPA positions without hitting French troops as well. Caldera himself noted the absence of navigation aids necessary for precision bombing. US airpower could, no doubt, have broken the siege by taking out the flak batteries and pummeling Giáp's supply line, but annihilating the besiegers was simply impossible. An FEAF study concluded that B-29s using conventional bombs could not have achieved decisive results, and this is no doubt why Eisenhower considered employing atomic weapons. Dulles is alleged to have toyed with the notion of "loaning" several A-bombs to the French, but thankfully nothing came of it.

Historian Mark Moyar contends that *Vulture* could have been decisive because "A variety of Communist sources subsequently revealed that nearly all of the Viet Minh's mobile forces had been sent to Dien Bien Phu, contradicting the dominant belief in the West that the Viet Minh had a vast number of soldiers hidden elsewhere in Vietnam."[169] Moyar asserts that this erroneous notion dissuaded Eisenhower from intervening unilaterally because he was convinced that *Vulture* would have little impact on the VPA's total force structure. However, Vietnamese and Western sources alike agree that the bulk of the VPA's regular troops were indeed deployed elsewhere. At peak strength, the siege force included 31 regular infantry battalions. VPA official histories report there were 127 in existence at the time, while the Deuxième Bureau estimated 109 regular battalions and 26 regional battalions.[170] And even if only Giáp's regular divisions are considered "mobile" (a debatable assumption) two of the six (the 320th and 325th) sent no troops to Điện Biên Phủ, and just one regiment of the 304th was present until the last week of the siege.

Operation *Condor*

While *Vulture*'s fate still hung in the balance, General Navarre tried to aid GONO by launching a relief operation from Laos. As originally conceived in December 1953, this operation – codenamed *Condor* – was designed to pursue retreating VPA troops after a failed assault on Điện Biên Phủ. Now *Condor*'s primary objective would be to deceive Giáp into withdrawing forces from the valley, though the notion of breaking the siege was not entirely abandoned until after the operation was under way. Colonel Jean Boucher de Crèvecœur, the senior French commander in Laos, could spare only four battalions for *Condor*. These were the II/2 REI (whose sister battalion was fighting on Huguette), and three low-quality Laotian Army units – the 4th and 5th Laotian Chasseur Battalions and the 1st Laotian Parachute Battalion. An 800-man "Commando Groupement" of Meo and Laotian tribesmen raised the total strength to just 3,088. Under command of Lieutenant-Colonel Yves Godard, this force began advancing up the Nậm Ou Valley on April 14, but was too weak even to mount a convincing diversion – much less break the siege.[171]

Small detachments from other CEFEO battalions were airlifted in to convince the enemy that major reinforcements were on their way. But to give *Condor* real "teeth," an entire GAP and a 75mm recoilless rifle battery were supposed to jump in and link up with the ground column just short of the border. However, a three-battalion jump would require 115 Dakota sorties, and supplying the enlarged, 5,500-strong force would consume another 24 sorties every day. To divert so many aircraft at a time when GONO needed every man and shell it could get was simply unthinkable. The two airlifts could have been conducted simultaneously only if large numbers of US transport planes had been deployed to Indochina. Moreover, Langlais was demanding that 1 BPC reinforce GONO, which would leave only 1 BPVN and 3 BPVN available for *Condor*.[172]

Condor's first phase went reasonably well despite mounting resistance by the VPA's 148th Independent Infantry Regiment and Vietnamese "volunteers" serving alongside Laotians in Communist Pathet Lao units. But Navarre signaled on April 22 that the airborne phase of the operation would have to be delayed, and Crèvecœur had to change his plans. He ordered Godard to leave his partisan troops behind to deceive the enemy, while the regular battalions headed east. This slower, less direct route to Điện Biên Phủ would accommodate a later linkup with the paratroops at Mường Nhà, a village near the Nậm Nứa River about 40km southeast of the Main Position. But on April 29, Godard had to halt his advance after Navarre advised that the airdrop would have to wait another seven or eight days. For reasons of morale, GONO's leadership let the rest of the garrison believe that the *Condor* force was just a few days away, though in fact there were never less than 80km of twisting mountain trails between the valley and Godard's foremost positions.[173]

Isabelle in April

Throughout April, CR Isabelle continued to perform its vital mission of firing artillery barrages around the Main Position. This required large quantities of ammunition, and Isabelle was not an easy target for supply planes because, even when flying just above stall speed, a Dakota would cross the entire perimeter in just two seconds. It accordingly took eight days to replace the 105mm shells expended between March 30 and April 1.[173] And since Isabelle's perimeter was so small, it was even more important to keep enemy trenches at a distance than at the Main Position. Fortunately for the defenders, the 57th

Regiment had no numerical advantage over them after the 888/176 departed in the second week of the month. On April 3, the garrison's total strength was about 1,600 (II/1 RTA (545), III/3 REI (426), V/7 RTA (116), II/10 RAC (116), and 410 Tai).[175] The 57th probably did not have 1,600 troops left and never fully encircled Isabelle. Its 346th Battalion was west of the river, while the 418th and 265th Battalions threatened Wieme from the northeast and southeast (respectively). However, the CR's southern flank remained open.[176]

The layout and numbering of Isabelle's strongpoints remains a mystery, as no two maps show them in the same places. Which units held which is also uncertain. By one account, II/1 RTA and III/3 REI were originally dispersed, side by side, among Isabelles 1 through 4. This would have allowed each battalion to sortie without requiring the other to redeploy to cover the vacated defensive sectors. But on April 8, II/1 RTA was evidently concentrated in the CR's eastern half (including the bridge strongpoint and Wieme), while III/3 REI was massed in the west. Yet, some veterans indicate that II/1 RTA was in the north and III/REI in the south. In any event, both battalions had absorbed troops from BT3's disbanded companies, and Lieutenant Wieme's Tai auxiliaries, 9/BT3 and V/7 RTA's remnants were in II/1 RTA's sector.[177]

Isabelle's tanks and infantry "aerated" trenches almost every day. II/1 RTA stumbled into a major battle when two of its companies went out with the Green Platoon and elements of V/7 RTA to fill in 300 meters of trench west of Isabelle on April 7. The mission was accomplished at the cost of 24 casualties (including nine officers and NCOs), but 50 enemy bodies were counted. Six days later, a "partially successful" sortie north of strongpoint Wieme cost the battalion another ten casualties, including two lieutenants. Since enemy pressure in this area was particularly strong, Colonel Lalande ordered troops of 9/BT3 to what was now known as the "airfield strongpoint." He reported that the entire company relieved Lieutenant Wieme's depleted CSMs, but Wieme himself insisted that only a single platoon was sent and that his auxiliaries remained in place. In any event, 9/BT3's commander, Captain Desire, was badly wounded while scouting the position and was replaced by Lieutenant Robert Siauve – who would be killed by a head wound on April 21.[178]

The fighting around Isabelle became increasingly costly during the second half of April, as practically every daylight sortie now triggered a battle and nighttime patrol clashes became legion. Mortars and ĐKZs deployed in the 57th Regiment's foremost trenches were a constant threat, and VPA snipers fired at anything that moved. *Bộ đội* would sometimes plant DRVN flags close to Isabelle's strongpoints at night so the defenders would be tempted to expose themselves trying to remove them. Giáp claims that the French eventually learned that it was best to leave the flags flying. The Green Platoon's Bisons continued to be an invaluable asset for the garrison, supporting sorties, intervening in crises, and daily "making the rounds" of the perimeter to destroy enemy bunkers. Generally, all three of its tanks were operational.[179]

On April 17, Colonel Lalande suggested that he facilitate a linkup with Operation *Condor* by establishing an outpost on Hill 944, which was located on the rim of the valley about 5km away.[180] Nothing came of this proposal, but Lalande was justifiably anxious for the siege to be broken, since the monsoon rains were making conditions on Isabelle truly desperate. Parachuting supplies and reinforcements became even more difficult, and before long the low-lying CR would be almost completely underwater. The garrison had its last warm meal on April 19 and temporarily ran out of food the next day.[181] And the daily drip of casualties was steadily eroding Lalande's manpower. On April 24, his infantry strength was just 1,400 (490 in II/1 RTA, 400 in III/3 REI, 140 in V/7 RTA, and 370 Tai).[182]

The deteriorating conditions on Isabelle strengthened the arguments of those who believed that the CR should be evacuated. Langlais, desperate for combat manpower on the Main Position, argued that at least one battalion be ordered to break through from Isabelle. De Castries disagreed, since he considered the flanking artillery barrages indispensable and feared that the CR could not survive if either II/1 RTA or III/3 REI was withdrawn.[183] He opposed having the entire garrison join the Main Position since III/10 RAC's 105s would have to be destroyed. General Cogny concurred, radioing on April 25 that abandoning Isabelle "does not seem desirable to me."[184]

The daily "grind" of aerating Isabelle's perimeter continued. On April 26, a four-platoon march company of II/1 RTA launched a dawn attack east of strongpoint Wieme. Encountering two trenches where the Deuxième Bureau had reported only one, the company was driven back by a VPA counterattack and lost six men killed and 22 wounded. Although it claimed to have killed 30 *bộ đội*, and captured a bazooka, a 60mm mortar, and several automatic rifles, Colonel Lalande was incensed by the repulse. Convinced that the Algerians were guilty of cowardice, he ordered that two men from each platoon be tried and executed by firing squad. Lieutenant Chiek Belabiche, commander of 8/II/1 RTA and one of the few African officers in the garrison, warned Lalande that his men would kill their French cadres if these orders were carried out. Unwilling to back down entirely, Lalande insisted that the court martial go ahead, but promised that all the accused would be acquitted. The charade was duly played out and a "civil war" inside Isabelle thus avoided.[185]

Since the start of the siege, aircraft flying over Isabelle at high altitude had been quite safe, because the only VPA flak weapons nearby were short-ranged antiaircraft machine guns. That changed on the night of April 26–27, when the 383rd AA Battalion's 816th Battery shifted its 37mm guns to a position northeast of Wieme so it could interdict the route French transport planes were using for night drops over the Main Position. Approaching Isabelle from the south, they would employ its runway as a reference point, then follow the river northward to CR Claudine. From its new position, the 816th Battery also threatened the airspace over Isabelle itself, and made supply drops there even more difficult. This was one reason why Isabelle received an average of just 348 105mm shells per day in late April, instead of the 1,700 it requested.[186]

Like the Algerians the day before, the Legionnaires of III/3 REI failed to aerate the trenches strangling Wieme on April 27 – though their repulse did not prompt a court martial. The battalion was supposed to receive a substantial number of replacements that night, but due to bad weather only a single "stick" of nine Legionnaires arrived. Another 63 jumped on the night of April 28–29 while two companies of III/3 REI and one from II/1 RTA guarded the drop zone south of Isabelle. Though this infusion of fresh troops boosted the garrison's morale, at 2225hrs on April 29, the 805th Howitzer, 112th Mortar, and 756th Mountain Batteries, and over a hundred 60mm and 81/82mm mortars started pummeling Isabelle. 75mm ĐKZs or mountain guns firing at point-blank range systematically destroyed Wieme's bunkers. Two Bisons rushed across the river to silence them, but Ratisbonne was knocked out by a pair of 105mm shellbursts and the enemy weapons remained in action. Colonel Lalande had been rotating "fresh" troops onto the exposed strongpoint at regular intervals, and on April 29 it was held by a march company of Algerians and Legionnaires commanded by Captain Botella of V/7 RTA. He and Lieutenant Jean Thymen were both wounded after their bunker collapsed. To escape the inferno, Wieme's defenders retreated to the western side of the strongpoint. This left the eastern face wide open to assault, but none came, though bộ đội cut three breaches in the barbed wire and pushed trenches into them.[187]

The eve of destruction

Anticipating the imminent capture of Huguette-1, on April 22 Giáp issued orders for another major offensive which would begin on May 1 (or "May Day" – international Communism's greatest holiday). To ensure its success, he brought up reinforcements from the 304th Division. Its 840th Artillery Battalion probably arrived by April 23, when the French detected several new 75mm howitzer batteries east of Isabelle.[188] The division's 9th Regiment was also ordered to the valley. To facilitate this move, the 57th Regiment was to send a reinforced company to replace the 400th Battalion's 83rd Company at the Tây Trang border crossing 15km south-southwest of Isabelle and prepare to rush an entire battalion there if the *Condor* force broke through. By way of compensation, it would receive the 938th Battalion from the 316th Division.[189]

VPA flak at Điện Biên Phủ was also reinforced. During the last week of April, the entire 381st Antiaircraft Battalion shifted into the valley from the supply lines, raising the number of 37mm antiaircraft guns to nearly three-dozen – an increase of more than 50 percent. By the night of April 30, its 811th and 812th Batteries were in position just north of Huguette-6 and Dominique-2 (respectively), while the 813th was emplaced near Bản Ta Po on the right bank of the Nậm Yum level with Béatrice. With the 396th Flak Battalion deployed west of the Main Position, the 383rd Flak Battalion to the east, and the detached 816th Battery covering the approach from Isabelle, what remained of the main DZ was now boxed in on all sides by heavy antiaircraft guns.[190]

In addition, VPA firepower was boosted by two brand-new artillery battalions that were hastily established in the field using personnel drawn from the 45th and 675th Artillery Regiments and novel weapons that had just arrived from China. One (whose numerical designation is not given) was armed with a dozen 75mm ĐKZs. Since VPA gunners were already familiar with 57mm ĐKZs, they quickly learned how to use these new weapons. Giáp's orders of April 22 directed that the 308th and 312th Divisions each be given four of them, while the 316th Division and 57th Regiment got two apiece. The 312th deployed its 75mm ĐKZs on the hills of Dominique, and one was in action against French tanks as early as April 24. Other units deployed theirs in the foremost trenches so French bunkers could be engaged at point-blank range.[191]

The second new battalion was equipped with a dozen multiple rocket launchers which Western historians usually describe as "Katyushas" – the nickname given to Russian MRLs of World War II. Yet, these towed, sextuple 102mm weapons were Chinese Type-506s manufactured at Military Factory 724 in Shenyang Province during 1953.[192] At full strength the new 224th Rocket Artillery Battalion (so designated because it was formed on April 22) would have three batteries of six "H6" (*Hỏa tiễn 6 nòng* – "rocket 6-barrel") launchers apiece. But although the crews were rushed through an abbreviated training program lasting only a week, just two batteries would be ready in time to participate in the last 48 hours of the siege. And the gunners had learned only the rudiments of operating their new weapons. Chinese advisors would be responsible for tactics, and aiming and firing the rockets.[193] Before the new battalion was formed, the advisors brought a launcher up to Điện Biên Phủ and gave Giáp a firing demonstration which ignited a forest fire. This incident probably occurred on the night of April 21, when a Dakota flying 5km east of the valley was bracketed by what the pilot thought was a salvo of antiaircraft rockets.[194]

Having learned the hard way how effective the flanking artillery barrages from Isabelle were, Giáp decided to devote half of his 105s to silencing its batteries during the new offensive. The 805th Battery, deployed in the mountains northeast of Isabelle, had done little but fire counterbattery missions on III/10 RAC's positions since the siege began. Now it would be joined by the 801st and 802nd Batteries, which shifted down into newly built casemates west of Isabelle. New emplacements were also being constructed near Françoise for a pair of 105s from the 803rd Battery. When in position, these guns would be able to fire directly at GONO headquarters from less than 2km away.[195]

Yet Giáp's artillery was still incapable of destroying the underground bunkers on Eliane-2, which rumor had inflated to epic proportions. Many *bộ đội* believed that the entire hill was honeycombed with tunnels, and some even claimed there was one big enough to accommodate tanks running all the way down to the Nậm Yum! The 316th Division's chief intelligence officer, Bùi Xuân Linh, knew this was nonsense since intercepted radio messages proved that French troops making their way to Eliane-2 were being hit by VPA shells. But his superiors insisted that patrols be sent out night after night to find the entrances to this non-existent passage and many elite *trinh sát* personnel were lost. These casualties and much demoralizing rumormongering could have been avoided if anyone had bothered to interview *bộ đội* who had visited Eliane-2 while it was in friendly hands the year before. Some had even been billeted in the bunkers![196]

In mid-April, the 316th Division decided to resort to another World War I tactic by digging a mineshaft under Eliane-2's summit so the bunkers could be blown up from below. The mission was given to the 151st Engineer Regiment's

25-strong 83rd Special Engineer Company, which normally disarmed unexploded ordnance. On the night of April 16, five engineers started tunneling from a trench on the Champs-Élysées, but Legionnaires just 25 meters away detected this activity and wounded four of them with (rifle?) grenades. Since intense shelling prevented digging on the next three nights, work only began in earnest on April 20. Men could spend no more than an hour in the meter-square shaft before they passed out from oxygen deprivation. Candles could not be used for the same reason, and the diggers labored in darkness until a senior officer donated a flashlight to the company commander, Nguyễn Phú Xuyên. The project understandably progressed slowly and would not be completed (after a fashion) until May 6.[197]

The torrential downpours of late April threatened to derail the new offensive before it even began. Giáp recalled, "I worried every time I saw a dark cloud over the mountains or a flash of lightning. We had made every preparation to fight through the rainy season. But it would be best if we could seal the enemy's fate before the rains truly began."[198] But the siege had dragged on, forcing VPA troops to live and fight in a waterlogged landscape. Digging tunnels for "creeping siege" assaults became increasingly difficult and VPA trenches opposite Claudine and Huguettes-4 and -5 were almost completely submerged. Worse yet, the rains proved far more destructive to the crude supply roads than French bombing, and greatly increased wear and tear on trucks which were already breaking down in considerable numbers after months of incessant use without proper maintenance. The flow of supplies to the front began to sputter, and Giáp noted with alarm that on one day in late April just a single metric ton of rice was delivered to the valley. Desperate measures had to be taken to keep the troops fed.

> We could not rely only on the Central Supply Council and the Strategic Logistics Supply Service, which the campaign's demands had already overtaxed. The various units worked to resolve such problems on their own. The divisions' logistics departments organized pack bicycles to transport salted meat, salted vegetables, sugar, milk, tobacco, and cigarettes from their rear bases in the Midlands or Northern Delta. The regiments' logistics departments sent supply teams to various hamlets to collect vegetables, especially kale, which the H'Mong ethnic minority people often planted with their opium poppies. Troops dug up yams in the forests and gathered forest greens along the streams. Regiment and battalion cadre signed

receipts to buy buffaloes from the local population, with the accounts to be settled after the campaign.[199]

Artillery shells were also in very short supply, and VPA gunners had to strictly curtail ammunition consumption in late April so that stocks could be built up before May 1. To maintain pressure on GONO during this period, Giáp circulated a "Letter Calling on Soldiers on the Dien Bien Phu Battlefield to Promote the Sniping of Enemy Troops" on April 22. It ordered machine-gun, mortar, and artillery crews to emulate the tactics of infantry snipers by patiently targeting the enemy with precisely aimed single shots. "Each shot should kill an enemy soldier!"[200]

Relief for the shell crisis was already on the way, however, in the form of an ammunition convoy that set out from the Chinese border on April 17. It was ordered to travel even in daylight, given top priority at ferry crossings, and authorized to make the trip to the front without halting at any of the intermediate logistical way stations (as all other convoys had to). It arrived at Điện Biên Phủ on April 25. Yet while VPA official histories assert that this single convoy relieved the ammunition crisis by "providing a timely resupply of artillery shells to meet the campaign's requirements"[201] it's hard to see how it could have since it comprised just a dozen trucks! The Deuxième Bureau estimated that it carried 4,000 105mm shells, 3,000 75mm shells, 1,600 120mm shells, 1,000 rockets, and another thousand shells of unspecified calibers[202] – which would have required far more vehicles. But these figures were likely inflated, since they suggest that over a third of the 120mm mortar shells and four-fifths of the 75mm howitzer shells allocated during the entire siege (see table, Chapter 2) arrived just a dozen days before it ended. And although the Chinese had scraped together another 7,400 105mm shells, none of them arrived in time.[203]

Giáp was also confronted by a morale crisis in late April. All his infantry regiments, and many artillery batteries, had been decimated in the fighting since March 30. The infantry losses were being made good with new draftees, but these poorly trained, novice soldiers were no match for the battle-hardened veterans they replaced, and *esprit de corps* and tactical proficiency suffered accordingly. Morale was also eroded by battle fatigue and poor living conditions. The Front Military Committee had already begun a "Three Wells" campaign (Eat Well, Sleep Well, Fight Well) to improve health and living conditions on the front line,[204] but achieving its aims became increasingly difficult as the torrential rains of late April produced knee-deep mud even in relatively well-drained trenches on the eastern hills.

The most significant factor degrading VPA morale was, however, the apparent lack of progress in the siege. After the rapid successes of March 13–17 and March 30–April 3, VPA troops had expected that final victory was just around the corner. Yet, only two strongpoints had been taken since April 3 while another had been lost, yielding a net gain of just one strongpoint in nearly three weeks of ceaseless and costly battles. Since most *bộ đội* did not realize how decisive their victory in the battle for Huguette had been, Giáp worried that they might not attack with sufficient ardor during the upcoming offensive. He recalled, "it was precisely at this time that a *rightist and negative tendency* [emphasis in original] appeared among our officers and men, in various forms: fear of casualties, losses, fatigue, difficulties and hardships, underestimation of the enemy, subjectivism and self-conceit."[205] To remedy these errors, the Front Military Committee summoned all departmental, divisional, and regimental political officers to a conference on April 27 that launched "a campaign for moral mobilization and 'rectification' of Rightist tendencies."[206] This would be integrated with an "emulation campaign" that would last from International Labor Day on May 1 to Hồ Chí Minh's birthday on May 19. The 316th Division launched a supplementary campaign marking the third anniversary of its establishment on May 1, 1951. The commissars returned to their units on April 29 to indoctrinate the rank and file.[207]

CHAPTER 8

GIÁP'S FINAL OFFENSIVES

The mood of GONO's defenders at the end of April was grim, but defiant. On the 30th, they had an "emulation campaign" of their own in the form of the Foreign Legion's annual celebration of the legendary 1863 Battle of Camerone. Fought during Napoleon III's ill-fated effort to install the puppet "Emperor" Maximilian as ruler of Mexico, the battle pitted a 65-man convoy escort against 2,000 Republican Mexican troops. Surrounded in a walled hacienda, the Legionnaires fought to the death and when the last six men ran out of ammunition, they fixed bayonets and charged their astounded foes. The Foreign Legion made the anniversary of this incident its greatest holiday, which features feasting, a recitation of the grim tale, and the honorary induction of a few non-Legionnaires into the ranks. At Điện Biên Phủ, this honor was granted to de Castries, Langlais, Bigeard, and the stranded nurse Geneviève de Galard, who had won accolades for her cheerful and tireless labors in the hellish, overcrowded charnel house that was GONO's main hospital. Indeed, on April 29 she had been awarded the Légion d'honneur. Yet the Legionnaires had a sparse feast, since the whole garrison went on half rations the day before, and most had to do without the traditional wine and blood sausage.[1]

Giáp expected the defenders to fight to the bitter end and planned accordingly, sticking to the cautious Steady Attack–Steady Advance formula. The new offensive starting on May 1 did not even aim to complete GONO's destruction.

Instead, Giáp planned to conduct a sequence of meticulously planned assaults and "creeping sieges" that would finally achieve the objectives of the March 30 offensive and further tighten the encirclement.

[T]he High Command has decided that between 1 May and 5 May the mission of Phase 2 must be basically completed, meaning the destruction of a number of additional eastern hill positions and of a number of western strong-points to achieve our goal of totally cutting off the delivery of enemy reinforcements and supplies. During the next five days, from 6 to 10 May, the primary mission will be to strengthen and consolidate the positions that have been captured, move our siege positions in closer, organize our heavy weapons firepower to gain control of the airspace, conduct destructive shelling of the enemy's central position, and conduct increased small operations and efforts to seize enemy supplies in preparations for attacking the enemy's central position.[2]

Only after this operational pause would a fourth offensive finish off GONO once and for all. And even the third offensive would be conducted slowly and incrementally, since it was divided into two sub-phases. A series of preliminary assaults on May 1 would pave the way for a second wave of attacks extending from May 2 to May 5. The specific missions for May 1 were:

- The 308th Division was to prepare to take Huguette-5. If conditions were not ripe to seize the strongpoint on May 1, the division was to subject it to an "aggressive siege."
- The 312th Division would capture the rest of Dominique-3, and use its infantry and heavy weapons to block the movement of enemy reinforcements toward Eliane-1.
- The 316th Division would capture Eliane-1, defend it against counterattacks, and mount a "creeping siege" against Eliane-4.
- The 304th Division was to "mount aggressive attacks" on Isabelle and suppress its artillery.
- The 351st Division's missions were unchanged, except that it would also be "responsible for coordinating with the infantry during the attacks on the strong-points and during battles against enemy counterattacks on the night of the attacks and during the following day."[3]

This new mission highlighted the importance attached to defeating counterattacks. Giáp knew from bitter experience how small bodies of paras and Legionnaires supported by tanks could rob him of the fruits of hard-won victories – and even turn them into bloodbaths. He would tolerate no recurrence of the errors of a month before, when VPA commanders had often been taken aback by counterattacks. All units "must prepare plans to fight off enemy counterattacks at night and during the day after they overrun a position; they must prepare a plan to repair and improve enemy fortifications in order to hold and defend the position; and they must have prepared a plan to take the position a second time if the enemy should retake it."[4] Repelling counterattacks also became the primary mission of all heavy weapons units, which were to pre-register targets along routes French reinforcements were likely to take. Yet destroying and suppressing French artillery would also be a priority, and Giáp noted that "firing methods must be changed and the previous pattern must be changed, temporarily at least." What he had in mind was a greater emphasis on counterbattery missions, but it would be difficult for VPA gunners to accomplish all their assigned tasks, since "All units must monitor ammunition usage, [and] economize on the expenditure of ammunition."[5]

"We will win the battle without you and in spite of you"

Colonel Vaillant's staff nonetheless estimated that 800 105mm, 500 120mm, 400 81/82mm and 100–300 75mm shells were fired at GONO on April 30 – almost certainly an exaggeration (at least with respect the calibers of the incoming shells).[6] In addition, several VPA infantry regiments "jumped the gun" by launching ground assaults. Shortly after 0600hrs, Dominique-3 was suddenly rushed by a party of bộ đội who struck without artillery preparation. The coup de main failed and 20 of the attackers were killed, but 3/6 BPC nonetheless had to reinforce Dominique-3 during a rainstorm that same night to help repulse a more conventional assault.[7]

Huguette-5 was also attacked on April 30. During the afternoon, several Bisons had dueled with the 754th Mountain Battery – which occupied new casemates just 50 meters from the strongpoint's outermost barbed wire – and killed one of its gun captains.[8] But if the mountain guns were knocked out, it wasn't for long, since they were back in action again before midnight targeting

8/BMEP (the survivors of 2 BEP's 6th and 8th Companies) on Huguette-5. By 0200hrs, the 88th Regiment had penetrated the perimeter from the southwest. Supported by two Bisons, Captain Luciani's 4/BMEP (the remnants of 1 BEP's 1st and 4th Companies) counterattacked from Huguette-3. The interlopers were ejected, but rallied and pierced the perimeter a second time while others tried to sever the communications trenches east of Huguette-5. Langlais fed a company of I/2 REI into the battle at 0600hrs, and the perimeter was cleared in bitter fighting that lasted until 1000hrs. The battle had cost the BMEP a dozen killed, 68 wounded, and eight missing – an entire company. 8th Company's survivors were relieved by Luciani's troops, though they too had suffered heavily.[9]

The victories at Dominique-3 and Huguette-5 did little to lift the spirits of GONO's leaders. They knew that another major offensive was imminent, and the pitiless equations of their logistical and personnel staffs proved that GONO could not survive it. The garrison had weathered Giáp's second offensive due to massive ammunition expenditures, sizeable reserves, and the fact that its battalions generally still had strengths over 500. None of these conditions now applied. Thanks to the return of the CAT pilots and good weather during the daylight hours of April 30 and May 1, there were now 14,000 105mm shells, 5,000 120mm shells, and 275 155mm shells on hand. These were riches that VPA gunners could only dream of, but experience had taught the French that they would be expended within 48 hours during a major offensive. And once that happened, poor weather, flak, and an ever-shrinking drop zone would ensure that Colonel Vaillant's gunners never again had an adequate supply of shells.[10]

The personnel situation was even worse. Between April 17 and the morning of May 1, GONO had lost 1,537 men killed, seriously wounded or captured, and received just 783 replacements. Langlais blamed Colonel Sauvagnac for this dismal balance sheet and on the afternoon of May 1 again demanded immediately reinforcement by another full-strength battalion. He concluded, "We will win the battle without you and in spite of you. This message, copy of which [sic] I shall transmit to all airborne battalion commanders here, will be the last I shall address to you."[11] Langlais' vitriol is excusable since most of his battalions now had combat strengths of little more than 300. And all the defenders were physically and psychologically exhausted by hunger, sleep deprivation, and incessant combat stress. For while many VPA units were at least briefly withdrawn from the trenches to rest and absorb replacements, there was no respite for the defenders.

But the chief reason why Langlais wanted 1 BPC was because GONO's reserves had been gutted. The dozen strong reserve companies that had given him the confidence to retake Eliane-1 on April 10 had withered away to just five weak ones by April 25[12] and had shrunk even further by the end of the month. To put this in perspective, one should recall that five companies had reinforced Eliane-2 alone on the night of March 30–31. The failure to drop in 1 BPC before the end of April meant that the Main Position would have only about four weak companies' worth of reserves for its entire perimeter when the storm broke on May 1. Whether withholding the battalion was the correct decision or not, responsibility for it rested with Cogny (and indirectly, Navarre), not Sauvagnac.

In the past, the Bisons had often tipped the scales in favor of weak counterattacks, but by now the tank squadron was operating at barely half strength. As we have seen, Ratisbonne was damaged on April 29 and would take some time to repair. That same day, Douaumont was hit by a 105mm shell and permanently immobilized. It was towed to Huguette-3 where, like Conti and Bazeilles, it would serve as a static bunker. Since Smolensk had been out of action since early April due to transmission trouble, this left the Main Position with just three mobile tanks. Mulhouse was in reasonably good shape, but both Ettlingen and Posen had turret damage that considerably reduced their combat effectiveness (one could not rotate). And all the remaining tanks were experiencing frequent main gun breakdowns due to recoil system failures and excessive barrel wear.[13]

The May Day offensive

VPA gunners opened the May Day festivities with a bombardment that lasted three hours and focused much of its fury on the opposing batteries. Five of Isabelle's 11 105s were put out of action that night.[14] When the fireworks ended, troops of the 36th Regiment overran part of Lily-3 (probably its long southern extension) and infiltrated into the communications trenches behind it. However, this appears to have merely been a diversion, and by 0600hrs Lily's small reserves had cleaned up the penetration and exterminated the infiltrators.[15] The 308th Division's main effort that night targeted Huguette-5, which was hit by the 88th Regiment's 29th and 322nd Battalions. The strongpoint's obstacles had been breached the night before, enemy trenches were just 20–30 meters away, and the defenders were greatly outnumbered – though not as badly as indicated by some Western historians who believe that Captain Luciani commanded only 30 men that night. The actual number was double that since Lieutenant Pierre Jauze had led about another 30 troops to Huguette-5's western bastion earlier in the day. Interestingly, the 88th Regiment's official history indicates there were at least 140 defenders![16]

The preparatory bombardment, in which the 806th Howitzer Battery played a leading role, left Huguette-5 leaderless.[17] For, in a replay of the disasters at Béatrice and Gabrielle, a shell destroyed the headquarters bunker and seriously wounded both Luciani and his executive officer, Lieutenant Alain de Stabenrath. This blow decapitated the strongpoint and each of its three bastions was left to fight on in isolation. The 88th Regiment's pioneers began breaching the wire at 2100hrs, following paths that had been marked in advance with pieces of white parachute cord to ensure they stayed on course in the darkness.[18] The sprawling perimeter was swiftly penetrated, and many of Lieutenant Jauze's troops were captured by bộ đội who fell upon them from behind. Yet the remaining Legion paras grimly fought on, and around midnight Major Guiraud ordered Captain Michel Brandon's 2/BMEP (the remnants of 1 BEP's 2nd and 3rd Companies) and a party of I/2 REI troops to reinforce them. It was to no avail, however, since the reinforcements were pinned down by small-arms and artillery fire, and never reached the strongpoint. By 0200hrs, all of Huguette-5 was in enemy hands and only a couple of dozen escapees linked up with Brandon's troops, who soon fell back. The BMEP lost 18 killed, five wounded, and 14 missing, including Luciani and Jauze. The badly wounded de Stabenrath was dragged to safety by his radioman, but would die in captivity on May 12.[19]

Over in the Five Hills, the 316th Division attacked both Elianes-1 and -2, but the latter operation was merely intended to drive the defenders away from the entrance to the still-incomplete mineshaft.[20] The French had discovered the tunnel's existence and repeatedly tried to destroy it with explosives during swift trench raids. These all failed, but the troops of I/13 DBLE (which had taken over the defense of Eliane-2 about a week before) constantly interfered with the work.[21] On the night of May 1, the 174th Regiment captured two bunkers on the Champs-Élysées and destroyed several more with 75mm ĐKZs, pushing the Legionnaires back beyond hand-grenade range from the entrance. It also tried to eliminate the main underground bunker with a "death volunteer" draped in parachute cloth who allowed himself to be captured in hopes of being led up to the summit. Béatrice survivor Sergeant Simon Kubiak of 10/III/13 DBLE (which was also deployed on Eliane-2) spotted explosives strapped to the man's body under his ghostly shroud and foiled the bizarre scheme. Over the coming days, a stream of death volunteers would try unsuccessfully to destroy the summit bunker and another under the mangled banyan tree atop Mannequin Hillock.[22]

The 98th Regiment had made meticulous preparations to capture Eliane-1; it even rehearsed the assault on a full-scale reproduction of the French defenses. The position was held by II/1 RCP, which rotated its three weak companies on and off the deadly hilltop every 48 hours. On the night of May 1, Lieutenant Yves Périou's 1st Company held the summit, with Lieutenant René Leguéré's 3rd Company in reserve in the communications trenches running back to Eliane-4. On the other side of the hill, the 888th Battalion's 811th Company fell back 200 meters to avoid being hit by the preparatory bombardment. Since the 804th Howitzer Battery was allotted just 30 shells for this crucial fire mission, two guns of the 752nd Mountain Battery firing down from Dominique-2 may have caused more damage. The 811th attacked at 2330hrs, but was halted by a flamethrower that was firing into its breach through the barbed wire. The impasse was broken when the 439th Battalion's 1480th Company launched a flank attack from the direction of Honeycomb Hill (brushing aside 5 BVPN's *sonnette* if it was still in place).[23]

Périou's paras were reinforced by Leguéré's and then by a detachment of 2/II/1 RCP that was sent up at 2200hrs, though these reinforcements had to pass through a barrage that the 804th Howitzer Battery was laying across the saddle from Eliane-4. The defenders also benefited from the support of Ettlingen and Mulhouse, which rushed over to Eliane-10, but the tanks could accomplish little after the battle degenerated into a close-quarters melee in which the enemy's superior numbers eventually proved decisive. Vietnamese historians claim that Eliane-1 fell within 60 minutes, but, according to French documents, the fighting lasted until 0200hrs, when the few survivors were ordered to retreat. Only 17 of 1st Company's troops escaped; the other 97 were killed or captured, and Lieutenant Périou was among the slain. Since 3rd Company had been reduced to just 25 men (Leguéré was badly wounded in the head) and 2nd Company's detachment also took losses, II/1 RCP was mostly destroyed that night.[24] *Bộ đội* following close on the heels of the retreating Chasseurs Parachutistes probed Eliane-4's defenses. The situation was so complex and confusing that GONO radioed several situation updates which falsely indicated that it too had fallen.[25]

Meanwhile, Dominique-3 was under attack by the 312th Division, which, like all the others, had formed "honor units" from headquarters and staff units to keep its combat troops supplied and evacuate the wounded. Only the strongpoint's two southern sub-positions were still in French hands, and had been garrisoned by the remnants of III/3 RTA since early April, joined on April 20 by 5/BT2. Since both units were exhausted and understrength (the Tai company had just 40–50 men left out of its original 200), Langlais decided to relieve them before nightfall on May 1. Lieutenant de la Malène's 5/BT2 switched places with 8/BT2 on Eliane-12,[26] while the Algerians redeployed to Eliane-4 and were replaced by 3/6 BPC. One Algerian platoon was left behind, however, because VPA artillery harassment delayed its relief. The incoming para commander, Lieutenant Robert Perret, was appalled by the poor state of the fortifications.[27]

VPA artillery began shelling Dominique-3 at 1630hrs, and 75mm ĐKZs proved particularly destructive. Bernard Fall suggests that they were emplaced in tunnels bored straight through the hills of Dominique,[28] but this was not true. The VPA dug only one deep tunnel during the siege – the Eliane-2 mineshaft – and the difficulties and delays encountered there prove that it would have been impossible for others to have been dug elsewhere. And, of course, had it been done, Vietnamese historians would have celebrated the feat. "Creeping siege" tunnels were much simpler affairs. Typically dug less than a meter underground, it was far easier to light and ventilate them, and remove the spoil, and many sections were, in truth, merely covered trenches. They could be constructed so quickly that the 36th Regiment had to erect signposts in junctions so its troops could find their way around the rapidly expanding tunnel network.

Tunnels had been dug before the final assault on Eliane-1, though it's unlikely they penetrated its perimeter. Others may have been present around Dominique-3, but here too the May 1 attack seems to have been a more conventional affair than the stealthy assault on Huguette-1. The 209th Regiment struck at 1930hrs, sending its 154th Battalion against the southeast bastion and the 166th Battalion against the southwestern one. Unfortunately, the regiment's official history only details the latter unit's operations. Its failure to address the 154th Battalion's operations during the closing days of the siege was debated in the pages of *Tạp chí Lịch sử Quân sự* (*Military History Magazine* – an official publication of the Vietnamese Defense Ministry) back in 2004–05.[29]

All accounts agree that the defenders bloodily repulsed the first assault, thanks to accurate artillery barrages and supporting fire from Elianes-10 and -12. A second attack at 2000hrs also went awry, and it was only after several pauses to reorganize that the 166th Battalion's 606th and 618th Companies finally entered the perimeter at 2045hrs. But the defenders disputed every inch of ground in savage close-quarters fighting.[30] Giáp admitted, "A company of the 6th Foreign Legion [sic] Parachute Battalion and units of Algerian and Tai soldiers ... put up a fierce resistance. We had to wrestle with the enemy to take each gun nest and every trench."[31] The battle was so fierce that Lieutenant Perret risked ordering Dominique-3's mortars to fire on his own troops' positions even though he knew their fortifications were weak. The gamble paid off since the exposed *bộ đội* suffered heavy casualties while the defenders sheltered in their bunkers.[32]

The 166th Battalion committed two more companies (including one from the 209th Regiment's 130th Battalion) at 2137hrs. Lieutenant Perret also requested reinforcements, and Major Chenel dipped deep into his meager reserves, committing Lieutenant de la Malène's 5/BT2 and a platoon of 2/6 BPC to the battle. When de la Malène neared Dominique-3, he found the communications trench clogged with defenders who had been pushed back from the strongpoint and ordered his men into the open to counterattack *bộ đội* just 30 meters away. They recaptured his old command post but took many casualties, and de la Malène himself was wounded twice. Major Thomas sent the rest of 2/6 BPC (which had a total strength of just 57), but it arrived after Dominique-3 had fallen at 0200hrs, and was ordered back to Eliane-10. The outnumbered defenders had stood their ground for more than six hours and inflicted severe casualties on their foes. The 166th Battalion alone had 40 men killed and 55 wounded.[33] The defending units were nearly wiped out, and both Lieutenant Perret and 8/BT's commander, Lieutenant Louis Pagès, were captured, though the latter soon escaped. 5/BT2's executive officer, Lieutenant Jacques Daussy, rallied the company's survivors and established a blocking position in the communications trench north of Eliane-12. Lieutenant Gérard Richard did the same with 8/BT2's escapees in the trench leading to Eliane-10.[34]

While battles were raging all around the Main Position, down at the other end of the valley, strongpoint Wieme was assaulted by the 57th Regiment's 418th Battalion while the 265th Battalion's 18th Company feinted against Isabelle proper from the southwest. Wieme was held by a mixed bag of Algerians from II/1 RTA and V/7 RTA, and a composite platoon of Legionnaires. Although breaches had been opened in the strongpoint's barbed wire the night before, the 418th Battalion's primary attack, made from the northeast by its

60th Company, stalled in front of uncleared obstacles. The defenders had done what they could to seal the breaches, but the chief problem was that the pioneers had veered off course and expended all their Bangalores without penetrating the innermost entanglement. A secondary attack from the southeast was also pinned down because its trenches ended too far from the perimeter. 60th Company finally broke into Wieme after Squad Leader Vệ threw a blanket over the last strands of barbed wire and then charged into the strongpoint. Inspired by Ve (who was promoted to platoon leader on the spot) *bộ đội* poured through the narrow gap and drove the small band of defenders back, step by step, until the entire position was captured shortly before 0400hrs. The few survivors retreated across RP41 to the "bridge strongpoint" on the eastern bank of the Nậm Yum.[35]

It had been a disastrous night for GONO. Four strongpoints were gone, the remaining Five Hill positions were now completely outflanked, and 331 men had been killed or gone missing, and another 158 wounded – the equivalent of an entire battalion (though none of those at Điện Biên Phủ had so many men left).[36] Even before he knew the final butcher's bill, de Castries radioed "No more reserves left. Fatigue and wear and tear on the units terrible. Supplies and ammunition insufficient. Quite difficult to resist one more such push by Communists, at least without bringing in one brand-new battalion of excellent quality."[37] On April 22, a half-dozen C-124 "Globemasters" of the US Air Force's 62nd Troop Carrier Wing had landed in Da Nang carrying 514 French troops who had been airlifted directly from France in a four-day-long odyssey. Among them were about 350 troops of the newly established 7 BPC who had just completed jump school. However, the battalion would need several weeks to coalesce into an effective combat unit and assimilate its many Indochinese personnel, including two ANV parachute companies. The equally new 3 BEP would have the same problem, and its 408 European troops would not arrive in Indochina until May 7 on a second wave of American "Operation Blue Star" aircraft.[38] Thus, the only "battalion of excellent quality" immediately available was Captain Guy de Bazin de Bezons' 1 BPC, and Cogny decided to start dropping it in that very night.

Having refused to provide another battalion in late March when it might have decisively tipped the scales, or even in late April to rebuild Langlais' reserves before the current offensive began, why did Cogny send one to certain destruction now? We don't know for sure, but he probably hoped that 1 BPC would enable GONO to hold out long enough to be saved by the diplomats in

Geneva. Then again, Cogny may have feared that his reputation would suffer even more if he denied aid to GONO when its commanders were filling the historical record with angry denunciations of those who refused to send reinforcements. If so, Cogny's action was inexcusable, since it would have been more humane to drop 1 BPC straight into one of the VPA's infamous prison camps and spare its men several days of deadly, but futile, combat and many hellish weeks of marching into captivity.

The (mostly) missing offensive of May 2–5

Giáp expected that the French would try to retake the lost strongpoints on May 2, and may have anticipated a major counteroffensive like that of March 31. Yet although his troops on Eliane-1, Dominique-3, and Huguette-5 furiously girded themselves for the French riposte, it never came. The battles of the two preceding nights had eliminated a company of 6 BPC, and a pair each from the BMEP, II/1 RCP and BT2, and attrited many other units, completely depleting the Main Position's reserves. All Langlais could do that morning was to have the Bisons on Eliane-10 pound the enemy-occupied heights (especially a new VPA base of fire on Honeycomb Hill), though Ettlingen had to do most of the work to spare Muhouse's worn-out main gun. After Ettlingen withdrew to resupply with ammunition, Mulhouse climbed up onto Eliane-4 to gain a better firing position. VPA observers may have mistaken this for the start of a counterattack.[39]

Only CR Isabelle had sufficient reserves to counterattack, and Colonel Lalande launched one at 0500hrs, just an hour after strongpoint Wieme was lost. This gave the 418/57 no time to reorganize itself or rebuild the shattered defenses before shells from the Main Position's batteries began raining down. When the barrage lifted, Captain Bernard Fournier's 11/III/3 REI, a platoon of II/1 RTA, and the Green Platoon attacked from the bridge strongpoint. By 1600hrs, they had ejected the enemy from Wieme at a cost of five killed and 24 wounded (including Fournier); Isabelle's overall losses for May 2 were nine killed, 42 wounded, and two missing. The fleeing enemy left behind many corpses, four prisoners, and large quantities of weaponry. Yet Wieme's flimsy defenses had been so thoroughly smashed by friendly and enemy shells, grenades, satchel charges, and bangalores that Lalande decided there was no point installing a new garrison. Instead the strongpoint would be held only as a *sonnette*.[40]

One might expect that the success of the May Day assaults and the absence of French counterattacks on the Main Position's lost strongpoints would have prompted Giáp to accelerate the pace of his offensive, but in fact, the exact opposite happened. The orders he issued back on April 22 had designated the following objectives for the period of May 2–5: [41]

- The 308th Division was to capture Lily-3 while simultaneously using "creeping siege" tactics against Claudine-5.
- The 312th Division would overrun Dominique-4 and the artillery positions south of it.
- The 316th Division would capture the underground bunkers on Eliane-2, defend them, conduct siege operations against Eliane-4, and overrun it if conditions were favorable.
- The 304th Division was to suppress Isabelle's artillery, employ "creeping siege" tactics against strongpoint Wieme, and overrun it if conditions were favorable.
- The 351st Division's missions were the same as those for May 1.

As it turned out, only the first of these objectives would be attained on schedule, and no serious attempt was made to achieve any of the others by May 5. Since no Vietnamese author addresses this anomaly, one can only speculate about its causes. The likeliest explanation is that Giáp drafted his plans before the rainy season had arrived in full force and he did not realize just how much it would disrupt his overstretched supply lines. And the clear skies that had prevailed on April 30 and May 1 were succeeded by several days of heavy downpours that caused even more disruption. It's also safe to assume that the lengthy bombardments of April 29 to May 1 had seriously depleted VPA ammo dumps – especially if the 351st Division's gunners were dependent on the one convoy of April 25 (and misdropped French shells) to keep their howitzers and heavy mortars in action. If so, a pause would have been necessary to allow additional shipments to arrive. Finally, the assault on Eliane-2 had to be delayed because the mineshaft still had not been finished and the 174th Regiment's "death volunteers" were probably a desperate gambit to get back on schedule.

The return of bad weather on May 2 also intensified GONO's logistical difficulties, since more and more planes aborted their missions or misdropped their cargoes. On most days, pilots had to "fly blind" through the mountains while being buffeted by heavy winds and rain, and then plunge down through thick overcast to find the valley. Armée de l'Air Dakotas successfully completed all 17 missions flown on May 2, but just 18 of 25 attempted on May 3, and 16 of 29 on May 4. The American CAT pilots were no less brave or skillful, but were dropping from high altitude and, as mercenaries, did not have the same sense of commitment to their employer's cause. Thus, only 14 out of 34 C-119 missions flown on May 1 dropped their loads inside the perimeter, an appallingly low two out of 30 on May 2, and seven out of 34 on May 3. And as if things weren't bad enough already, on May 1 it was the turn of French civilian pilots to refuse to continue flying to Điện Biên Phủ, and their "strike" would last several days at the worst possible time.[42]

Only 107 men of Lieutenant Marcel Edme's 2/1 BPC jumped in on the night of May 2. As usual, the latest newspapers came with them, revealing that a highly placed source at FTNV headquarters had told journalists that GONO was unlikely to survive more than a few days. Navarre rightly suspected that Cogny himself was responsible for the leak, and launched a formal investigation that brought relations between the two generals to a new low. Yet Navarre himself had ordered FTNV to plan a breakout from Điện Biên Phủ, although this was a desperate option that could be considered only as a last resort when GONO was on the verge of being overrun. Code-named *Albatros*, this operation would have sacrificed most of the garrison to give 2,000–3,000 paras and Legionnaires a slim chance of piercing the siege lines and linking up with the *Condor* force. Cogny opposed *Albatros* because he believed the underfed and exhausted defenders were physically incapable of making a fighting withdrawal over the mountains, and feared the retreat would degenerate into an unseemly rout. It was better, he thought, to fight to the end at Điện Biên Phủ and tie down Giáp's divisions as long as possible. In any case, Lieutenant-Colonel Godard's partisan troops, who would have to infiltrate north to screen the retreat and guide the escapees to safety, could not be in place until May 20![43]

Navarre flew to Hanoi on May 3 to meet with Cogny and Colonel de Crèvecœur. Although relations between the two principal players could not have been more poisonous, Navarre concurred with Cogny's decision to send 1 BPC to Điện Biên Phủ. He had no illusions that the battalion would turn the tide of battle, but hoped that it might allow GONO to hold out until the Geneva Conference produced a ceasefire. The two generals also agreed that if the worst came to the worst and GONO had to end its resistance to avoid a futile bloodbath, honor demanded that there be no formal act of surrender. They could not reach consensus, however, on Operation *Albatros*, and "passed the buck" to de Castries by authorizing him to attempt a breakout at his own discretion.[44]

GONO's personnel situation was so desperate that a call went out to the teeming hospitals asking lightly wounded men to return to combat duty. Incredibly, hundreds of men – including some with missing limbs – answered the call, and, in addition to those who returned to their units, Eliane-11 and Junon would henceforth be garrisoned mainly by walking wounded. But the garrison's fighting spirit generally remained strong, and many defenders still held out hope for victory through their own exertions and relief by Operation *Condor*. The paras and Legionnaires remained as aggressive as ever. On May 3, a sally on Eliane-2 succeeded in blowing up an enemy bunker on the Champs-Élysées, while a sortie by Isabelle's Legionnaires killed eight *bộ đội* and captured a 57mm ĐKZ and 21 small arms.[45] However, after dark, Isabelle was harassed by enemy mortars and several of its *sonnettes*, including that on Wieme, were driven in. By midnight all had been reestablished by Legionnaires and Tai partisans. This ritual would be repeated almost every night for the remainder of the siege.[46]

The fall of Lily-3

Meanwhile, 5km to the north, Lily-3 was under attack by the 36th Regiment, which employed the same "creeping siege" tactics it had perfected against Huguette-1. Here again, three different axes of attack were used in order to confuse and disorganize the defenders. The 80th Battalion's 63rd Company would deliver the main blow, while the 84th Battalion's 43rd Company and the 89th Battalion's 397th Company made diversionary attacks.[47] It's unclear why elements of three different battalions were employed, since this violated the principle of unity of command, making it far more difficult for the regimental leadership to exercise command and control. However, if one assumes that all three battalions had at least a company in close reserve to exploit a penetration by their vanguard companies, the odds against the defenders were at least six to one.

Although the strongpoint had been part of CR Lily for three weeks, most Western accounts of the battle label it "Huguette-4" and claim that it was garrisoned by Captain Luciani's BMEP company reinforced by some Moroccans of I/4 RTM.[48] This is contradicted by multiple French documents and witnesses (including Luciani himself), which indicate that Lily-3 (unsurprisingly) belonged to CR Lily and was defended exclusively by 1/I/4 RTM.[49] The Moroccan battalion had never been considered fully reliable after its 3rd Company fled from Eliane-1 on March 30, though its troops had fought steadfastly ever since. They had laid the foundation for the successful defense of Eliane-2; played an important role during the battles for Huguette; and handily repulsed the May 1 attack on Lily-3. On the night of May 3–4, Lily-3's defenders gave another demonstration of the reasons why Moroccans were renowned as fearsome and skillful warriors.

The 36th Regiment's assault began at 0030hrs with a brief bombardment, after which all three spearheads quickly entered the perimeter. However, they found that the Moroccans had taken precautions against *bộ đội* tunneling inside their lines. The regiment's official historian explains: "They, too, had learned lessons from our use of the siege attack tactic at 106, 206, and 311A [Huguettes-6, -1, and -5]. They had planted mines and booby-traps throughout the base, including around their gun positions and bunkers. We were surprised by this new enemy tactic, which inflicted casualties on our troops and prevented our troops from advancing quickly."[50]

Despite these difficulties, the 36th Regiment supposedly finished off Lily-3 within an hour. This is contradicted by French sources, but shortly after 0130hrs the strongpoint's northern salient was overrun and its central portion penetrated.[51] 1st Company's commander, Lieutenant Robert Perrin, had been stunned and partially incapacitated by a nearby shellburst the day before, and 2nd Company's leader, Captain Maurice Nicod, was sent out to replace him temporarily. At 0200hrs, Nicod was surprised to see enemy troops approaching the command bunker and had to beat a hasty retreat with his staff. Lieutenant Perrin could not move quickly enough and was captured. The remaining Moroccans fought on, however, and intercepted radio messages revealed that there was mounting confusion within the attackers' ranks that caused several VPA commanders to be replaced. Lily-3 was finally submerged at 0335hrs, when the last surviving junior officer was killed while he was speaking on the radio with GONO headquarters.[52]

This macabre conversation was overheard by Captain Jean Pouget, who had just jumped in with his 3/1 BPC. In January 1954, Pouget had chosen to leave a safe post as Navarre's aide-de-camp and join the paratroops, and some would later claim that he went to Điện Biên Phủ as a form of penance for his old boss's sins. This is nonsense, since Pouget had parted ways with Navarre well before the siege began and he jumped in simply because he was assigned to 1 BPC. Since he would have to wait until morning to lead his company across the river to Eliane-3, Pouget visited Langlais' and de Castries' headquarters to familiarize himself with the situation and was on hand to listen to Lily-3's death throes. De Castries said, "You see, there goes another strongpoint. There is nothing we can do about it. We are just constantly shrinking."[53]

Langlais did not agree that nothing could be done and ordered a counterattack, although the camp's western sector was so denuded of reserves that he had to summon Lieutenant Roger Ulpat (a survivor of the disastrous retreat from Lai Châu) all the way from Eliane-3 with his 3/I/13 DBLE. The counterattack was also delayed by the need to terminate flare-dropping while reinforcements were jumping. Accompanied by Ettlingen, Mulhouse, and some Moroccan riflemen, Ulpat's 50 Legionnaires finally attacked at 0500hrs during a violent rainstorm. The sodden moonscape of shell craters stretching toward Lily-3 was impassable to the tanks, and without them the advance bogged down at the edge of the strongpoint. Some survivors of 1/I/4 RTM were rescued, but with a mere hundred men, Ulpat could accomplish nothing more. Indeed, the situation was so perilous that without the tanks (including immobilized Douaumont) firing in support, his troops would not have been able to extricate their many wounded. Ulpat directed the Bisons to smash Lily-3's bunkers so they could not be used by the enemy.[54]

Across the river, artillery and mortar barrages had sufficed to repulse two tentative probes of Eliane-4 with little loss to the defenders.[55] But all told, the night's fighting had cost GONO about two companies' worth of troops – 164 men killed and missing, and another 58 wounded. On the other side of the balance sheet, it had received just 128 parachuted reinforcements overnight, for a net loss of 94 men. The 36th Regiment's casualties were also considerable, but it had accomplished its mission and was now ensconced just 750 meters from de Castries' command bunker.[56] There was now only a single line of fortifications barring the way to the headquarters area from the west, though Claudine-5 still guarded the southwestern approach. The Legionnaires of I/2 REI tried to convert the communications trench running back to Claudine-4 into a proper fighting position so the two strongpoints would present a continuous, fortified front against attack from the south. However, it was a Sisyphean task because the area was waist deep in water and the new entrenchments were constantly collapsing.[57]

La Cuvette

In French, the word *cuvette* (i.e., "bowl" or "basin") could be used without irony to describe the valley of Điện Biên Phủ. But as the siege progressed, it was increasingly employed in the sense of a *cuvette des toilettes* – that is, a "toilet bowl." And indeed, by late April GONO's shattered strongpoints resembled heaps of garbage dumped into reeking lakes of mud and water polluted with festering corpses and all manner of filth which were regularly "flushed" by torrential rains. It was a testament to the efficiency of the medical staff and water purifiers that the garrison was not decimated by cholera and other diseases. The term *la cuvette* proved even more apt in May, when it became clear that reinforcements were being "flushed down the toilet" when they were dropped in. Amazingly, jump refusals remained rare, even though most of the reinforcements knew they were being sent to their doom, and many had several opportunities to reconsider their options. A total of 260 reinforcements were supposed to jump on the night of May 4–5, but owing to flak and bad weather, most of them had to return to Hanoi.[58] Only 74 paras of 1 BPC's Headquarters and 4th Companies arrived, including the battalion commander, who did not try to conceal his displeasure at how his unit was being sacrificed.

> Captain de Bazin's frank complaint on his arrival at the [GM9] command post that he could not understand why they had been dropped into this toilet, since his tired men could do nothing to save the camp, triggered an equally frank outburst from Colonel Langlais. According to Bigeard's memoir, Langlais told Bazin to keep his opinions to himself – he was there simply to fight and if necessary die alongside them.[59]

As fate would have it, Captain Pouget had to assume command of 1 BPC just a few hours later when de Bazin's leg was smashed by an enemy shell. But although he was now out of the picture, the image of the Điện Biên Phủ garrison as a Shakespearean "band of brothers" cheerfully standing shoulder to shoulder in the face of impossible odds was obviously wearing a bit thin. And although de Bazin had been taken to task for his resentful pessimism, de Castries and Langlais were no less bitter in their messages to Hanoi. Supply drops were still too few and misdrops too frequent; the high-flying C-119s were particularly inaccurate. Overcome by frustration at his inability to satisfy his subordinates' pleas for even the most basic supplies, on May 4 de Castries sent an anguished message to FTNV in which he notably departed from his habitual, aristocratic reserve.

Our provisions of all kinds are at their lowest, for 15 days they have been reduced little by little. We don't have enough ammunition to stop enemy attacks or for the harassing fire that must continue without pause; it appears that no effort is being made to remedy the situation. I am told of the risks to the aircrew, but every man here runs infinitely greater risks – there cannot be a double standard. Night supply drops must begin at 2000 instead of 2300. The morning hours are lost because of the fog, and due to the planning of night drops with long intervals between aircraft the results are ridiculous. I have absolute need of provisions in massive quantities.

The very small size of the center of resistance, and the fact that the elements holding the perimeter cannot leave their shelters without coming under fire from snipers and recoilless guns, means that more and more of the [supply] cases dropped are no longer retrievable. The lack of vehicles and porters obliges me to employ exhausted units for recovery tasks; the result is detestable – it also causes casualties. I cannot count on recovering even half of what is dropped, though the quantities sent to me represent only a very small proportion of what I have requested. This situation cannot go on.[60]

De Castries was not exaggerating GONO's plight. The sides of its rain-eroded trenches were falling in and its bunkers were collapsing under the weight of the waterlogged earth covering their poorly supported roofs. Others were being destroyed, one by one, by heavily fortified ĐKZs and mountain guns firing at point-blank range; they also made it impossible to reinforce or resupply some peripheral strongpoints in daylight. GONO's artillery did not have enough ammunition either to eliminate these weapons or to interfere with enemy troops who were laboring day and night to construct new siegeworks in the recently captured terrain.[61] The batteries expended 2,600 105mm shells, 1,180 120mm shells, and 40 155mm shells on May 4, leaving just enough ammunition for one more day of firing at the same rate.[62] Fortunately for the defenders, no new attacks came on the night of May 4, and by 1800hrs the next day, the Main Position had a more reassuring three units-of-fire on hand for its 105s and 2.3 for Isabelle's howitzers. However, ammunition for the heavy mortars and last operational 155 remained scarce (just 1.8 and 1.1 units-of-fire respectively), and was obviously insufficient to deal with another "big push" like the May Day offensive.[63]

And although GONO had three days' rations stockpiled on the afternoon of May 5, poor nutrition was beginning to erode the combat efficiency of even the garrison's best troops. The problem wasn't merely the inadequate quantity of food the troops were receiving now that they were on half-rations, but also its quality. Since it was no longer possible to collect and centrally distribute supplies, men had to subsist on whatever parachuted rations chanced to land within reach. Thus, throughout the first week of May, II/1 RCP's paras ate nothing but a decidedly imbalanced diet of bread and tomato sauce.[64]

Langlais deployed 1 BPC's well-fed paras on the most vital strongpoints. Captain Jean Tréhiou's incomplete 4th Company was ordered up to Eliane-4, while Pouget's Headquarters and 2nd and 3rd Companies went to Eliane-2. The departing Legionnaires warned Pouget about the enemy mineshaft, whose progress could be tracked using rudimentary "geophones" jury-rigged from canteens and medical stethoscopes. The sound of the VPA engineers burrowing underfoot was strangely reassuring, since no major attack was likely to come until after the digging stopped and the tunnel had been packed with explosives. 2nd Company tried to eliminate the looming threat on May 6, but a raiding party led by Sergeant André Glinel was wiped out before it could reach the tunnel entrance.[65]

More than 200 troops of 1 BPC were supposed to jump in on the night of May 5–6,[66] but yet again, most of them did not arrive. Dense flak slowed operations and the DZ was now so small that each plane had to make three or four passes to deliver all its passengers. Thus, only 94 men of the Headquarters and 4th Companies jumped before the first light of dawn forced personnel drops to cease at 0520hrs. The rest returned to Hanoi after spending most of the night vainly circling over the valley. One can only imagine what they were thinking as their planes droned back to the Delta. For although they had been spared, for the moment, they knew the whole nerve-wracking experience would have to be repeated in less than 24 hours. They had no way of knowing that GONO had just received its final reinforcements and would have to make do with just 383 of 1 BPC's paras (155 of whom were Indochinese).[67]

AIR COMBAT SORTIES DURING MAY[68]						
Period	Direct support	Counterbattery	Flak suppression	Interdiction	Vs. Depots & cantonments	TOTAL
May 1–7	91	40	123	53	26	333

Yet the spirits of GONO's defenders were lifted on May 6 by bright, clear skies that prompted GATAC Nord to put an impressive 127 combat sorties over the valley and allowed the garrison to receive its first good supply lift in four days. Twenty-nine Dakotas and 25 C-119s dropped 195 tons (including 50 tons of artillery ammunition – mostly 120mm shells) that day, and de Castries noted with approval that the CAT pilots were delivering their loads more accurately.[69] Indeed, several of them volunteered to fly low-altitude missions carrying artillery ammunition to Isabelle, the DZ of which was too small to hit from high altitude. This courageous act cost the CAT contingent its only fatalities of the siege. Pilot Art Wilson's plane was hit by a 37mm shell, but managed to limp back to base. The plane piloted by James B. McGovern (a huge, heavily bearded man nicknamed "Earthquake McGoon" after a character in the *Li'l Abner* comic strip) was not so lucky. It took two hits, one in the left engine, and although McGovern and his copilot Wallace Buford managed to keep the C-119 airborne for another 40 minutes, they crashed just short of a crude airstrip at Mường Het, Laos 112km northwest of Điện Biên Phủ. Both Americans were killed, though one of their French cargo-handlers survived the crash and his subsequent capture by Pathet Lao troops.[70]

GONO was still in dire straits on May 6, since it had virtually no reserves and several hours of heavy firing by its artillery would empty the ammo dumps. There was some cause for hope, however, since negotiations at Geneva would commence in less than 48 hours, the good weather should allow the rest of 1 BPC to jump in overnight, and the ammunition situation would improve considerably after the thousands of freshly parachuted shells lying in exposed positions around the perimeter were recovered during the hours of darkness. Langlais highlighted these hopeful points at a conference with GONO's battalion commanders on the morning of May 6, but his rather forced upbeat tone was based upon the assumption that Giáp would let a third night in a row pass without launching any new attacks. Instead, Captain Jacques Noël of the Deuxième Bureau interrupted the meeting with the news that intercepted VPA radio messages revealed another wave of assaults would begin that very night. Everyone present realized this meant the end was nigh, since there would be no time to collect the supplies or receive reinforcements before the blow landed. Captain Hervouët, who had been out of action for several weeks with two broken arms, had his casts removed prematurely so he could lead his Bisons into their final battle.[71]

Giáp's fourth offensive

Whatever the problems that had caused Giáp to delay most of the attacks scheduled for May 2–5 had evidently been resolved by the evening of May 6. His subordinates had used the respite to rush additional supplies to the front and absorb still more replacements into their depleted ranks. Moreover, the 304th Division's 9th Regiment was now on hand and the newly minted 224th Rocket Artillery Battalion had also arrived and spent the preceding five days reconnoitering and occupying firing positions.[72] The rockets' deafening moan was unnerving (American GIs called a similar German weapon the "Screaming Meemie") and the simultaneous blast of a full salvo could shake even the best troops. Giáp hoped their shock effect would help compensate for his shortage of ammunition.[73] Last, but not least, the Eliane-2 mineshaft had been declared complete when it attained a length of 49 meters on May 5, and, during the night, over a ton of explosives had been packed into a T-shaped gallery at its western extremity. More than half of the total (600kg) had been extracted from bombs pulled from the wreckage of a PB4Y "Privateer" shot down on April 12 and then defused by the 83rd Special Engineer Company. The mine's detonation would be the signal for simultaneous ground assaults on Claudine-5 by the 308th Division, Elianes-10 and -12 by the 312th Division, and Elianes-2 and -4 by the 316th Division.[74]

VPA gunners harassed GONO throughout May 6, and the H6 rocket launchers revealed themselves for the first time, individually firing ranging shots at targets marked by a 105mm howitzer. In the afternoon, the 105s began hitting the strongpoints that would be assaulted that night with carefully rationed allotments of shells that were intended to range in on and destroy specific bunkers. At 1510hrs, the 801st and 804th Batteries each fired 21 shells at Eliane-4 – equally split between the hill's eastern and western summits – and the 802nd targeted Claudine-5 with 30 precisely aimed shells at 1630hrs, collapsing five of its waterlogged bunkers. An hour later, the 802nd Battery dropped another 30 rounds on Eliane-2's summit. After the 105s fell silent, the H6 rocket launchers fired another series of ranging shots.[75] The final bombardment began at 2000hrs and continued for 45 minutes, with the H6s concentrating their fire on French artillery positions. Although a tube on one launcher had burst, they fired six devastating, full-battalion volleys that made the earlier test shots seem tame by comparison. A seventh volley was aimed at de Castries' headquarters just as the ground assaults were beginning at 2100hrs.[76]

The fuses on the mine under Eliane-2 were ignited at 2030hrs after *bộ đội* had been ordered to face the other way, lift their buttocks off the ground, open their mouths, and close their eyes. Rumor had it that anyone within 300 meters who did not take these precautions would be killed. But instead of the huge, earsplitting blast they all expected, there was only a flash of flame and a heavy thud. Since the field telephone wire running to Eliane-2 had been removed to avoid damage, it took about 15 minutes to confirm that the mine had indeed exploded. It had blown a crater 10 meters deep and about twice as wide in the Champs-Élysées, but was perhaps 30 meters short of the summit bunker (as is readily apparent in photos of Eliane-2's preserved fortifications that are available online). VPA commanders must have known the mineshaft was too short, but evidently believed that concussion alone would suffice to collapse the underground fortifications further up the hill.[77]

The fall of Claudine-5

The rebuilt 102nd Regiment, which had seen no major action since its withdrawal from Eliane-2 a month earlier, was tasked with capturing Claudine-5. The position was held by Captain Jean Schmitz's 2/I/2 REI, which had only two platoons left. Two days earlier it had been reinforced by a platoon of I/4 RTM, but five of the Moroccans had deserted on the night of May 4–5. Like the Béatrice survivors that fled from Huguette-6 back on April 3, these men made their escape by cutting a gap through the barbed wire. Since this breach could prove fatal to Claudine-5, the defenders desperately tried to seal it off. But that meant working in the open under fire from enemy automatic weapons dug in just a few meters away, and eight Legionnaires were killed and another dozen wounded in failed attempts to repair the wire. Although this mass desertion was almost as unusual for the Moroccans as it had been for the Legionnaires a month before, the African platoon's remaining troops were disarmed and forcibly ejected from the strongpoint. A platoon of Legionnaires replaced them, but the breach still had not been closed by the evening of May 6. And owing to its low-lying position, Claudine-5's defenses had been further compromised by flooding. Most of its remaining bunkers were flattened by a pair of mountain guns that had been emplaced within 300 meters of its perimeter during the afternoon.[78]

The ground assault began at 2100hrs. The 18th Battalion's 259th Company made the main attack through a tunnel that extended inside Claudine-5, while 79th Battalion's 277th Company mounted a diversion from trenches that had been pushed within 15 meters of the perimeter. Bridgeheads were quickly captured, and the 102nd Regiment's official history states that a "deep penetration platoon" from the 263rd Company overran Schmitz's headquarters just 20 minutes later. French sources are silent on this point, but indicate that the battered 3rd Platoon was unable to hold out long in front of the main breach since the fortifications in that area had been totally destroyed. It was quickly replaced, however, by Sergeant Chief Gossens' platoon of 10/III/13 DBLE brought over from Claudine-4. And when his troops were also driven back, the pioneer platoon of I/2 REI's Headquarters Company counterattacked and retook the lost ground. But at midnight, the 102nd Regiment began attacking everywhere at once and the few remaining pioneers had to fall back an hour later when they ran out of ammunition. Their retreat allowed the enemy to overrun the rest of Claudine-5 by 0130hrs. To protect Claudine-4, a "cork" was installed in the trench linking it to Claudine-5. This was defended by the few Claudine-5 survivors, some I/2 REI Headquarters Company troops, a weak platoon of Moroccans from BG31, and a 155mm gun crew fighting as infantry. It was supported for a time by Ettlingen.[79]

Junon was "seriously probed"[80] while the battle for Claudine-5 was raging nearby. This appears to have been a diversion, and was most likely conducted by elements of the 102nd Regiment. The attackers were eventually seen off by the Air Force Detachment and "Tonton Carabine" Duluat's CTB – which everyone agreed was the best Tai unit serving at Điện Biên Phủ. Otherwise, Junon was garrisoned only by walking wounded.

Bazeilles

As we have seen, the Eliane-2 mine did not even dent the redoubtable bunkers under the summit. Most of 3/1 BPC's 2nd Platoon was buried under tons of earth and rock, but in every other respect, the result was the worst-case scenario foreseen by the 249th Battalion's commander, Vũ Đình Hoè: "If the enemy bunkers are not touched and the hill devastated, our attempts to attack will be a thousand times more difficult because of the obstacles created by the debris."[81] Based on past experience, the attackers could expect the defenders to retreat into the bunkers, call down artillery on themselves, and then counterattack with the aid of reinforcements sent up by way of Eliane-3. But for several reasons, this scene would not be played out again. Firstly, the effort invested in silencing Isabelle's batteries was paying dividends.[82] Secondly, Colonel Vaillant's gunners were rapidly running out of ammunition. At midnight, the Legion heavy mortars would have only 500 120mm shells remaining. By 0200hrs, the figure would be down to 100, while the Main Position's seven operational 105s would have just 500 shells between them, and the solitary 155 would have a mere 13.[83] Only the three surviving Quad-50s (one had been knocked out by a mortar on May 6[84]) were still amply supplied with ammunition and continued to blaze away from firing positions that were waist-deep in .50-caliber shell casings.

Finally, the 174th Regiment did not repeat past mistakes by merely battering its way frontally up the Champs-Élysées; it also launched a secondary attack designed to sever the communications trench from Eliane-3 and strike Eliane-2 from the rear. To open this new axis of attack, a trench had been dug running southwest from Bald Hill to RP41, where it turned north toward Mannequin Hillock. Much blood was spilt excavating this trench, which was dominated by enemy positions atop Eliane-2, and partly sandwiched between the hill and Eliane-3. Each successive portion of the final stretch started as a shallow tunnel whose roof would be knocked down after dark and the now open excavation carefully camouflaged before sunup. The diggers were hidden from direct fire by screens of straw and even wore "armored vests" made of the same material.[85]

Captain Pouget claims that his troops easily repulsed an attack at 1845hrs thanks to effective artillery support.[86] But it's likely that what he took for an assault wave was merely the 249th Battalion moving up to relieve the 255th Battalion, which withdrew to Bald Hill after 34 hellish days on Eliane-2. Vietnamese authors insist no attack was made until after the mine was detonated. As Hoè feared, the explosion had turned the Champs-Élysées into a rubble-strewn obstacle course. Since the rain-slick crater barred the way up the center and debris clogged the trenches on either side, his 316th and 317th Companies had to pick their way along the flanks of the hill, offering easy targets for the opposing paras. Meanwhile, the "Lopped-Off Banyan Tree Blockhouse" thwarted every attempt to breach the wire in front of Mannequin Hillock. After a prolonged delay, it was finally destroyed by a ĐKZ, but when the pioneers went forward again, they were mowed down by a well-camouflaged machine gun sited right next to the wrecked bunker. Another lengthy delay ensued before this weapon was destroyed by a "death volunteer" and the 251st Battalion's 674th Company finally entered the perimeter. While a detachment peeled off westward to block the communications trench from Eliane-2, the rest of the company advanced east.[87]

Under pressure from three directions, Pouget radioed an urgent request for reinforcements. He was convinced that one more company would suffice to restore the perimeter, but Elianes-4 and -10 were also begging for reinforcements and there were virtually no reserves left. In this crisis, Langlais took the risk of stripping strongpoints west of the river that were not under attack to reinforce the eastern bank. Just before midnight, each of 8 BPC's companies was ordered to surrender a platoon; these were hastily assembled into two march companies under Lieutenants Bailly and Maurice Jacquemet, and set out for Eliane-10. By now the BMEP had just two companies, one containing all 1 BEP's survivors, and the other, all of 2 BEP's. The 1 BEP company was ordered to send two platoons to Claudine-5 (they did not arrive in time to save it) while Captain Brandon led the other two toward Eliane-4. Lieutenant Lecour-Grandmaison's 2 BEP company was directed to Eliane-2, but left a platoon behind to maintain a façade of defense on Huguette-2. Its place was taken by a march platoon of BMEP headquarters personnel which brought Grandmaison's total strength to 80. All four of these units were considerably weakened and slowed by artillery harassment, and would be delayed still further by enemy infantry ambushes once they crossed the river.[88]

As Pouget impatiently followed Grandmaison's progress on the radio, his troops were fighting with what the 316th Division's official historian described as "insane fervor."[89] Sergeants Bruni and Ballait of 2nd Company recklessly climbed into an exposed position atop the hulk of Bazeilles and used its machine gun to spray .50-caliber bullets at *bộ đội* just a few meters away. The tank's name commemorated the 1870 battle of Bazeilles, whose anniversary had become a holiday for French colonial troops just as Camerone was for the Foreign Legion. Caught up in the disastrous French defeat at the far larger battle of Sedan during the Franco-Prussian War, 60 colonial troops surrounded by the 15th Bavarian Infantry Regiment had fought until they ran out of ammunition in the legendary "Last Cartridge House."[90]

Pouget's colonial paras fought just as stubbornly on Eliane-2, halting the enemy advance short of the summit in incredibly vicious, close-quarters combat. The 174th Regiment's commander, Nguyễn Hữu An, personally visited the front to assess the situation, and ordered the 249th Battalion to break the impasse by committing its reserve 315th Company. These reinforcements finally captured the summit and linked up with the 251st Battalion, but the paras merely fell back to the mortar positions on the reverse slope and the VPA advance ground to a halt yet again. Determined to restore the attack's momentum, An summoned the 255th Battalion's 924th Company back up to Eliane-2 at 2300hrs, but it must have taken at least an hour or two to arrive.[91]

As the battle dragged on toward dawn, Pouget learned to his dismay that Grandmaison's troops had been redirected to Eliane-4 after they spent several hours vainly attempting to break through to Eliane-2. Yet, although by 0400hrs there were only 34 able-bodied paras left and their ammunition was almost exhausted, Pouget still believed that he could hold out with a company of reinforcements and radioed a last, desperate plea to Langlais. Instead, he found himself speaking to Major Vadot, who replied, "Come on, be reasonable. You know the situation as well as I do. Where do you want me to find a company? I can't give you a single man or a single shell, my boy."[92] When Pouget then asked for permission to retreat, Vadot refused, saying, "After all you're a paratrooper and you must resist to the death – or at least until morning." After acknowledging this grim order, Pouget destroyed his radio. He was stunned by a grenade and captured just before all resistance ended at 0440hrs. His men had fought to the last cartridge.[93]

Undaunted, Langlais ordered a counterattack on Eliane-2. At that point, it still seemed that Elianes-4 and -10 would hold out, and if Eliane-2 could be retaken, GONO would gain a new lease on life. And although his remaining "reserves" (in fact, troops extricated from frontline positions west of the Nâm Yum) were laughably inadequate, there was still a small chance that a counterthrust might succeed if it struck before the 174th Regiment could consolidate on and reinforce the strongpoint. Lieutenant Ulpat's 3/I/13 DBLE was sent across the river from Lily-1, and Captain Bizard was ordered to leave a platoon behind on the Nameless Strongpoint and bring the rest of 1/5 BPVN down to Junon to join in the counterattack. The operation was stillborn, however, because Elianes-4 and -10 fell before it really got under way. Ulpat's troops were recalled at 0900hrs and sent to Junon, while Bizard's took up position just west of the Bailey bridge.[94]

The fall of Eliane-10

The fate of Eliane-10 was decided by an equally epic and even more protracted battle in which echoes of Bazeilles could also be heard. It may seem odd that this low-lying mudhole of a strongpoint lasted longer than towering Eliane-2 with its indestructible bunkers, but it was attacked from only one direction, received several infusions of reinforcements, and was garrisoned by the last remnants of Bigeard's elite 6 BPC. On May 6, these amounted to about 120 combat troops organized into two march companies commanded by Captains Trapp and LePage, plus a small Headquarters Company.[95] In addition, the remnants of 8/BT2 were still blocking the communications trench from Dominique-3.

Since many of the strongpoint's bunkers had been smashed earlier in the day by ĐKZs and 120mm mortars (and ammunition was scarce), the 115/165 attacked after a very brief artillery preparation in which the supporting batteries fired just two volleys apiece to keep the paras' heads down. The 501st Company entered the perimeter just 15 minutes after the assault began, driving back the para platoon that was defending Eliane-10's northern sector, and killing its commander, Lieutenant André Samalens. Then, although just a platoon's worth of bộ đội remained on their feet, they attacked in two different directions to fragment the defense.[96] A counterattack drove the two groups back together and reduced their combined strength to that of a squad. The 115th Battalion's commander, Thiết Cương, hastily assembled a platoon of reinforcements and personally led it into the breach. Yet when he linked up with the 501st Company's survivors, Cương found that, all told, he had just a dozen men left. By 0030hrs, he would have only five able-bodied men. If we are to believe the 312th Division's commander, Lê Trọng Tấn, these were the only VPA troops inside Eliane-10 until just before dawn, when the 165th Regiment committed a makeshift unit thrown together from regimental and battalion headquarters staff personnel.[97] It's unclear why this improvisation was necessary, since the regiment had two other battalions and had not made an assault in a month. Since it seems that the 564th Battalion was not involved in the May offensives, perhaps it was still recovering from earlier losses.

Tấn's account cannot be reconciled with those of French witnesses who describe superior enemy forces driving Sergeant-Chief Ménage's platoon (which had lost all but seven of its original 15 paras) back toward the center of Eliane-10 at 2300hrs. Enemy troops flooding into the strongpoint then split the defenders into three isolated groups led by Major Thomas in the center, Captain Hervé Trapp in the west, and Captain René LePage in the east. Needless to say, all this was not accomplished by a half-dozen bộ đội! The 312th Division's official history reports that two companies of the 115th Battalion and the 542nd Battalion's 918th Company fought on Eliane-10 that night.[98]

Close to midnight, Bigeard faced an agonizing choice. Dakotas carrying 133 paras of 1 BPC were circling overhead, waiting for a lull in flare-dropping to descend to jump altitude. Since each plane would have to make several passes, dropping the entire force could take as much as two hours. Yet enemy pressure on Eliane-10 was so severe that it might not survive even a brief period of full darkness. Bigeard deferred this hard decision to the commander closest to the scene of action – Captain LePage. He radioed, "LePage from Bruno [Bigeard's *nom de guerre*]. Our friends are above you in the air. We've got to stop the 'fireflies' to drop them. Can we do it?" After a brief pause LePage tersely replied, "Priority to 'fireflies.' Out."[99] 1/1 BPC had dodged the bullet a second time, and its troops – surely the luckiest paras in the world – again returned to Hanoi. Soon after this exchange, LePage's command post was threatened by advancing *bộ đội*. When a counterattack by Lieutenant Michel Datin's platoon failed to halt the enemy, LePage and a few other survivors managed to slip away to Major Thomas' position.[100]

Most of Eliane-10 was overrun during the pre-dawn hours of May 7, but the remnants of Captain Trapp's company fought on in the strongpoint's western tip even though their commander was seriously wounded. Lieutenant Bailly had also been hit, and when his 8 BPC march company finally arrived, its few dozen exhausted survivors were incapable of counterattacking. The other 8 BPC march company commanded by Lieutenant Jacquemet did not appear because it had been diverted to Eliane-12 to replace two weak platoons of 3/I/2 REI that were sent over to Eliane-10 at about this same time. Yet, the situation was so hopeless that the Legionnaires did not fight with their usual zeal.[101]

Eliane-10 was still holding at dawn, but its defenders were too few, too exhausted, and too short of ammunition to last much longer, and Langlais could do nothing to help them. He had no reserves to spare and Colonel Vaillant's batteries were falling silent as their last shells were expended. And while some of the defenders were starting to succumb to despair, the attackers were spurred on by the sight of the "Determined to Fight, Determined to Win" flag floating triumphantly over nearby Eliane-2 – and Giáp was prodding their commanders to finish the job quickly. The 209th Regiment's improvised unit of staff personnel proved sufficient to decide the issue and Eliane-10 finally fell at 0930hrs. The 542/165 immediately relieved the shattered 115th Battalion, and began planning an assault on Eliane-11 even while it prepared to repel a French counterattack.[102]

Eliane-10's defenders had been authorized to retreat at the last minute, but few escaped. LePage was one them, and suddenly appeared in GM9 headquarters as an unrecognizable, mud-caked apparition to bring Bigeard the grim news that his beloved 6 BPC had ceased to exist. He got a measure of revenge when Eliane-10 was hit by several napalm attacks later that morning. For once the mist lifted, the day was bright and sunny, and French aircraft appeared in strength. Corsairs would put 16 sorties over the valley that day while B-26s would fly 25 and Bearcats 30.[103]

The fall of Eliane-4

Eliane-4 was held by burned-out shells of II/1 RCP, III/RTA, and 5 BPVN, which could now muster just a company's worth of troops apiece. These had been reinforced on May 5 by Captain Tréhiou's newly arrived 4/1 BPC, but just 86 of its 142 paras ever jumped into the valley. These fresh troops were posted in the most endangered, northeastern sector; while 5 BPVN's 2nd and 3rd "Companies" (each only a couple of platoons in size) held the southeastern and southwestern sectors; and the Algerians defended the northwestern quadrant. II/1 RCP's remnants (essentially Captain Clédic's 2nd Company), were mostly in reserve near Major Bréchignac's headquarters.[104] Major Botella and 5 BPVN's headquarters were also present. Feeble though each of its components was, this garrison was several times larger than Claudine-5's and Eliane-10's, and even exceeded Pouget's on Eliane-2. It also benefited from the fact that Eliane-4 had two summits with obstacles in between; the western one could continue to hold out even if the eastern one was lost. Finally, Captain Hervouët sent Posen up to reinforce the position at 1800hrs.[105]

The 98th Regiment attacked on three axes at 2030hrs. The 215th Battalion's 38th Company made the main attack from the southeast, while the 35th advanced across the saddle from Eliane-1, and the 439th Battalion's 1480th Company delivered a flank attack from Honeycomb Hill. French fire was so intense that only a single squad of the 35th Company and an "assault cell" of the 38th managed to enter the perimeter through 5 BPVN's sector. They linked up and infiltrated to 3rd Company's headquarters, but were eliminated by the Nungs (ethnic Chinese) of its mortar platoon. Meanwhile, the 1480th Company had been caught in a crossfire between Eliane-4 and a Quad-50 west of the Bailey bridge. The company would remain pinned down all night; its commander and executive officer were both wounded, and the pioneer platoon reduced to just three men.[106]

Captain Phu's 2/5 BPVN had been badly hurt and gaps in its sector had to be filled by headquarters personnel. Worse yet, 5 BPVN had only 50 81mm shells left, was running out of hand grenades, and Captain Vaillant's batteries could no longer spare any shells for Eliane-4. At midnight, the 38th Company launched another attack that overran Phu's sector and penetrated to the second-line trenches. 3/5 BPVN counterattacked up the frontline trenches and sealed the breach, while Lieutenant Francis Pottier's platoon of 2/II/1 RCP cleared the second line. The *bộ đội* made no attempt to retreat and were all wiped out. Yet despite being repulsed twice with heavy losses, the 38th Company refused to give up. Sometime between 0200 and 0300hrs, a squad led by the company's political officer penetrated deep inside the perimeter, drove down into the gully separating Eliane-4's two crests, and overran 5 BPVN's mortars. Regimental Commander Vũ Lăng had no communications with this unit, but the sound of its battle convinced him to throw in the reserve 34th Company. Ettlingen arrived at about the same time.[107]

The 34th Company could not pass through the curtain of fire sweeping the breach, but the 38th Company's remaining troops did and overran much of Eliane-4's eastern half. Phu was wounded and what was left of his company fought in isolated pockets surrounded by *bộ đội*. 3/5 BPVN counterattacked again, but was too weak to accomplish much and Captain Guilleminot was wounded. Captain Trehiou of 4/1 BPC was also wounded and his company severely attrited. Yet just in the nick of time, Captain Brandon's now platoon-sized 1 BEP march company reached Eliane-4. Since Brandon had been hit, Lieutenant Georges Roux led the counterattack, which was joined by some Algerians and benefited from the timely arrival of a master sergeant and two PIMs carrying six boxes of grenades.[108] Aided by the remnants of Pottier's platoon and the Nungs, Roux drove the enemy out yet again. One Vietnamese author admits, "Virtually all of our troops fighting inside the enemy strongpoint were killed or wounded."[109] Grandmaison finally arrived at first light with a dozen men of 2 BEP. The rest were hopelessly pinned down outside Eliane-4 and the Headquarters Company march platoon had vanished after its leader proclaimed that Grandmaison was dead and turned back.[110]

Frustrated by Eliane-4's stubborn resistance, Giáp "pulled out all the stops" to ensure that it did not hold out much longer. He authorized the 316th Division's commander, General Lê Quảng Ba, to commit a battalion of the 9th

Regiment to the battle and instructed him to have the 174th Regiment troops on Eliane-2 redirect their heavy weapons fire to rake Eliane-4's southern flank. Finally, Giáp allocated an impressive 200 105mm shells to the preparatory bombardment that would precede the new assault.[111] Vũ Lăng was ecstatic when he heard the news: "All I could do was howl with delight. I felt indescribably happy. I thought to myself, 'This time we are being really extravagant with our ammunition.' Only later did I learn that in fact the Command's stockpile of artillery ammunition was quite limited."[112] The tables had truly been turned, since when Captain Clédic spotted the 375/9 assembling in plain view on neighboring Eliane-1, Colonel Vaillant could spare only three shells for this tempting target.[113]

The final assault began at 0730hrs, but fighting dragged on for another two hours since the defenders contested every meter of ground. A little after 0900hrs, Bréchignac and Botella radioed that resistance was about to collapse and sought permission for their remaining men to retreat. Although this was granted, the two commanders had decided to stay behind with the many wounded, and asked, for their sake, that the hill not be bombed or shelled. Botella was last to speak: "It's all over. They're at the CP. Goodbye. Tell that Young Pierre [Langlais' *nom de guerre*] we liked him a lot."[114] The two Bisons drove down to the crossroads below Eliane-4 to cover the retreat, which occurred in broad daylight in full view of enemy infantry and artillery observers who poured fire on the fugitives from all directions. The 224th Rocket Artillery Battalion's political officer, Hoàng Khoát, recalled that two volleys of rockets were fired at the Bailey bridge at about this time, though he says they were aimed at counterattacking troops trying to cross over to the eastern bank.[115] Few escaped this gauntlet of fire. Captain Clédic reached Eliane-10 with Lieutenants Pottier and Charles Césarini only to find that the strongpoint had just fallen. Pottier alone managed to avoid capture – for a few hours. Ettlingen's engine was destroyed by a bazooka and Posen had to hitch up the tank under the very noses of enemy infantry and drag it back across the river.[116]

The unknown victory

There was one French victory on the night of May 6–7, but GONO's commanders were so distracted by the rising tide of disaster that they barely noticed it. The 312th Division was supposed to have captured both Eliane-10 and Eliane-12 that night. As we have seen, the 165th Regiment's attack on the former ultimately succeeded, but the 209th Regiment's attempt to take the latter completely miscarried. Jumping off simultaneously with the rest of the attacking units, the 130th Battalion sent its 363rd Company forward at 2100hrs. Yet the pioneers expended all their Bangalores without opening a breach, since the concertina wire was simply lifted off the ground by the explosions and fell back into place. Boards, sandbags, and blankets were brought up to lay across the barbed wire, but the entire night passed without any penetration of Eliane-12's perimeter.[117] Major Chenel thought it secure enough that he sent Lieutenant Eric Weinberger over to Eliane-10 with two platoons of Legionnaires.[118]

Since the 363rd Company had suffered severe casualties, it was replaced at dawn by the 366th Company, which managed to open a breach on a different axis of attack (west of the "dead arm" of the Nậm Yum?). Yet that was the extent of its good fortune. The company commander and his executive officer were both seriously wounded, and Platoon Commander Trần Can had to assume command though he had been hit himself while leading an unsuccessful charge through the gap. Can was killed leading another assault and was posthumously made a "Hero of the People's Armed Forces" for his bravery. Although the 209th Regiment's official history asserts that a portion of Eliane-12 was captured, the penetration must have been small and brief, because GONO's situation reports make no mention of it. In any event, the 366th Company was reduced to just a half-dozen able-bodied troops.[119]

The last day

The failure of the Eliane-12 attack was probably one of the factors that caused Giáp to remain cautious on the morning of May 7. For although he was no longer thinking in terms of an operational pause lasting until May 10, he remained hesitant to shift over to a General Offensive. "Logistics comrades intended to leave to prepare ammunition for the general assault. I noticed that several places had not reported full details of their situation. I felt we should sit back and wait. Many enemy soldiers remained in Mường Thanh... We had driven the French into a critical situation. We needed to make diligent preparations for our general attack."[120] In retrospect, it's easy to say that Giáp was being too cautious, but things weren't so clear at the time. The good weather had brought French aircraft out in force, his ammunition was limited, and seven of the nine regiments around the Main Position had been decimated for a second (or third) time in the battles since April 30. Only the 304th Division's 9th Regiment and the 312th Division's 141st Regiment had seen no fighting over the preceding week and were still close to full strength (though the latter had mostly green troops filling its ranks). And since the entire 312th Division had been brought east of the river, the western siege lines were manned solely by the battered 308th Division.

If Giáp could not bring himself to believe that the siege was finally coming to an end, Langlais and de Castries were certain of it. Except for two remaining 105s on Isabelle, which had about 1,700 shells left,[121] the artillery was almost completely out of ammunition; all reserves had been expended; the last shreds of high ground were lost; and casualties had been catastrophically high. 1 BPC, II/1 RCP, III/3 RTA, 5 BPVN, and 6 BPC had all been destroyed overnight, and I/2 REI, the BMEP, and 8 BPC had also lost much of their remaining strength. The destruction of the elite para and Legion units shocked the entire garrison and shattered the morale of its Tai and Moroccan troops. At about 1000hrs, de Castries went on the radio to give Cogny a stiffly formal and rambling update on the hopeless situation. Cogny lamely suggested that GONO might hold on the line of the Nậm Yum, but de Castries knew that was impossible and had decided to try *Albatros* that night. He was encouraged to attempt a breakout by an erroneous Deuxième Bureau report that placed both the 88th and 102nd Regiments east of the Nậm Yum. In fact, the entire 308th Division was still west of the river. Cogny concurred with the decision to try *Albatros*, though, as we've seen, he had objections to it.[122]

Instead of the 2,000–3,000 paras and Legionnaires envisioned less than a week before, the Main Position's breakout would now involve little more than 600 men organized into eight march companies of 70–80 men apiece. The remaining African and Tai units, and 200–300 paras and Legionnaires would remain behind to cover the escapees, who would march in two columns – one comprising the paras under Bigeard and the other consisting of all "leg" infantry units under Lemeunier. According to Bernard Fall, the two commanders would draw straws to determine which route they took. The winner would aim straight for the valley's western rim while the loser would head south toward the *Condor* force. The latter route was considered suicidal since it was the obvious one and Giáp had already taken steps to block it; the troops that used it would be sacrificed as a diversion so that the western column could make its escape. Isabelle's garrison would form a third column.[123]

Anticipating a breakout that night, some French units must have started burning classified documents and destroying equipment, since Giáp began receiving reports of such activity on the morning of May 7. Encouraged by these signs of French weakness, he gave his approval when the 209th Regiment requested permission to launch a daylight attack on Eliane-12 that afternoon. By noon, the accumulating evidence that GONO was on the verge of collapse convinced Giáp to issue orders for a General Offensive – though H-hour would be delayed until dusk.[124]

Just what happened at Điện Biên Phủ on the afternoon of May 7 remains an enigma despite the best efforts of this book's authors to unravel it. One mystery concerns Operation *Albatros*. It had always been a desperate venture and Bigeard had accordingly nicknamed it Operation *Percée de Sang* ("Bloodletting"). What made the breakout seem practical was that the siege lines south of Junon remained invitingly loose. Even in the last week of April, patrols had often scouted out 800 meters before meeting resistance, and aerial photos taken on May 6 showed only one enemy trench barring the way south. Yet just as Langlais began a final planning conference at 1200hrs, a Corsair dropped a pouch of photos taken that morning which revealed that two additional trenches had materialized overnight. Bernard Fall claims that all those present immediately agreed that a breakout from the Main Position now had no chance of success, and that de Castries canceled it by 1330hrs. This is unlikely, since at 1400hrs his chief of staff, Major Séguin-Pazzis, was still coordinating plans for *Albatros* with Colonel Lalande, who would not be told that the Main Position's breakout had been canceled for another two hours.[125]

Another riddle concerns the Low Elianes. Vietnamese authors claim that the 154/209 assaulted Eliane-12 at 1400hrs and overran it within an hour. The vanguard 520th Company reportedly needed just four Bangalores to breach the barbed wire and had little difficulty entering the strongpoint because the Tai of BT2 had mostly lost their will to fight and either fled south or surrendered (the few paras who were also present are not mentioned). Clusters of white flags then appeared on Eliane-11 and entrenchments just north of it known to the VPA as Position 508. The 209th Regiment immediately organized attacks on these vulnerable positions with the 130th and 154th Battalions, and quickly captured both.[126] However, almost the only French source that supports any part of this story is an unlabeled FTNV situation map that shows Elianes-11 and -12 crossed out to indicate they had been overrun, but gives no times. There appear to be no radio messages from GONO reporting that either strongpoint was lost at this time, and several French witnesses (including some still alive in 2017) insist that the Low Elianes held out until they were caught up in GONO's general collapse several hours later.[127]

The fate of Eliane-3, on the other hand, is no mystery. It was evacuated at 1500hrs because the position was clearly untenable and under constant fire from enemy heavy weapons on the dominating heights of Eliane-2. It was not an easy retreat for the remnants of 2/I/4 RTM and 2/I/13 DBLE, especially under fire, since the rain-swollen river could be crossed only with the aid of a cable strung from bank to bank.[128] The evacuation offered further proof of French weakness and may have influenced Giáp's decision to order an immediate General Offensive at 1500hrs. "No need to wait for dusk. Start general attack on Muong Thanh immediately. The units in the east will attack straight toward the enemy's Command Post. The units in the west will launch a coordinated attack toward the Command Post. The strike must be strong, the siege must remain tight. Do not let de Castries or any other enemy escape."[129] A slightly different version of this order which was addressed only to the 308th and 312th Divisions can be found in other Vietnamese books.[130] And French historian Pierre Rocolle claims that the Điện Biên Phủ Front's deputy chief of staff actually issued the order because Giáp was absent from his headquarters at the time.[131]

Sometime between 1500 and 1600hrs, de Castries' subordinates informed him that what was left of the Main Position would be overrun before nightfall, eliminating any chance of a breakout. The only option left was to bring a quick and orderly end to resistance in order to avoid a bloodbath. De Castries agreed, and at 1600hrs canceled all requests for combat air support and asked that thereafter only food and medical supplies be dropped – not ammunition. To avoid the ignominy of a formal surrender, a radio message would be broadcast "in the clear" announcing that GONO would "cease fire" at 1730hrs. Séguin-Pazzis began phoning the strongpoint commanders at 1630hrs to inform them of the ceasefire and order the destruction of all weapons, ammunition, and equipment (apart from that necessary to keep the camp supplied with electricity and drinking water). Small arms were beaten to pieces or had their barrels burst by firing a round with the muzzle stuck in the ground. Artillery pieces were "spiked" with thermite grenades that melted the inside of their barrels, sights were smashed, and breechblocks were thrown in the river. The tanks raced their engines without oil until they were reduced to scrap. Thus, though the ceasefire would not take effect until 1730hrs, most defenders had nothing left to shoot with at least half an hour earlier.[132]

Just before 1700hrs, de Castries made one last call to Hanoi over a secure voice radio. He initially spoke with Navarre's adjutant, Colonel Pierre Bodet, informing him that he was about to broadcast the ceasefire announcement and planned to send emissaries to make direct contact with the enemy at 1730hrs. It was probably this revelation that caused Cogny to take over the microphone, since he knew that this delegation would have to carry a white flag as it crossed the front lines. He insisted there could be no hint of surrender: "Old boy, it had to finish now, of course; but not in the form of a capitulation. That is forbidden to us. There mustn't be any raising of the white flag; the firing must be allowed to die away – but don't surrender. That would debase everything magnificent that you've done up to now."[133]

Bernard Fall argues that no white flag was ever raised over GONO headquarters – though he admits that Béatrice survivor Sergeant Kubiak claimed to have seen one. Other Western historians disagree, since it's at this point that several sentences seem to have been edited out of the transcript and audio recording of the conversation. When it picks up again, de Castries said: "All right, general, only I wished to protect the wounded."[134] Martin Windrow concludes that his use of the past tense suggests that a white flag had been displayed, but was taken down. And even if none was raised over de Castries' command bunker, French witnesses report that white flags were sprouting up all over the camp. But Cogny seems to have been more interested in an abstract point of honor than saving lives, and ended the conversation at 1730hrs with another admonition against surrender: "Do whatever's best. But this mustn't finish with a white flag. What you've achieved is too good for that. Do you understand old boy?" De Castries replied: "All right, general," then Cogny signed off with "Well ... au revoir, old boy."[135]

De Castries' emissaries were never sent, because just minutes later he was a prisoner of the VPA. For as GONO's resistance died away after 1630hrs, bộ đội began closing in from all sides. Their advance was tentative at first, but as white flags proliferated and it became clear that few defenders were still fighting, they started moving with less caution. Before long, some were advancing in the open and not bothering to shoot anymore. The 209th Regiment's official history describes the 130th Battalion's 360th Company

"Bypassing three enemy strong-points" (Elianes-11 and -12, and Position 508?) as it raced toward the Bailey bridge under fire from a Quad-50 on the other side. But enemy fire withered away after the lead platoon stormed across to the western bank and Company Commander Tạ Quốc Luật ordered his men to leave the trenches (blocked by non-resisting enemy troops) and head straight for de Castries' headquarters.[136] Finding the command bunker was no easy matter, but this problem was overcome with the assistance of a Vietnamese or Tai prisoner who pointed it out. After a small explosive charge was thrown into each of the bunker's two entrances, Luật entered with Privates Vinh and Nho, and captured de Castries along with his entire staff.[137]

When word of de Castries' capture was received, Giáp's headquarters went mad. "All the cadre at our General Headquarters had been somber for so long. Suddenly everyone burst into shouts that sounded like a rough sea. Cadre and soldiers alike shouted, slapped their thighs, and hugged one another. They jumped for joy like little kids. Some people cried. Others stood with their mouths gaping. The faces of others turned pale."[138] Their joy only intensified when it soon became clear that all resistance on the Main Position had ended at roughly the same time. *Bộ đội* at the front celebrated by jumping, dancing, lighting flares, and firing their weapons in the air. The dejected defenders were quickly formed into columns and sent marching northeast along RP41.The only immediate exceptions were some of those too badly wounded to move under their own power (the rest had to be carried by their comrades) and the medical staffs in the hospitals. BG31's engineers would soon be brought back to the camp since only they had the expertise necessary to keeps its infrastructure running.

The last night

Colonel Lalande had been informed about the Main Position's imminent ceasefire a little after 1600hrs and authorized to attempt *Albatros* on his own. He had been intending to surprise the enemy by breaking out northward east of the Nậm Yum, veering left to ford the river about 2km south of the Main Position, and then racing for the western mountains. But GONO advised him instead to go south and then follow the Nậm Nứa River (which intersected with the Nậm Yum at the bottom of the valley) downstream to the southeast. This longer route to Laos was thought best because it avoided known VPA troop concentrations southwest of the valley – especially those on the road to the Tây Trang border crossing.[139]

Isabelle's tanks and automatic weapons were sabotaged at 1900hrs, but the last remaining 105 was left intact to support the breakout. It began at 2000hrs, when 12/III/3 REI (with Lieutenant Wieme and 30 Tai of CSM 432 acting as guides), slipped out of the perimeter southward down the eastern bank of the Nậm Yum. Half an hour later, the Legion battalion's 9th and 10th Companies headed south on the western bank, and shortly thereafter, the 11th Company, CSM 431, and the Green Platoon's dismounted tank crews took the eastern route. These units were to be followed, at intervals, by the remnants of V/7 RTA, Lalande's headquarters, and II/1 RTA, in that order (BT3's place in the column is not mentioned in Isabelle's reconstructed war diary).[140]

The enemy quickly detected the breakout and responded decisively.

Comrade Nguyen Can, the commander of the 57th Regiment, ordered his battalions to light torches and to move out to pursue and capture the fleeing enemy troops. At approximately 2000hrs on the night of 7 May 1954 the 57th Regiment's 418th and 346th Battalions, together with the 9th Regiment's 400th Battalion which had just been sent down from Muong Thanh to reinforce the 57th Regiment, clashed with enemy forces south of Hong Cum and captured one entire enemy company.[141]

According to Lieutenant Wieme all was quiet until 2105hrs, when the second wave of units following the eastern route fell into an ambush just south of Isabelle. The Tai of CSM 431, the Green Platoon's crews, and a few troops of 11/III/3 REI escaped by fleeing across the river westward, but the rest of the Legionnaires were driven back into Isabelle. *Bộ đội* pursued the survivors back to the perimeter and fell upon the Algerians of V/7 RTA who were just exiting it.[142]

The western column had also come to grief. Although a few individuals – including 9th Company's commander, Lieutenant Maurice Surbier[143] – broke through southward, many were killed or captured, and the rest also had to flee back to Isabelle. There they became thoroughly intermingled with the eastern column's survivors and troops who had never departed. Fearing that the southern route was thoroughly blocked, Lalande considered reviving his original plan to break out northward. According to Lieutenant Wieme, he ordered the still unmolested 12/III/3 REI and CSM 432 to halt in their tracks at 2130hrs and kept them waiting for nearly two hours while he debated his options with Cogny. At 2315hrs, Lalande finally decided to stick to the southern route, although he thought that the northern route "seems more favorable."[144] Why Lalande did not follow his own judgment is unclear; perhaps he concluded that it would be impossible to brief his officers and reorient his units given the chaos that now reigned on Isabelle.

In any event, it does not appear that a second breakout from Isabelle was even attempted (though some individuals and small groups may have tried). By midnight, Lalande was trying to have his units reoccupy Isabelle's defenses, but was foiled by a breakdown in communications and mounting disorder. At 0100hrs, a delegation of VPA officers approached under a white flag and demanded Isabelle's immediate surrender. Recognizing how hopeless the situation was, Lalande reluctantly ordered his troops to lay down their arms and radioed a last message to Hanoi at 0150hrs: "Sortie failed. Cannot communicate with you anymore."[145]

The siege of Điện Biên Phủ had finally ended before sunrise on its 56th day, but Operation *Albatros* continued. The Green Platoon, CSM 431, and some fragments of III/3 REI's 9th, 10th, and 11th Companies that had broken through the ambushes were now generally west of the river fleeing toward the mountains in small parties. Most were quickly captured by pursuing *bộ đội*, but much of the Green Platoon hung together and escaped by heading straight west for the valley rim.[146] Meanwhile, east of the Nậm Yum, 12/III/3 REI and CSM 432 initially fared better because they were much farther south and had not been detected by the enemy. They began moving again at 2315hrs, though the delay had given the 265/57 time to beat them to the three-way junction at Bản Cang where RP41 intersected with the road to Tây Trang.[147] But the column had left the open rice fields behind and entered a region covered with brush and woods abutting on the valley's southern foothills. Moving stealthily through this concealing terrain, the escapees reached the confluence of the Nậm Yum and Nậm Nứa just south of Bom Lót at about 0100hrs. They had marched 9km from Isabelle without encountering any enemy troops.[148]

The column's next hurdle was to cross the Nậm Nứa. This was done in two stages, since the crossing spot straddled an island of shingle in midstream. Although the Tai and Legionnaires were spotted by VPA sentries patrolling the northern bank as they swam and waded to the island, their odds of getting away still looked good since they would soon be on the other side of the river from their enemies. These hopes were dashed when they found that on its southern bank the river washed up against a sheer, 7-meter cliff. The troops desperately tried to climb it using their weapons as mountaineers' axes while *bộ đội* lining the northern bank hammered them with mortars and automatic weapons. Less than half of the 200 men who attempted the crossing escaped by scaling the cliff or floating downstream.[149]

The survivors of this massacre fragmented into small parties that fled southward in various directions, hotly pursued by *bộ đội*. A group of 45 coalesced around 12th Company's commander, Captain Jean Michot, though this included 15 PIMs transporting supplies and equipment. The prisoners slipped away before 0700hrs, taking with them the radios they had been carrying, and Michot therefore could not contact two aircraft that were spotted overhead. Since it proved impossible to move in a straight line through the rugged, densely foliated terrain, the party advanced in zigzags, taking the path of least resistance, but the point men still had to be replaced every five minutes because they were tired out so quickly by the exertion of hacking a path through the underbrush. Michot therefore tried to stay on course by roughly paralleling the Nậm Nứa, but at midmorning his group encountered a series of bends in the river that slowed its progress and allowed the pursuing enemy to close in. It gradually disintegrated as men were killed, wounded or dropped out because of exhaustion, and Operation *Albatros* sputtered to an inglorious end by 1300hrs on May 8, when the last survivors were cornered on a hill west of Bản Na Ti, 13km from Isabelle.[150]

CHAPTER 9

CONCLUSION

No one knows how many men escaped the valley during Operation *Albatros* or slipped away from the POW columns over the coming days. But it's generally accepted that just 78 successfully reached friendly lines. This became far more difficult after General Cogny ordered the *Condor* force to fall back to Mường Sai on May 8 to avoid destruction by the now unrestrained VPA units at Điện Biên Phủ. Most of those who got clean away were Tai troops who spoke the local language, knew how to survive in the jungle, and could blend in with the civilian population. The odds for other Indochinese fugitives were less good, but still far better than for Europeans, who were generally "fish out of water" in this environment and stood out like the proverbial sore thumb. Only 19 made the trek successfully.[1]

While the lucky 78 made their escape, another 11,721 men were captured. Less than a quarter of these were effective combat troops; the rest were either wounded, "Rats of the Nậm Yum," or non-combat support troops.[2] The wounded numbered about 4,500, and the French hoped to gain Giáp's permission to repair the runway and evacuate them by air. But the VPA dragged its heels trying to extract the maximum French concessions before it agreed to permit this and directed all the medical supplies that were being airdropped each day to its own overcrowded and pitifully ill-equipped hospitals. It was not until May 13 that the first Red Cross plane landed, carrying Professor Pierre

Huard, the widely respected dean of the Hanoi Medical University, to open face-to-face negotiations. Four more days passed before the terms were settled, and a total of 858 wounded and 27 uninjured medical personnel were flown out by the end of May. In exchange, the French had to halt all combat air operations within 10km of the valley and over lengthy portions of RP41 that were crowded not only with POW columns, but also VPA troops marching back toward the Delta.[3]

The plight of the prisoners was terrible. The VPA barely had the means to keep its own troops fed and could spare only a few trucks to carry senior officers to POW camps as far as 480km away in the Việt Bắc. Other prisoners had to walk the whole way in forced marches lasting up to six weeks with little food and virtually no medical care. Few of the roughly 3,500 wounded who set out on this death march survived it, and many uninjured men also died since they were exhausted and poorly nourished even before the trek began. Conditions in the POW camps were little better, since food and medical care remained scarce and were doled out primarily to those prisoners who proved most receptive to Communist propaganda and brainwashing. The mental stress of trying to resist their captors' persistent "thought control" efforts (which ultimately proved futile) further weakened men who were already in terrible shape physically. Only about 3,900 were released in August–September 1954, but not all the rest had died. Perhaps a thousand Legionnaires were forcibly repatriated to their native countries that were under Communist rule, and an untold number of Indochinese prisoners simply were never released.[4]

The French estimated enemy casualties at 23,000 – with 7,900 dead and 15,000 wounded.[5] The VPA official figures are 4,020 killed, 9,118 wounded, and 792 missing – for a total of 13,930.[6] However, substantially higher figures for wounded can be found in *Công tác bảo đảm hậu cần trong Chiến dịch Điện Biên Phủ: Bài học kinh nghiệm và thực tiễn [Rear Services Support Operations During the Điện Biên Phủ Campaign: Lessons from Experience and Practice]*, which was published on the siege's fiftieth anniversary in 2004. It consists of a series of articles written by different authors who sometimes provide inconsistent data. Three different articles variously give the figures of 10,139, 15,000, and 16,130 for total wounded (i.e., evacuated to medical facilities). It's possible that the second number includes sick troops that are excluded from the first – which gives a separate figure of 4,489 *bộ đội* who were evacuated on account of illness. However, the same article that gives the highest figure says that in addition there were 4,492 sick troops.[7] Since the figure of 10,139 wounded covers the entire campaign from November 1953 through May 1954, it seems reasonable to conclude that the two higher numbers do as well.[8] Yet there can be little doubt that most of these thousands of additional casualties occurred during the siege rather than before it. Thus, even if one accepts the figure of 4,812 killed and missing as definitive, total losses would still be closer to the French estimate than the official VPA figure. Moreover, the official numbers seem to tally only casualties in those military units that actually fought at Điện Biên Phủ. They certainly don't include casualties among the civilian *dân công* toiling on the supply lines, who must have suffered heavily from French air attacks.

Yet debating casualty figures is pointless, since the VPA had won a decisive victory that was well worth the cost whether it was 13,930 or 23,000 casualties (or higher). When the Geneva Conference's Indochina talks opened on May 8, the DRVN delegation held all the cards. The humiliated French delegation was weakened still further when the political fallout from the defeat at Điện Biên Phủ caused the collapse of Prime Minister Joseph Laniel's right-wing government. He was succeeded on June 19 by leftist Pierre Mendès France, who promised to resign if he could not produce a ceasefire within a month. The Final Declaration of the Geneva Conference was actually signed on July 21, but backdated a day to accommodate his deadline. Thanks to support from the Chinese and Soviet delegations, whose masters desired peace and normalization of relations with the West for economic reasons, he got a better deal than anyone expected. The frustrated DRVN delegation had to accept the division of Vietnam pending elections in 1956 and was, in the meantime, given control of only half the country, although the military situation entitled them to about two-thirds. And both the United States (covertly) and the State of Vietnam rejected elections which Hồ Chí Minh was almost certain to win and they never took place. Vietnam would not be unified until the Second Indochina War ended two decades later.[9]

Apologiae

All nations and peoples are reluctant to accept humiliating defeats and often seek to construct, *ex post facto*, alternative narratives that turn defeats into noble sacrifices against impossible odds or even into victories of a sort. This is, for example, a central motif in the long, generally sad history of Irish rebellions against British rule. It also manifested itself in the "Lost Cause" mythology embraced by Southerners after the American Civil War, and, more recently, in the "Better War" or "Lost Victory" narrative which claims that the US actually won its Vietnam War militarily, only to throw the victory away on account of a loss of political will on the home front. Likewise, some French commentators have constructed a narrative that tries to make GONO's heroic sacrifice seem worthwhile. They argue that while only 5 percent of Navarre's order of battle was destroyed at the siege, 60 percent of Giáp's regular divisions (four out of six) were decimated at Điện Biên Phủ and took a full year to recover from their losses. And, by tying down the bulk of Giáp's Main Force *corps de bataille* in the remote mountains of northwest Tonkin for five months, GONO supposedly saved the Red River Delta from being overrun.

This argument is just as specious as the "Lost Victory" narrative that many Americans have used to make their humiliation in Vietnam more palatable. It's true that three of Giáp's regular divisions lost most of their veteran troops at Điện Biên Phủ (the 351st Heavy Division did not), but it was immaterial, since they'd won a decisive victory that ended the war in a few months. As for saving the Delta, the French would have fought under far more advantageous terms if Giáp had made the mistake of attacking there again – and could possibly have won a major victory, though not the war. In any event, the Delta had been so thoroughly infiltrated by VPA guerrillas and regulars that, apart from the major towns and transportation routes, very little of it was still truly under French control. On June 28, FTNV launched Operation *Auvergne*, which evacuated the entire southern half of the Delta in just six days.[10]

French veterans of Điện Biên Phủ (especially senior officers) have also offered self-exculpatory rationales for their defeat that have been echoed in the works of Western historians. Some have implied that GONO's non-European troops were chiefly to blame. Langlais wrote:

> In fact, of the thirteen strongpoints lost by the first of May, eight had been [lost] by the defection of their garrisons without costing the enemy a single man. These garrisons represented a total of three battalions [BT3, I/4 RTM and III/3 RTA]. A fourth [BT2] was left throughout the entire battle sitting in the middle of the camp totally annihilated [psychologically]. It may not be good to tell the whole truth, however these defections cannot be ignored.[11]

This is hyperbole, to say the least, since at most five strongpoints were lost due to routs and defections (Anne Maries-1 and -2, Dominique-2, Eliane-1, and Françoise); the entire I/4 RTM and elements of III/3 RTA and BT3 continued to serve until the end of the siege; and BT2 did, in fact, make important contributions to GONO's defense. But the non-European troops make easy scapegoats, since who could dispute that the mass desertions, routs, and 5 BPVN's failure at Bàn Khe Phai greatly influenced the siege's outcome? And blaming the Algerian, Moroccan, Tai, and Vietnamese troops also served a more subtle purpose. In the 1950s, white supremacy was still taken for granted in most of the Western world, and to be defeated by an inferior, Asian foe was disgraceful. It was simply inconceivable that a French (i.e., white) army could be trounced by an army of primitive, technologically backward, yellow-skinned Vietnamese. But it was quite another thing if three-fifths of the "French" troops were themselves black- and yellow-skinned. A decade later, Bigeard famously told a historian – perhaps with no conscious racial overtones – "If you had given me 10,000 SS troopers, we'd have held out."[12]

Yet if GONO fell because 60 percent of its garrison was non-European, how did Giáp win when the figure in his army was 100 percent? And how was it that elite parachute battalions like Bigeard's 6 BPC ranked above Legion infantry battalions when 50 percent of their personnel were non-European, while the Legion units had few or no non-Europeans in their ranks? And while Algerian and Moroccan battalions ranked below the Legionnaires, they were recruited from notoriously warlike populations, and in past wars had often been thought superior to run-of-the-mill units of the lily-white metropolitan French Army. No such comparison was possible in Indochina, of course, because only a handful of elite metropolitan units ever served there. BT2 and BT3 ranked last among GONO's regular battalions when it came to fighting positional battles, but were far superior to every other unit in the garrison in junglecraft and familiarity with the local terrain, language, and culture. Their tragedy was that the circumstances of the siege offered them no opportunity to exploit these unique capabilities. The CSMs, of course, had never been intended to fight VPA regulars, and were neither trained nor equipped for the role. It was bad enough that they had to be positioned on exposed outposts such as Françoise and Wieme, but to leave one on a crucial strongpoint like Dominique-2 was an act of criminal negligence.

The mass desertions and combat failures of non-European units are among the most famous episodes of the entire siege, while incidents that show them in a better light are virtually unknown. Thus, 5/BT's crucial victory at Dominique-5 has been totally overlooked, though it deserves to be celebrated just as much as Lieutenant Brunbrouck's famous and contemporaneous stand on Dominique-3. The doomed, but steadfast and skillful, defense of "Huguette-4" is well known, but has usually been credited to imaginary Legion paras rather than the company of Moroccans that actually fought to the last cartridge on Lily-3. The important role that I/4 RTM played during the battles for Huguette has likewise been almost completely overlooked. II/1 RTA served on Isabelle from start to finish without a single stain on its reputation (including the sortie of April 26), sharing the most difficult missions equally with the Legionnaires of III/3 REI. Then there was 5 BPVN, which – apart from a single incident on March 15 – fought just as well as any other parachute unit in the valley. It did not "disintegrate" on March 15, as Fall suggests, and he and Langlais are unjustly making scapegoats of the Vietnamese paras when they suggest that 5 BPVN contributed little to GONO's defense. Finally, there were the African gunners who kept GONO's artillery in action despite increasingly deadly VPA counterbattery fire. II/4 RAC alone had 48 men killed and 179 wounded out of a total strength of 465 (including 117 replacements).[13]

However, the most popular and persistent excuse offered for the disaster at Điện Biên Phủ has been that the defenders were defeated by superior firepower. Since the French had been counting on superior firepower to overcome their considerable numerical and positional disadvantages at Điện Biên Phủ, the argument goes, all their plans were upended when the VPA unexpectedly trumped them in that department. Now this is a curious argument, since the Deuxième Bureau produced accurate estimates of the artillery and flak that Giáp would bring to Điện Biên Phủ well before the siege and de Castries, Cogny, and Navarre were all familiar with this data. And French authors writing during the first decade after the siege generally stuck with the Deuxième Bureau's numbers, which showed the VPA with no advantage in heavy artillery – though General Navarre, no doubt desperate to salvage his reputation, added "The [VPA] artillery strength was augmented by the probable intervention of two additional battalions of 105s."[14]

The storyline changed dramatically in 1967 with the posthumous publication of Bernard Fall's *Hell in a Very Small Place*, which bluntly claimed that GONO had been outgunned four-to-one:

> While exact figures will no doubt forever remain unknown, French ground and air observation (which was far from perfect) estimated that the enemy finally fielded at Điện Biên Phủ at least forty-eight field howitzers of 105mm caliber, forty-eight pack howitzers of the 75mm caliber, forty-eight heavy 120mm mortars, and at least as many 75mm recoilless rifles... In all, then, the Communists possessed at least 200 guns above the 57mm caliber. On

the French side, the maximum number of such guns ever available amounted to sixty and dropped to an average of less than forty within a week after the battle had begun.[15]

Fall's book was the first-full length study on the subject in English and quickly became the standard Western account of Điện Biên Phủ.[16] As a result, his conclusions about Giáp's artillery strength have gained wide acceptance and been incorporated into the prevailing Western narrative of the siege. And for several decades, it was nearly impossible to challenge that narrative because Vietnamese publications offered few details about the VPA's order of battle and weaponry at Điện Biên Phủ. The veil only began to lift in the 1980s, and not until the siege's fiftieth anniversary was all the information necessary to disprove Fall's conclusions publicly available – though only in Vietnamese-language works.

The following table compares peak strengths including weapons in units that arrived after the siege began, but not replacement weapons (an area in which the French had a decided advantage). If one counts only artillery pieces above 60mm, the VPA's superiority was just 1.6 to 1 (254 to 157), and 81/82mm mortars, which were not impressive bunker-killers, accounted for fully two-thirds of the VPA's advantage. Excluding them, it enjoyed only a 1.3-to-1 advantage (92 to 70). And discounting weapons that were not present when the siege began (i.e., four French 75mm ĐKZs, and at least 34 VPA heavy weapons – a dozen 75mm ĐKZs, a dozen H6s, at least six 75mm mountain guns, and four 120mm mortars), the VPA was actually at a slight disadvantage (58 to 62) on March 13! The dozen VPA 75mm ĐKZs were in action only for the last two weeks of the siege, and the H6s merely for its final 24 hours.

HEAVY WEAPONRY COMPARISON		
Weapon	VPA	French[17]
155mm howitzer		4
105mm howitzer	24	24
75mm howitzer	24	10
102mm mrl	12	
120mm mortar	20	28
81/82mm mortar	162	87
60mm mortar	179	113
50mm mortar		36
Bomb-thrower	Unknown	

75mm recoilless rifle	12	4
57mm recoilless rifle	57	56
90mm bazooka	72	
Flamethrower		88
TOTAL (1.25 to 1)	562	450

Yet, even French authors who credit the VPA with only modest numbers of artillery pieces still claim that GONO was outgunned because they believe the besiegers fired more shells than the besieged. In 1956, a French journalist claimed that Giáp's gunners had fired an astounding 350,000 shells![18] Two years later, Navarre put the figure at over 200,000 shells, though in a 1963 interview he raised it to 250,000.[19] Bernard Fall estimated VPA expenditures at 103,000 shells of 75mm or larger, while claiming that GONO fired just 93,000 (both numbers exclude a great many smaller-caliber shells).[20] Here again, most Western historians followed Fall's lead just as they had when accepting his estimate of VPA artillery strength. And again, in the absence of published Vietnamese logistical data, there was no way of challenging Fall's conclusions.

As discussed in Chapter 2, this gap in the literature was finally closed in 2004 with the publication of *Điện Biên Phủ, Mốc Vàng Thời Đại [Điện Biên Phủ: Landmark of the Golden Era]*. It reveals that only 69,000 shells of 75mm+ were allocated to VPA gunners during the Điện Biên Phủ campaign – and over half of them (37,300) were 81/82mm mortar rounds. These were supplemented by shells recovered from misdropped parachute loads. The following table shows the number of shells of each caliber that were airdropped during the siege. No comprehensive data is available on how many were misdropped, though Fall reports that 12,000 75mm+ shells went astray (including at least 3,500 105mm and 7,000 120mm).

AIRDROPPED AMMUNITION*	
Caliber	**Quantity[21]**
155mm howitzer	5,081
105mm howitzer	76,768
75mm tank gun	1,874
75mm recoilless rifle	190
120mm mortar	21,414
81mm mortar	74,007
60mm mortar	52,886
50mm mortar	5,300
57mm recoilless rifle	752

TOTAL	238,272
TOTAL 75mm+	179,334
*Excludes smoke and illumination shells	

Fall's figures for misdrops and French ammunition expenditures are both certainly too low. For on one hand, Giáp claims that his troops recovered 5,000 misdropped 105mm shells, while on the other, even if we double Fall's estimate of 12,000, that still leaves GONO with 157,000 75mm+ shells![22] And that's only ammunition that arrived after the siege began, and ignores the tens of thousands of rounds that were already in GONO's dumps on March 13. In contrast, even if one assumes that 24,000 shells were misdropped and all captured and used, that only brings the VPA's 75mm+ shell consumption to 93,000 – which is the same number that Fall reports GONO fired. But, according to Colonel Vaillant, GONO expended 5,000 155mm, 70,000 105mm, and 28,000 120mm rounds during the siege (for a total of 103,000 75mm+ shells not including Bison main gun, 75mm recoilless, and 81mm mortar shells).[23] No figures are available for consumption of these other calibers, but considering that 76,000 of them were airdropped, it must have been very high.

GONO ARTILLERY AMMUNITION CONSUMPTION[24]				
Shell caliber	Typical consumption on days without major battles	Typical consumption on days when major battles occurred	Total consumption during siege	Shells destroyed by VPA artillery
105mm	1,000*	2,700–10,500 total	70,000	3,000
120mm	500		28,000	2,000
155mm	40		5,000	400**

* Including 250 'credited' to forward observers, 400 for flak suppression, and 350 for other missions.
** Plus 600 propellant charges.

Thus, Vietnamese authors who describe French artillery firing far more shells than their own are simply telling the plain truth. During both Giáp's first and second offensives, the French fired as many 105mm shells in just a few days as his logistical system delivered to the valley during the entire campaign. Overall, GONO's 105s expended 70,000 shells while the VPA's fired at most 20,000. Ratios for 120mm mortar and 75mm howitzer ammunition expenditures were also lopsided, and the VPA did not even possess a weapon comparable to the French 155s, which were literally in a class by themselves. A 105mm warhead contained about 2.18kg of explosive, while a 155mm shell held 7.6kg.

Finally, in the siege's opening weeks, many VPA shells that had been in storage for years proved to be duds. On the night of March 13–14, for example, as much as 40 percent of the shells that fell upon 8/III/10 RAC failed to explode.[25] And none of these calculations takes airpower into account. When it's factored into the equation, there can be no doubt whatsoever that – just as planned – GONO's firepower exceeded the VPA's several times over.

Another common apologia argues that it was really the Chinese that defeated the French at Điện Biên Phủ, by unexpectedly supplying the primitive VPA with the equipment and technical expertise necessary to prevail in a conventional siege. This canard may be easily dispensed with. De Castries, Cogny, and Navarre cannot have been surprised by the trucks, heavy artillery, and flak that China supplied before the siege began because the Deuxième Bureau had given them plenty of advance warning. Intelligence was an area in which the CEFEO excelled throughout the Điện Biên Phủ campaign. What truly surprised French commanders was not that the VPA possessed this new equipment and weaponry, but that it proved so proficient at using it. In an April 5 meeting with Prime Minister Laniel, US Ambassador to France Douglas Dillon was told that it was "fully established" that there were 40 radar-controlled 37mm antiaircraft guns at Điện Biên Phủ operated by Chinese crews, and that all 1,000 supply trucks operating on the supply roads were driven by Chinese army personnel.[26]

In fact, there were only 628 trucks on the supply lines, and nearly 800 Vietnamese military and civilian drivers were mobilized to operate them. The official history of VPA rear support operations during the Điện Biên Phủ campaign reports, "the High Command transferred to the Transportation Department 228 trucks, 600 drivers, and 200 mechanics who had been trained in Class II at the Progressive School [probably in China]. In addition, the Transportation Department's units were able to conduct on-the-job training that provided 121 more drivers and recruited a total of 74 more drivers and mechanics from local areas."[27] And it was never "fully established" that the 37mm flak guns were radar-controlled since there was (and still is) no evidence for it. Neither Vietnamese authors, who are always anxious to celebrate the VPA's mastery of technical skills, nor Chinese historians, who are determined to claim as much credit as possible for the triumph at Điện Biên Phủ, make any mention of radar. And although a Chinese advisor was present with each 37mm gun (and H6 rocket launcher), the rest of their crews were Vietnamese. Langlais ridiculed those who suggested that Chinese aid had unfairly tipped the odds against the French.

Our enemies had, over the past seven years, exchanged peasants' rags for combat dress, and their handmade grenades for Russian or Czechoslovakian arms that were comparable to our American weapons. Moralists were offended. This Chinese aid is scandalous! It would have been great to keep on fighting peasants armed with sticks. I got quite a kick out of this. What is more natural than to get aid from an ally? If we are to be honest with ourselves, Chinese aid was only a drop in the bucket compared to the flood of US materiel on our side.[28]

And even if there had been Chinese truck drivers and mechanics on the supply lines in addition to the CMAG staff and engineering and artillery advisors at the front, one must recall the hundreds of Americans that supported GONO. In addition to several advisors who served in the valley before the siege began (and were withdrawn soon after March 13), there were dozens of US pilots ferrying planes and a torrent of supplies to Vietnam, dozens more flying desperately needed reinforcements direct from France to Indochina, hundreds of mechanics keeping French planes in the air, dozens of parachute packers rigging loads to be dropped into Điện Biên Phủ, and, of course, the American CAT pilots who flew hundreds of combat missions over the valley. And all this was in addition to massive material, logistical, and financial assistance without which the French would have had to abandon the war years earlier. The fact of the matter is that neither side could have fought at Điện Biên Phủ without the wholehearted support of its Cold War patron.

Some French historians – most notably Bernard Fall – took the United States to task for not intervening directly to save GONO. But the French had always been chary about allowing too large a US presence in Indochina because they rightly feared that the Americans wanted to rid the war of its detrimental colonial context by forcing them to grant true independence to the State of Vietnam. The Americans also wanted to build a self-sufficient VNA that was not dependent on French leadership and technical and logistical support. The French threw obstacles in the way of this policy by refusing to allow Americans to train Indochinese troops and obstructing efforts by members of the US Military Assistance Advisory Group (MAAG) to ascertain just how American-supplied funds and military equipment were being used.[28] Not until the eleventh hour did the French seek direct US military intervention to avoid a humiliating defeat.

A few American historians have suggested that the United States missed an opportunity to save Vietnam from Communism by choosing not to intervene at Điện Biên Phủ. Mark Moyar, for instance, argues that a couple of massive US airstrikes could have wiped out practically all of the VPA's regular troops and won the war in a matter of days. But this opinion was not shared by most senior US and French military commanders, who believed that, while American aerial intervention could probably have saved GONO, it would not have decided the war and was likely to have provoked massive Chinese intervention that they would have had to match with hundreds of thousands of American troops on the ground. General Ridgway also recognized that the French were finished in Indochina with or without direct US intervention, and were trying to get the Americans to assume responsibility for a colonial war that was already lost. President Eisenhower truly "dodged a bullet" when he chose not to jump into the Indochinese quagmire where the United States would be bogged down by the legacies of French imperialism. The tragedy is that Senator Lyndon Johnson, who played a significant role in US Indochinese policy deliberations in 1954, did not follow Eisenhower's example when he was president himself a decade later.

Missed opportunities

There were missed opportunities at Điện Biên Phủ, but for France, not the United States. First and foremost, Navarre missed an opportunity to avoid a decisive battle there. Had GONO merely been a lightly fortified "mooring point" for GMI guerrillas and Tai auxiliaries, as Cogny intended, it could easily have been evacuated with little injury to the CEFEO's morale or overall strategic position. Abandoning a major *base aéro-terrestre* at Điện Biên Phủ – especially after Cogny proclaimed "We've taken the place and we shall stay there" – would have undermined faith in Navarre's leadership and been politically embarrassing (especially with the Americans), but still would have been the wise move. By choosing to accept battle, Navarre merely resolved Giáp's dilemma about where to employ his strategic reserves. Had he not done so, Giáp might eventually have been tempted to take another try at the Red River Delta, where the French could have fought under far more advantageous circumstances.

Another opportunity was missed when de Castries, Cogny, and Navarre failed to recast their plans after Giáp's cancelation of the January offensive dashed hopes that the outcome at Điện Biên Phủ would be decided in a brief battle lasting only a few days. As the calendar rolled on into February and March, evidence mounted that Giáp was now preparing for a protracted siege, and had upended French assumptions by deploying and sustaining four divisions in the Tai country and northern Laos, and hauling heavy artillery and flak to the valley along with impressive stocks of ammunition. The wise response would have been to launch a "crash program" to strengthen GONO's fortifications (including communications trenches and new strongpoints on Phony Hill and around the airfield), replace the two BTs with units better suited for positional battles, and reinforce the garrison with another battalion or two plus additional medical and artillery units. But while nearly all these steps were proposed – including by de Castries and Navarre themselves in certain cases – none of them was implemented. Instead, everyone in real authority seems to have clung to reassuring, but outdated, assumptions that the battle would be short, the airfields would remain in operation, and reinforcements and supplies could be lifted in and wounded flown out at will. Thus, the fact that the air transport fleet was inadequate to sustain a prolonged siege was simply ignored, the impact of the rainy season on air operations was not honestly addressed, and no effort was made to stockpile parachutes in anticipation of prolonged airfield closures.

It seems clear that these rose-tinted assumptions were rooted in the perceived lessons of the French victory at the siege of Nà Sản in November–December 1952. There, over the space of just about a week, 11 CEFEO battalions had repulsed, at great cost to the attackers, a series of assaults launched by a VPA siege force comprising six regiments of the 308th, 312th, and 316th Divisions (not all of which became engaged). And they had done so with fortifications constructed so hastily that many strongpoints even lacked barbed-wire obstacles, had no tanks and only limited artillery support. When the first wave of attacks began on November 23, the heaviest French weapons at Nà Sản were four 120mm mortars. But since the solitary runway remained in operation throughout the brief siege, these were quickly supplemented by a dozen 105mm howitzers, and reinforcements and supplies were landed on it daily, while the wounded were evacuated by the same means. Although the Điện Biên Phủ *base aéro-terrestre* had only one more battalion than Nà Sản's it was far stronger in every other way. It was better fortified, had twice as many 105s and seven times as many 120s, plus four 155s, ten tanks, its own permanent detachment of fighter-bombers and spotter planes, and two runways located 5km apart. But such simplistic comparisons miss the differences in terrain that allowed Nà Sản's defenders to occupy the heights overlooking the airport, and ignore the fact that the VPA artillery there was even weaker than the garrison's and included only the standard mix of mortars, 75mm mountain guns, and AA machine guns.[30]

In retrospect, it should have been obvious to senior French commanders that their optimistic assumptions would not apply at Điện Biên Phủ since it was about 150km farther from French airbases, the terrain was vastly different, and the VPA would have heavy artillery and flak weapons this time round. It's hard to explain how they failed to recognize this without factoring racism into the equation. They knew all about the VPA's new truck fleet and heavy weaponry, but simply assumed that it was incapable of using these game-changing capabilities effectively. Worse yet, as the VPA disproved one assumption after another in the months preceding the siege, instead of reconsidering those that had yet to be overturned, French commanders generally clung to them all the more fiercely. At the end of the day, they simply could not conceive that an army of primitive Asians (no matter how brave and skilled in other forms of warfare) could ever best them in a conventional, Western-style battle.

When French commanders' last, most cherished illusions were demolished in the siege's opening hours, the pendulum suddenly swung from blind optimism to an excessive pessimism that was manifested in Piroth's suicide, Keller's mental breakdown, de Castries' abdication of authority, Tourret's "excessive nervousness," and Langlais' indecision. This, in turn, led to another series of missed opportunities. The first was the Gabrielle counterattack, which could have altered the siege's psychological balance by exploiting Giáp's faulty decision to press ahead with the assault although his meticulously crafted plan had fallen into chaos. If Langlais had made a firm decision to repulse the assault on Gabrielle and committed the entire 1 BEP or 8 BPC to the counterattack, the odds of success would have been very good. Likewise, if he'd been willing to replace or substantially reinforce BT3 on Anne Marie, that CR could have held out for some time. But although Langlais never gave way to despair, he was infected by pessimism insofar as he abandoned all hope of holding the Northern Subsector, and focused myopically on husbanding his reserves for the coming battles on the Main Position.

Bernard Fall observed that Langlais was so obsessed with manpower that he tended to overlook logistical considerations, and had to be reminded about them by de Castries. If so, it was never more apparent than in the case of Anne Marie, since Langlais obviously cared only about the likely cost in manpower of holding its outer hill strongpoints. This caused him to overlook

– or at least disregard – the many countervailing factors that argued in favor of trying to hold them. First and foremost, the hills kept enemy flak and infantry at arm's length from the airstrip and main drop zone, and every day they remained in friendly hands was a great boon to GONO (especially the wounded awaiting evacuation in its overcrowded hospitals). Secondly, holding Anne Marie preserved maneuver space for the Bisons, and the terrain between Anne Marie and the Main Position was tailor-made for armor. Finally, Langlais simply ignored the deleterious effect that losing a third CR in short order would inevitably have upon the garrison's morale – and especially the non-European units.

GONO's command crisis was overcome, however, in the latter half of March thanks to the prolonged lull in VPA attacks and the arrival of a half-dozen new senior commanders – including the unflappable and ever-aggressive Major Bigeard, whose presence boosted the entire garrison's morale. The same could not be said about FTNV and EMIFT, since despite a few fleeting periods of cautious optimism, Cogny and Navarre never overcame their initial pessimism. During the first days of the siege, Langlais had refused to make the hard choice between writing off Gabrielle and Anne Marie, and taking the steps necessary to hold them, but had tried without success to find some sort of middle ground where half-measures would suffice. Cogny and Navarre did this throughout the entire siege, and consequently missed several opportunities either to give GONO better odds for survival or to cut their losses dramatically. Thus, instead of reinforcing GONO with II/1 RCP in late March, when its presence might have turned the tide of battle, they waited until early April, when the battalion could merely stabilize an already desperate situation. Their joint decision to drop in 1 BPC when Giáp's May Day offensive had already pushed GONO to the brink of destruction was another half-measure born of desperation and indecisiveness rather than sober calculation. If the odds of saving Điện Biên Phủ through diplomacy at Geneva were good enough to warrant sacrificing another precious para battalion, it should have been sent before the new offensive began rather than after.

How did the VPA win?

To say that the French lost at Điện Biên Phủ owing to their own errors is true, but unfairly and inaccurately denies the VPA any role in achieving its own triumph. For, despite their mistakes, the French enjoyed numerous advantages (armor, airpower, elite troops, superior gunners, larger ammo dumps, and more experience in positional warfare) that the VPA had to overcome in order to win. CMAG helped the VPA accomplish this, but the key player was Giáp himself, who, though lacking experience in positional battles, did not slavishly follow Chinese advice, and learned a great deal as the siege progressed. He made several major errors that cost his troops dear and gave the French opportunities to reverse the tide of battle – some of which they seized and some not. However, his good command decisions outnumbered and certainly outweighed the bad ones.

Giáp's first and most crucial decision was to cancel the "Fast Strike–Fast Victory" offensive scheduled for January 26. If it had gone ahead as planned, Điện Biên Phủ would be remembered as a great French victory. Even if Giáp abandoned the offensive at the urging of his CMAG advisors (which is far from clear), the moral courage necessary for him to take this step was truly remarkable. As previously discussed, Communists view warfare as a scientific endeavor in which the outcomes of battles and campaigns can be predicted with mathematical precision. This reflects their devotion to the theory of "scientific socialism," pioneered by Karl Marx, which holds that the ultimate triumph of Communism is inevitable owing to the influence of immutable social, economic, and political forces upon the course of human history. Since the outcome is predestined, success is certain as long as the Party (or in this case, the People's Army) objectively weighs all the relevant factors beforehand and properly indoctrinates itself. Consequently, failures are never the fault of the institution, but only of individuals who fall prey to "subjectivism" and "rightist tendencies."

When Giáp suddenly reversed course on the morning of January 26, he skated dangerously close to admitting these sins, since otherwise how could the offensive that was certain to succeed the day before have become too risky to attempt just a few hours later? Indeed, merely taking a position contrary to the (inevitably) unanimous Party resolution that had authorized the offensive just weeks before could be seen as dangerously individualistic and thus "subjective." In short, by challenging the groupthink of his senior staff and commanders, Giáp was courageously putting his career at risk. Some might scoff at this and say that his rank and celebrity insulated Giáp from such worries, but in fact, both his career and reputation would later suffer significantly from his opposition to the 1968 Tet Offensive.

Giáp's "hardest decision of [his] entire life" denied the French the swift and certain victory they expected at Điện Biên Phủ, but left the VPA with the immense challenge of fighting and winning a prolonged siege, although it had almost no experience in that kind of warfare. It had far superior numbers of infantry at the front, but the French had always taken it for granted that they would be outnumbered and were certain that their firepower would overcome that disadvantage. Moreover, as shown in many places throughout this book, the actual VPA advantage at the point of contact during assaults was not always as pronounced as one might expect. There were times when "human waves" of *bộ đội* surged into strongpoints yelling the battle cry *"tiến lên!"* ("go forward!") but these were rare because such tactics were exceedingly dangerous in the face of French firepower, and the need to funnel troops through narrow gaps in minefields and barbed-wire obstacles generally prohibited massed charges.

The VPA did benefit from advantageous terrain at Điện Biên Phủ. Unlike at Nà Sản, its batteries could be emplaced anywhere on the heights dominating the airports and every other part of the *base aéro-terrestre*. This enabled it to confound key French assumptions by closing the runway during the first hours of the siege and making it impossible for aircraft to survive on the ground except at night. Deploying artillery on the forward slope of the ridges around the valley also simplified targeting for inexperienced VPA gunners by enabling them to use direct fire. Yet this was very risky, since the battery positions were within the defenders' line of sight and would, consequently, be easier to detect and more vulnerable to counterfire by French tanks, planes, and artillery. Colonel Piroth predicted that Giáp would be so anxious to protect his precious handful of heavy guns that he would have to make the safe – and conventional – choice by deploying them in defiladed positions behind the ridges where only French aircraft could spot them.

The VPA confounded this and many other assumptions by performing engineering prodigies. Siege warfare is largely about engineering, and although the French had more experience at it, they did not take into account Giáp's CMAG advisors, who had all fought in Korea. For its last two years (1951–53), the Korean War was essentially a vast, static siege that pitted superior Chinese (and North Korean) numbers against superior United Nations firepower. The Chinese had learned the hard way how to survive the torrent of high explosives that enemy tanks, artillery, and aircraft rained down on them, and passed this knowledge on to their Vietnamese comrades. Thus, like the Chinese in Korea, the VPA installed its artillery in expertly camouflaged casemates that were invulnerable to bombs and shells, and could be destroyed only by a direct hit on their embrasures – which were opened only during fire missions. Even greater engineering feats were accomplished in reconstructing hundreds of kilometers of supply and artillery roads, and keeping them functioning despite constant air interdiction and the steadily worsening effects of the rainy season. And since the VPA had none of the heavy construction and earthmoving equipment that a Western army would have employed, it had to rely upon sheer muscle-power provided by its troops and a quarter-million *dân công*. Victory at Điện Biên Phủ could not have been achieved without the General Mobilization – which obliged most of Tonkin's population to make personal sacrifices of some sort in support of the campaign. This was truly a "People's War," whether the sacrifices were made voluntarily or not.

The VPA also employed novel tactics at Điện Biên Phủ. None surprised the French more than Giáp's switch to trench warfare in the second half of March. Whether this idea was entirely his own (which seems unlikely) or was recommended by his staff and/or CMAG, it was a brave choice since it meant exposing his troops to GONO's superior firepower around the clock. This completely upset French expectations that the VPA would adhere to its familiar pattern of nighttime attacks followed by quick withdrawals before dawn to deny the French the chance to bring their planes, tanks, and artillery to bear. To their dismay, they found that *bộ đội* occupying well-constructed trench systems could resist the full weight of French firepower even in broad daylight. Trench warfare also enabled Giáp to turn the tables on the French by forcing them to attack heavily fortified positions every day in order to reinforce and resupply isolated strongpoints. Given the disparity in numbers between besiegers and besieged, this was an attritional contest that GONO simply could not win.

The VPA also responded creatively to the artillery ammunition crisis of April. Since the shell shortage ruled out large-scale infantry assaults for much of the month, a Western army would have halted operations until its supply dumps were replenished. Instead, Giáp intensified his attack on GONO's aerial supply line by tightening the noose of trenches and flak around its remaining strongpoints, and relying upon sniping, small arms, and infantry heavy weapons to attrite French manpower. The 36th Regiment took things a step further by developing its unique "creeping siege" tactics, which allowed strongpoints to be assaulted by stealth with minimal expenditure of artillery ammunition. Finally, Giáp encouraged VPA gunners – even those manning his 105s – to employ sniper tactics to wear down enemy strength with precisely aimed single shots. None of these tactical innovations owed much to the CMAG advisors, and were either developed on the spot or passed on by VPA guerrillas who were sent up to fill gaps in the ranks.

Bernard Fall wrote, "Dien Bien Phu, like almost all other besieged fortresses, eventually died from its supply deficiencies."[31] This is absolutely correct, since the siege was essentially a contest between two utterly different logistical systems. The French accepted battle at Điện Biên Phủ largely because they believed that logistical factors favored them there. They took it for granted that the VPA could not sustain a lengthy siege hundreds of kilometers away from its logistical bases. Thus, an assault on Điện Biên Phủ could last no more than a week, and for that, their small air transport fleet was more than adequate. It also meant that they did really have to worry about combat in the valley dragging on into the rainy season.

These predictions were fatally wrong, of course. They would have been accurate had Giáp still been dependent upon porters to transport his supplies, but thanks to Chinese aid he was able for the very first time to establish a motorized supply system. That meant restoring and maintaining hundreds of kilometers of road, but once that was accomplished, the truly decisive battle was fought between the French pilots who sought to interdict Giáp's supply lines and VPA flak gunners who tried to interdict GONO's. The Armée de l'Air and Aéronavale never had enough aircraft to do the job, even if they had not been under pressure from GONO to fly flak suppression, counterbattery, and close air support missions in the valley itself. But aided by worsening weather and the sacrifice of thousands of *bộ đội* who died or were maimed in order to encroach upon the DZs and tighten the flak envelope, VPA antiaircraft gunners did eventually choke off GONO's aerial lifeline – and won the battle. As Bernard Fall put it, "If any particular group of enemy soldiers should be considered indispensable to victory, then it must be the Viet-Minh antiaircraft gunners and their Chinese instructors."[32]

Vietnamese authors claim that 62 aircraft were shot down at Điện Biên Phủ, which is much higher than the losses reported by the French. Even if this figure covers the entire period of the campaign starting on November 20, 1953, rather than just the duration of the siege, it's still inflated. The number of planes shot down between March 13 and May was relatively low, but the number hit by flak (several times in some cases) was immense when one considers that the French had just 220 combat and military transport aircraft available when the siege began. Historically, the effectiveness of antiaircraft defenses has been measured less in terms of planes shot down than in terms of the deterrent effect they had on enemy air operations. Such was the case at Điện Biên Phủ, where VPA flak units decisively influenced the siege's outcome by forcing French pilots to fly higher and more cautiously than they would have otherwise – greatly reducing the accuracy of their bombing and supply drops. Another interesting fact that emerges from the data is that, compared with the B-26s, five times as many transport planes were hit or shot down. It has been alleged that the Armée de l'Air bomber crews took fewer risks than the French and American transport pilots, and these figures would seem to support that contention.[33]

MILITARY AIRCRAFT LOST AND DAMAGED AT ĐIỆN BIÊN PHỦ[34]				
Type	Hit by flak	Shot down	Missing in action	Destroyed on ground
F6F Bearcat	12	1	4	6
F6F Hellcat	10	3	1	0
SB2C Helldiver	1	2	0	0
B-26 Invader	22	1	3	0
PB4Y Privateer	1	1	1	0
C-47 Dakota	68	4	0	3
C-119 Packet	42	1	0	0
MS.500 Cricket	2	1	0	5
Helicopters	0	0	0	2
TOTAL	158	14	9	16

MILITARY AIRCREW CASUALTIES AT ĐIỆN BIÊN PHỦ[35]				
TYPE	Killed	Wounded	Missing	TOTAL
F6F Bearcat	4	1	1	6
F6F Hellcat	2	1	1	4
SB2C Helldiver	1	0	1	2
B-26 Invader	1	0	14	15
PB4Y Privateer	0	0	18	18
C-47 Dakota	12	0	14	26
C-119 Packet	0	0	6	6
MS.500 Cricket	1	0	0	1
Helicopters	1	2	0	3
TOTAL	22	4	55	81
Most of the missing were killed. Many of those taken prisoner died in captivity.				

French flak suppression efforts failed due to insufficient numbers of aircraft, poor bombing accuracy, and the fact that Giáp was constantly shifting his antiaircraft guns. By May, the Deuxième Bureau had identified 40 37mm battery positions and 45 12.7mm battery positions, which were occupied intermittently.

Postscript

This book aimed to answer many crucial questions about the showdown at Điện Biên Phủ that have remained unanswered for more than six decades. Although this task has involved correcting errors and filling gaps in Western accounts of the siege, it was chiefly a matter of presenting the other, Vietnamese, side of the story for the first time, for the recollections of Vietnamese veterans and the works of Vietnamese historians often challenge the prevailing Western narrative about Điện Biên Phủ. According to the Vietnamese authors, the popular image of the garrison being pulverized by a deluge of artillery shells and submerged by screaming hordes of *bộ đội* is nonsense. They describe the siege as a much more finely balanced contest in which, despite its numerical superiority, the VPA had to overcome daunting challenges – most notably, superior French firepower – in order to win. We can now say with great confidence that the VPA's victory owed more to superior engineering, novel tactics, and the judicious employment of limited resources – and French errors – than to the crude application of superior force.

BIBLIOGRAPHY

Books

Antoine, Jacques, *Il y a cinquante ans: Le 8e Choc à Diên-Biên-Phu, 21 novembre 1953 – 7 mai 1954* (l'Amicale du 8e RPIMA, 2004)

Bail, René, *Dernier baroud à Điên Biên Phu* (Paris: J. Grancher, 1990)

Bauer, Heinrich, *Les chemins de Diên Biên Phu* (Paris: Nimrod, 2015)

Bergot, Erwan, *Les Cent soixante-dix jours de Diên Biên Phu* (Paris: Presses de la Cité, 1979)

Bergot, Erwan, *Bataillon Bigeard* (Paris: Presses de la Cité, 1977)

Bertin, Marc, *Packet sur Diên Biên Phu: la vie quotidienne d'un pilote de transport* (Paris: Presses universitaires de France, 1991)

Bigeard, Marcel, *Pour Une Parcelle de Gloire* (Paris: Libraire Plon, 1975)

Brancion, Henri de, *Diên Biên Phu: artilleurs dans la fournaise* (Paris: Presses de la Cité, 1993)

Bruge, Roger, *Les hommes de Dien Bien Phu* (Paris: Perrin, 1999)

Cadeau, Ivan, *Diên Biên Phu: 13 mars–7 mai 1954* (Paris: Tallandier, 2013)

Cadeau, Ivan, *Le Génie au combat: Indochine 1945–1956* (Paris: Service Historique de la Defense, 2013)

Chief of Ordnance, *Technical Manual 9-1940: Land Mines* (Washington, DC: US War Department, 1943)

Chomsky, Noam & Zinn, Howard, eds., *The Pentagon Papers (The Senator Gravel Edition), Volume I* (Boston: Beacon Press, 1971)

Collet, Jean, *Avoir 20 ans à Dien Bien Phu* (Paris: Les éditions de la Bruyère, 1994)

Croizat, Col. V.J., trans., *A Translation from the French: Lessons of the War in Indochina, Memorandum RM-5271-PR* (Santa Monica: Rand Corporation, 1967)

Daillier, Général Pierre, *Le 4eme RTM: les bataillons de marche en Indochine 1947–1954* (Paris, Château de Vincennes: Service historique de la defense, 1990)

Đặng Việt Thủy, Trần Ngọc Đoàn and Nguyễn Thúy Cúc, *Hỏi Đáp về Các Binh Chủng Trong Quân đội Nhân dân Việt Nam [Frequently Asked Questions About the Branches of the Vietnamese People's Army]* (Hanoi: People's Army Publishing House, 2009)

Đặng Việt Thủy, Trần Ngọc Đoàn and Nguyễn Thúy Cúc, *Hỏi Đáp về Các Quân Chủng Trong Quân đội Nhân dân Việt Nam [Frequently Asked Questions About the Armed Services in the Vietnamese People's Army]* (Hanoi: People's Army Publishing House, 2009)

David, Michel, *Guerre secrète en Indochine – les maquis autochtones face au Viet-Minh 1950–1955* (Paris: Lavauzelle 2005)

Davidson, Phillip B., *Vietnam at War: The History 1946–1975* (Novato, CA: Presidio Press, 1988)

Demélas, Marie-Danielle, *Parachutistes en Indochine* (Paris: Vendémiaire 2016)

Duluat, Michel, *Mémoires de tonton Carabine* (Paris: A. Casalis, 2012)

Fall, Bernard, *Hell in a Very Small Place: The Siege of Dien Bien Phu* (Philadelphia: Lippincott, 1967)

Fall, Bernard, *Street Without Joy* (Harrisburg, PA: Stackpole, 1964)

Fall, Bernard, *Viet-Nam Witness, 1953–1966* (New York: Praeger, 1966)

Favreau, Jacques & Dufour, Nicolas, *Nasan: La Victoire Oubliée (1952–1953), Base Aéroterrestre au Tonkin* (Paris: Economica, 1999)

Fleury, Georges, *Le Para* (Paris: Grasset 1982)

Gaujac, Paul, ed., *Histoire des Parachutistes Français, Volume II* (Paris: SPL, 1975)

Gia Đức Phạm; et al., *Điện Biên Phủ, Mốc Vàng Thời Đại [Điện Biên Phủ: Landmark of the Golden Era]* (Hanoi: People's Army Publishing House, 2004)

Gras, Philippe, *L'Armée de l'air en Indochine, 1945–1954: l'impossible mission* (Paris: Harmattan, 2001)

Grauwin, Paul, *Doctor at Dien Bien Phu* (New York: The John Day Company, 1955)

Grintchenko, Michel, *Atlante-Arethuse: Une Operation de Pacification en Indochine* (Paris: Economica, 2001)

Journod, Pierre and Hugues, Tertrais, *Paroles de Dien Bien Phu, les survivants témoignent* (Paris: Texto, 2004–2012)

Juteau, Jean-Marie, *Quand les canons se taisent* (Montpellier: Imprimerie du progrès, 1994)

Kemencei, Janos, *Légionnaire en avant!* (Paris: Jacques Grancher, 1985)

Kim Lê & Huy Tỏan Lê, *Lịch sử Trung đoàn 36 (Sư đoàn 308, quân đoàn 1) [History of Regiment 36 (Division 308, Corps I)]* (Hanoi : Cực chính trị Quân Đòan I, 1990)

Langlais, Pierre, *Dien Bien Phu* (Paris, Éditions France-Empire, 1963)

Leboudec, Général Lucien, *Elevé à la dignité, mémoires 1923–1954, 2e edition* (Paris: Lavauzelle, 2015)

Lê Huy Toàn, Nguyễn Văn Nam & Hoàng Phú Cường, *Lịch sử Trung đoàn 88 Tu Vũ (1949–2009) [History of Regiment 88 Tu Vu (1949–2009)]* (Hanoi: People's Army Publishing House, 2009)

Lê Huy Toàn, *Trung đoàn Thủ Đô [Capital Regiment]* (Hanoi: People's Army Publishing House, 1992)

Le Mire, Henri, *Epervier: Le 8e Choc à Dien Bien Phu* (Paris: Editions Albin Michel S.A., 1988)

Leonetti, Guy, *Lettres de Dien Bien Phu* (Paris: Fayard, 2004)

Lê Trọng Tấn, *Từ Đồng Quan Đến Điện Biên [From Dong Quan to Dien Bien]* (Hanoi: People's Army Publishing House, 2002)

Logevall, Fredrik, *Embers of War: The Fall of an Empire and the Making of America's Vietnam* (New York: Random House, 2013)

Luciani, Jean & de Maleissye, Philippe, *Qui es-tu? Où vas-tu? souvenirs d'un officier parachutiste corse à la Légion Etrangère* (Paris: Indo-Editions, 2016)

Lưu Trọng Lân, *Lịch sử Sư đoàn 367, tập I [History of Division 367, Volume I]* (Air Defense Service, Vietnam, 1988)

Mengelle, André, *Diên-Biên-Phu: des chars et des hommes* (Paris: Éditions Lavauzelle, 2006)

Ministry of Defense, Artillery Command, *Biên Niên Sự Kiện Lịch Sử Ngành Kỹ Thuật Pháo Binh Quân đội Nhân dân Việt Nam 1945–1975 [Chronicle of Historic Events in Building the Vietnamese People's Army's Artillery, 1945–1975]* (Hanoi: People's Army Publishing House, 1997)

Ministry of Defense, Artillery Command Headquarters, *Pháo binh Quân đội nhân dân Việt Nam trong chiến dịch Diện Biên Phủ [Artillery of the People's Army of Vietnam During the Dien Bien Phu Campaign]* (Hanoi: People's Army Publishing House, 2004)

Ministry of Defense, Central Military Party Committee, *Một số văn kiện chỉ đạo chiến cuộc Đông Xuân 1953-1954 và chiến dịch Điện Biên Phủ [Selected War Guidance Documents from the Winter-Spring Campaign of 1953–1954 and the Battle of Dien Bien Phu]* (Hanoi: People's Army Publishing House, 2004)

Ministry of Defense, General Logistics Department, *Công tác bảo đảm hậu cần trong chiến dịch Điện Biên Phủ: bài học kinh nghiệm và thực tiễn [Rear Services Support Operations During the Dien Bien Phu Campaign: Lessons from Experience and Practice]* (Hanoi: People's Army Publishing House, 2004)

Molinier, Jacques, *les guerres d'un artilleur* (Paris: Les éditions de la Bruyère, 1999)

Morgan, Ted, *Valley of Death: The Tragedy at Dien Bien Phu That Led America into the Vietnam War* (New York: Random House, 2010)

Moyar, Mark, *Triumph Forsaken: the Vietnam War, 1954–1965* (Cambridge & New York: Cambridge University Press, 2009)

Muelle, Raymond, *Combats en pays thaï: Document* (Paris: Presses de la Cité, 1999)

Muzzati, Georgio Adamo, *Là où l'on meurt... Peut être* (Paris: Editions Italiques, 2004)

Navarre, Henri, *Agonie de l'Indochine (1953–1954)* (Paris: Libraire Plon, 1958)

Nguyễn Công Luận, *Nationalist in the Viet Nam Wars: Memoirs of a Victim Turned Soldier* (Bloomington: Indiana University Press, 2012)

Nguyen Khac Tinh, Phung Luan, & Truong Nguyen Tue, *Pháo binh Nhân dân Việt Nam: Những chặng đường chiến đấu, tập một [People's Artillery of Vietnam: Combat History, Volume I]* (Hanoi: People's Army Publishing House, 1982)

Nguyễn Tiến Hùng, *Lịch Sử Sư Đoàn 316 (1951–2001) [History of Division 316 (1951–2001)]* (Hanoi: People's Army Publishing House, 2001)

Phạm Văn Chiến & Phạm Văn Chanh, *Lịch sử Sư đoàn 304, Tập I (1950–1975) [History of Division 304, Volume I (1950–1975)]* (Hanoi: People's Army Publishing House, 2011)

Phan Chi Nhan, Le Kim, Le Huy Toan, & Nguyen Dinh Khuong, *Sư đoàn 308 Quân tiên phong [The 308th "Vanguard" Division]* (Hanoi: People's Army Publishing House, 1999)

Porch, Douglas, *The French Secret Services: from the Dreyfus Affair to the Gulf War* (New York: Farrar, Straus, and Giroux, 1995)

Prados, John, *Operation Vulture* (New York: ibooks, inc., 2002)

Quốc Dũng Nguyễn, *Lịch sử Trung đoàn bộ binh 209, Sư đoàn 312, 1947-2007: lưu hành nội bộ [History of Infantry Regiment 209 Division 312 (1947–2007) Internal Distribution Only]* (Hanoi: People's Army Publishing House, 2007)

Renaud, Patrick-Charles, *Aviateurs en Indochine: Diên Biên Phu, de novembre 1952 à juin 1954* (Paris: Grancher, 2003)

Rocolle, Pierre, *Pourquoi Dien Bien Phu?* (Paris: Flammarion 1968)

Roy, Jules, *The Battle of Dien Bien Phu* (New York: Harper & Row, 1965)

Roy, Jules, *La Bataille de Dien Bien Phu* (Paris: Rene Julliard, 1963),

Sergent, Pierre, *Paras-Légion, le 2eme BEP en Indochine* (Paris: Presses de la Cité 1982)

Sergent, Pierre, *Je ne regrette rien: la poignante histoire des légionnaires-parachutistes du 1er REP* (Paris: Fayard, 1972)

Shrader, Charles, *A War of Logistics: Parachutes and Porters in Indochina, 1945–1954* (Lawrence: University Press of Kansas, 2015)

Simon, Jean-Pierre, *Les aviateurs dans la guerre d'Indochine, 1945–1957: Témoignages* (Paris: Éditions du Grenadier/ANVOI, 2016)

Tanham, George K., *Communist Revolutionary Warfare* (New York: Praeger, 1967)

Thanh Huyền Đào, Duc Tue Dang, & Xuân Mai Nguyễn, *Chuyện những người làm nên lịch sử - Hồi ức Điện Biên Phủ 1954–2009 [Stories of People Who Made History: Memories of Dien Bien Phu, 1954–2009]* (Hanoi: National Political Publishing House, 2009)

Thanh Huyền Đào, Duc Tue Dang, & Xuân Mai Nguyễn, *Diên Biên Phu vu d'en face: paroles de bô dôi* (Paris: Nouveau Monde, 2010)

Thánh Nhân Nguyễn, *Lịch sử Trung đoàn 209, Sư đoàn 7, Quân đoàn 4 (1947–2003) [History of Regiment 209, Division 7, Corps 4 (1947–2003]* (Hanoi: People's Army Publishing House, 2004)

Thanh Tam Pham & Buchanan, Sherry, *Carnet de guerre d'un jeune Viêt-minh à Diên Biên Phu: 21 février–28 août 1954* (Paris: Armand Colin, 2011)

Thieu Tuong & Nguyễn Trung Kiên, *Ký ức pháo binh [Artillery Memories]* (Hanoi: People's Army Publishing House, 2007)

Trần Hanh, ed., *Một số trận đánh trong kháng chiến chống Pháp, kháng chiến chống Mỹ, 1945–1975, Tập II [Selected Battles During the Resistance Wars Against the French and the Americans, 1945–1975, Volume II]* (Hanoi: People's Army Publishing House, 1991)

Trinquier, Roger, *Les Maquis d'Indochine (1952–1954)* (Paris: Éditions Albatros, 1976)

Văn Cẩn Phan, *Lịch sử Bộ Tổng tham mưu trong kháng chiến chống Pháp 1945–1954 [History of the General Staff in the Resistance War against the French 1945–1954]* (Hanoi: People's Army Publishing House, 1999)

Văn Hùng Nguyễn, Duy Cường Hà, Điền Sinh Trần, & Trường Hải Nguyễn, *Lịch sử Trung đoàn bộ binh 174 anh hùng (1949–2012) [History of "Hero" Infantry Regiment 174 (1949–2012)]* (Hanoi: People's Army Publishing House, 2013)

Various, *Contribution to the History of Dien Bien Phu, Vietnamese Studies #3* (Hanoi: Foreign Languages Publishing House, 1965)

Various, *DBP, il y a quarante ans* (l'Amicale des Anciens Légionnaires Parachutistes, no date)

Various, *Le Bélier - Amicale du 7eme RTA No 7* (Atelier d'Impression de l'Armée de Terre, 1982)

Various, *Lịch sử sư đoàn bộ binh 312 [History of Infantry Division 312]* (Hanoi: People's Army Publishing House, 1995)

Various, *Vài Hồi Ức Về Điện Biên Phủ, Tập I [A Few Memories About Dien Bien Phu, Volume I]* (Hanoi: People's Army Publishing House, 1977)

de Verdelhan, Eric, *Au capitaine de Dien Bien Phu* (Paris: SRE-Editions, 2013)

Võ Nguyên Giáp, *Dien Bien Phu (5th Edition)* (Hanoi: Thế Giới Publishers, 1994)

Võ Nguyên Giáp, *Điện Biên Phủ (8th Edition)* (Hanoi: Thế Giới Publishers, 2007)

Võ Nguyên Giáp, Hữu Mai & Lady Borton, *Dien Bien Phu: Rendezvous with History* (Hanoi: Thế Giới Publishers, 2004)

Võ Nguyên Giáp, *Tổng Tập Luận Văn [Collected Essays]* (Hanoi: People's Army Publishing House, 2006)

Wieme de Ruddere, Reginald, *Journal des Marches et Opérations du Groupement Wieme (Groupement mobile Tai no 5) à Dien Bien Phu Pendant la Campagne du 1er Décembre 1953 au 31 Mai 1954* (publisher unidentified, 1999)

Windrow, Martin, *The Last Valley: Dien Bien Phu and the French Defeat in Vietnam* (Cambridge, MA: Da Capo Press, 2004)

Ysquierdo, Antoine, *Ces hommes de la Légion... Qui meurent pour la gloire!* (Paris: Editions du Camelot & de la Joyeuse Garde, 1993)

Zhai, Qiang, *China and the Vietnam Wars, 1950–1975* (Chapel Hill: University of North Carolina Press, 2000)

Articles

Allaire, Guillaume, "Dien Bien Phu (30 Mars 1954)," *Ancre d'Or-Bazeilles: La Revue des Troupes de Marine,* Nᵒ 339 (Mars–Avril 2004)

Gavin, James M., "The Easy Chair – A Communication on Vietnam from Gen. James M. Gavin," *Harpers* (Feb 1966)

Isabelle, Marc, "Dien Bien Phu – les raisons d'une défaite" (self-published, 2017)

Kubiak, Simon, "Operation Castor… Verdun 1954," *Képi blanc, la vie de la Légion étrangère*, n°186 (October 1962)

Langlais, Pierre, "La dernière nuit de DBP," *Béret Rouge*, n°39 (Avril–Mai 1962) [accessed online May 27, 2017 at http://fr.calameo.com/read/0014251177f4a8ce1e152]

Loiseau, Yves, "La 1e Compagnie Etrangère parachutiste de mortiers lourds," *Képi blanc, la vie de la Légion étrangère*, n°654 (Avril 2004) and n°655 (Mai 2004)

Muller, Lieutenant Guillaume, "Essai de microhistoire: la destruction au sol de six Bearcat au début de la bataille de Diên Biên Phu," *Revue historique des armées*, n° 286 (1er trimester 2017)

Ngọc An, "Tiểu Đoàn Hóa Tiên 224" ["Rocket Battalion 224"], *Tạp chí Lịch sử Quân sự [Military History Magazine]*, Issue 4 (July–Aug 1997)

Tập chí trí thực phát triển [Knowledge Development Magazine], *Huyền thoại Điện Biên [Legends of Dien Bien Phu]* [Special issue] (Hanoi: Vietnam News Agency, 2013)

Theses

Cournil, Laure, "Diên Biên Phu, Des tranchées au prétoire: 1953–1958" (Doctoral Thesis: Université de Paris I Panthéon – Sorbonne, 2014)

Jackson, Maj. Peter D., "French Ground Force Organizational Development for Counterrevolutionary Warfare Between 1945 and 1962" (Master's Thesis: US Army Command and General Staff College, 2005)

Online Sources

Armchair General, *Dien Bien Phu and Operation Vulture*, http://www.armchairgeneral.com/forums/showthread.php?t=75459&page=21 (accessed Nov 26, 2016)

Aviation Safety Network, *Database 1954*, https://aviation-safety.net/database/dblist.php?Year=1954 (accessed June 17, 2017)

Báo Cựu Chiến Binh Việt Nam [Vietnam Veterans Newspaper], *Bắn rơi máy bay Pháp ở Điện Biên Phủ: Kỷ niệm khó quên [French aircraft shot down at Dien Bien Phu: Unforgettable Anniversary]*, http://cuuchienbinh.com.vn/index.aspx?Menu=1370&Style=1&ChiTiet=5381 (accessed July 21, 2010)

Baomoi.com [New Newspaper.com], *Bảo đảm vận tải theo yêu cầu thay đổi phương châm tác chiến [Guaranteed On-Demand Transportation Changed Warfare]*, http://www.baomoi.com/bao-dam-van-tai-theo-yeu-cau-thay-doi-phuong-cham-tac-chien/c/14008098.epi (accessed Feb 12, 2017)

Cảnh Sát Toàn Cầu Online [Worldwide Police Newspaper Online], *Bí ẩn "Đồi khâm liệm" [The Secrets of "Shroud Hill"]*, http://cstc.cand.com.vn/Phong-su-Tieu-diem/Bi-an-Doi-kham-liem-318001/ (accessed March 2, 2017)

Điện Biên Phủ Online, *Bài 2: Điện Biên Phủ, "điểm hẹn" của lòng yêu nước" [Lesson 2: Dien Bien Phu, "rendezvous" of patriotism"]*, http://www.baodienbienphu.com.vn/tin-tuc/tu-lieu-va-lich-su/145343/bai-2-dien-bien-phu-%E2%80%9Cdiem-hen%E2%80%9D-cua-long-yeu-nuoc (accessed June 6, 2017)

Dossier Indochine – Site des Troupes de Marine, *Les Missions du 31e BMG au Combat, (Mai–Juin 2015)* http://www.fng.asso.fr/Module_Actualites/wp-content/uploads/2015/09/2-LA-CHARTE_LE-GENIE-%C3%A0-D.B.P..pdf (accessed July 29, 2016)

Foreign Legion Info, *2nd Foreign Legion Mortar Mixed Company*, http://
foreignlegion.info/units/2e-cmmle/ (accessed Dec 29, 2015)

Forum laguerreenindochine, *Le parcours d'un marsouin du 3e bataillon
thaï,* http://laguerreenindochine.forumactif.org/t1542p50-le-parcours-
d-un-marsouin-du-3e-bataillon-thai (accessed Dec 28, 2015)

James Madison University, Center for International Stabilization and
Recovery, *Munitions Reference Guide*, http://www.jmu.edu/cisr/_
pages/research/munitions.shtml and Wikipedia, *Tellermine 43*
(accessed April 13, 2006)

La Bataille de Điện Biên Phủ (le devoir de mémoire), *Souvenirs du
Capitaine Armandi*, http://dienbienphu.soforums.com/t1420-
Souvenirs-du-Capitaine-Armandi.htm#p13328 (accessed Nov 28,
2016)

More Majorum, *1° Bataillon du 2° REI*, http://more-majorum.de/
einheiten/2rei/bat1/index.html (accessed Nov 16, 2016)

One Project Too Far, *Indochina War Ressources*, http://1project2far.
blogspot.com/p/indochina-war-ressources.html (accessed Sept 2,
2016)

Sở vân húa, thể thao và du lịch tỉnh điện biên [Department of Culture,
Sports and Tourism Dien Bien Province], *Dũng sĩ đánh bộc phá
Nguyễn Văn Ty trong trận đánh Đồi Độc Lập,* http://svhttdldienbien.
gov.vn/chitietls/2392/Dung-si-danh-boc-pha-Nguyen-Van-Ty-trong-
tran-danh-Doi-Doc-Lap.html (accessed Oct 24, 2016)

Trái Tim Việt Nam online [Heart of Vietnam online], *Điện Biên Phủ và
những điều chưa biết - Phần 1 [Dien Bien Phu and the Unknown –
Part I]*, http://ttvnol.com/threads/dien-bien-phu-va-nhung-dieu-chua-
biet-phan-1.246189/page-57 (accessed Sept 6, 2016)

Vietnam Breaking News.com, *Dien Bien Phu and the Art of Artillery*,
https://www.vietnambreakingnews. com/2016/05/dien-bien-phu-and-
the-art-of-artillery/ (accessed Sept 22, 2016)

vnmilitaryhistory.net, *Tóm tắt các chiến dịch trong kháng chiến chống
Pháp [A summary of the campaign in the war against France]*, http://
www.vnmilitaryhistory.net/index.php?topic=24429.90 (accessed Nov
30, 2016)

vnmilitaryhistory.net, *Trận Đồi A1 (từ đêm 30 tháng 3 đến sáng ngày 3
tháng 4 năm 1954) [Battle for Hill A1 (from the night of 30 March to
the morning of April 3, 1954)]*, http://www.vnmilitaryhistory.net/

index.php?topic=1936.170 (accessed May 15, 2017)

vnmilitaryhistory.net, *Vũ Khí Việt Nam Trong Hai Cuộc Kháng Chiến [Vietnamese Weapons in the Two Resistance Wars]*, http://www.vnmilitaryhistory.net/index.php/topic, 41.170/wap2.html (accessed Jan 8, 2014)

vnmilitaryhistory.net, *Trận Điện Biên Phủ 20/11/1953 – 7/5/1954 [Overwhelming Dien Bien Phu 20/11/1953 – 7/5/1954]*, http://www.vnmilitaryhistory.net/index.php?topic=1936.210;wap2 and http://www.vnmilitaryhistory.net/index.php?topic=1936.200 (both accessed Oct 24, 2017)

Wikipedia, *M2 Mine*, https://en.wikipedia.org/wiki/M2_mine (accessed April 13, 2016)

Wikipedia, *M14 Mine*, https://en.wikipedia.org/wiki/M14_mine (accessed April 13, 2016)

www.reds.vn, *Chùm ảnh: Chứng tích vụ Pháp thảm sát 444 người ở Điện Biên Phủ [In pictures: Memorial to 444 people massacred by the French at Dien Bien Phu]*, www.reds.vn/index.php/dat-viet/10788-vu-tham-sat-noong-nhai (accessed June 22, 2016)

APPENDICES

Appendix 1: GONO personnel strength on March 10, 1954[1]

Although this data was assembled and reported by FTNV's personnel staff, several units are missing from the table, most notably GAP 2 headquarters and 1 CEPML. Some combat service support units may also be missing. Several hundred PIMs are not included in these figures either.

Unit	French	Africans	Foreign Legion	Indochinese regulars	Indochinese auxiliaries	TOTAL
GONO HQ	14	15				29
ZONO HQ, CTB, GMPT 1	96	1		137	1,126	1,360
GM 9 HQ (Central)	1	15	226	3		245
I/13 DBLE	1		519	1	55	576
III/13 DBLE			535	3	58	596
III/3 RTA	81	470		7	89	647
GM 6 HQ (Isabelle)	3		92			95
II/1 RTA	70	538		6		614
V/7 RTA	80	543		3		626
III/3 REI			561			561
I/2 REI			566	3		569
8 BPC	318			337		655
1 BEP			332	266		598
1 CMMLE			62			62
2 CMMLE			41	23		64
BT 2	92			608		700
BT 3	90	2		705	90	887
I/4 RTM	84	566		12		662
III/10 RAC	125	172				297
II/4 RAC	156	245				401
4/I/4 RAC	26	49				75
31 BG	63	210	3	2		278
RICM (Blue Platoon)	9			4		13
1 RCC (Other Bisons)	27			25		52
Communications	52	22			10	84
Material	2		32	1		35
Supply	13	1		4		18
SM	2					2
Medical	7	5				12
TOTAL	1,412	2,854	2,969	2,150	1,428	10,813
PERCENTAGE	13%	26%	27%	20%	13%	

Appendix 2: GONO order of battle on March 13, 1954

This is a 'snapshot' detailing GONO's organization and deployment as they stood when the siege began. Changes that occurred as it progressed are discussed in individual chapters, but took place so frequently after March 30 that it is impossible to mention all of them.

Groupement Opérationnel Nord-Ouest (GONO)

Colonel Christian Marie Ferdinand de la Croix de Castries
71st Headquarters Company (HQ Area)

ARTILLERY

"Fire" Command Post (GONO HQ)
Colonel Charles Piroth

GROUPEMENT A

Major Jean Alliou
3rd Battalion, 10th Colonial Artillery Regiment (III/10 RAC)
   Headquarters Battery (HQ Area)
   7th and 8th Batteries, 8 x 105mm (Isabelle)
   9th Battery, 4 x 105mm (HQ Area)
1st Foreign Legion Parachute Heavy Mortar Company (1 CEPML), 12 x 120mm (HQ Area, D-2)
2nd Foreign Legion Composite Mortar Company (2 CMMLE), 8 x 120mm (AM-3, G-5)

GROUPEMENT B

Major Guy Knecht
2nd Battalion, 4th Colonial Artillery Regiment (II/4 RAC)
   Headquarters Battery (D-4)
   4th Battery, 4 x 105mm (D-3)
   5th and 6th Batteries, 8 x 105mm (D-4)
11th Battery, 4th Battalion, 4th Colonial Artillery Regiment (11/IV/4 RAC), 4 x 155mm (HQ Area, E-4)
1st Foreign Legion Composite Mortar Company (1 CMMLE), 8 x 120mm (D-1)

Platoon, 1st Far Eastern Colonial Antiaircraft Battalion (1 GAACEO), 4 x Quad-50 (Épervier)

TANK COMPANY
Captain Yves Hervouët
Provisional Company, 1st Light Cavalry Regiment (Bisons)
    Headquarters "Conti" (HQ Area)
    1st Platoon "Blue:" Bazeilles, Douaumont, Mulhouse (Junon)
    2nd Platoon "Red:" Ettlingen, Posen, Smolensk (HQ Area)
    3rd Platoon "Green:" Auerstaedt, Ratisbonne, Neumach (Isabelle)

RESERVES
Groupement Aéroporté 2 (GAP 2) (HQ Area)
Lieutenant-Colonel Pierre Langlais
1st Foreign Legion Parachute Battalion (1 BEP)
    Headquarters Company (Junon)
    1st Company (Junon)
    2nd Company (C-7)
    3rd Company (C-7)
    4th Company (Junon)
8th Assault Parachute Battalion (8 BPC)
    Headquarters Company (Épervier)
    1st Company (Épervier; to D-4 on Mar 14)
    2nd Company (E-10)
    3rd Company (Épervier)
    4th Company (Épervier)

- *Some GAP 2 companies were "dual-tasked" since they also garrisoned strongpoints in the Central Subsector.*
- *On March 13, the 2nd Tai Battalion (BT2) was a reserve unit in GAP 2, which it had joined when the 5th Vietnamese Parachute Battalion (5 BPVN) left Điện Biên Phủ in January. But 5 BPVN resumed its place in GAP 2 after jumping back into the valley on March 14 and BT2 was subordinated to the Central Subsector.*

OTHER UNITS
8th Commando Group, Groupes Mixte d'Intervention (GMI) (HQ Area) *Tai guerrillas*

Headquarters, 1st Tai Partisan Mobile Group (GMPT 1) (HQ Area)

    417th Tai Auxiliary Company (CSM 417) (HQ Area)

    418th Tai Auxiliary Company (CSM 418) (HQ Area)

    433rd Tai Auxiliary Company (CSM 433) (HQ Area)

31st Engineer Battalion (BG 31)

    Headquarters Company (HQ Area)

    1st Company (HQ Area)

    2nd Company (E-11)

2nd Platoon, 5th Foreign Legion Medium Repair Company (2/5 CRALE) (HQ Area) *Auto repair*

    Detachment, 2nd Foreign Legion Tank Repair Company (HQ Area) *Tank repair*

    Detachment, 11th Medium Maintenance Company (HQ Area) *Artillery repair*

2nd Company, 822nd Signal Battalion (HQ Area)

2nd Company, 823rd Signal Battalion (HQ Area)

342nd Parachute Signal Company (HQ Area)

403rd Postal Detachment (HQ Area)

3rd Transportation Company (HQ Area) *Trucks*

712th Traffic Control Company (HQ Area)

Depot 81, 730th Fuel Supply Company (HQ Area) *Fuel dump*

1st Quartermaster Operational Exploitation Group Commissariat (HQ Area)

Detachment, 3rd Ammunition Supply Company (HQ Area) *Ammunition dump*

3rd Composite Legion, Republican Guard/Gendarmerie *Military Police* (HQ Area)

29th Mobile Surgical Team (HQ Area)

44th Mobile Surgical Team (VNA) (HQ Area)

FRENCH AIR FORCE UNITS

Air Intervention Control Post "Torri Rouge" (Red Tower)

Major Jacques Guérin

195th Airbase Detachment (Main Airfield)

21/374 Signal Company (Main Airfield)

Detachment, Fighter Group 1/22 "Saintonge," 6 x F8F "Bearcat" (Main Airfield)

Detachment, 21st Artillery Observation Group, 6 x Morane 500 "Cricket" (Main Airfield)

Detachment, 1st Light Medical Evacuation Company, 1 x Sikorsky S-51 (Main Airfield)

NORTHERN SUBSECTOR
Zone Opérationnel Nord-Ouest (ZONO) HQ Area
Lieutenant Colonel André Trancart

CR ANNE MARIE
Major Léopold Thimonnier
3rd Tai Battalion (BT3)
   Headquarters Company (AM-2)
   9th Company (AM-4)
   10th Company (AM-2)
   11th Company (AM-1)
   12th Company (AM-3)
   272nd Auxiliary Company (CSM 272) (AM-2)
Platoon, 2 CMMLE (AM-3)

CR GABRIELLE
Major Roland de Mecquenem / Major Edouard Kah
5th Battalion, 7th Algerian Rifle Regiment (V/7 RTA)
   Headquarters Company (G-5)
   1st Company (G-1)
   2nd Company (G-4)
   3rd Company (G-3)
   4th Company (G-2)
416th Tai Auxiliary Company (CSM 416) (G-5)
Platoon, 2 CMMLE (G-5)

CENTRAL SUBSECTOR
Mobile Group 9 (GM 9)
Lieutenant Colonel Jules Gaucher
9th Command & Service Company (HQ Area)

CR BÉATRICE
Major Paul Pégot
3rd Battalion, 13th Foreign Legion Half-Brigade (III/13 DBLE)
   Headquarters Company (B-2)
   9th Company (B-1)
   10th Company (B-2)

11th Company (B-3)
12th Company (B-2)
245th Auxiliary Company (CSM 245) (B-1, B-2, B-3)

CR CLAUDINE

Major Roger de Brinon
1st Battalion, 13th Foreign Legion Half-Brigade (I/13 DBLE)
    Headquarters Company (C-2)
    1st Company (C-3)
    2nd Company (C-4)
    3rd Company (C-5)
    4th Company (C-1)
    424th Auxiliary Company (CSM 424) (C-2?)
White Tai Company (CTB) (C-6)
2nd Company, 1 BEP (C-7)
3rd Company, 1 BEP (C-7)

CR DOMINIQUE

Captain Jean Garandeau
3rd Battalion, 3rd Algerian Rifle Regiment (III/3 RTA)
    Headquarters Company (D-2)
    9th Company (D-1)
    10th Company (D-4; to D-2 on Mar 14)
    11th Company (D-2)
    12th Company (D-3)
    425th Auxiliary Company (CSM 425) (D-2)
1 CMMLE (D-1)
4th Battery, II/4 RAC (D-3)
5th and 6th Batteries, II/4 RAC (D-4)
7th Company, 2nd Tai Battalion (D-4)
5th Company, 2nd Tai Battalion (D-5)
Platoon, 1 CEPML (Behind D-5)

CR ELIANE

Major Jean Nicholas
1st Battalion, 4th Moroccan Rifle Regiment (I/4 RTM)
    Headquarters Company (E-2)

1st Company (E-2)
2nd Company (E-2)
3rd Company (E-1)
4th Company (E-3)
2nd Tai Battalion (-) (BT2)
    Headquarters Company (E-12)
    6th Company (E-12)
    8th Company (E-12)
Groupement "Martinez"
    414th Tai Auxiliary Company (CSM 414) (E-3)
    415th Tai Auxiliary Company (CSM 415) (E-4)
11th Battery, IV/4 RAC (3 guns) (E-10)
2nd Company, 8 BPC (E-10)
2nd Company, 31st Engineer Battalion (E-11)

CR FRANÇOISE

Adjutant Clément Cante
Groupement "Cante"
    413th Tai Auxiliary Company (CSM 413)
    434th Tai Auxiliary Company (CSM 434)

CR HUGUETTE

Major Pierre Clémençon
1st Battalion, 2nd Foreign Legion Infantry Regiment (I/2 REI)
    Headquarters Company (H-3)
    1st Company (H-4)
    2nd Company (H-5)
    3rd Company (H-2)
    4th Company (H-1)

SOUTHERN SUBSECTOR

Mobile Group 6 (GM 6)
Lieutenant Colonel André Lalande
    6th Command & Service Company (Isabelle)
7th and 8th Batteries, III/10 RAC (Isabelle)
3rd (Green) Tank Platoon (Isabelle)
3rd Battalion, 3rd Foreign Legion Infantry Regiment (III/3 REI)

Headquarters Company (Isabelle)

9th Company (I-3)

10th Company (I-2)

11th Company (I-1)

12th Company (I-4)

2nd Battalion, 1st Algerian Rifle Regiment (II/1 RTA)

Headquarters Company (Isabelle)

5th Company (I-1)

6th Company (I-4)

7th Company (I-3)

8th Company (I-2)

Groupement "Wieme"

431st Tai Light Company (CSM 431) (Wieme)

432nd Tai Light Company (CSM 432) (Wieme)

Appendix 3: GONO orders of battle on March 30 and May 1, 1954

The following orders of battle include only combat infantry, artillery and engineer units. Virtually all of the units listed in the May 1 column were considerably understrength.

Position	March 30	May 1
Bald Hill	3rd Pltn 2/I/4 RTM	
Claudine-1 / Lily-2	4/I/4 RTM	2/I/4 RTM
Claudine-2	CSM 424	CSM 424 (-)
Claudine-3	1/I/13 DBLE (-), Pltn 1/I/4 RTM	4/I/2 REI (-), CSM 424 (-)
Claudine-4	2/I/13 DBLE (-), Pltn 2/I/4 RTM	3/I/2 REI
Claudine-5	3/I/13 DBLE (-), Pltn 3/I/4 RTM	2/I/2 REI, Pltn 3/I/4 RTM
Claudine-7 / Lily-1	3/1 BEP	4/I/4 RTM (-), Pltn 3/I/4 RTM
Dominique-1	4/5 BPVN, 12/III/3 RTA (-)	
Dominique-2	10/III/3 RTA (SE), 11/III/3 RTA (NE), CSM 425 (W)	
Dominique-3	9/III/3 RTA (S), 12/III/3 RTA (-) (N), 4/II/4 RAC (N)	3/6 BPC, 8/BT2, Pltn 12/III/3 RTA
Dominique-4	1/8 BPC, 1 CMMLE, 5/II/4 RAC, 6/II/4 RAC,	1/8 BPC, 5/II/4 RAC, 1 CMMLE
Dominique-5	5/BT2	
Dominique-6	2/5 BPVN	
Eliane-1	3/I/4 RTM (-), Pltn 3/I/13 DBLE	1/II/1 RCP, 3/II/1 RCP

Eliane-2	1/1 BEP (center), 1/I/4 RTM (-) (W), 2/I/4 RTM (-) (E), Pltn 1/1/13 DBLE (W),Pltn 2/I/13 DBLE (Champs Elysées)	2/I/13 DBLE, 10/III/13 DBLE
Eliane-3	4/I/13 DBLE, CSM 414, CSM 415	3/I/13 DBLE, CSM413 (?)
Eliane-4	1/6 BPC (SW), 3/6 BPC (NW), 4/6 BPC (NE), 3/5 BPVN (SE), 2/1 CEPML (NW)	2/II/1 RCP (NE), 12/III/3 RTA (NW), 2/5 BPVN (SE), 3/5 BPVN (SW)
Eliane-10	2/8 BPC	1/6 BPC, 2/6 BPC
Eliane-11	2/BG31	2/BG31, Wounded
Eliane-12	6/BT2, 7/BT2 (-), 8/BT2 (-)	5/BT2, 6/BT2, 7/BT2 (-), Pltn 4/I/2 REI
Epervier	3/8 BPC, 4/8 BPC, 2/1 BEP, Pltn 1 GAACEO	3/8 BPC, 4/8 BPC, 1 GAACEO
Francoise	CSM 413, CSM 434	
Junon	CTB, 4/1 BEP, Pltn 1 GAACEO	CTB, Wounded
HQ Area	11/IV/4 RAC, 1/1 CEPML, 2/2 CMMLE, 3/BG31, CSM 417, CSM 418, CSM 433	11/IV/4 RAC, 6/II/4 RAC, 1/1 CEPML, 2/2 CMMLE, 3/BG31, CSM 418, CSM 433
Honeycomb Hill	2/6 BPC	Pltn 2/5 BPVN ?
Huguette-1	4/I/2 REI	
Huguette-2	12/BT3 (-), 10/III/13 DBLE (-)	2/BMEP, 7/BMEP
Huguette-3	10/III/13 DBLE (-)	8/BMEP
Huguette-4 / Lily-3	1/I/2 REI	1/I/4 RTM
Huguette-5	2/I/2 REI	4/BMEP
Huguette-6	3/I/2 REI	
Huguette-7	1/5 BPVN	
Nameless	7/BT2 (-)	1/5 BPVN, Pltn 7/BT2
Opera ?	2 Pltns BT2	

Appendix 4: Munitions landed at or parachuted to GONO[2]

Munition type	11/20/53 12/7/53	12/8/53 12/25/53	12/26/53 1/25/54	1/26/54 3/12/54	3/13/54 5/8/54	TOTAL	Metric tons
7.65mm	32,122	71,528	69,848		262,643	436,141	5.231
7.5mm (Model 29C MG)	974,650	1,426,950	2,495,325	3,036,375	5,497,075	13,430,375	1,200.630
9mm	471,348	570,592	2,354,992	32,768	2,254,686	5,684,386	95.750
.38 & .380 caliber			2,004			2,004	0.046
.45 caliber	48,200	10,800				59,000	1.475
.30 cal (M-1 rifle)	90,800	85,800	680,400		16,200	873,200	13.971
.30 cal (M-2 carbine)	66,400	235,696	788,088		788,500	1,878,684	65.754
.303 caliber	112,632					112,632	3.942
.50 caliber	25,070	59,931	123,210	116,820	181,510	506,541	81.062
OF 37 grenade	3,060	5,436	38,542		1,600	48,638	39.000

DF 37 grenade	3,860	6,087	48,408		80,472	138,827	166.592
Mk 2 grenade	3,235	3,650				6,885	10.052
Tear gas grenade			120			120	0.120
M14 thermite grenade	144	192	1,296	490		2,122	2.546
Smoke grenade	336		324			660	0.924
Model 48 rifle grenade	3,400	7,200	24,660		64,948	100,208	100.208
Model 32 XO rifle grenade					23,275	23,275	35.8431
M19 WP rifle grenade	200				400	600	0.600
50mm mortar	1,908	7,500	10,040		5,300	24,748	27.222
60mm HE (French)	2,400			4,920		7,320	18.300
60mm HE (US)	4,876	9,220	9,250	11,360	52,886	87,592	140.000
60mm illumination	208	984	2,372		11,423	14,987	37.467
60mm smoke	80		936			1,016	2.540
81mm HE (US) light	4,513	3,954		896	72,207	81,570	407.850
81mm HE grand capacité	624				1,800	2,424	21.216
81mm smoke (US)	156				216	372	3.162
81mm illumination (US)	342	72	638		1,356	2,408	12.040
120mm HE	2,472	210	12,475	6,960	21,414	43,531	957.682
2.36" bazooka rocket		480				480	1.440
57mm recoilless rifle	704	1,240	3,198	1,000	752	6,894	34.470
75mm recoilless rifle	1,532		1,806		190	3,528	59.976
75mm tank shell		518	8,182	500	1,874	11,074	254.702
105mm HE	2,356		5,725	8,500	76,768	93,349	2,613.772
105mm illumination					96	96	2.592
105mm M-4 smoke			180			180	3.960
155mm HE			3,410	1,727	5,081	10,218	613.080
M4A1 155mm propellant charge			1,393	1,446	2,488	5,327	74.578
Hand signal flare	725	900	2,000	1,000	1,000	5,625	1.969
Illumination flare	1,180		1,141		640	2,961	1.658
GP 32 flare	32		192	96		320	1.200
T-6 and M-49 trip flares			2,300	1,000	7,400	10,700	32.100
2" smoke pot	210				296	506	0.101
Bangalore torpedo					500	500	0.100
M-2 and M-3 mines	1,191			22	6,260	7,473	29.892
Model 48 mine	900		4,904	10		5,814	5.814
M-14 mine					17,190	17,190	3.438
10kg plate charge		60	120	110		290	5.800
Plate charge detonator		7	12	10		29	0.015

Appendix 5: Distribution of total air combat sorties[3]

Category	Place	Combat sorties	Percentage total sorties	Bombload (metric tons)	Percentage total bombload
By day	Valley	3,510	57%	3,725	59%
	Supply lines	2,356	38%	2,270	36%
By night	Valley	172	3%	180	3%
	Supply lines	112	2%	122	2%
Day and night	Valley	3,682	60%	3,905	62%
	Supply lines	2,468	40%	2,392	38%
TOTAL		6,150		6,297	

Appendix 6: French weapons lost at Điện Biên Phủ[4]

The most complete data on the weaponry available to GONO is provided by French Army accountants, who tallied the cost of every single weapon lost at the siege. The total value of the lost equipment was between $1.9 million and $2.2 million in 1954 US dollars.

Type	Quantity	Unit cost (francs)	Total cost (francs)
Automatic pistols	1,200	12,000	14,400,000
Submachine guns	5,116	20,500	104,878,000
Rifles and carbines	5,297	16,900	89,519,300
Automatic rifles	1,048	105,000	110,040,000
Light machine guns	240	129,000	30,960,000
Heavy machine guns	30	252,000	7,560,000
50mm mortars	36	40,700	1,465,200
60mm mortars	113	291,200	32,905,600
81mm mortars	87	523,000	45,501,000
120mm mortars	49	2,144,600	105,085,400
57mm recoilless	56	476,000	26,656,000
75mm recoilless	4	560,000	2,240,000
105mm howitzer	27	5,413,800	146,172,600
155mm howitzer	4	10,372,950	41,491,800
Flamethrower	88	125,000	11,000,000
TOTAL			769,874,900

Appendix 7: VPA strongpoint designations

The VPA had its own set of codenames for French strongpoints. In January 1954, each was assigned a three-digit numerical identifier (e.g., 201) and (perceived) satellite positions were sometimes given the same number as an existing position, but with an alphabetic qualifier attached (e.g., 311B). But before the siege began in March, the Five Hills strongpoints received new alpha-numeric identifiers (e.g., A1), though on rare occasions the old designation was still used. Finally, the outlying strongpoints Anne Marie, Béatrice, Gabrielle, and Isabelle were commonly referred to by the name of the closest village rather than by their numerical designations. This tangle of VPA codenames has confounded Western historians (particularly in cases where both sides used the same designation (e.g., D1) for different hills). Some still cannot be identified.

Anne Marie-1	*Bản Kéo, 104B*	Eliane-1	*301, C1*
Anne Marie-2	*Bản Kéo, 104A*	Eliane-2	*302, A1*
Anne Marie-3 (Huguette-6)	*105*	Eliane-3	*304, A3*
Anne Marie-4 (Huguette-7)	*106*	Eliane-4	*324, C2*
Beatrice-1	*Him Lam, 101A*	Eliane-10	*506*
Beatrice-2	*Him Lam, 102*	Eliane-11	*509, 511*
Beatrice-3	*Him Lam, 101B*	"Island" within E-11	*510*
Claudine-1	*309*	Between E-11 & E-12	*508*
Claudine-2	*?*	Eliane-12	*507*
Claudine-3	*?*	Between E-11 & E-3	*512*
Claudine-4	*?*	Épervier	*305?*
Claudine-5	*310*	Françoise	*311*
Claudine-6	*322*	Gabrielle	*Độc Lập, 103*
Claudine-7	*307? 327?*	GONO Headquarters	*?*
Dominique-1	*202, E, E1*	Huguette-1	*206*
Dominique-2	*201, D1*	Huguette-2	*208*
Old Reserve Position	*201A*	Huguette-3	*309A?*
1 CEPML Mortar Position	*D2*	Huguette-4	*311B*
Dominique-3 (north)	*Artillery Position 210*	Huguette-5	*311A*
Dominique-3 (south)	*505*	Isabelle-1	*Hồng Cúm A*
Dominique-3 (southeast)	*505A*	Isabelle-2	*Hồng Cúm A*
Honeycomb Hill	*Rice Tray Hill*	Isabelle-3	*Hồng Cúm A*
Dominique-4	*203*	Isabelle-4	*Hồng Cúm A*
II/4 RAC Artillery Position	*204*	Isabelle-5 / Wieme	*Hồng Cúm B*

Dominique-5	D3	Isabelle-3 Bridgehead	Hồng Cúm C
Dominique-6 (old)	E-2	Junon	318
Dominique-6 (new)	?	Marcelle	?

Appendix 8: Điện Biên Phủ siege force order of battle

It's impossible to assemble a flawless VPA order of battle because no Vietnamese source presents a detailed, comprehensive list of the units that participated in the siege. The one shown here is based primarily on Deuxième Bureau documents from June 1954, cross-indexed against unit identifications for VPA soldiers buried in the military cemeteries at Điện Biên Phủ and other Vietnamese sources. But although every effort has been made to ensure that this order of battle is as accurate as possible, some errors undoubtedly remain. Unit designations and weapons inventories at the battalion level and above are highly reliable, but those at the company level are less certain since, for deceptive purposes, the VPA routinely assigned multiple designations to the same unit. Thus, while the heavy weapons company of the 439th Infantry Battalion was officially numbered the 1481st, it was given the cover designation of 84th for the Điện Biên Phủ Campaign.

Support units (transport, commo-liaison, engineer, etc.) are problematic since they were far less likely than infantry units to yield prisoners who could be interrogated by the French, or fatalities that would be interred in the cemeteries. Consequently, some divisional- and regimental-level support units (including heavy weapons units) are missing entirely, while others are identified by designation but not by type (e.g., "254th ? Company"). Still other units are classified by type but their designations are unknown (e.g., "? ĐKZ Battalion"). Underlined companies in the infantry battalions are heavy weapons units, but since the French did not identify all of them, many are not marked. Underlined companies in the 367th Antiaircraft Regiment were armed with 12.7mm (.50-caliber) antiaircraft machineguns. There was one such company per battalion, but not all are marked due to gaps in source data. The text in quotes after unit names are honorific titles if in English and cover names if in Vietnamese.

ĐIỆN BIÊN PHỦ FRONT

Võ Nguyên Giáp
426th General Staff Intelligence-Reconnaissance Battalion (62, 63 Companies)

304TH INFANTRY DIVISION "NAM ĐỊNH"

Hoàng Minh Thảo
DIVISIONAL TROOPS
    20th Intelligence-Recon Company (*presence uncertain*)
    41st ? Company (*presence uncertain*)
    77th Guard Company (*presence uncertain*)
    128th Engineer Company (*presence uncertain*)
    161st Commo-Liaison Company (*presence uncertain*)
    505th R&R Battalion (*presence uncertain*)
    620th Transport Company (*presence uncertain*)
    650th ? Company (*presence uncertain*)
840th Artillery Battalion, 6 x 75mm howitzer
    (91, ?, ? Companies), (*Final weeks of siege only?*)
9TH INFANTRY REGIMENT "NINH BINH" (*Entire regiment present only for last few days of the siege*)
    353rd Infantry Battalion (11, 12, 87, <u>50</u> Companies)
    375th Infantry Battalion (71, 73, 138, <u>75</u> Companies)
    400th Infantry Battalion (83, 84, 86, <u>56</u> Companies)
    10th Intelligence-Recon Company
    90th ? Company
    93rd ? Company
    94th Infantry Gun Company, 4-6 x 57mm ĐKZ
    126th Engineer Company
    157th Guard Company
    162nd Commo-Liaison Company
57TH INFANTRY REGIMENT "NHO QUAN"
    265th Infantry Battalion (17, 18, 19, 98 Companies)
    346th Infantry Battalion (50, 52, 53, <u>51</u> Companies)
    418th Infantry Battalion (54, 59, 60, <u>61</u> Companies)
    30th Intelligence-Recon Company
    55th ĐKZ Company, 4-6 x 57mm ĐKZ
    127th Engineer Company
    158th Guard Company
    164th Commo-Liaison Company

308TH INFANTRY DIVISION "VIỆT BẮC"

Vương Thừa Vũ

DIVISIONAL TROOPS

    ĐKZ Company ?, 57mm ĐKZs?

    127th Commo-Liaison Company

    168th Intelligence-Recon Company

    172nd Guard Company

    195th ? Company

    309th Engineer Company

    317th Transport Company

387th Antiaircraft Battalion, 18 x 12.7mm AAMG?

    (74, 78, 241, 322 Companies) West side of valley

36TH INFANTRY REGIMENT "SA PA"

    80th Infantry Battalion (61, 62, 63, 64 Companies)

    84th Infantry Battalion (41, 42, 43, <u>44</u> Companies)

    89th Infantry Battalion (395, 397, 399, 401 Companies)

    11th Commo-Liaison Company

    12th Transport Company

    14th Support Company, 6 x 81/82mm mortar

    15th ? Company

    16th ĐKZ Company, 4-6 x 57mm ĐKZ

    25th ? Company

88TH INFANTRY REGIMENT "TAM ĐẢO"

    23rd Infantry Battalion (209, 211, 213, <u>215</u> Companies)

    29th Infantry Battalion (217, 219, 221, <u>223</u> Companies)

    322nd Infantry Battalion (225, 227, 229, <u>231</u> Companies)

    13th ĐKZ Company, 4-6 x 57mm ĐKZ

    201st Intelligence-Recon Company

    203rd Commo-Liaison Company

    205th ? Company

    207th ? Company

    238th Support Company, 6 x 81/82mm mortar

    240th ? Company

102ND INFANTRY REGIMENT "BA VI"

    18th Infantry Battalion (259, 261, 263, <u>265</u> Companies)

    54th Infantry Battalion (267, 269, 271, <u>273</u> Companies)

    79th Infantry Battalion (275, 277, 279, <u>281</u> Companies)

251st Intelligence-Recon Company

252nd ? Company

253rd Commo-Liaison Company

255th Guard Company

257th Transport Company

283rd Support Company, 6 x 81/82mm mortar

285th ? Company

312TH INFANTRY DIVISION "BẾN TRE"

Lê Trọng Tấn

DIVISIONAL TROOPS

ĐKZ Company ?, 57mm ĐKZs?

72nd Intelligence-Recon Company

232nd R&R Battalion

240th Engineer Company

244th ? Company

248th Guard Company

531st Antiaircraft Battalion, 18 x 12.7mm AAMG?

(26, 266, 267, 268 Companies) East side of valley

141TH INFANTRY REGIMENT "ĐẦM HÀ"

11th Infantry Battalion (241, 243, 245, <u>247</u> Companies)

16th Infantry Battalion (18, 19, 20, 21 Companies)

428th Infantry Battalion (39, 58, 77, <u>670</u> Companies)

76th Intelligence-Recon Company

252nd ? Company

254th ? Company

260th Infantry Gun Company, 4-6 x 57mm ĐKZ

261st Guard Company

262nd ? Company

165TH INFANTRY REGIMENT "ĐÔNG TRIỀU"

115th Infantry Battalion (501, 503, 505, <u>914</u> Companies)

542nd Infantry Battalion (915, 918, 924, 942 Companies)

564th Infantry Battalion (527, 946, 950, 964 Companies)

168th ? Company

401st ĐKZ ? Company, 4-6 x 57mm ĐKZ

405th Commo-Liaison Company

407th Intelligence-Recon Company

409th Transport Company

509th ? Company

209TH INFANTRY REGIMENT "HỒNG GAI"

130th Infantry Battalion (360, 363, 366, <u>280</u> Companies)

154th Infantry Battalion (520, 525, 530, <u>270</u> Companies)

166th Infantry Battalion (606, 612, 618, <u>290</u> Companies)

74th Intelligence-Recon Company

202nd Engineer Company

256th ĐKZ Company, 4-6 x 57mm ĐKZ

288th Commo-Liaison Company

294th ? Company

300th Transport Company

303rd ? Company

316TH INFANTRY DIVISION "BIÊN HOÀ"

Lê Quảng Ba

DIVISIONAL TROOPS

ĐKZ Company ?, 57mm ĐKZs?

150th Engineer Company

160th Commo-Liaison Company

170th Intelligence-Recon Company

180th Transport Company

444th ? Company

630th Guard Company

536th Antiaircraft Battalion, 18 x 12.7mm AAMG?

(676, 677, 764, 765 Companies) East side of valley

98TH INFANTRY REGIMENT "BA ĐỒN"

215th Infantry Battalion (34, 35, 36, 38 Companies)

439th Infantry Battalion (81, 82, 83, <u>84</u> Companies)

938th Infantry Battalion (91, 92, 93, 94 Companies)

15th Guard Company

19th Commo-Liaison Company

50th Intelligence-Recon Company

56th ĐKZ Company, 4-6 x 57mm ĐKZ

58th ? Company

75th ? Company

174TH INFANTRY REGIMENT "SÓC TRĂNG"
249th Infantry Battalion (315, 316, 317, 318 Companies)
251st Infantry Battalion (671, 672, 673, 674 Companies)
255th Infantry Battalion (924, 925, 926, 653 Companies)
151st Commo-Liaison Company
153rd Intelligence-Recon Company
508th Support Company, 6 x 81/82mm mortar
509th Guard Company
567th ? Company

888th Battalion/176TH INFANTRY REGIMENT (811, 812, 813, 319 Companies)

351ST ARTILLERY-ENGINEER DIVISION "LONG CHÂU"
Đào Văn Trường
DIVISIONAL TROOPS
3rd ? Company
5th ? Company
7th ? Company
37th Antiaircraft Company
120th Engineer Company
121st Transport Company
128th Commo-Liaison Company
140th ? Company

45TH ARTILLERY REGIMENT "EVER VICTORIOUS," 24 x 105mm howitzer
632nd Howitzer Battalion (801, 802, 803 Batteries)
954th Howitzer Battalion (804, 805, 806 Batteries) *805th targeted Isabelle throughout siege*

675TH ARTILLERY REGIMENT "HEROIC," * 18 x 75mm howitzer, 20 x 120mm mortar
83rd Mortar Battalion (112, 113, 114, 115, 116 Batteries) *116th formed with captured mortars*
175th Mountain Gun Battalion (752, 753, 754 Batteries)** *754th joined siege in late March*
275th Mountain Gun Battalion (755, 756, 757 Batteries)** *755th joined siege in late March*

237TH ARTILLERY REGIMENT, 36 or 54 x 81/82mm mortar, 12 x 102mm

MRL, 12 x 75mm ĐKZ
    413th Mortar Battalion (201, 202, 203 Companies)*
    224th Rocket Battalion (two companies) *In action only last 24 hours of siege*
    ? ĐKZ Battalion (three companies) *** *In action starting April 24*
367TH ANTIAIRCRAFT REGIMENT (-), Maximum 36 x 37mm AA gun, 48 x 12.7mm AAMG
    381st AA Battalion (811, 812, 813, 814 Batteries) *Joined siege force in late April*
    383rd AA Battalion (815, 816, 817, <u>818</u> Batteries)
    394th AA Battalion (827, <u>828</u>, 829, 830 Batteries)
    396th AA Battalion (-) (<u>834</u> Battery) *Joined siege force in mid-March*
151ST ENGINEER REGIMENT
    106th Engineer Battalion (52, 53, 54 Companies)
    333rd Engineer Battalion (226, 250, 260, 270 Companies)
    444th Engineer Battalion (309, 311, 313, 315 Companies)
    555th Engineer Battalion (124, 130, 515 Companies)
    83rd Special Engineer Company (Explosives Ordnance Disposal)
* Fought as detached companies and even platoons subordinated to individual infantry divisions.
** Different sources disagree about which batteries were assigned to the 175th and 275th Mountain Gun Battalions. A 751st Battery had served with the 675th Artillery Regiment in prior years, but there is little evidence that it was at Điện Biên Phủ. Perhaps it still belonged to the regiment, but was deployed elsewhere during the siege. If so, this may explain why some Vietnamese authors report that the 675th had 20 mountain guns.
*** When the ĐKZ Battalion arrived, its dozen guns were immediately parceled out to the infantry divisions – four each to the 308th and 312th, and two apiece to the 304th and 316th.

Appendix 9: VPA rear area forces

Although the Điện Biên Phủ Front's rear area extended back only as far as Sơn La, for the sake of completeness, some security and air defense units that operated east of that point (at least during the first phase of the siege) are listed below. The company-level unit designations presented below are taken from the same sources that were discussed above in Appendix 7 and are likewise problematic in some cases.

ĐIỆN BIÊN PHỦ FRONT REAR AREA COMMAND

Đặng Kim Giang
77th Infantry Regiment
Logistical Sector Headquarters (x3) *Sơn La, Tuần Giáo, Nà Tấu*
Commo-Liaison Companies (x2)
Main Traffic Control Stations (x18)
Road Construction Engineer Battalions (x4)
Medical Companies (non-divisional) (x7) *679 total personnel*
Automobile Transport Companies (10) *446 trucks (including 94 from artillery units)*
Civilian Workers (33,500) *Contributed 3 million workdays*

AIR DEFENSE FORCES
367TH ANTIAIRCRAFT REGIMENT (-), Maximum 48 x 37mm AA gun, 48 x 12.7mm AAMG
   381st AA Battalion (811, 812, 813, 814 Batteries) *Joined siege force in late April*
   385th AA Battalion (819, 820, 821, 822 Batteries) *Defended Việt Bắc*
   392nd AA Battalion (823, 824, 825, 826 Batteries) *Defended Việt Bắc*
   396th AA Battalion (831, 832, 833, <u>834</u> Batteries) *834th left to join siege force on March 17. 833rd was used to reconstitute the 394th AA Battalion's decimated 827th Battery.*
533rd Antiaircraft Battalion (35, 93, 100, 110 Batteries), 18 x 12.7mm AAMG? *Detached from 304th Division*
681st Antiaircraft Battalion (?, ?, ?, ? Batteries), 18 x 12.7mm AAMG? *VPA High Command asset*

SECURITY FORCES
9TH INFANTRY REGIMENT "NINH BINH" *Detached from 304th Division. Joined the siege force in first week of May. See 304th Division above for the regiment's full order of battle.*

148TH SEPARATE INFANTRY REGIMENT "TÂY BẮC"

910th Infantry Battalion (220, 221, 225, <u>634</u> Coys)

920th Infantry Battalion (250, 254, 255, <u>256</u> Coys)

930th Infantry Battalion (511, 513, 515, <u>509</u> Coys)

125th Intelligence-Recon Company

226th Support Company, 6 x 81/82mm mortar

519th ? Company

523rd Commo-Liaison Company

565th ? Company

176TH INFANTRY REGIMENT (-) "LẠNG SƠN" *Detached from 316th Division*

970th Infantry Battalion (628, 632, 636, 580 Companies)

999st Infantry Battalion (320, 321, 323, 324 Companies)

300th Intelligence-Recon Company

325th Commo-Liaison Company

326th Engineer Company

327th ĐKZ Company, 4-6 x 57mm ĐKZ

328th ? Company

329th Transport Company

ENDNOTE ABBREVIATIONS

AALP	l'Amicale des Anciens Légionnaires Parachutistes (The Friendly [Association] of Former Legion Paratroops)
BQR	Bulletin Quotidien de Renseignements (Daily Information Bulletin). In effect, a stack of radio messages bound together in the order in which they were received. All GONO BQR documents are from SHD records group 10H1166.
Bruge Collection	An extensive collection of documents about Điện Biên Phù and letters written by French veterans of the siege assembled by the late Roger Bruge in preparation for writing his 2003 book *Les Hommes de Dien Bien Phu*. It is stored in SHD records group 1K594.
Catroux Commission	Commission d'enquête militaire sur la bataille de Dien Bien Phu
CDHLE	Centre de documentation historique de la Légion étrangère, Aubagne, France
CHETOM	Centre d'Histoire et d'Étude des Troupes d'Outre-Mer, Quartier Lecocq, Fréjus, France (Center for the Study of the Overseas Troops – i.e., Colonial Troops)
EMIFT	État-major Interarmées et des Forces Terrestres (Inter-arms and Land Forces Headquarters – i.e., General Navarre's headquarters for all of Indochina)
FTNV	Forces Terrestres du Nord Vietnam (Land Forces North Vietnam [Headquarters] – i.e., General Cogny's

	headquarters for Tonkin)
GONO	Groupement Opérationnel Nord-Ouest
JMO	Journal de Marche et des Opérations
SHD	Service historique de la defense, Château de Vincennes, Vincennes, France

ENDNOTES

Chapter 1

1   Fredrik Logevall, *Embers of War: The Fall of an Empire and the Making of America's Vietnam* (New York: Random House, 2013), 137.

2   Bernard Fall, *Street Without Joy* (Harrisburg, PA: Stackpole, 1964), 33.

3   Pierre Rocolle, *Pourquoi Dien Bien Phu?* (Paris: Flammarion 1968), 101 fn.

4   Charles Shrader, *A War of Logistics: Parachutes and Porters in Indochina, 1945–1954* (Lawrence: University Press of Kansas, 2015), 161.

5   Jacques Favreau and Nicolas Dufour, *Nasan: La Victoire Oubliée (1952–1953), Base Aéroterrestre au Tonkin* (Paris: Economica, 1999).

6   Shrader, *A War of Logistics*, 278–282.

7   Logevall, *Embers of War*, 343–344, 354–357; Bernard Fall, *Viet-Nam Witness, 1953–1966* (New York: Praeger, 1966), 30–31; Shrader, *A War of Logistics*, 287–288.

8   Douglas Porch, *The French Secret Services: from the Dreyfus Affair to the Gulf War* (New York: Farrar, Straus, and Giroux, 1995), 332; Roger Trinquier, *Les Maquis d'Indochine (1952–1954)* (Paris: Éditions Albatros, 1976), map 'Evacuation de Nà Sản.'

9   Shrader, *A War of Logistics*, 288–290.

10 Michel Grintchenko, *Atlante-Arethuse: Une Opération de Pacification en Indochine* (Paris: Economica, 2001); Bernard B. Fall, *Hell in a Very Small Place: The Siege of Dien Bien Phu* (Philadelphia: Lippincott, 1967) 46–47; Phillip B. Davidson, *Vietnam at War: The History, 1946–1976* (New York & Oxford: Oxford University Press, 1988), 204–213.

11 Võ Nguyên Giáp, Hữu Mai and Lady Borton, *Dien Bien Phu: Rendezvous with History* (Hanoi, Thế Giới Publishers, 2004), 22.

12 Qiang Zhai, *China and the Vietnam Wars, 1950–1975* (Chapel Hill: University of North Carolina Press, 2000), 42–45.

13 Giáp, *Rendezvous*, 15.

14   *ibid.*, 19.
15   Fall, *Hell*, 19.
16   *ibid.*, 31–39.
17   *ibid.*, 53.
18   *ibid.*, 20.
19   Giáp, *Rendezvous*, 45, 58–59.
20   *ibid.*, 86–87.
21   Fall, *Hell*, 63–64.
22   Raymond Muelle, *Combats en pays thaï: Document* (Paris: Presses de la Cité, 1999), 37–128. Some of these units were formally titled Tai Light Auxiliary Companies (Compagnies Légères de Supplétifs Tai – or CLSTs), but there was no real difference in how they were organized, trained, and equipped.
23   *ibid.*, 111.
24   Giáp, *Rendezvous*, 52–55; Fall, *Hell*, 68–71.
25   Giáp, *Rendezvous*, 17–18.
26   *ibid.*, 46, 86, 88.
27   *ibid.*, 96.
28   Thanh Huyền Đào, Duc Tue Dang, Xuân Mai Nguyễn, *Diên Biên Phu vu d'en face: paroles de bô dôi* (Paris: Nouveau Monde, 2010), 104.
29   Ministry of Defense, Central Military Party Committee, *Một số văn kiện chỉ đạo chiến cuộc Đông Xuân 1953-1954 và chiến dịch Điện Biên Phủ [Selected War Guidance Documents from the Winter-Spring Campaign of 1953–1954 and the Battle of Dien Bien Phu]* (Hanoi: People's Army Publishing House, 2004), 315–321.
30   Giáp, *Rendezvous*, 98.
31   Martin Windrow, *The Last Valley: Dien Bien Phu and the French Defeat in Vietnam* (Cambridge, MA: Da Capo Press, 2004), 258.
32   *ibid.*, 100–102.
33   GONO, *Nº91: Fiche Sur le Dispositif Brise-Lame, 21 Jan 1954* (10H1166, SHD), 1.
34   Giáp, *Rendezvous*, 103.
35   Fortifications as depicted in a French Army map of January 1954.
36   Roger Bruge, *Les hommes de Dien Bien Phu* (Paris: Perrin, 1999), 98.
37   Zhai, *China and the Vietnam Wars*, 46.
38   Giáp, *Rendezvous*, 112.
39   *ibid.*, 111–112, 119–132; Fall, *Viet-Nam Witness*, 36–38; Shrader, *A War of Logistics*, 309–311, 337.

Chapter 2

1   Charles Shrader, *A War of Logistics: Parachutes and Porters in Indochina, 1945–1954* (Lexington: University Press of Kentucky, 2015), 171.
2   *ibid.*, 294, 393; Bernard B. Fall, *Hell in a Very Small Place: The Siege of Dien Bien Phu* (Philadelphia: Lippincott, 1967), 44, 51.
3   Võ Nguyên Giáp, Hữu Mai and Lady Borton, *Dien Bien Phu: Rendezvous with History* (Hanoi, Thế Giới Publishers, 2004), 186.

4   Gia Đức Phạm; et al, *Điện Biên Phủ, Mốc Vàng Thời Đại [Điện Biên Phủ: Landmark of the Golden Era]* (Hanoi: People's Army Publishing House, 2004), 401–402.

5   Shrader, *A War of Logistics*, 347–348; Giáp, *Rendezvous*, 47, 93, 187–190.

6   Giáp, *Rendezvous*, 184–185.

7   Điện Biên Phủ Online, *Bài 2: Điện Biên Phủ, "điểm hẹn" của lòng yêu nước" [Lesson 2: Dien Bien Phu, "rendezvous" of patriotism"]*, http://www. baodienbienphu.com.vn/tin-tuc/tu-lieu-va-lich-su/145343/bai-2-dien-bien-phu-%E2%80%9Cdiem-hen%E2%80%9D-cua-long-yeu-nuoc (accessed June 6, 2017)

8   Giáp, *Rendezvous*, 184.

9   Martin Windrow, *The Last Valley: Dien Bien Phu and the French Defeat in Vietnam* (Cambridge, MA: Da Capo Press, 2004), 266; Ministry of Defense, General Logistics Department, *Công tác bảo đảm hậu cần trong chiến dịch Điện Biên Phủ: bài học kinh nghiệm và thực tiễn [Rear Services Support Operations During the Dien Bien Phu Campaign: Lessons from Experience and Practice]* (Hanoi: People's Army Publishing House, 2004), 156 gives the improbably precise figure of 261,451 civilian workers.

10 *[Rear Services Support]*, 137.

11 *ibid.*, 297.

12 Giáp, *Rendezvous*, 188.

13 Armée d'Afrique, 2e Bureau, *Bulletin de Renseignements N°1590: Occupation de Dien Bien Phu, 1 Jun 1954* (10H1160, SHD).

14 Oral History Interview of Đinh Xuân Bá, Entrepreneur and Former Assault Youth Member by Merle Pribbenow, 5 June 2007.

15 Giáp, *Rendezvous*, 84.

16 Shrader, *A War of Logistics*, 277–278.

17 Nguyễn Công Luận, *Nationalist in the Viet Nam Wars: Memoirs of a Victim Turned Soldier* (Bloomington: Indiana University Press, 2012), 118–121.

18 *ibid.*

19 Qiang Zhai, *China and the Vietnam Wars, 1950–1975* (Chapel Hill: University of North Carolina Press, 2000), 41.

20 FTNV, 2e Bureau, *N°6771: Message Postalisé, 22 Dec 1953* (10H1160, SHD), 5.

21 Giáp, *Rendezvous*, 185.

22 *ibid.*, 256–257.

23 Phạm Văn Chiến, Phạm Văn Chanh, *Lịch sử Sư đoàn 304, Tập I (1950–1975) [History of Division 304, Volume I (1950–1975)]* (Hanoi: People's Army Publishing House, 2011), 148.

24 Gia, *[Landmark of the Golden Era]*, 405.

25 Giáp, *Rendezvous*, 101.

26 *ibid.*, 115.

27 Zhai, *China and the Vietnam Wars*, 47; Giáp, *Rendezvous*, 137.

28 Giáp, *Rendezvous*, 154–155.

29 Department of Defense, Artillery Command Headquarters, *Pháo binh Quân đội nhân dân Việt Nam trong chiến dịch Điện Biên Phủ [Artillery of the People's Army of Vietnam During the Dien Bien Phu Campaign]* (Hanoi: People's Army Publishing House, 2004), 61–62.

30   Thieu Tuong and Nguyễn Trung Kiên, *Ký ức pháo binh [Artillery Memories]* (Hanoi: People's Army Publishing House, 2007), 60.

31   Pierre Langlais, *Dien Bien Phu* (Paris, Éditions France-Empire, 1963), 47–48.

32   Fall, *Hell*, 133.

33   Shrader, *A War of Logistics*, 370.

34   *[Rear Services Support]*, 162.

35   Gia, *[Landmark of the Golden Era]*, 404–405. The pack animal figure is too low, since *[Rear Services Support]*, 68, reports that 17,000 were used in all. The boat figure, on the other hand, seems too high. Perhaps it actually tallies boatloads?

36   Shrader, *A War of Logistics*, 129; Công Tác, 167.

37   George K. Tanham, *Communist Revolutionary Warfare* (New York: Praeger, 1967), 70–71.

38   Shrader, *A War of Logistics*, 126–127.

39   Giáp, *Rendezvous*, 127.

40   *ibid.*, 80, 189.

41   Shrader, *A War of Logistics*, 351.

42   Baomoi.com [New Newspaper.com], *Bảo đảm vận tải theo yêu cầu thay đổi phương châm tác chiến [Guaranteed On-Demand Transportation Changed Warfare]*, http://www.baomoi.com/bao-dam-van-tai-theo-yeu-cau-thay-doi-phuong-cham-tac-chien/c/14008098.epi (accessed Feb 12, 2017).

43   *[Rear Services Support]*, 165, 297.

44   *ibid.*, 68.

45   Giáp, *Rendezvous*, 11.

46   Fall, *Hell*, 127; Windrow, *Last Valley*, 149.

47   Artillery Command, *Biên Niên Sự Kiện Lịch Sử Ngành Kỹ Thuật Pháo Binh Quân đội Nhân dân Việt Nam 1945–1975* [Chronicle of Historic Events in Building the Vietnamese People's Army's Artillery, 1945–1975] (Hanoi: People's Army Publishing House, 1997), various.

48   Ministry of Defense, Central Military Party Committee, *Một số văn kiện chỉ đạo chiến cuộc Đông Xuân 1953-1954 và chiến dịch Điện Biên Phủ [Selected War Guidance Documents from the Winter–Spring Campaign of 1953–1954 and the Battle of Dien Bien Phu]* (Hanoi: People's Army Publishing House, 2004), 227.

49   Thanh Huyền Đào; et al., *Chuyện những người làm nên lịch sử - Hồi ức Điện Biên Phủ 1954–2009 [Stories of People Who Made History: Memories of Dien Bien Phu, 1954–2009]* (Hanoi: National Political Publishing House, 2009), 106.

50   Đặng Việt Thủy; Trần Ngọc Đoàn; Nguyễn Thúy Cúc, *Hỏi Đáp về Các Binh Chủng Trong Quân đội Nhân dân Việt Nam [Frequently Asked Questions About the Branches of the Vietnamese People's Army]* (Hanoi: People's Army Publishing House, 2009), 22.

51   Artillery Command, *[Chronicle of Historic Events]*, 22.

52   Shrader, *A War of Logistics*, 163.

53   Trái Tim Việt Nam online [Heart of Vietnam online], "Điện Biên Phủ và những điều chưa biết – Phần 1" [Dien Bien Phu and the Unknown – Part I], http://ttvnol.com/threads/dien-bien-phu-va-nhung-dieu-chua-biet-phan-1.246189/page-57 (accessed September 6, 2016).

54 Vietnam Breaking News.com, *Dien Bien Phu and the Art of Artillery,* https://www. vietnambreakingnews. com/2016/05/dien-bien-phu-and-the-art-of-artillery/ (accessed Sept 22, 2016).

55 *[Rear Services Support],* 321.

56 Lưu Trọng Lân, *Lịch sử Sư đoàn 367, tập I [History of Division 367, Volume I]* (Air Defense Service, Vietnam, 1988), 58–62, 111, 171; vnmilitaryhistory.net, "Vũ Khí Việt Nam Trong Hai Cuộc Kháng Chiến" [Vietnamese Weapons in the Two Resistance Wars], http://www.vnmilitaryhistory.net/index.php/topic, 41.170/wap2. html (accessed Jan 8, 2014).

57 Giáp, *Rendezvous,* 189; Lưu, *Lịch sử Sư đoàn 367,* 58–62, 111; Đặng Việt Thủy; Trần Ngọc Đoàn; Nguyễn Thúy Cúc, *Hỏi Đáp về Các Quân Chủng Trong Quân đội Nhân dân Việt Nam [Frequently Asked Questions About the Armed Services in the Vietnamese People's Army]* (Hanoi: People's Army Publishing House, 2009), 25.

58 Ministry of Defense, *[Rear Services Support],* 160.

59 Phillip B. Davidson, *Vietnam at War: The History 1946–1975* (Novato, CA: Presidio Press, 1988), 201.

60 Fall, *Hell,* 266, 337; Windrow, *Last Valley,* 671.

61 Shrader, *A War of Logistics,* 175, 356–357.

62 Zhai, *China and the Vietnam Wars,* 46–47; Howard Simpson, "Très Secret," *Army,* 44:4 (April 1994) 47–49.

63 Jules Roy, *The Battle of Dien Bien Phu* (New York: Harper & Row, 1965), 203.

64 United Press, 'French Say Chinese Troops Helped Capture Fortress,' *Canberra Times,* 11 May 1954, p. 1. It's possible that the "Chinese artillery regiment" did not actually refer to an *additional* artillery unit, but was rather a deliberate exaggeration based upon the undeniable fact that the two VPA 105mm battalions were organized, trained and equipped by the PLA.

65 *Email from Dr Sherman Lai to Kevin Boylan,* April 12, 2018

Chapter 3

1 GONO, 2e Bureau, *Fiche de mise au point quotidienne, 12 janvier 1954* (10H1161, SHD); III/3 REI, *JMO du III e Bataillon du 3 e REI: Période du 1 Janvier 1953 au 32 Mars inclus,14 mai 1954* (CDHLE), 9.

2 I/4 RTM, *JMO, Mois de Février 1954* (7U565, SHD), 5.

3 Bernard B. Fall, *Hell in a Very Small Place: The Siege of Dien Bien Phu* (Philadelphia: Lippincott, 1967), 112.

4 *ibid.,* 45–48.

5 *ibid.,* 54–56.

6 *ibid.,* 39–40.

7 *ibid.,* Chapter III; Martin Windrow, *The Last Valley: Dien Bien Phu and the French Defeat in Vietnam* (Cambridge, MA: Da Capo Press, 2004), 333–339, 359–360.

8 Pierre Langlais, *Dien Bien Phu* (Paris: Éditions France-Empire, 1963), 72.

9 Ivan Cadeau, *Le Génie au combat: Indochine 1945–1956* (Paris: Service Historique de la Défense, 2013), 401–402.

10   Windrow, *Last Valley*, 314–316.

11   II/4 RAC, *Rapport sur les opérations de Dien Bien Phu du 13 Mars au 7 Mai 1954* (Bruge Collection, Box 26), 10.

12   Fall, *Hell*, 119; Captain Maurice Nicod, *Les Combats de la 2e Compagnie du I/4 R.T.M. sur Eliane II du 6 Mars au 1er Avril 1954 Inclus, 10 février 1964* (Bruge Collection, Box 25), 1.

13   *ibid.*, 192. Several authors erroneously identify Bald Hill as the crest immediately between Phony Hill and Eliane-2.

14   Jacques Favreau & Nicolas Dufour, *Nasan: La Victoire Oubliée (1952–1953), Base Aéroterrestre au Tonkin* (Paris: Economica, 1999), Chapter 8.

15   Cảnh Sát Toàn Cầu Online [Worldwide Police Newspaper Online], *Bí ẩn "Đồi khâm liệm" [The Secrets of "Shroud Hill"]*, http://cstc.cand.com.vn/Phong-su-Tieu-diem/ Bi-an-Doi-kham-liem-318001/ (accessed March 2, 2017).

16   Cadeau, *Le Génie*, 410.

17   *ibid.*, 420.

18   FTNV, Commandement du Génie, État-Major – 3e Bureau, *Nº13715: Rapport du Colonel Legendre, 19 Mai 1954* (SHD, 10H1169), 2.

19   *ibid.*, Appendix 1–2.

20   *ibid.*, 1-5.

21   Cadeau, *Le Génie*, 416.

22   Windrow, *Last Valley*, 390.

23   Cadeau, *Le Génie*, 408.

24   *Rapport du Colonel Legendre*, 3.

25   Langlais, *Dien Bien Phu*, 237.

26   Artillery Command, *Biên Niên Sự Kiện Lịch Sử Ngành Kỹ Thuật Pháo Binh Quân đội Nhân dân Việt Nam 1945–1975 [Chronicle of Historic Events in Building the Vietnamese People's Army's Artillery, 1945–1975]* (Hanoi: People's Army Publishing House, 1997), various.

27   Fall, *Hell*, 175.

28   Windrow, *Last Valley*, 317.

29   Fall, *Hell*, 91.

30   GONO BQR, *Nº91: Fiche Sur le Dispositif Brise-Lame, 21 Jan 1954*.

31   FTNV, Commandement, Direction du Matériel, Section Munitions, *Des Munitions Posées Ou Parachutées Au Profit du G.O.N.O.*, no date (10H1164, SHD), 12.

32   *ibid.*

33   Chief of Ordnance, *Technical Manual 9-1940: Land Mines* (Washington, DC: US War Department, 1943), 27–30.

34   Wikipedia, *M2 Mine*, https://en.wikipedia.org/wiki/M2_mine (accessed April 13, 2016).

35   Cadeau, *Le Génie*, 377–378; *Des Munitions Posées Ou Parachutées Au Profit du G.O.N.O.*, 12; James Madison University, Center for International Stabilization and Recovery, *Munitions Reference Guide*, http://www.jmu.edu/cisr/_pages/research/ munitions.shtml and Wikipedia, *Tellermine 43*, https://en.wikipedia.org/wiki/ Tellermine_43 (both accessed April 13, 2016).

36 Cadeau, *Le Génie*, 378–379; Dossier Indochine – Site des Troupes de Marine, *Les Missions du 31e BMG au Combat, (Mai–Juin 2015)*, http://www.fng.asso.fr/ Module_Actualites/wp-content/uploads/2015/09/2-LA-CHARTE_LE-GENIE- %C3%A0-D.B.P..pdf (accessed July 29, 2016); Roger Bruge, *Les hommes de Dien Bien Phu* (Paris: Perrin, 1999), 258.

37 *Des Munitions Posées Ou Parachutées Au Profit du G.O.N.O.*, 12.

38 Wikipedia, *M14 Mine*, https://en.wikipedia.org/wiki/M14_mine (accessed April 13, 2016).

39 FTNV, 1e Bureau, *Effectifs présents à Dien Bien Phu à la date du 10 mars 1954* (10H1157, SHD).

40 6 BPC, *Extrait du JMO Novembre 1953* (7U3037, SHD), 1.

41 FTNV, État Major, *Constitution d'une Compagnie de Thai Blancs, 19 nov 1953* (10H1157, SHD); Michel Duluat, *Mémoires de Tonton Carabine* (Meudon: A. Casalis, 2012).

42 Raymond Muelle, *Combats en Pays Tai* (Paris: Presses de la Cité, 1999), 205.

43 GONO, *Répartition et Utilisation des Supplétifs, 1 jan 1954* (10H1164, SHD).

44 Col. V.J. Croizat, trans., *A Translation from the French: Lessons of the War in Indochina, Memorandum RM-5271-PR* (Santa Monica: Rand Corporation, May 1967), 196–198.

45 *ibid.*, 198–199, 217–218.

46 *ibid.*, 224–225.

47 *Ibid.*, 223–226.

48 One Project Too Far, *Indochina War Ressources*, http://1project2far.blogspot.com/p/ indochina-war-ressources.html (accessed September 2, 2016), 1954 parachute battalion TO&E; Forces Terrestres Navales et Aériennes en Indochine, État-Major Interarmées et des Forces Terrestres, 1e Bureau, *Fiche: Aspect financier de l'opération de DIEN BIEN PHU, 1955* (10H1177, SHD), I Armement.

49 Croizat, *Lessons of the War in Indochina*, 226.

50 Maj. Peter D. Jackson, "French Ground Force Organizational Development for Counterrevolutionary Warfare Between 1945 and 1962" (Master's Thesis: US Army Command and General Staff College, 2005), 56–57.

51 Favreau & Dufour, *Nasan*, 116.

52 II/4 RAC, *JMO, 22 Avril 1954* (7U3130, SHD); III/10 RAC, *Extrait du JMO, 1 Mai 1954* (7U3154, SHD).

53 Artillery Command Headquarters, *Pháo binh Quân đội nhân dân Việt Nam trong chiến dịch Diện Biên Phủ [Artillery of the People's Army of Vietnam in the Dien Bien Phu Campaign]*, 209; *Des Munitions Posées Ou Parachutées Au Profit du G.O.N.O.*, 12.

54 Steve Zaloga, *US Field Artillery of World War II* (Oxford: Osprey Publishing, 2007).

55 Jacques Molinier, *Livre-roman écrit en 1992 pour ses enfants et petit-enfants de la Tunisie (1943) à l'Algérie (1962)* (Bruge Collection, Box 28); Docteur Yves Loiseau, "*La 1e Compagnie Etrangère parachutiste de mortiers lourds,*" *Képi blanc, la vie de la Légion étrangère*, n°654 (Avril 2004) and n°655 (May 2004); Windrow, *Last Valley*, 305.

56 Windrow, *Last Valley*, 376.

57   Henri de Brancion, *Diên Biên Phu: artilleurs dans la fournaise* (Paris: Presses de la Cité, 1993), 101–102.

58   Charles R. Shrader, *A War of Logistics: Parachutes and Porters in Indochina, 1945–1954* (Lawrence, Kansas: University Press of Kansas, 2015), 336.

59   Brancion, *artilleurs dans la fournaise*, 88–89, 94–95.

60   *ibid.*, 268.

61   FTNV, *N°4/06: Situation GONO 13 mars* (10H1164, SHD).

62   Windrow, *Last Valley*, 679 fn.

63   Fall, *Hell*, 101–102.

64   Ted Morgan, *Valley of Death: The Tragedy at Dien Bien Phu That Led America into the Vietnam War* (New York: Random House, 2010), 269–270.

65   Windrow, *Last Valley*, 363.

66   Cadeau, *Le Génie*, 413–414.

67   *ibid.*, 414; *Rapport du Colonel Legendre*, 4.

68   GONO BQR, *N°85/40: Situation à 1200h, 19 Mars.*

69   Shrader, *A War of Logistics*, 300–301.

70   Favreau & Dufour, *Nasan*, Chapter 9.

71   Jules Roy, *La Bataille de Dien Bien Phu* (Paris: Rene Julliard, 1963), 568.

72   Windrow, *Last Valley*, 268–274, 704–705.

73   Shrader, *A War of Logistics*, 294–295, 307.

74   Windrow, *Last Valley*, 706.

75   *ibid.*, 268–274, 704–705.

76   Jean-Pierre Simon, *Les aviateurs dans la guerre d'Indochine, 1945–1957: Témoignages* (Paris: Éditions du Grenadier/ANVOI, 2016), 202.

77   John Prados, *Operation Vulture* (New York: ibooks, inc., 2002), 53–64.

78   *ibid.*, 82–85; Lieutenant Guillaume Muller, *"Essai de microhistoire: la destruction au sol de six Bearcat au début de la bataille de Diên Biên Phu"* Revue historique des armées, No 286 (1er trimester 2017), 126; Simon, *Les Aviateurs*, 203; Phillip B. Davidson, *Vietnam at War: The History*, 1946–1976 (New York & Oxford: Oxford University Press, 1988), 219.

79   Aviation Safety Network, *Database 1954*, https://aviation-safety.net/database/dblist.php?Year=1954 (accessed June 17, 2017); Fall, *Hell*, 227.

80   Muller, *"Essai de microhistoire,"* 122–124.

Chapter 4

1   Lưu Trọng Lân, *Lịch sử Sư đoàn 367, tập I [History of Division 367, Volume I]* (Air Defense Service, Vietnam, 1988), 123, 164.

2   Võ Nguyên Giáp, Hữu Mai and Lady Borton, *Dien Bien Phu: Rendezvous with History* (Hanoi, Thế Giới Publishers, 2004), 212.

3   Jules Roy, *La Bataille de Dien Bien Phu* (Paris: Rene Julliard, 1963), 426.

4   Bernard B. Fall, *Hell in a Very Small Place: The Siege of Dien Bien Phu* (New York & Philadelphia: Lippincott, 1967), 115.

5   FTNV, 1e Bureau, *Effectifs présents à Dien Bien Phu à la date du 10 mars 1954* (10H1157, SHD).

6   GONO BQR, *B.A. GONO 13–14 Mars 1954*; Pierre Rocolle, *Pourquoi Dien Bien Phu?* (Paris: Flammarion 1968), 352–353 fn; Marcel Philippe, *Peloton d'élèves grades*, (Cartons de 40 ans DBP, CDHLE), 2.

7   *Lettre de Renault à Bruge, 3 Janvier 1998* (Bruge Collection, Box 26).

8   I/2 REI, *JMO pour la période du 1er Mars 1954 au 7 Mai 1954* (7U625, SHD), 2.

9   Groupement Administratif de la Légion Etrangère (GALE), *Rapport de Lieutenant Etienne Turpin* (DBP 40eme Anniversaire Box, CDHLE), 1.

10   *Rapport du Capitaine Philippe Nicolas*, 1.

11   *Lettre de Cruz à Bruge, 2 novembre 1996* (Bruge Collection, Box 26).

12   Lê Trọng Tấn, *Từ Đồng Quan Đến Điện Biên [From Dong Quan to Dien Bien]* (Hanoi: People's Army Publishing House, 2002), 298.

13   III/3RTA, *JMO 1er trimestre 1954, 13 mars 1954*, 2; Commissariat Général de France et Commandement en Chef en Indochine, *Citation à l'ordre de l'Armée du capitaine Franchet, 18 janvier 1955* (Copy provided by Madame Franchet in 2015).

14   Lê, *[From Dong Quan to Dien Bien]*, 304.

15   Tran Hanh, ed., *Một số trận đánh trong kháng chiến chống Pháp, kháng chiến chống Mỹ, 1945–1975, Tập II [Selected Battles During the Resistance Wars Against the French and the Americans, 1945–1975, Volume II]* (Hanoi: People's Army Publishing House, 1991), 60; Nguyen Khac Tinh, Phung Luan, and Truong Nguyen Tue, *Pháo binh Nhân dân Việt Nam: Những chặng đường chiến đấu, tập một [People's Artillery of Vietnam: Combat History, Volume I]* (Hanoi: People's Army Publishing House, 1982), 324.

16   Henri de Brancion, *Dien Bien Phu: artilleurs dans la Fournaise* (Paris: Presses de la Cité, 1993), 110–111.

17   Martin Windrow, *The Last Valley: Dien Bien Phu and the French Defeat in Vietnam* (Cambridge, MA: Da Capo Press, 2004), 382.

18   Tran, *[Selected Battles, Vol II]*, 57–59; Thanh Tam Pham and Sherry Buchanan, *Carnet de guerre d'un jeune Viêt-minh à Diên Biên Phu: 21 février–28 août 1954* (Paris: Armand Colin, 2011), 77–82; Thieu Tuong and Nguyễn Trung Kiên, *Ký ức pháo binh [Artillery Memories]* (Hanoi, People's Army Publishing House, 2007), 65.

19   Simon Kubiak, *Operation Castor… Verdun 1954, Képi blanc, la vie de la Légion étrangère*, n°186 (Octobre 1962), 36.

20   GONO, *B.A. GONO 13–14 mars*.

21   Windrow, *Last Valley*, 381.

22   Tran, *[Selected Battles, Vol II]*, 58–59.

23   Windrow, *Last Valley*, 383–384.

24   Quốc Dũng Nguyễn, *Lịch Sử Trung Đoàn Bộ Binh 209 Sư Đoan 312 (1947–2007) Lưu Hành Nội Bộ [History of Infantry Regiment 209 Division 312 (1947–2007) Internal Distribution Only]* (Hanoi: People's Army Publishing House, 2007), 116.

25   *Rapport du Lieutenant Etienne Turpin*, 5.

26   Tran, *[Selected Battles, Vol II]*, 68.

27   *ibid.*, 65–66; Giáp, *Rendezvous*, 220–224 & map 452.

28   Lê, *[From Dong Quan to Dien Bien]*, 310.

29   Nguyen, *[People's Artillery of Vietnam]*, 325.

30   Tran, *[Selected Battles, Vol II]*, 67–68; *Rapport du Capitaine Philippe Nicolas*, 4.

31   *Rapport du Capitaine Philippe Nicolas*, 4.

32   Windrow, *Last Valley*, 381.

33   Tran, *[Selected Battles, Vol II]*, 66; Nguyen, *[People's Artillery of Vietnam]*, 325.

34   *ibid.*, 69–71; Lê, *[From Dong Quan to Dien Bien]*, 310; and GONO, *BA GONO 13–14 mars.*

35   *Rapport de Capitaine Philippe Nicolas*, 5.

36   III/3 RTA, *JMO 1er trimestre 1954* (7U425, SHD), 2.

37   Rocolle, *Pourquoi*, 358 fn.

38   I/2 REI, *JMO pour la période du 1 Mars 1954 au 7 Mai 1954*, 4; *Lettre Lt Huguenin à Bruge, 17 Novembre 1995* (Bruge Collection, Box 26).

39   Philippe, *Peloton d'élèves grades*, 4–6.

40   Kubiak, *Operation Castor... Verdun 1954*, 37.

41   *Lettre de Chataignier à Bruge*, 18 Avril 1990 (Bruge Collection, Box 27). After this mission was completed, 10th Company was stationed on D-2. It was replaced on D-4 by 1/8 BPC.

42   Windrow, *Last Valley*, 388; and Giáp, *Rendezvous*, 226–227.

43   Catroux Commission, *Témoignage de Général De Castries, 25 juin 1955* (1R230, SHD), 26.

44   Kubiak, *Operation Castor... Verdun 1954, Képi blanc, la vie de la Légion étrangère*, n°187 (Novembre 1962), 44.

45   Roy, *La Bataille*, 572; Tran, *[Selected Battles, Vol II]*, 71.

46   Thanh, *vu d'en face*, 150.

47   *ibid.*, 147–148.

48   Capitaine Daniel Carré, *Rapport officiel établi en septembre 1954 à son retour de captivité* (Bruge Collection, Box 26), 1.

49   René Bail, *Dernier baroud à Điên Biên Phu* (Paris: J. Grancher, 1990), 121.

50   FTNV, 1e Bureau, *FTNV, Effectifs présents à Dien Bien Phu à la date du 10 mars 1954.*

51   Roland de Mequenem, *Reconstitution des actions du bataillon [V/7 RTA] du 3 au 15 Mars 1954, redige par le Commandant de MECQUENEM apres son retour de captivite, septembre 1954* (7U465, SHD); Various, *Le Bélier - Amicale du 7eme RTA no 7* (Atelier d'Impression de l'Armée de Terre, 1982), 40.

52   V/7RTA, *JMO au 28 janvier 1954* (7U465, SHD); and *Le Bélier no7*, 34.

53   Windrow, *Last Valley*, 395; and Capitaine Daniel Carré, *Rapport officiel*, 2.

54   Mequenem, *Reconstitution des actions du bataillon*, map.

55   Roland de Mequenem, *Compte-rendu rédigé en captivité par le lieutenant Gilbert Clerget {Copied from a handwritten document}*, Undated (Bruge Collection, Box 26, Archives personnelles du général Roland de Mecquenem Folder), 1.

56   *Lettre de Decorse à Bruge, 8 Octobre 1996*; and *Lettre de Botella à Bruge, 10 Octobre 1996* (both Bruge Collection, Box 26).

57   Capitaine Daniel Carré, *Rapport officiel*, 2.

58   At this point, there were apparently just 12x75mm guns present, since the 675th
      Artillery Regiment was missing two detached mountain batteries and it seems that
      the 304th Division's 840th Artillery Battalion only joined the siege force in late April.

59   Giáp, *Rendezvous*, 224–225, 230.

60   *ibid.*, 224–225, 231.

61   Thanh, *vu d'en face*, 151.

62   Giáp, *Rendezvous*, 210.

63   GONO BQR, *Situation 11h30, 14 mars*; Lưu, *[History of Division 367, Vol I]*,
      131–134.

64   Giáp, *Rendezvous*, 231.

65   *ibid.*, 230; Nguyen, *[People's Artillery of Vietnam]*, 329.

66   *ibid.*, 231.

67   Thanh, *vu d'en face*, 152.

68   Lê Huy Toàn, Nguyễn Văn Nam, Hoàng Phú Cường, *Lịch sử Trung đoàn 88 Tu Vũ
      (1949–2009) [History of Regiment 88 Tu Vu (1949–2009)]* (Hanoi, Nhà xuất bản
      Quân đội nhân dân, 2009), 108, map.

69   Fall, *Hell*, 146.

70   *Le Bélier no7*, 43.

71   Mequenem, *Reconstitution des actions du bataillon*, 5.

72   *Le Bélier no7*, 38.

73   Windrow, *Last Valley*, 398.

74   Thanh, *vu d'en face*, 151.

75   Nguyen, *[People's Artillery of Vietnam]*, 329.

76   Windrow, *Last Valley*, 400.

77   Mequenem, *Reconstitution des actions du bataillon*, 5–8; Capitaine Daniel Carré,
      rapport officiel, 6–9; *Le Bélier no7*, 33–55; *Lettres de Monneau, Sanselme, Botella,
      Decorse and Carré à Roger Bruge, 1996–1998* (Bruge Collection, Box 26).

78   Giáp, *Rendezvous*, 232.

79   Sở vân hứa, thể thao và du lịch tỉnh điện biên [Department of Culture, Sports and
      Tourism Dien Bien Province], *Dũng sĩ đánh bộc phá Nguyễn Văn Ty trong trận đánh
      Đồi Độc Lập*, http://svhttdldienbien.gov.vn/chitietls/2392/Dung-si-danh-boc-pha-
      Nguyen-Van-Ty-trong-tran-danh-Doi-Doc-Lap.html (accessed Oct 24, 2016); Phan
      Chi Nhan, Le Kim, Le Huy Toan, and Nguyen Dinh Khuong, *Sư đoàn 308 Quân tiên
      phong [The 308th "Vanguard" Division]* (Hanoi: People's Army Publishing House,
      1999), 120–121.

80   Fall, *Hell*, 147.

81   Capitaine Daniel Carré, *rapport officiel*, 8; and Mequenem, *Reconstitution des
      actions du bataillon*, 7.

82   Capitaine Daniel Carré, *rapport officiel*, 8.

83   *ibid.*; and *Le Bélier no7*, 46–48.

84   Catroux Commission, *2e Audition De Castries à commission d'enquête, 25 juin 1955*
      (1R229, SHD), 27.

85   5 BPVN, *JMO Période du 14 Mars au 7 Mai 1954* (7U2971, SHD), 1–2.

86   Windrow, *Last Valley*, 393.

87   Catroux Commission, *2e Audition De Castries à commission d'enquête*, 27.

88   Catroux Commission, *Rapport Trancart pour la commission d'enquête, 29 juin 1955* (1R229, SHD), 4.

89   *ibid.*

90   André Mengelle, *Diên-Biên-Phu: des chars et des hommes* (Paris: Éditions Lavauzelle, 2006), 102; *Le Bélier no7*, 48–49; and Roger Bruge, *Les hommes de Dien Bien Phu* (Paris: Perrin, 1999), 182.

91   Giáp, *Rendezvous*, 234; Lê, et al., *Lịch sử Trung đoàn 88 Tu Vũ (1949–2009)*, 108 map.

92   *Le Bélier no7*, 102–106; Catroux Commission, *Rapport Trancart pour la commission d'enquête*, 3–4; Capitaine Daniel Carré, *rapport officiel*, 9.

93   Mengelle, *des chars et des hommes*, 101–105; and Bruge, *Les hommes*, 182.

94   Giáp, *Rendezvous*, 234.

95   Mengelle, *des chars et des hommes*, 105–106.

96   *ibid.*, 107; and Bruge, *Les hommes*, 183–184.

97   5 BPVN, *JMO Période du 14 Mars au 7 Mai 1954*, 2; Catroux Commission, *Témoignage de Colonel Langlais, 17 Octobre 1955* (1R230, SHD), 23–25.

98   *Rapport de Capitaine Daniel Carré*, 9; *Lettre de Botella à Bruge, 14 mars 1996* (Bruge Collection, Box 16).

99   Fall, *Hell*, 150; Windrow, *Last Valley*, 403; and Rocolle, *Pourquoi*, 372–375.

100   Catroux Commision, *Rapport Trancart pour la commission d'enquête, 29 juin 1955*, 3–4; *Trancart's Reply to the commission from a letter of 7 July 1955* (1R229, SHD), 1.

101   Pierre Langlais, *Dien Bien Phu* (Paris, Éditions France-Empire, 1963), 31.

102   Windrow, *Last Valley*, 441–444.

103   Mengelle, *des chars et des hommes*, 111.

104   Windrow, *Last Valley*, 403; Fall, *Hell*, 150.

105   *Rapport du Colonel Langlais pour la commission d'enquête, suivi d'une audition le Octobre 17, 1955* (1R229, SHD).

106   Catroux Commission, *Trancart's Reply to the Catroux Commission from a letter of 7 July 1955*, 1; *Rapport Trancart pour la commission d'enquête, 29 juin 1955*; *Rapport Langlais pour la commission d'enquête*.

107   Rocolle, *Pourquoi*, 372–375.

108   *Phone conversation Jean Luciani and Luc Olivier, 8 December 2015.*

109   Roy, *La Bataille*, 477.

110   Thanh, *vu d'en face*, 152–153.

111   Fall, *Hell*, 146.

112   Mequenem, *Reconstitution des actions du bataillon*, 11; and Capitaine Daniel Carré, *rapport officiel*, 9.

113   Fall, *Hell*, 154.

114   Andre Botella, *Quelques Souvenirs d'Indochine* (Archives personnelles de Guy Leonetti), 5.

115   GONO BQR, *du 18 au 19 mars – 17 heures*.

116   Fall, *Hell*, 156–157.

117   Giáp, *Rendezvous*, 334.

118   1 BEP, *JMO Mois de Novembre 1953* (7U659, SHD).

119 Michel Duluat, *Mémoires de tonton Carabine* (Paris: A. Casalis, 2012), 17.

120 *FTNV,* 1e Bureau, *Effectifs présents à Dien Bien Phu à la date du 10 mars 1954, 13 Mai 1954* (10H1157, SHD).

121 *Phone Conversation Raymond Legoubé and Luc Olivier*, January 2, 2016.

122 Foreign Legion Info, *2nd Foreign Legion Mortar Mixed Company*, http://foreignlegion.info/units/2e-cmmle/ (accessed Dec 29, 2015).

123 Raymond Legoubé, *"Un bataillon obscur dans une bataille célébre: Le BT3 à Dien Bien Phu,"* April 2000 (1KT1218, SHD), Booklet 1, 48.

124 *ibid.*, Booklet 1, 53; Forum laguerreenindochine, *Le parcours d'un marsouin du 3e bataillon thaï,* http://laguerreenindochine.forumactif.org/t1542p50-le-parcours-d-un-marsouin-du-3e-bataillon-thai (accessed Dec 28, 2015).

125 BT3, *JMO 1er et 2eme Trimestre 1954* (Bruge Collection, Box 29), 2.

126 Legoubé. *"Un bataillon obscur,"* Booklet 1, 55–56.

127 BT3, *JMO 1er et 2eme Trimestre 1954*, 3.

128 *ibid.*

129 Georgio Adamo Muzzati, *Là où l'on meurt... Peut être* (Paris: Editions Italiques, 2004), 292.

130 Fall, *Hell*, 159.

131 Erwan Bergot, *Les Cent soixante-dix jours de Diên Biên Phu* (Paris: Presses de la Cité, 1979), 151.

132 Mengelle, *des chars et des hommes*, 113.

133 GONO BQR, *Evènements GONO – Nuit 16 au 17-3.*

134 BT3, *JMO 1er et 2eme Trimestre 1954*, 4.

135 Nguyen, *[People's Artillery of Vietnam]*, 333.

136 GONO, *Evènements GONO – Nuit 16 au 17-3.*

137 Legoubé. *"Un bataillon obscur,"* Booklet 1, 57–58.

138 Giáp, *Rendezvous*, 236–237.

139 BT3, *JMO 1er et 2eme Trimestre 1954*, 4.

140 Pierre Langlais, *Dien Bien Phu* (Paris: Éditions France-Empire, 1963), 29.

141 Legoubé, *"Un bataillon obscur,"* Booklet 1, 59.

142 Mengelle, *des chars et des hommes*, 116.

143 Nguyen, *[People's Artillery of Vietnam]*, 333; BT3, *JMO 1er et 2eme Trimestre 1954*, 4–5.

144 BT3, *JMO 1er et 2eme Trimestre 1954*, 5.

145 6 BPC, *JMO Mois de Mars 1954* (7U3037, SHD), 3; Bergot, *Les Cent soixante-dix jours de Diên Biên Phu*, 153; 1 BEP, *JMO Mois de Mars 1954* (7U659, SHD), 9; Rocolle, *Pourquoi*, 384.

146 Giáp, *Rendezvous*, 237.

147 *Contribution to the History of Dien Bien Phu, Vietnamese Studies #3* (Hanoi: Foreign Languages Publishing House, 1965), 191.

148 Legoubé, *"Un bataillon obscur,"* Booklet 1, tableau n⁰ 29.

149 BT3, *JMO 1er et 2eme Trimestre 1954*, 6.

150 Catroux Commision, *Audition de Lieutenant-Colonel Lalande, 2 July 1955* (1R229, SHD), 20–21.

151 Legoubé, *"Un bataillon obscur,"* Booklet 1.

152 *ibid.*, Booklet 1, 60.

153 Rocolle, *Pourquoi*, 331.

154 Catroux Commission, *2e Audition de Général De Castries, 25 juin 1955*, 1.

155 Catroux Commission, *1e Audition de Général De Castries, 23 juin 1955*, 8.

156 GONO, *Message à FTNV 23h35, 20 mars* (1R235, SHD).

157 Giáp, *Rendezvous*, p. 217.

158 Fall, *Hell*, 102.

159 *Tập chí trí thực phát triển [Knowledge Development Magazine]*, Huyền thoại Điện Biên *[Legends of Dien Bien Phu]* (Hanoi: Vietnam News Agency, 2013), 114–244.

160 Rapport sur l'appui aérien en Indochine, *De Répartition des Sorties "FEU" Selon les Périodes et Selon Les Différentes Missions, Mai 1954* (10H1170, SHD).

161 Windrow, *Last Valley*, 707.

162 Qiang Zhai, *China and the Vietnam Wars, 1950–1975* (Chapel Hill: University of North Carolina Press, 2000), 46.

163 Henri de Brancion, *Diên Biên Phu: artilleurs dans la fournaise* (Paris: Presses de la Cité, 1993), 280.

Chapter 5

1 *Contribution to the History of Dien Phu – Vietnamese Studies #3* (Hanoi: Foreign Languages Publishing House, 1965), 191. This should not be confused with the commanders' conference that Giáp describes taking place the following day.

2 *ibid.*, 63.

3 Võ Nguyên Giáp, Hữu Mai and Lady Borton, *Dien Bien Phu: Rendezvous with History* (Hanoi, Thế Giới Publishers, 2004), 244–247, 392.

4 Giáp, *Rendezvous*, 251.

5 *Contribution*, 85–86.

6 Langlais, *Dien Bien Phu* (Paris, Éditions France-Empire, 1963), 58–59.

7 Artillery Command Headquarters, *Pháo binh Quân đội nhân dân Việt Nam trong chiến dịch Diện Biên Phủ [Artillery of the People's Army of Vietnam During the Dien Bien Phu Campaign]* (Hanoi: People's Army Publishing House, 2004), 139–140.

8 Nguyen Khac Tinh, Phung Luan, and Truong Nguyen Tue, *Pháo binh Nhân dân Việt Nam: Những chặng đường chiến đấu, tập một [People's Artillery of Vietnam: Combat History, Volume I]* (Hanoi: People's Army Publishing House, 1982), 337–338.

9 Lưu Trọng Lân, *Lịch sử Sư đoàn 367, tập I [History of Division 367, Volume I]* (Air Defense Service, Vietnam, 1988), 172; Báo Cựu Chiến Binh Việt Nam [Vietnam Veterans Newspaper], 'Bắn rơi máy bay Pháp ở Điện Biên Phủ: Kỷ niệm khó quên' *[French aircraft shot down at Dien Bien Phu: Unforgettable Anniversary]*, http://cuuchienbinh.com.vn/index.aspx?Menu=1370&Style=1&ChiTiet=5381 (accessed July 21, 2010).

10 Catroux Commission, *2e Audition de Castries à commission d'enquête, 25 juin 1955* (1R230, SHD), 40.

11   Bernard B. Fall, *Hell in a Very Small Place: The Siege of Dien Bien Phu* (Philadelphia, Lippincott, 1967), 175.

12   GONO BQR, *N°102/40: Situation à 08h00, 20 mars*.

13   GONO BQR, Chef d'État-Major, *N°2/1: 28 mars*.

14   5 BPVN, *JMO Période du 14 Mars au 7 Mai 1954* (7U2971, SHD), 2; *Emails from Pierre Latanne to Luc Olivier*, June 12, 2015.

15   *Interview of Sergent-Chef Michel Sleurs & Caporal-Chef Gérard Thieulin by Luc Olivier*, August 10, 2014.

16   *Lettre de Chataignier à Bruge, 11 Novembre 1990* (Bruge Collection, Box 27).

17   Patrick-Charles Renaud, *Aviateurs en Indochine: Diên Biên Phu, de novembre 1952 à juin 1954* (Paris: Grancher, 2003), 329.

18   *Lettre de Capitaine Franchet à Bruge, 5 Septembre 1997* (Bruge Collection, Box 27).

19   André Mengelle, *Diên-Biên-Phu: des chars et des hommes* (Paris: Éditions Lavauzelle, 1996), various; Pierre Rocolle, *Pourquoi Dien Bien Phu?* (Paris: Flammarion, 1968), 284. The 32 heavy mortars included four reserve tubes. The 50 percent decline in operational 120s by March 16 must reflect personnel losses, since only eight had been destroyed or captured by that date. On all the specified dates there were three operational tanks at Isabelle, though the Green Platoon had some out of action on other dates. A tank was considered "operational" if it could move and fire even if damage impaired its effectiveness. Of the five operational on May 7, three had serious damage to their turrets – one of which could no longer rotate.

20   FTNV, General Commandant, *N°7/1, 14 mars* (1R235, SHD).

21   Henri de Brancion, *Diên Biên Phu: artilleurs dans la fournaise* (Paris: Presses de la Cité, 1993), 141–142.

22   Charles Schrader, *A War of Logistics: Parachutes and Porters in Indochina, 1945–1954* (Lexington: University Press of Kentucky, 2015), 335.

23   *Rapport du Colonel de Winter, Commandant l'Artillerie des FTNV, 20 Mai 1954* (10H1174, SHD), Annexe IX: Recapitulation de l'Artillerie; Forces Terrestres Navales et Aériennes en Indochine, État-Major Interarmées et des Forces Terrestres, 1e Bureau, *Fiche: Aspect financier de l'opération de DIEN BIEN PHU, 1955* (10H1177, SHD), I Armement.

24   GONO BQR, *Situation à 1800 H, 27 mars*.

25   AALP, *Dien Bien Phu, il y a quarante ans*, 99–100; and Docteur Yves Loiseau, *"La 1e Compagnie Etrangère parachutiste de mortiers lourds,"* Képi blanc, la vie de la Légion étrangère, N°654 (Avril 2004) and N°655 (May 2004); Roger Bruge, *Les hommes de Dien Bien Phu* (Paris: Perrin, 1999), 234.

26   Brancion, *artilleurs dans la fournaise*, 268.

27   GONO BQR, *N°58/40, 26 mars*.

28   Jules Roy, *La Bataille de Dien Bien Phu* (Paris: Rene Julliard, 1963), 209.

29   Lieutenant Guillaume Muller, *"Essai de microhistoire: la destruction au sol de six Bearcat au début de la bataille de Diên Biên Phu"* Revue historique des armées, *n°286* (1er trimester 2017), 128.

30   Fall, *Hell*, 165–171; Roy, *La Bataille*, 569; Marcel Philippe, *Peloton d'élèves grades* (Cartons de 40 ans DBP, CDHLE), 5.

31   Fall, *Hell*, 190.

32   Raymond Muelle, *Combats en pays thai: Document* (Paris: Presses de la Cité, 1999), 143–144.

33   Mengelle, *des chars et des hommes*, 117.

34   Phạm Văn Chiến, Phạm Văn Chanh, *Lịch sử Sư đoàn 304, Tập I (1950–1975) [History of Division 304, Volume I (1950–1975)]* (Hanoi: People's Army Publishing House, 2011), 158; Catroux Commission, *Document Nº13c: Rapport du Colonel Lalande sur les combats du Centre de Resistance "Isabelle," JMO du C.R. Isabelle* (1R227, Dossier II-40, SHD), 2.

35   Captain Maurice Nicod, *Les Combats de la 2e Compagnie du I/4 R.T.M. sur Eliane II du 6 Mars au 1er Avril 1954 Inclus, 10 Février 1964* (Bruge Collection, Box 29), 1–2.

36   Fall, *Hell*, 192.

37   *ibid.*, 174; GONO BQR, *Nº7/40, 21 Mars*; 6 BPC, *JMO Mois de Mars 1954* (7U3037, SHD), 4.

38   5 BPVN, *JMO Période du 14 Mars au 7 Mai 1954*, 3.

39   Bruge, *Les hommes*, 234.

40   *ibid.*; Jacques Antoine, *Il y a cinquante ans: Le 8e Choc à Diên-Biên-Phu, 21 novembre 1953 – 7 mai 1954* (Amicale du 8e RPIMA, 2004), 131–133; 8 BPC, *JMO 1 Janvier à 8 Mai 1954* (7U3059, SHD); Mengelle, *des chars et des hommes*, 128.

41   Fall, *Hell*, 181–182; Mengelle, *des chars et des hommes*, 128; Pierre Sergent, *Je ne regrette rien: la poignante histoire des légionnaires-parachutistes du 1er REP* (Paris: Fayard, 1972), 174.

42   GONO BQR, *Nº58/40, 26 mars*.

43   6 BPC, *JMO Mois de Mars 1954*, 4.

44   Bataillion Bigeard, *1954: L'Année du Sacrifice*, http://bataillonbigeard.wifeo.com/1954.php (accessed June 22, 2016).

45   I/2 REI, *JMO pour la période du 1er Mars 1954 au 7 Mai 1954* (7U625, SHD), 4; GONO BQR, *Nº12/40, 22 mars*.

46   GONO BQR, *Journée du 24 Mars au 25 Mars – 17H.00*; Bruge, *Les hommes*, 224.

47   GONO BQR, *Nº36/40: Situation à 11H30, 24 mars*; Mengelle, *des chars et des hommes*, 122.

48   Mengelle, *des chars et des hommes*, 129–131; AALP, *DBP, il y a quarante ans*, 113–118; 1 BEP, *JMO Mois de Mars 1954* (7U659, SHD), 12.

49   GONO BQR, *Nº76/40, 27 mars*; 5 BPVN, *JMO Période du 14 Mars au 7 Mai 1954*, 3; *Interview of William Schillardi by Luc Olivier*, 25 May 2015; Bruge, *Les hommes*, 235–236; *Dien Bien Phu, une carrière brisée par René de Salins*, self-published (1KT1440, SHD), 18; Mengelle, *des chars et des hommes*, 132.

50   BG 31, *JMO Décembre 1953* (7U1402, SHD).

51   13 DBLE, *Additif au JMO de la 13ºD.B.L.E., 17 Septembre 1954* (CDHLE).

52   GONO BQR, *Nº68/40 : Situation 14h30, 18 Mars 1954*.

53   GONO, 2e Bureau, *Nº13/24, 19 mars* (10H1166, SHD).

54   *JMO du C.R. Isabelle*, 3; III/3 RTA, *JMO 1er trimestre 1954* (7U425, SHD), 3; GONO BQR, *Nº3/40, 21 mars*; AALP, *Dien Bien Phu, il y a quarante ans*, 126.

55   Mengelle, *des chars et des hommes*, 118–120.

56   *ibid.*, 120–121; GONO BQR, *N°25/40: Bilan du 22 Mars* and *Nuit du 21 au 22 Mars 1954.*

57   Phạm, *Lịch sử Sư đoàn 304*, 149.

58   8 BPC, *JMO 1 Janvier à 8 Mai 1954*; Antoine, *Il y a cinquante ans*, 127–128; Mengelle, *des chars et des hommes*, 121.

59   Laure Cournil, "Diên Biên Phu, Des tranchées au prétoire: 1953–1958" (Doctoral Thesis: Université de Paris I Panthéon – Sorbonne, 2014), 199–200.

60   *Lettre de de Castries à Cogny, 22 Mars* (10H1161, SHD).

61   Jules Roy, *La Bataille de Dien Bien Phu* (Paris: Rene Julliard, 1963), 237.

62   *JMO du C.R. Isabelle*, 3.

63   GONO BQR, *N°50/40: Intentions Pour le 26 Mars.*

64   GONO BQR, *Situation à 18 heures 00, 24 mars*; 6 BPC, *JMO Mois de Mars 1954*, 4; Mengelle, *des chars et des hommes*, 123–124.

65   GONO BQR, *N°48/40: Situation à 17H30, 25 mars*; Mengelle, *des chars et des hommes*, 127–128.

66   GONO BQR, *N°2/40: Situation à 1130 heures, 29 mars.*

67   GONO BQR, *N°9/40, 30 mars*; 1 BEP, *JMO Mois de Mars 1954*, 13; 6 BPC, *JMO Mois de Mars 1954*, 5.

68   Thanh Huyền Đào; Duc Tue Dang; Xuân Mai Nguyễn, *Diên Biên Phu vu d'en face: paroles de bô dôi* (Paris: Nouveau Monde, 2010), 157–158 ; Lưu, *Lịch sử Sư đoàn 367*, 143–146.

69   Rapport sur l'appui aérien en Indochine, *De Répartition des Sorties "FEU" Selon les Périodes et Selon Les Différentes Missions, Mai 1954* (10H1170, SHD). Since French and Vietnamese accounts both describe intensive efforts to knock out VPA flak, sorties targeting AA positions must be included in the "Counterbattery" column.

70   Lưu, *Lịch sử Sư đoàn 367*, 160–161.

71   *ibid.*, 162–163.

72   Ministry of Defense, General Logistics Department, *Công tác bảo đảm hậu cần trong Chiến dịch Điên Biên Phủ: Bài học kinh nghiệm và thực tiễn [Rear Services Support Operations During the Dien Bien Phu Campaign: Lessons from Experience and Practice]* (Hanoi: People's Army Publishing House, 2004), 75.

73   Philippe Gras, *L'Armée de l'air en Indochine, 1945–1954: l'impossible mission* (Paris: Harmattan, 2001), 517.

74   Marc Bertin, *Packet sur Diên Biên Phu: la vie quotidienne d'un pilote de transport* (Paris: Presses universitaires de France, 1991), 95–108; Martin Windrow, *The Last Valley: Dien Bien Phu and the French Defeat in Vietnam* (Cambridge, MA: Da Capo Press, 2004), 439–441.

75   Fall, *Hell*, 176.

76   Reginald Wieme de Ruddere, *Journal des Marches et Opérations du Groupement Wieme (Groupement mobile Tai n° 5) à Dien Bien Phu Pendant la Campagne du 1er Décembre 1953 au 31 Mai 1954* (publisher unidentified, 1999); www.reds.vn, *Chùm ảnh: Chứng tích vụ Pháp thảm sát 444 người ở Điện Biên Phủ [In pictures: Memorial to 444 people massacred by the French at Dien Bien Phu]*, www.reds.vn/index.php/dat-viet/10788-vu-tham-sat-noong-nhai (accessed June 22, 2016).

77   Jean Beguin, *Lettre du 25 Oct 2000* (1KT596 Private Collection of Général de Champeaux, SHD), 1.

78   *JMO du C.R. Isabelle*, 3.

79   Fall, *Hell*, 176–179.

80   Ivan Cadeau, *Diên Biên Phu: 13 mars–7 mai 1954* (Paris: Tallandier, 2013), 127–128; Windrow, *The Last Valley*, 431, 441–444.

81   Fall, *Hell*, 171.

82   Windrow, *The Last Valley*, 442.

83   *ibid.*, 443, 527, 577; Fall, *Hell*, 178.

84   Marcel Bigeard, *Pour Une Parcelle de Gloire* (Paris: Libraire Plon, 1975), 161–163.

85   Fall, *Hell*, 177.

86   Bigeard, *Pour Une Parcelle de Gloire*, 165–166.

87   Marcel Bigeard, *Dégagement à Ouest du C.R. Principal de Dien Bien Phu, Sep 1954* (Cartons des 40 ans de DBP, CDHLE), 1–2 ; Henri Le Mire, *Epervier: Le 8e Choc à Dien Bien Phu* (Paris: Editions Albin Michel S.A., 1988), 209–211; Rocolle, *Pourquoi*, 402–403.

88   Le Mire, *Epervier*, 212–213 ; Mengelle, *des chars et des hommes*, 133–138.

89   Le Mire, *Epervier*, 213.

90   Langlais, *Dien Bien Phu*, 59–61; Mengelle, *des chars et des hommes*, 136–138; Franck Mirmont and Heinrich Bauer, *Les chemins de Diên Biên Phu* (Paris: Nimrod, 2015), 336.

91   Langlais, *Dien Bien Phu*, 59–61; Mengelle, *des chars et des hommes*, 140–143; *Phone conversation Luc Olivier and Général Guy Ménage*, 7 July 2016.

92   Giáp, *Rendezvous*, 240–251; *Huyền thoại Điện Biên [Legends of Dien Bien Phu]*, 114–244; Lê Huy Toàn, Nguyễn Văn Nam, Hoàng Phú Cường, *Lịch sử Trung đoàn 88 Tu Vũ (1949–2009) [History of Regiment 88 «Tu Vu» (1949–2009)]* (Hanoi, Nhà xuất bản Quân đội nhân dân, 2009), 114–115.

93   Thanh, *vu d'en face*, 161.

94   Phan Chi Nhan, Le Kim, Le Huy Toan, and Nguyen Dinh Khuong, *Sư đoàn 308 Quân tiên phong [The 308th "Vanguard" Division]* (Hanoi: People's Army Publishing House, 1999), 125.

95   6 BPC, *JMO Mois de Mars 1954*, 5.

96   Mengelle, *des chars et des hommes*, 141.

97   GONO BQR, *Situation 15 Heures 30, 28 mars*.

98   GONO BQR, *Le 29 Mars à 10h50*.

99   Le Mire, *Epervier*, 213.

100   Bigeard, *Dégagement à Ouest du C.R. Principal de Dien Bien Phu*, 4.

101   Langlais, *Dien Bien Phu*, 59–60.

102   GONO BQR, Chef E.M., *N°2/01, 28 mars*; Võ Nguyên Giáp, *Tổng Tập Luận Văn [Collected Essays]* (Hanoi: People's Army Publishing House, 2006), 349.

103   Fall, *Hell*, 169–170.

104   *ibid.*, 172.

105   Catroux Commission, *Rapport du Colonel Langlais pour la commission d'enquête, suivi d'une audition le Octobre 17, 1955* (1R229, SHD), 15.

Chapter 6

1   Bernard B. Fall, *Hell in a Very Small Place: The Siege of Dien Bien Phu* (New York & Philadelphia: Lippincott, 1967), 195.

2   Ministry of Defense, Central Military Party Committee, *Một số văn kiện chi đạo chiến cuộc Đông Xuân 1953-1954 và chiến dịch Điện Biên Phủ [Selected War Guidance Documents from the Winter–Spring Campaign of 1953–1954 and the Battle of Dien Bien Phu]* (Hanoi: People's Army Publishing House, 2004), 468–476.

3   *ibid.*, 474.

4   Pierre Langlais, *Dien Bien Phu* (Paris: Éditions France-Empire, 1963), 80–82.

5   Andre Botella, *Quelques Souvenirs d'Indochine* (Personal Archive of Guy Leonetti), 8.

6   6 BPC, *JMO Mois de Mars 1954* (7U3037, SHD), 5.

7   Henri de Brancion, *Diên Biên Phu: artilleurs dans la fournaise* (Paris: Presses de la Cité, 1993), 103.

8   I/13 DBLE, *Additif an JMO de la 13°D.B.L.E.*, *17 Septembre 1954* (CDHLE), 4; Général Pierre Daillier, *Le 4eme RTM: les bataillons de marche en Indochine 1947–1954* (Paris, Château de Vincennes: Service Historique de l'Armée de Terre, 1990), 310: Serge Fantinel, *Une section de Marocains à DBP*, no date (1KT1155, SHD), 14; *Interview of Antoine Cerlini by Luc Olivier*, 28 Aug 2015; *Interview of Josef Unterlechner by Luc Olivier*, 27 Sept 2016; *Phone Interview of Jean Luciani (1/1 BEP) by Luc Olivier*, 18 Sept 2016; *Phone Interview of Jack Horniak by Luc Olivier*, 27 Sept 2016.

9   Tran Hanh, ed., *Một Số Trận Đánh Trong Kháng Chiến Chống Pháp, Kháng Chiến Chống Mỹ, 1945–1975, Tap II [Selected Battles During the Resistance Wars Against the French and the Americans, 1945–1975, Volume II]* (Hanoi: People's Army Publishing House, 1991), 125–126.

10 Võ Nguyên Giáp, Hữu Mai and Lady Borton, *Dien Bien Phu: Rendezvous with History* (Hanoi, Thế Giới Publishers, 2004), 270; GONO BQR, *Message à FTNV 17h30, 30 Mars*; *Message à FTNV 18h45, 30 Mars* and *Message à FTNV 07h15, 31 Mars*.

11 Fall, *Hell*, 195–196.

12 Guillaume Allaire, "*Dien Bien Phu (30 Mars 1954)*," *Ancre d'Or-Bazeilles: La Revue des Troupes de Marine*, N° 339 (Mars–Avril 2004), 41; Lieutenant Guy Filaudeau, *Rapport de Lieutenant Filaudeau 1 Janvier 1955 à Argenton-Château* (Bruge Collection, Box 31).

13 Roger Bruge, *Les hommes de Dien Bien Phu* (Paris: Perrin, 1999), 11, Ivan Cadeau, *Dien Bien Phu: 13 mars – 7 mai* (Paris: Editions Tallardier, 2013), 129 & 186 fn 9; *Handwritten document "Dominique 1 jusqu'au 29 mars" found in envelope with JMO of 1 CMMLE/1 CEML* (CDHLE).

14 Guillaume Allaire, "*Dien Bien Phu (30 Mars 1954)*," 41.

15 Nguyen Khac Tinh, Phung Luan, and Truong Nguyen Tue, *Pháo binh Nhân dân Việt Nam: Những chặng đường chiến đấu, tập một [People's Artillery of Vietnam: Combat History, Volume I]*, (Hanoi: People's Army Publishing House, 1982), 341.

16   *Letter from Jean Martinais to Luc Olivier*, 18 Jan 2015; Giáp, *Rendezvous*, 271.

17   Martin Windrow, *The Last Valley: Dien Bien Phu and the French Defeat in Vietnam* (Cambridge, MA: Da Capo Press, 2004), 459.

18   Letter from Jean Martinais to Luc Olivier.

19   *ibid.*; *Lettre de Martinais à Bruge*, 3 Février 1996 (Bruge Collection, Box 26); Giáp, *Rendezvous*, 271–272; GONO BQR, *Message à FTNV 21h50, 30 Mars*.

20   *Rapport du Lieutenant Jean Chataigner*, 10 Septembre 1954 (Bruge Collection, Box 27), 1; *Rapport de Lieutenant Filaudeau*, 1.

21   *Lettre de Joseph Cadiou à son frère, 20 Mars 1954* (Bruge Collection, Box 26).

22   Giáp, *Rendezvous*, 272; Thánh Nhân Nguyễn, *Lịch sử Trung đoàn 209, Sư đoàn 7, Quân đoàn 4 (1947–2003) [History of Regiment 209, Division 7, Corps 4 (1947–2003)]* (Hanoi: People's Army Publishing House, 2004), 63–64.

23   Allaire, "*Dien Bien Phu (30 Mars 1954),*" 40–41; *Rapport du Lieutenant Jean Chataigner*, 1–2; *Rapport du Lieutenant Lentsch, 10/9/54* (Bruge Collection, Box 35) 1-2; *Lettres de Jean Garandeau à Colonel de Badts*, 8 Mars 1990 (Bruge Collection, Box 25); Windrow, *Last Valley*, 460; GONO BQR, *Message à B3, 20h00, 30 Mars*.

24   Lê Trọng Tấn, *Từ Đồng Quan Đến Điện Biên [From Dong Quan to Dien Bien]* (Hanoi: People's Army Publishing House, 2002), 321; Various, *Contribution to the History of Dien Phu – Vietnamese Studies #3* (Hanoi: Foreign Languages Publishing House, 1965), 194.

25   Andre Botella, *Quelques Souvenirs d'Indochine*, 8.

26   GONO BQR, *Message à FTNV 01h14, 1 Avril*; Pierre Rocolle, *Pourquoi Dien Bien Phu?* (Paris: Flammarion 1968), 508.

27   André Mengelle, *Diên-Biên-Phu: des chars et des hommes* (Paris: Éditions Lavauzelle, 2006), 151–156.

28   *Interview of Guy de la Malène by Luc Olivier*, 5 Dec 2014.

29   *ibid.*; *Contribution*, 195; vnmilitaryhistory.net, *Tóm tắt các chiến dịch trong kháng chiến chống Pháp [A summary of the campaign in the war against France]*, http://www.vnmilitaryhistory.net/index.php?topic=24429.90 (accessed Nov 30, 2016).

30   *Interview of Guy de la Malène*; Erwan Bergot, *Les Cent soixante-dix jours de Diên Biên Phu* (Paris: Presses de la Cité, 1979), 308; Fall, *Hell*, 196.

31   Rocolle, *Pourquoi*, 422.

32   *Rapport de Lieutenant Filaudeau*, 1.

33   Võ Nguyên Giáp, *Điện Biên Phủ* (Hanoi: Nhà xuất bản Chính trị quốc gia, 1998), 172 fn 2.

34   Armchair General, *Dien Bien Phu and Operation Vulture*, http://www.armchairgeneral.com/forums/showthread.php?t=75459&page=21 (accessed Nov 26, 2016).

35   *Lịch sử sư đoàn bộ binh 312 [History of Infantry Division 312]* (Hanoi: People's Army Publishing House, 1995), 71; BG 31, *Message à Commandement Génie 12h10, 28 Mars* (10H2624, SHD).

36   *Telephone interview of Gérard Thieulin by Luc Olivier*, 10 Aug 2014.

37   Quốc Dũng Nguyễn, *Lịch sử Trung đoàn bộ binh 209, Sư đoàn 312, 1947-2007: lưu hành nội bộ [History of Infantry Regiment 209 Division 312 (1947–2007) Internal*

Distribution Only] (Hanoi: People's Army Publishing House, 2007), 121–122. This book actually states that the 130th attacked Position D2, but that was the CEPML's now vacant mortar position behind Dominique-5. The 166th Battalion's two companies may have aided the assault on Dominique-6.

38 Giáp, *Rendezvous*, 281.

39 Brancion, *artilleurs dans la fournaise*, 161–165.

40 *ibid.*, 165–171.

41 Fall, *Hell*, 196.

42 *Contribution*, 195.

43 Brancion, *artilleurs dans la fournaise*, 172; *Rapport de Lieutenant Filaudeau*, 1–4.

44 Langlais, *Dien Bien Phu*, 110.

45 *[History of Infantry Division 312]*, 72. By the morning of April 1, the 243rd Company would have just 20 men left, seven of them wounded.

46 *Rapport de Lieutenant Filaudeau*, 4–5.

47 Phạm Vĩnh Phúc, Nguyễn Tuấn Doanh, Cao Xuân Lịch, *Một Số Trận Đánh Trong Kháng Chiến Chống Pháp, Kháng Chiến Chống Mỹ, 1945–1975, Tạp III [Selected Battles During the Resistance Wars Against the French and the Americans, 1945–1975, Volume III]* (Hanoi: People's Army Publishing House, 1992), 123–124.

48 Giáp, *Rendezvous*, 268–269.

49 Nguyen, *[People's Artillery of Vietnam]*, 339–340; Pham, *[Selected Battles, Vol III]*, 128–129; Various, *Vài Hồi Ức Về Điện Biên Phủ, Tập I [A Few Memories About Dien Bien Phu, Volume I]* (Hanoi: People's Army Publishing House, 1977), 139–140.

50 Phúc, *[Selected Battles, Vol III]*, 119, 129-13; Nguyễn Tiến Hùng, *Lịch Sử Sư Đoàn 316 (1951–2001) [History of Division 316 (1951–2001)]* (Hanoi: People's Army Publishing House, 2001), 106.

51 Jules Roy, *La Bataille de Dien Bien Phu* (Paris: Rene Julliard, 1963), 425.

52 Daillier, *Le 4eme RTM*, 305–349; GONO BQR, *Message à FTNV 19h25, 30 Mars*.

53 I/4 RTM, *Extrait du JMO du 1er Bataillon de Marche du 4eme R.T.M.* (7U565, SHD), 4; I/4 RTM, *Liste nominative du personnel à Dien Bien Phu le 7 Mai 1954* (7U565, SHD), 5; *Lettre de Nicod à Bruge, 1 Fervier 1997* (Bruge Collection, Box 28).

54 Phúc, *[Selected Battles, Vol III]*, 130.

55 Various, *[A Few Memories About Dien Bien Phu, Volume I]*, 142.

56 Hùng, *[History of Division 316]*, 107.

57 6 BPC, *JMO Mois de Mars 1954* (7U3037, SHD), 5.

58 Phúc, *[Selected Battles, Vol III]*, 132–133; *Contribution*, 88.

59 Phúc, *[Selected Battles, Vol III]*, 133–134; 5 BPVN, *JMO Période du 14 Mars au 7 Mai 1954* (7U2971, SHD), 4; Thanh Huyền Đào; Duc Tue Dang; Xuân Mai Nguyễn, *Diên Biên Phu vu d'en face: paroles de bô dôi* (Paris: Nouveau Monde, 2010), 227.

60 5 BPVN, *JMO Période du 14 Mars au 7 Mai 1954* (7U2971, SHD), 4.

61 Brancion, *artilleurs dans la fournaise*, 212–213; Docteur Yves Loiseau, *"La 1e Compagnie Etrangère parachutiste de mortiers lourds,"* Képi blanc, la vie de la Légion étrangère, N°655 (May 2004).

62 *Contribution*, 88–89.

63   Daillier, *Le 4eme RTM*, 309.
64   Nguyen, *[People's Artillery of Vietnam]*, 342; vnmilitaryhistory.net, *Trận Đồi A1 (từ đêm 30 tháng 3 đến sáng ngày 3 tháng 4 năm 1954) [Battle for Hill A1 (from the night of 30 March to the morning of 3 April 1954)]*, http://www.vnmilitaryhistory.net/index.php?topic=1936.170 (accessed May 15, 2017).
65   *Trận Đồi A1*; *Contribution*, 90.
66   Fantinel, *Une section de Morocains à DBP*, 15.
67   Giáp, *Rendezvous*, 273.
68   *Trận Đồi A1*; Văn Hùng Nguyễn, Duy Cường Hà, Điền Sinh Trần, Trường Hải Nguyễn, *Lịch sử Trung đoàn bộ binh 174 anh hùng (1949–2012) [History of 'Hero' Infantry Regiment 174 (1949–2012)]* (Hanoi: People's Army Publishing House, 2013), 96–97.
69   Thanh, *vu d'en face*, 175–176.
70   *Lettre de Premillieu à Bruge, 14 Janvier 1997* (Bruge Collection, Box 29).
71   *Trận Đồi A1*.
72   *Contribution*, 91–92.
73   *Trận Đồi A1*.
74   *Contribution*, 92.
75   *Lettre de Premillieu à Bruge*.
76   Fall, *Hell*, 199.
77   *Contribution*, 92–93; Thanh, *vu d'en face*, 177–178; Hùng, *[History of Division 316]*, 113.
78   I/13 DBLE, *Additif an JMO de la 13°D.B.L.E., 4; Lettre de Rancoule à Bruge*, 6 novembre 1995 (Bruge Collection, Box 26).
79   Mengelle, *des chars et des hommes*, 156.
80   6 BPC, *JMO Mois de Mars 1954*, 5. Guy Leonetti, *Lettres de Diên Biên Phu* (Paris: Fayard, 2004), 254.
81   Giáp, *Rendezvous*, 274; Kim Lê and Huy Tỏan Lê, *Lịch sử Trung đoàn 36 (Sư đoàn 308, quân đoàn 1) [History of Regiment 36 (Division 308, Corps I)]* (Hanoi, Cực chính trị Quân Đòan I, 1990), 101.
82   Phan Chi Nhan, Le Kim, Le Huy Toan, and Nguyen Dinh Khuong, *Sư đoàn 308 Quân tiên phong [Division 308 Military Vanguard]* (Hanoi: People's Army Publishing House, 1999), 126.
83   *Lettre de Bizard à Bruge, 23 Octobre 1995* (Bruge Collection, Box 26); Heinrich Bauer, *Les chemins de Diên Biên Phu* (Paris: Nimrod, 2015), 350; I/2 REI, *JMO pour la période du 1er Mars 1954 au 7 Mai 1954* (7U625, SHD), 6.
84   GONO BQR, *Message à FTVN 0.00h, 31 Mars*; *Lettre de Bizard à Bruge*; I/2 REI, *JMO pour la période du 1er Mars 1954 au 7 Mai 1954, 6*; Mengelle, *des chars et des hommes*, 158–159.
85   Raymond Muelle, *Combats en Pays Tai* (Paris: Presses de la Cité, 1999), 151–155; Fall, *Hell*, 284.
86   Windrow, *Last Valley*, 472.
87   GONO BQR, *N°9/01: Message à FTNV 8h45, 31 Mars*.
88   FTNV, *Message à GONO 09h25, 31 Mars* (1R235, SHD).

89   Phạm Văn Chiến, Phạm Văn Chanh, *Lịch sử Sư đoàn 304, Tập I (1950–1975)*
      [History of Division 304, Volume I (1950–1975)] (Hanoi: People's Army Publishing
      House, 2011), 150–153; Catroux Commission, *Document Nº 13c: Rapport du
      Colonel Lalande sur les combats du Centre de Résistance "Isabelle," JMO du C.R.
      Isabelle* (1R227, Dossier II-40, SHD), 4; Mengelle, *des chars et des hommes*,
      156–158; GONO BQR, *Message à FTNV 11h50, 31 Mars.*

90   *Trận Đồi A1*; Daillier, *Le 4eme RTM*, 310–313.

91   5 BPVN, *JMO Période du 14 Mars au 7 Mai 1954*, 4.

92   Phúc, *[Selected Battles, Vol III]*, 135–136.

93   *Interview of Pierre Flamen by Luc Olivier, 2 Aug 2016.*

94   Général Lucien Leboudec, *Elevé à la dignité, mémoires 1923–1954*, 2e edition (Paris:
      Lavauzelle, 2015), 423–424.

95   GONO BQR, *Message à FTNV 11h50, 31 Mars.*

96   FTNV, *Message à GONO 12h50, 31 Mars* (1R235, SHD).

97   GONO BQR *Chef d'E.M. 13h05, 31 Mars.*

98   GONO BQR *Message à FTNV 1645h, 31 Mars* and *Message à FTNV 1727h, 31 Mars.*

99   Phúc, *[Selected Battles, Vol III]*, 137.

100   *ibid.*, 138; *Lettre de Thomas à Bruge, 8 Octobre 1996* (Bruge Collection, Box 25);
      Giáp, *Rendezvous*, 280; GONO BQR *Message à FTNV 14h30, 31 Mars* and *Message
      à FTNV 18h15, 31 Mars.*

101   *Lettre de Desmons à Franceschi, 22 Janvier 1987* (Bruge Collection, Box 27).

102   Jacques Antoine, *Il y a cinquante ans: Le 8e Choc à Diên-Biên-Phu, 21 novembre
      1953 – 7 mai 1954* (Amicale du 8e RPIMA, 2004), 146.

103   Mengelle, *des chars et des hommes*, 160 map.

104   *[History of Division 312]*, 71.

105   Giáp, *Rendezvous*, 279; Antoine, *Il y a cinquante ans*, 147.

106   *Réponse détaillée du Colonel Franceschi au Colonel Le Mire, sur son livre Épervier,
      le 8eme Choc à DBP, 24 Mars 1997* (Bruge Collection, Box 27).

107   Quốc Dũng Nguyễn, *Lịch sử Trung đoàn bộ binh 209, Sư đoàn 312, 1947-2007: lưu
      hành nội bộ [History of Infantry Regiment 209 Division 312 (1947–2007) Internal
      Distribution Only]* (Hanoi: People's Army Publishing House, 2007), 123.

108   *Réponse détaillée du Colonel Franceschi; Email from Aimé Trocmé to Luc Olivier,
      16 Aug 2016.*

109   Fall, *Hell*, 204.

110   Mengelle, *des chars et des hommes*, 164–165.

111   GONO BQR *Nº22/40: Situation à 18 Heures 00, 31 Mars.*

112   *Réponse détaillée du Colonel Franceschi.*

113   8 BPC, *JMO du 14 Novembre 1953 au 1er Juin 1954* (7U3059, SHD).

114   Marcel Bigeard, *Dien Bien Phu* (CDHLE), 11; *Interview of Guy de la Malène.*

115   *Rapport de Lieutenant Filaudeau*, 4; Brancion, *artilleurs dans la fournaise*, 174.

116   Giáp, *Rendezvous*, 276; *Contribution*, 93–94.

117   Lê Huy Toàn, *Trung đoàn Thủ Đô [Capital Regiment]* (Hanoi: People's Army
      Publishing House, 1992), 131–132. These were the 263rd, 265th, 267th, and 269th
      Companies.

118 *Trận Đồi A1.*

119 Thanh, *vu d'en face*, 178.

120 *Contribution*, 94.

121 Marcelle Bigeard, *Pour une parcelle de gloire* (Paris: Librairie Plon, 1975), 169.

122 GONO BQR *N° 28/40: Situation à 1 Heure 45, 1 Avril.*

123 *[History of Division 312]*, 72.

124 *Réponse détaillée du Colonel Franceschi*, 121–127; *Lettre de Krumenacker à Bruge, January 1997* (Bruge Collection, Box 27); *Lettre de Lecué à Bruge, 4 Juillet 1997* (Bruge Collection, Box 27); Mengelle, *des chars et des hommes*, 170–173.

125 Giáp, *Rendezvous*, 277.

126 *Lettre de Bizard à Bruge.*

127 *ibid.*

128 *Lettre de Huguenin à Bruge, 17 Novembre 1995* (Bruge Collection, Box 26).

129 GONO BQR *N°24/40 2113h, 31 Mars.*

130 GONO BQR *Message à FTNV 0114h, 1 Avril.*

131 Jean Pouget, *Nous étions à Dien-Bien-Phu* (Paris: Presses de la Cité, 1964), 270.

132 FTNV, General Commandant, *Message à GONO BQR Pour Colonel de Castries Personnellement, 1630h, 1 April* (1R235, SHD).

133 Lê, *[Capital Regiment]*, 133–134; *Trận Đồi A1.*

134 *Lettre de Nicolas à Bruge 6 Janvier 1997* (Bruge Collection, 26); *Lettre de Rancoule à Bruge*; GONO BQR *Message à FTNV 1250, 1 Avril* and *N° 34/40: Situation à 1400h, 1 Avril*; Bauer, *Les chemins de Diên Biên Phu*, 385; I/13 DBLE, *Additif au JMO de la 13°D.B.L.E.*, 5; François Bernot, *Souvenirs et Réflexions*, handbound 1989 (1KT1109, SHD), 15.

135 *Trận Đồi A1.*

136 Giáp, *Rendezvous*, 283; *Contribution*, 95–96; 6 BPC, *JMO Mois de Avril 1954* (7U3037, SHD), 2; Mengelle, *des chars et des hommes*, 187; *Trận Đồi A1.*

137 Kim, *[History of Regiment 36]*, 101–102; Nguyen, *[People's Artillery of Vietnam]*, 343.

138 Giáp, *Rendezvous*, 284–285; Kim, *[History of Regiment 36]*, 102–103; *Lettre de Huguenin à Bruge.*

139 GONO BQR *N°44/40: Situation 4 Heures, 2 Avril*; *Lettre de Bizard à Bruge*; Mengelle, *des chars et des hommes*, 187–188.

140 Giáp, *Rendezvous*, 284; GONO BQR *Message à FTNV 14h10, 2 Avril.*

141 Reginald Wieme de Ruddere, *Journal des Marches et Opérations du Groupement Wieme (Groupement mobile Tai n° 5) à Dien Bien Phu Pendant la Campagne du 1er Décembre 1953 au 31 Mai 1954* (publisher unidentified, 1999).

142 *ibid.*, 113.

143 *JMO du C.R. Isabelle*, 4; GONO BQR *N°47/40, Situation le 2 Avril a 10 Heures 00*; *N°28/40: Situation à 1 Heure 45, 1 Avril* and *Message à FTNV 14h10, 2 Avril* (all 10H1166, SHD).

144 GONO BQR *Message à FTNV, 2 Avril.*

145 Fall, *Hell*, 201–211.

146 Thanh, *vu d'en face*, 178.

147 *Contribution*, 96; Lê, *[Capital Regiment]*, 135.

148 Thanh, *vu d'en face*, 180–181; Lê, *[Capital Regiment]*, 137; Phan, *[Division 308 Military Vanguard]*, 132.

149 Fall, *Hell*, 214.

150 *Trận Đồi A1*; Lê, *[Capital Regiment]*, 135.

151 GONO BQR *N°57/40: Situation à 2230h, 2 Avril* and *N°56/40: Situation à 20h15, 2 Avril.*

152 *Trận Đồi A1.*

153 GONO BQR *N°57/40: Situation à 2230h, 2 Avril.*

154 More Majorum, *1° Bataillon du 2° REI*, http://more-majorum.de/einheiten/2rei/bat1/index.html (Accessed Nov 16, 2016).

155 GONO BQR *N°61/40: Situation à 0215, 3 Avril*; Fall, *Hell*, 216; Rocolle, *Pourquoi*, 434.

156 Võ Nguyên Giáp, *Điện Biên Phủ, 8th Edition* (Hanoi: Thế Giới Publishers, 2007), 108; GONO BQR *N°64/40: Situation à 1000 Heures, 3 Avril*; Mengelle, *des chars et des hommes*, 175. Most Western historians date the evacuation of Françoise to April 1 or 2, but French documents and Vietnamese authors make it clear that it actually occurred on April 3.

157 Mengelle, *des chars et des hommes*, 195. A hole in the turret was closed by welding a mortar baseplate over it!

158 Fall, *Hell*, 215; GONO BQR *Message à FTNV 1635h, 3 Avril.*

159 Lê, *[Capital Regiment]*, 138.

160 *Trận Đồi A1.*

161 1 BEP, *JMO Mois d'Avril 1954* (7U659, SHD), 4; Mengelle, *des chars et des hommes*, 196.

162 GONO BQR *Message à FTNV 06h45, 4 Avril.*

163 Nguyen, *[People's Artillery of Vietnam]*, 344.

164 Francis Pencreac'h, *"La première compagnie du I/2REI à DBP, "* handwritten 11 Février 1990 (Bruge Collection, Box 28).

165 GONO BQR *Message à B3 19h20, 3 Avril.*

166 Mengelle, *des chars et des hommes*, 197–198.

167 Windrow, *Last Valley*, 488.

168 *Lettre de Cousin à Bruge, 21 juin 1997* (Bruge Collection, Box 26); I/2 REI, *JMO pour la période du 1er Mars 1954 au 7 Mai 1954* (7U625, SHD), 8.

169 *Contribution*, 98–99; Giáp, *Rendezvous*, 300–301; GONO BQR *No 08/40: Situation à 1200 Heures, 4 Avril.*

170 Fall, *Hill*, 217.

171 II/4 RAC, *Rapport sur les opérations de Dien Bien Phu du 13 Mars au 7 Mai 1954* (Bruge Collection, Box 26), 2, 11.

172 GONO BQR *Message à FTNV B3 21h15, 5 Avril.*

173 I/2 REI, *JMO pour la période du 1er Mars 1954 au 7 Mai 1954)*, 8–9; GONO BQR *Message à FTNV 2115, 5 Avril.* vnmilitaryhistory.net, *Đường binh nghiệp của tôi - Thiếu tướng Nguyễn Chuông [My military career – Major General Nguyen Choung]*, http://www.vnmilitaryhistory.net/index.php?topic=10102.20 (Accessed 25 Sept 2018)"

174 Bernot, *Souvenirs et Réflexions*, 16; Mengelle, *des chars et des hommes*, 204–207.

175 Marcel Philippe, *Peloton d'élèves grades* (Cartons de 40 ans DBP, CDHLE), 7.

176 Mengelle, *des chars et des hommes*, 207–209.

177 *ibid.*, 209; *Synthèse des renseignements recueillis auprès des blessés libérés par le VM après la chute de DBP, Hanoi le 16 juin 1954* (10H179, SHD), 5.

178 Marcel Bigeard, *Opération Reprise de Huguette VI, Sep 1954* (CDHLE), 1–2.

179 Mengelle, *des chars et des hommes*, 210; I/2 REI, *JMO pour la période du 1er Mars 1954 au 7 Mai 1954*, 8–9.

180 Võ Nguyên Giáp, *Điện Biên Phủ* (Hanoi: Thế Giới Publishers, 2007), 108.

181 Giáp, *[Collected Essays]*, 351.

182 *[History of Division 312]*, 73.

183 I/2 REI, *JMO pour la période du 1er Mars 1954 au 7 Mai 1954*, 8–9; GONO BQR *Message à FTNV 2115, 5 Avril.*

184 GONO BQR *Nº27/40: Message à FTNV 14h45, 5 Avril* and *Nº41/40: Message à FTNV 16h24, 6 Avril.*

185 Phạm, *[History of Division 304, Vol I]*, 154; Windrow, *Last Valley*, 418.

186 Rocolle, *Pourquoi*, 300; Windrow, *Last Valley*, 436, 521.

187 FTNV, General Commandant, *Nº14/07: 1215h, 3 April* (1R235, SHD).

188 FTNV, Cabinet, *Nº1/07, 1015h, 5 April* (1R235, SHD).

189 Fall, *Hell*, 227.

190 *Tập chi trí thực phát triển [Knowledge Development Magazine], Huyền thoại Điện Biên [Legends of Dien Bien Phu]* [Special issue], (Hanoi: Vietnam News Agency, 2013), 114–244. Since many deaths are recorded by month but not by date, just 385 of the March fatalities indisputably occurred on or after the 13th. The number of burials identified only by month for April is 415. There is no way of telling how many died before April 6.

191 Thanh, *vu d'en face*, 180.

192 Giáp, *Rendezvous*, 335.

193 Fall, *Hell*, 200–201.

194 Cadeau, *Dien Bien Phu: 13 mars – 7 mai*, 194.

195 Langlais, *Dien Bien Phu*, 116.

196 Rapport sur l'appui aérien en Indochine, *De Repartition des Sorties "FEU" Selon les Périodes et Selon Les Différentes Missions, Mai 1954* (10H1170, SHD).

197 *Trận Đồi A1.*

198 *[A Few Memories About Dien Bien Phu, Volume I]*, 62.

199 Guy Vaillant, *Rapport du Colonel Vaillant sur l'artillerie dans la bataille de Dien Bien Phu*, 12 Octobre, 1954 (1K233, SHD), Part III, 8.

Chapter 7

1 Võ Nguyên Giáp, *Tổng Tập Luận Văn [Collected Essays]* (Hanoi: People's Army Publishing House, 2006), 349.

2 For example, Võ Nguyên Giáp, Hữu Mai and Lady Borton, *Điện Biên Phủ: Rendezvous with History* (Hanoi, Thế Giới Publishers, 2004), 214.

3   Giáp, *[Collected Essays]*, 353.

4   *ibid.*, 354.

5   Giáp, *Rendezvous*, 293.

6   Lưu Trọng Lân, *Lịch sử Sư đoàn 367, tập I [History of Division 367, Volume I]* (Air Defense Service, Vietnam, 1988), 172–173, 210.

7   Pierre Langlais, *Dien Bien Phu* (Paris: Editions France-Empire, 1963), 167.

8   Ministry of Defense, Central Military Party Committee, *Một số văn kiện chỉ đạo chiến cuộc Đông Xuân 1953-1954 và chiến dịch Điện Biên Phủ [Selected War Guidance Documents from the Winter–Spring Campaign of 1953–1954 and the Battle of Điện Biên Phủ]* (Hanoi: People's Army Publishing House, 2004), 509–514.

9   So-called because Châu ("Prefect") Đèo Văn Ún's mansion had been located on the hill.

10   Giáp, *[Collected Essays]*, 357.

11   Ministry of Defense, *[Selected War Guidance Documents]*, 513.

12   Bernard B. Fall, *Hell in a Very Small Place: The Siege of Dien Bien Phu* (New York & Philadelphia: Lippincott, 1967), 223.

13   Thanh Huyền Đào; Duc Tue Dang; Xuân Mai Nguyễn, *Diên Biên Phu vu d'en face: paroles de bô dôi* (Paris: Nouveau Monde, 2010), 169, 179.

14   FTNV, *Messages à GONO, 17h, 6 Avril* and *20h40, 9 Avril* (both 1R235, SHD).

15   Phan Chi Nhan, Le Kim, Le Huy Toan, and Nguyen Dinh Khuong, *Sư đoàn 308 Quân tiên phong [The 308th "Vanguard" Division]* (Hanoi: People's Army Publishing House, 1999), 133; Kim Lê and Huy Tòan Lê, *Lịch sử Trung đoàn 36 (Sư đoàn 308, quân đoàn 1) [History of Regiment 36 (Division 308, Corps I)]* (Hanoi, Cực chính trị Quân Đòan I, 1990), 104

16   Langlais, *Dien Bien Phu*, 113.

17   Lieutenant Guy Filaudeau, *Rapport du Lieutenant Filaudeau 1 Janvier 1955 à Argenton-Château* (Bruge Collection, 35); *Interview of Jacques Daussy by Luc Olivier, 14 Jan 2015.*

18   Capitaine Jean Charnot, *JMO du détachement air* (Archives Armée de l'Air 4C849, SHD).

19   GONO BQR, *N°74/40: Message à FTNV 10h00, 9 Avril.*

20   Général Pierre Daillier, *Le 4eme RTM: les bataillons de marche en Indochine 1947–1954* (Paris, Château de Vincennes: SHD, 1990), 317–318.

21   13 DBLE, *Additif au JMO de la 13°D.B.L.E. (Mois de Mars, Avril et Mai 1954)* (CDHLE), 5.

22   I/13 DBLE, *JMO du Mois de Mars 1954*, 25 and *JMO du Mois d'Avril 1954*, 2 (both CDHLE).

23   *Phone Interview of Jack Horniak by Luc Olivier,* 27 Sept 2016.

24   6 BPC, *JMO Mois de Avril 1954* (7U3037, SHD).

25   Jacques Antoine, *Il y a cinquante ans: Le 8e Choc à Diên-Biên-Phu, 21 novembre 1953 – 7 mai 1954* (Amicale du 8e RPIMA, 2004), 155.

26   AALP, *Đien Bien Phu: il y a 40 ans,* (AALP, 1994), 168.

27   GONO BQR, *N°54/40: Message à FTNV 10h10, 7 April*; I/2 REI, *JMO pour la période du 1er Mars 1954 au 7 Mai 1954* (7U625, SHD), 10.

28   Marcel Philippe, *La 13e DBLE à Dien Bien Phu* (1KT935_1, SHD); Andre Botella, *Quelques Souvenirs d'Indochine* (archives personnelles de Guy Leonetti), 10.

29   *Lettres de Salaun à Bruge, 3 Août 1995* and *8 Octobre 1996* (Bruge Collection, Box 29).

30   Marcel Philippe, *Peloton d'élèves grades* (Cartons de 40 ans DBP, CDHLE), 9.

31   Langlais, *Dien Bien Phu*, 245.

32   *ibid.*, 115.

33   2 BEP, *JMO Période du 26 Mars au 25 Avril 1954* (7U664, SHD), 2; FTNV, *Message à GONO, 12 Avril* (1R235, SHD).

34   Martin Windrow, *The Last Valley: Dien Bien Phu and the French Defeat in Vietnam* (Cambridge, MA: Da Capo Press, 2004), 497.

35   Marcel Bigeard, *Reprise de Eliane-1, Sep 1954* (Cartons de 40 ans DBP, CDHLE), 1–2.

36   *ibid.*, 1–2; Martin Windrow, *The Last Valley*, 503.

37   *Interview of Jacques Daussy by Luc Olivier.*

38   GONO BQR, *N°86/40: Situation à 8h15, 10 Avril*; Bigeard, *Reprise de Eliane-1*, 2–3; Nguyễn Tiến Hùng, *Lịch Sử Sư Đoàn 316 (1951–2001) [History of Division 316 (1951–2001)]* (Hanoi: People's Army Publishing House, 2001), 115; Nguyen Khac Tinh, Phung Luan, and Truong Nguyen Tue, *Pháo binh Nhân dân Việt Nam: Những chặng đường chiến đấu, tập một [People's Artillery of Vietnam: Combat History, Volume I]* (Hanoi: People's Army Publishing House, 1982), 343.

39   Nguyễn, *[History of Division 316]*, 115.

40   EMIFT, *Fiche de Renseignements N°196, 10.4.1954 à 18h00* (10H179, SHD).

41   GONO BQR, *N°98/40: Situation à 1400 Heures, 10 Avril.*

42   6 BPC, *JMO Mois d'Avril* (7U3037, SHD), 3; GONO, *N°94/40: Situation à 2100h, 10 Avril.*

43   FTNV, *N°118/3 Message à GONO*, 10 Avril (10H1166, SHD).

44   GONO BQR, *N°20/01: Réservé General Cogny 1330h, 10 Avril.*

45   FTNV, *Texte N°07/01: Réservé Colonel de Castries, 10 Avril* (1R235, SHD).

46   GONO BQR, *N°22: Message à FTNV, 11 Avril.*

47   *ibid.*; GONO BQR, *N°97/40: Situation à 4 Heures, 11 Avril* and *N°96/40: Situation à 2 Heures, 11 Avril.*

48   GONO BQR, *N°91/40: Situation à 16 Heures, 10 Avril.*

49   Windrow, *Last Valley*, 507.

50   GONO BQR, *N°106/40: Message à FTNV 20h, 11 Avril.*

51   Various, *Vài Hồi Ức Về Điện Biên Phủ, Tập I [A Few Memories About Dien Bien Phu, Volume I]* (Hanoi: People's Army Publishing House, 1977), 160.

52   5 BPVN, *JMO Période du 14 Mars au 7 Mai 1954* (7U2971, SHD), 5.

53   GONO BQR, *N°106/40.*

54   AALP, *il y a 40 ans*, 141–142.

55   La Bataille de Điện Biên Phủ (le devoir de mémoire), *Souvenirs du Capitaine Armandi*, http://dienbienphu.soforums.com/t1420-Souvenirs-du-Capitaine-Armandi. htm#p13328 (accessed Nov 28, 2016).

56   *Contribution to the History of Dien Phu – Vietnamese Studies #3* (Hanoi: Foreign Languages Publishing House, 1965), 199.

57 *[A Few Memories]*, 161.

58 6 BPC, *JMO Mois d'Avril*, 3.

59 1 BEP, *JMO Mois de Avril* (7U659, SHD), 6.

60 II/1 RCP, *JMO Mois d'Avril*, 5–6.

61 AALP, *il y a 40 ans*, 149–151.

62 Giáp, *Rendezvous*, 53.

63 *ibid.*, 299–300.

64 Fall, *Hell*, 244.

65 Nguyen, *[People's Artillery of Vietnam, Volume I]*, 350–351.

66 Thanh, *vu d'en face*, 13.

67 Phan, *[The 308th "Vanguard" Division]*, 136; Lê Huy Toàn, Nguyễn Văn Nam, Hoàng Phú Cường, *Lịch sử Trung đoàn 88 Tu Vũ (1949–2009) [History of Regiment 88 "Tu Vu" (1949–2009)]* (Hanoi, Nhà xuất bản Quân đội nhân dân, 2009), 115–116.

68 *Lịch sử sư đoàn bộ binh 312 [History of Infantry Division 312]* (Hanoi: People's Army Publishing House, 1995), 73.

69 I/2 REI, *JMO pour la période du 1er Mars 1954 au 7 Mai 1954*, 10–12.

70 13 DBLE, *Additif au JMO de la 13ºD.B.L.E.*, 6; Philippe, *Peloton d'élèves grades*, 9–10; André Mengelle, *Diên-Biên-Phu: des chars et des hommes* (Paris: Éditions Lavauzelle, 2006), 227–230.

71 GONO BQR, *Nº112/40: Situation à 8h00, 12 Avril.*

72 GONO BQR, *Nº12/40: Situation à 8h30, 13 Avril*; Mengelle, *des chars et des hommes*, 230–231.

73 GONO BQR, *Nº41/05: Situation le 13 à 18h, 13 Avril.*

74 GONO BQR, *Nº14/40: Situation à 14h00, 13 Avril.*

75 GONO BQR, *Nº18/40: Situation à 2000h, 13 Avril.*

76 AALP, *Il y a 40 ans*, 163; Pierre Sergent, *Le 2e BEP en Indochine* (Paris: France Loisirs, 1983), 196; GONO BQR, *Nº31/40: Situation à 24h00, 15 Avril*; *Contribution*, 199.

77 *Contribution*, 120–130.

78 GONO BQR, *Nº26/40: Situation à 1200 heures, 14 Avril.*

79 Nguyen, *[People's Artillery of Vietnam, Volume I]*, 353–354.

80 Thanh Tam Pham & Sherry Buchanan, *Carnet de guerre d'un jeune Viêt-minh à Diên Biên Phu: 21 février-28 août 1954* (Paris: Armand Colin, 2011), 133–138.

81 Mengelle, *des chars et des hommes*, 233.

82 *Contribution*, 130–142; AALP, *Il y a 40 ans*, 163–164.

83 Mengelle, *des chars et des hommes*, 232; AALP, *Il y a 40 ans*, 165; *Contribution*, 143–144.

84 GONO BQR, *Nº29/40: Message à FTNV, 14 Avril; Nº28/40: Message à FTNV, 14 Avril*; and *Nº26/40: Situation à 1200 heures, 14 Avril.*

85 EDAP, *Résume de l'activité des unites de l'EDAP (Période du 1er Avril au 15 Avril 1954)* (10H1159, SHD), 8; EMIFT, *Fiche de Renseignements par Courants Porteurs Reçus de Hanoi le 15 Avril 1954 à 9 Heures 50* (10H179, SHD).

86 *Contribution*, 146.

87 I/2 REI, *JMO pour la période du 1er Mars 1954 au 7 Mai 1954*, 12.

88 GONO BQR, *Nº42/40: Message à FTNV, 15 Avril.*

89 Mengelle, *des chars et des hommes*, 235–239.

90 *Contribution*, 147–152; GONO, *Nº42/40: Situation à 16h00, 15 Avril* and *Situation à 1200h, 15 Avril* (both 10H1166, SHD). Some veterans claim this outpost was established on April 10, but the preponderance of evidence points to April 14.

91 8 BPC, *JMO du 14 Novembre 1953 au 1er Juin 1954* (7U3059, SHD).

92 GONO BQR, *Fiche de Situation 15 Avril.*

93 I/13 DBLE, *JMO du Mois d'Avril 1954,* 27; I/2 REI, *JMO pour la période du 1er Mars 1954 au 7 Mai 1954*, 12.

94 GONO BQR, *Activité G.O.N.O.: Période du 15 Avril à 20h00 au 16 Avril à 04h00.*

95 *[History of Infantry Division 312]*, 279.

96 GONO BQR, *Fiche de Situation 16 Avril.*

97 René de Salins, *Une carrière Brisée* (1KT1440, SHD), 20.

98 Kim, *[History of Regiment 36]*, 104–105.

99 *[History of Infantry Division 312]*, 273.

100 Ministry of Defense, *[Selected War Guidance Documents]*, 517–518.

101 Võ Nguyên Giáp, *Directive No. 134, 17 April 1954* (duplicated on Facebook, accessed Sept 11, 2017).

102 I/2 REI, *JMO pour la période du 1er Mars 1954 au 7 Mai 1954*, 12.

103 Henri Le Mire, *Épervier, Le 8e Choc à Dien Bien Phu* (Paris: Editions Albin Michel S.A., 1988), 253–254; EMIFT, *Fiche de Renseignements par Courants Porteurs Reçus de Hanoi le 17 Avril 1954 à 10h15* (10H179, SHD).

104 GONO BQR, *Activité G.O.N.O.: 16 Avril*; EDAP, *Résume de l'activité des unités de l'EDAP (Période du 16 Avril au 27 Avril 1954)* (10H1159, SHD), 1.

105 Mengelle, *des chars et des hommes*, 244–245; Le Mire, *Épervier*, 257–258; Antoine, *Il y a cinquante ans*, 178; Phan, *[The 308th "Vanguard" Division]*, 136.

106 Mengelle, *des chars et des hommes*, 246–247; 1 BEP, *JMO Mois de Avril*, 8.

107 *[History of Infantry Division 312]*, 279. The 88th Regiment's redeployment opposite Huguette-6 was probably never completed. The 312th Division's official history states that the 165th Regiment took it on April 18.

108 Fall, *Hell*, 259.

109 *ibid.*, 259–260.

110 Georges Fleury, *le Para* (Paris: Grasset, 1982), 333–336.

111 Mengelle, *des chars et des hommes*, 247.

112 Windrow, *Last Valley*, 518; EMIFT, *Fiche de Renseignements par Courants Porteurs* Reçus *de Hanoi le 19.4.1954 à 23h30* (10H179, SHD); I/2 REI, *JMO pour la période du 1er Mars 1954 au 7 Mai 1954*, 13.

113 Tran Hanh, ed., *Một số trận đánh trong kháng chiến chống Pháp, kháng chiến chống Mỹ, 1945–1975, Tập II [Selected Battles During the Resistance Wars Against the French and the Americans, 1945–1975, Volume II]* (Hanoi: People's Army Publishing House, 1991), 87–88.

114 Thanh, *vu d'en face*, 189–190; Lê, *[History of Regiment 36 (Division 308, Corps I)]*, 105–106.

115 Mengelle, *des chars et des hommes*, 252–253; 13 DBLE, *Additif an JMO de la 13oD.B.L.E.*, 7.

116 Le Mire, *Épervier*, 261.

117 Fall, *Hell*, 262.

118 Mengelle, *des chars et des hommes*, 256; Général Pierre Daillier, *Le 4eme RTM: les bataillons de marche en Indochine 1947–1954* (Paris, Château de Vincennes: Service Historique de l'Armée de Terre, 1990), 318.

119 I/2 REI, *JMO pour la période du 1er Mars 1954 au 7 Mai 1954*, 14; 13 DBLE, *Additif an JMO de la 13°D.B.L.E.*, 7–8; Daillier, *Le 4eme RTM*, 318; Fall, *Hell*, 267–269; *Rapport de Lieutenant Filaudeau*.

120 Tran, *[Selected Battles, Volume II]*, 95.

121 Lê Trọng Tấn, *Từ Đồng Quan Đến Điện Biên [From Dong Quan to Dien Bien]* (Hanoi: People's Army Publishing House, 2002), 323–324.

122 Tran, *[Selected Battles, Volume II]*, 91–92; Lê, *[From Dong Quan to Dien Bien]*, 324.

123 Kim, *[History of Regiment 36]*, 105.

124 Fall, *Hell*, 270.

125 Tran, *[Selected Battles, Volume II]*, 97–99.

126 *ibid.*, 99–100; Kim, *[History of Regiment 36]*, 106.

127 Fall, *Hell*, 269–270; *Sergeant Flamen interview with Luc Olivier, 16 February 2016*.

128 Tran, *[Selected Battles, Volume II]*, 100.

129 Langlais, *Dien Bien Phu*, 246.

130 Marcel Bigeard, *Opération Huguette 1, Sep 1954* (Cartons de 40 ans DBP, CDHLE).

131 GONO BQR, *Message de FTVN, N°3106/FTVN/3.AA, 23 Avril.*

132 Bigeard, *Opération Huguette 1*; Mengelle, *des chars et des hommes*, 259.

133 Windrow, *Last Valley*, 528–529.

134 Lê Huy Toàn, Nguyễn Văn Nam, Hoàng Phú Cường, *Lịch sử Trung đoàn 88 Tu Vũ (1949–2009) [History of Regiment 88 Tu Vu (1949–2009)]* (Hanoi, Nhà xuất bản Quân đội nhân dân, 2009), 118.

135 Nguyen, *[People's Artillery of Vietnam, Volume I]*, 354–355.

136 Mengelle, *des chars et des hommes*, 260.

137 *Relation des événements vécus par le 2ème B.E.P. à Dien-Bien-Phu le 23 avril 1954 faite par le Chef de Bataillon LIESENFELT, Chef de Corps*, no date (2 BEP, JMO documents associés, CDHLE); Bigeard, *Opération Huguette 1*.

138 Windrow, *Last Valley*, 530–531.

139 Nguyen, *[People's Artillery of Vietnam, Volume I]*, 358; Mengelle, *des chars et des hommes*, 261–262

140 *Relation des événements vécus par le 2ème B.E.P. à Dien-Bien-Phu le 23 avril 1954 faite par le Chef de Bataillon LIESENFELT, Chef de Corps*; Bigeard, *Opération Huguette 1*.

141 Windrow, *Last Valley*, 532–533; Mengelle, *des chars et des hommes*, 265–266.

142 2 BEP, *JMO Période du 26 Mars au 25 Avril 1954*, 4–5.

143 Mengelle, *des chars et des hommes*, 267–268; Fall, *Hell*, 330.

144 Thanh, *vu d'en face*, 184–186.

145 Fall, *Hell*, 267.

146 GONO BQR, *Fiche de Situation 23 Avril.*

147 Langlais, *Dien Bien Phu*, 176.

148 Lưu, *[History of Division 367, Volume I]*, 175, 210.

149 Jules Roy, *La Bataille de Dien Bien Phu* (Paris: Rene Julliard, 1963), 568.

150 *Rapport du Colonel Vaillant*, Part III, 123.

151 Rapport sur l'appui aérien en Indochine, *De Répartition des Sorties "FEU" Selon les Périodes et Selon Les Différentes Missions, Mai 1954* (10H1170, SHD).

152 Windrow, *Last Valley*, 553–562.

153 Fall, *Hell*, 356–357; Windrow, *Last Valley*, 577.

154 Windrow, *Last Valley*, 541–542, 550; John Prados, *Operation Vulture* (New York: ibooks, inc., 2002), 238–239.

155 GONO BQR, *Fiche de Situation 19 Avril*.

156 Windrow, *Last Valley*, 522–523, 542–545.

157 *ibid.*, 706.

158 Fall, *Hell*, 340.

159 *Revitaillement de Dien Bien Phu: Période du 14 Mars au 7 Mai 1954* (10H1176, SHD). This data was used because it all comes from a single source, produced retrospectively after the siege ended. It must be noted that documents generated during the siege often give significantly different figures for tonnages dropped and misdropped on specific dates.

160 1 BEP, *JMO Mois de Avril*, 7.

161 13 DBLE, *Additif an JMO de la 13°D.B.L.E.*, 7.

162 GONO BQR, *Fiche de Situation 23 Avril* and *N°107/40: Situation à 00.00 heures, 26 Avril*; Windrow, *Last Valley*, 548.

163 Fall, *Hell*, 481.

164 GONO BQR, *N°32/01, 29 Avril*.

165 *Map "Situation au C.R. de Dien Bien Phu du 25/Avril/1954"* (Cartes de Dien Bien Phu, SHD).

166 Prados, *Operation Vulture*, 92.

167 James M. Gavin, "The Easy Chair – A Communication on Vietnam from Gen. James M. Gavin," *Harpers* (Feb 1966).

168 Prados, *Operation Vulture*, 202.

169 Mark Moyar, *Triumph Forsaken: the Vietnam War, 1954–1965* (Cambridge & New York: Cambridge University Press, 2009), 26.

170 Thanh, *vu d'en face*, XIII; Noam Chomsky and Howard Zinn, eds., *The Pentagon Papers (The Senator Gravel Edition), Volume I* (Boston: Beacon Press, 1971), Map 193.

171 Fall, *Hell*, 315, 318.

172 *ibid.*, 315-317.

173 *ibid.*, 319–322; Windrow, *Last Valley*, 574.

174 Fall, *Hell*, 285; Windrow, *Last Valley*, 546.

175 Catroux Commission, *Document N°13c: Rapport du Colonel Lalande sur les combats du Centre de Resistance "Isabelle", JMO du C.R. Isabelle* (1R227, Dossier II-40, SHD), 4.

176 Phạm Văn Chiến, Phạm Văn Chanh, *Lịch sử Sư đoàn 304, Tập I (1950–1975) [History of Division 304, Volume I (1950–1975)]* (Hanoi: People's Army Publishing House, 2011), 155.

177 Commandant Jeancenell 3 2/1 RTA, *Quelques Dates Permettant la Mise a Jour du Journal de Marche du 2/1 RTA et GM.6 (en ce qui concerne ISABELLE), 10 Septembre 1954* (Bruge Collection, Box 35), 2.

178 *JMO du C.R. Isabelle*, 4–6; Reginald Wieme de Ruddere, *JMO du Groupement Wieme (Groupement mobile Tai n° 5) à Dien Bien Phu Pendant la Campagne du 1er Décembre 1953 au 31 Mai 1954* (publisher unidentified, 1999), 115.

179 *JMO du C.R. Isabelle*, 5–6; Giáp, *Rendezvous*, 311.

180 *JMO du Groupement Wieme*, 116.

181 Fall, *Hell*, 285.

182 *JMO du C.R. Isabelle*, 6.

183 Catroux Commission, *Général de Castries Réponse au Paragraphe N° 11, 25 Juillet 1955* (1R229, SHD), 4.

184 Fall, *Hell*, 271; FTNV, *N° 10355: 15h30, 25 Avril* (1R235, SHD).

185 *JMO du C.R. Isabelle*, 6; Fall, *Hell*, 286–288.

186 Luu, *[History of Division 367, Volume I]*, 210; Windrow, *Last Valley*, 548.

187 *JMO du C.R. Isabelle*, 6; *JMO du Groupement Wieme*, 119–120; Windrow, *Last Valley*, 547.

188 *JMO du Groupement Wieme*, 118; Thanh, *vu d'en face*, 197–198. Although the 840th served at Điện Biên Phủ for two weeks at most, its losses were considerable. A 30-man platoon of scouts, runners, and guard personnel lost nine killed and many wounded during that relatively brief period.

189 Ministry of Defense, *[Selected War Guidance Documents]*, 539–540.

190 Luu, *[History of Division 367, Volume I]*, 235.

191 Ministry of Defense, *[Selected War Guidance Documents]*, 539–540; Đặng, et al., *Hỏi Đáp Về Các Binh Chủng Quân đội Nhân dân Việt Nam [Frequently Asked Questions About the Branches of the Vietnamese People's Army]* (Hanoi: People's Army Publishing House, 2009), 37.

192 vnmilitaryhistory.net, *Vũ Khí Việt Nam Trong Hai Cuộc Khánh Chiến [Vietnamese Weapons in the Two Resistance Wars], http://www.vnmilitaryhistory.net/index. php?topic=41.360* (accessed Jan 8, 2014).

193 Ngọc An, "Tiểu Đoàn Hóa Tiên 224" [Rocket Battalion 224], *Tạp chí Lịch sử Quân sự [Military History Magazine]*, Issue 4 (July–Aug 1997), 58–60.

194 Fall, *Hell*, 268.

195 Nguyen, *[People's Artillery of Vietnam, Volume I]*, 370.

196 Thanh, *vu d'en face*, 173–174; Giáp, *[Collected Essays]*, 351.

197 Thanh, *vu d'en face*, 207–210.

198 Giáp, *Rendezvous*, 329.

199 *Ibid.*, 335.

200 Võ Nguyên Giáp, *Điện Biên Phủ (8th Edition)* (Hà Nội: Thế Giới Publishers, 2007), 206.

201 Nguyen, *[People's Artillery of Vietnam, Volume I]*, 370.

202 Pierre Rocolle, *Pourquoi Dien Bien Phu?* (Paris: Flammarion, 1968), 484.

203 Giáp, *Rendezvous*, 335.

204 *ibid.*, 336.

205 Võ Nguyên Giáp, *Dien Bien Phu (5th Edition)* (Hanoi: The Gioi Publishers, 1994), 130.

206 Fall, *Hell*, 342.

207 Văn Hùng Nguyễn, Duy Cường Hà, Điền Sinh Trần, Trường Hải Nguyễn, *Lịch sử Trung đoàn bộ binh 174 anh hùng (1949–2012) [History of "Hero" Infantry Regiment 174 (1949–2012)]* (Hanoi: People's Army Publishing House, 2013), 171.

Chapter 8

1 Bernard B. Fall, *Hell in a Very Small Place: The Siege of Dien Bien Phu* (New York & Philadelphia: Lippincott, 1967), 247, 346–348.

2 Ministry of Defense, Central Military Party Committee, *Một số văn kiện chỉ đạo chiến cuộc Đông Xuân 1953-1954 và chiến dịch Điện Biên Phủ [Selected War Guidance Documents from the Winter–Spring Campaign of 1953–1954 and the Battle of Điện Biên Phủ]* (Hanoi: People's Army Publishing House, 2004), 536.

3 *ibid.*, 537.

4 *ibid.*

5 *ibid.*, 538.

6 GONO BQR, *N⁰17/24: Message à FTNV 1916h, 30 avril.*

7 GONO BQR, *N⁰56/40: Situation à 08h00, 30 avril* and *Fiche de Situation 1 mai.*

8 Nguyen Khac Tinh, Phung Luan, and Truong Nguyen Tue, *Pháo binh Nhân dân Việt Nam: Những chặng đường chiến đấu, tập một [People's Artillery of Vietnam: Combat History, Volume I]* (Hanoi: People's Army Publishing House, 1982), 368.

9 GONO, *Fiche de Situation 1 mai*; EMIFT, *Fiche de Renseignements par Courants Porteurs N⁰335 reçus de Hanoi le 1er Mai 1954 à 12h15* and *Fiche de Renseignements par Courants Porteurs N⁰342 reçus de Hanoi le 2 Mai 1954 à 8h30* (both in 10H179, SHD).

10 Fall, *Hell*, 350.

11 *ibid.*, 351.

12 This counts only formed companies and (rightly) ignores detached platoons held in close reserve for specific CRs. By now, companies generally had 80–100 men and platoons only 15–20.

13 André Mengelle, *Diên-Biên-Phu: des chars et des hommes* (Paris: Éditions Lavauzelle, 2006), 281–282; *L'Escadron de chars M.24 dans le bataille de Dien Bien Phu* (10H1178, SHD), 7.

14 Martin Windrow, *The Last Valley: Dien Bien Phu and the French Defeat in Vietnam* (Cambridge, MA: Da Capo Press, 2004), 584.

15 GONO BQR, *N⁰79/40: Situation à 0000, 2 mai*; EMIFT, *Fiche de Renseignements par Courants Porteurs N⁰342.*

16 Lê Huy Toàn, Nguyễn Văn Nam, Hoàng Phú Cường, *Lịch sử Trung đoàn 88 Tu Vũ (1949–2009) [History of Regiment 88 Tu Vu (1949–2009)]* (Hanoi, Nhà xuất bản Quân đội nhân dân, 2009), 119; Fall, *Hell*, 354; Windrow, *Last Valley*, 583; *Lettre du Lt Roux à Bruge [based on his diary]* (Bruge Collection, Box 29).

17 Nguyen, *[People's Artillery of Vietnam: Volume I]*, 367.

18 Thanh Huyền Đào; Duc Tue Dang; Xuân Mai Nguyễn, *Diên Biên Phu vu d'en face: paroles de bô dôi* (Paris: Nouveau Monde, 2010), 217.

19 *Lettre de Jauze à Bruge, 2 Octobre 1995* (Bruge Collection, Box 26); Pierre Sergent, *Je ne regrette rien: la poignante histoire des légionnaires-parachutistes du 1er REP* (Paris: Fayard, 1972), 189; *Lettre de Nicod à Bruge, 26 Avril 1997* (Bruge Collection, Box 28); Roger Bruge, *Les hommes de Dien Bien Phu* (Paris: Perrin, 1999), 393–398.

20 Văn Hùng Nguyễn, Duy Cường Hà, Điền Sinh Trần, Trường Hải Nguyễn, *Lịch sử Trung đoàn bộ binh 174 anh hùng (1949–2012) [History of "Hero" Infantry Regiment 174 (1949–2012)]* (Hanoi: People's Army Publishing House, 2013), 171.

21 Windrow, *Last Valley*, 536.

22 Fall, *Hell*, 352, 368–369.

23 Lê Trọng Tấn, *Từ Đồng Quan Đến Điện Biên [From Dong Quan to Dien Bien]* (Hanoi: People's Army Publishing House, 2002), 334; Nguyễn Tiến Hùng, *Lịch Sử Sư Đoàn 316 (1951–2001) [History of Division 316 (1951–2001)]* (Hanoi: People's Army Publishing House, 2001), 122; Various, *Vài Hồi Ức Về Điện Biên Phú, Tập I [A Few Memories About Dien Bien Phu, Volume I]* (Hanoi: People's Army Publishing House, 1977), 165–166.

24 *Lettre de Dutel à Bruge, 16 Mars 1998* (Bruge Collection, Box 26); Mengelle, *des chars et des hommes*, 287; *Synthèse des renseignements reccueillis auprès des blessés libérés par le VM – 3eme partie récits de combat: Récit de l'adjudant Cordier* (10H179, SHD) 2–4; Georges Fleury, *le Para* (Paris: Grasset, 1982), 346–354.

25 GONO BQR, *N°79/40: Situation à 0000h, 2 mai.*

26 *Lettre de De la Malène à Bruge, 30 Avril 1996* (Bruge Collection, Box 27).

27 *Lettre de Perret à Bruge, 14 Février 1999* (Bruge Collection, Box 28).

28 Fall, *Hell*, 345.

29 vnmilitaryhistory.net, *Trận Điện Biên Phủ 20/11/1953 – 7/5/1954 [Overwhelming Dien Bien Phu 20/11/1953 – 7/5/1954]* http://www.vnmilitaryhistory.net/index.php?topic=1936.210;wap2 and http://www.vnmilitaryhistory.net/index.php?topic=1936.200 (both accessed on Oct 24, 2017). These posts discuss a series of articles dealing with the 209th Regiment at Điện Biên Phủ that were written by Trần Quân Lập and Nguyễn Hữu Tài, and published in *Tạp Chí Lịch Sử Quân Sự [Military History Magazine]* Issues 9–11 of 2004, and Issues 1 and 5 of 2005.

30 Thánh Nhân Nguyễn, *Lịch sử Trung đoàn 209, Sư đoàn 7, Quân đoàn 4 (1947–2003) [History of Regiment 209, Division 7, Corps 4 (1947–2003)]* (Hanoi: People's Army Publishing House, 2004), 126; EMIFT, *Fiche de Renseignements par Courants Porteurs N°342.*

31 Võ Nguyên Giáp, Hữu Mai and Lady Borton, *Điện Biên Phủ: Rendezvous with History* (Hanoi, Thế Giới Publishers, 2004), 360.

32 Lê, *[From Dong Quan to Dien Bien Phu]*, 335.

33 Thánh, *[History of Regiment 209]*, 126; *Lettre de De la Malène à Bruge, 26 Juin 1995* and *Lettre compte-rendu de Chenel à Bruge, 1995* (both in Bruge Collection, Box 27).

34 *Lettre de De la Malène à Bruge, 26 Juin 1995*; Bruge, *Les hommes*, 384–390; Windrow, *Last Valley*, 582.

35 Phạm Văn Chiến, Phạm Văn Chanh, *Lịch sử Sư đoàn 304, Tập I (1950–1975)* *[History of Division 304, Volume I (1950–1975)]* (Hanoi: People's Army Publishing House, 2011), 161–163; Catroux Commission, *Document N°13c: Rapport du Colonel Lalande sur les combats du Centre de Resistance "Isabelle", JMO du C.R. Isabelle* (1R227, Dossier II-40, SHD), 6–7.

36 Windrow, *Last Valley*, 583.

37 Fall, *Hell*, 354.

38 John Prados, *Operation Vulture* (New York: ibooks, inc., 2002), 156–159.

39 Mengelle, *des chars et des hommes*, 288.

40 *JMO du C.R. Isabelle*, 7; Reginald Wieme de Ruddere, *Journal des Marches et Opérations du Groupement Wieme (Groupement mobile Tai n° 5) à Dien Bien Phu Pendant la Campagne du 1er Décembre 1953 au 31 Mai 1954* (publisher unidentified, 1999), 121.

41 Ministry of Defense, *[Selected Docs]*, 538–539.

42 Fall, *Hell*, 357–359.

43 *ibid.*, 360–361; Windrow, *Last Valley*, 586–587.

44 Fall, *Hell*, 360–361.

45 EMIFT, *Fiche de Renseignements par Courants Porteurs N°358 reçus de Hanoi le 4 Mai 1954 à 9h30* (10H179, SHD).

46 Wieme, *JMO du Groupement Wieme*, 121.

47 Kim, *[History of Regiment 36]*, 108.

48 See Windrow, *Last Valley*, 589; Fall, *Hell*, 363.

49 *Luc Olivier conversation with Luciani, 11 December 2016.*

50 Kim Lê and Huy Tòan Lê, *Lịch sử Trung đoàn 36 (Sư đoàn 308, quân đoàn 1)* *[History of Regiment 36 (Division 308, Corps I)]* (Hanoi, Cực chính trị Quân Đòan I, 1990), 108.

51 *ibid.*, 109

52 Fall, *Hell*, 363; *Lettre de Nicod à Bruge, 27 Novembre 1997* (Bruge Collection, Box 28); *Lettre du Dr Premillieu à Bruge, 8 Décembre 1995* (Bruge Collection, Box 29).

53 Fall, *Hell*, 363.

54 *Lettre de Ulpat à Bruge, 17 Avril 1997* (Bruge Collection, Box 29); Mengelle, *des chars et des hommes*, 294; Bruge, *Les hommes*, 400–401.

55 GONO BQR, *N°15/40: Situation à 10h00, 4 mai.*

56 Windrow, *Last Valley*, 590.

57 Fall, *Hell*, 360.

58 FTNV, *Largages Nuit du 4 au 5 Mai 1954 sur Dien Bien Phu* (10H1166, SHD).

59 Windrow, *Last Valley*, 593.

60 *ibid.*, 592.

61 EMIFT, *Fiche à l'attention du Général Commandant en Chef, Réservé de G.O.N.O., Journée du 5 et nuit 5 au 6* (10H179, SHD).

62 Fall, *Hell*, 367.

63 EMIFT, *Fiche de Renseignements par Courants Porteurs N°383 reçus de Hanoi le 8.5.54 à 7h30* (10H179, SHD).

64 Windrow, *Last Valley*, 549.

65 *ibid.*, 593–594.

66 GONO, *Texte nº09/06, 5 mai* (10H116, SHD).

67 Windrow, *Last Valley*, 596–597.

68 Rapport sur l'appui aérien en Indochine, *De Répartition des Sorties "FEU" Selon les Périodes et Selon Les Différentes Missions, Mai 1954* (10H1170, SHD).

69 *ibid.*, 597; GONO BQR, *Nº45/40: Situation à 1200 heures, 6 mai.*

70 Windrow, *Last Valley*, 597–598.

71 *ibid.*, 598.

72 Thanh, *vu d'en face*, 205–206.

73 Giáp, *Rendezvous*, 353.

74 *ibid.*, 304; Văn, *["Hero" Infantry Regiment 174]*, 169.

75 Ngọc An, "Tiểu Đoàn Hóa Tiên 224" [Rocket Battalion 224], *Tạp chí Lịch sử Quân sự [Military History Magazine]*, Issue 4 (July–Aug 1997), 58; Nguyen, *[People's Artillery of Vietnam, Volume I]*, 371; Thanh, *vu d'en face*, 227.

76 Giáp, *Rendezvous*, 368–369; Thanh, *vu d'en face*, 227, asserts that H6s actually opened fire at 1930.

77 Văn, *["Hero" Infantry Regiment 174]*, 169–170; Thanh, *vu d'en face*, 219–220; Giáp, *Rendezvous*, 367–369. It's impossible to reconcile Vietnamese and French accounts of the mine's detonation, which the latter place at 2300.

78 Lê Huy Toàn, *Trung đoàn Thủ Đô [Capital Regiment], (Hanoi: People's Army Publishing House, 1992)*, 141; *Lettre de Schmitz à Bruge, 27Juillet 1997* (Bruge Collection, Box 26); Fall, *Hell*, 369–370.

79 Lê, *[Capital Regiment]*, 142; *Mémoire du capitaine Philippe au 4 mai 1954* (1KT935, SHD); I/2 REI, *JMO pour la période du 1er Mars 1954 au 7 Mai 1954* (7U625, SHD), 17; Mengelle, *des chars et des hommes*, 298–299.

80 GONO BQR, *Nº52/40: Situation à 2400 heures, 7 mai.*

81 *Thanh, vu d'en face*, 219.

82 Guy Vaillant, *Rapport du Colonel Vaillant sur l'artillerie dans la bataille de Dien Bien Phu*, 12 Octobre, 1954 (1K233, SHD), Part I, 11.

83 GONO, *Nº52/40: Situation à 2400 heures, 7 mai*; Fall, *Hell*, 388.

84 *Lettre de Redon à Bruge, 22 Août 1995* (Bruge Collection, Box 29).

85 Văn, *["Hero" Infantry Regiment 174]*, 170–171.

86 Fall, *Hell*, 374.

87 Văn, *["Hero" Infantry Regiment 174]*, 173–174.

88 Pierre Langlais, "La dernière nuit de DBP," *Bérêt Rouge*, n°39 (Avril–Mai 1962), 25 [accessed online May 27, 2017 at http://fr.calameo.com/ read/0014251177f4a8ce1e152]; *Agenda du Lt Georges Roux tenu journalièrement pendant la bataille et la captivité* (1K594, SHD); *Lettres de Lecour-Grandmaison à Bruge, 10 Décembre 1997 et 30 Janvier 1998* (both in Bruge Collection, Box 27).

89 Nguyễn, *[History of Division 316]*, 125.

90 Windrow, *Last Valley*, 603; Fall, *Hell*, 383.

91 Văn, *["Hero" Infantry Regiment 174]*, 174.

92 Quoted in Fall, *Hell*, 388.

93 Fall, *Hell*, 388–389.

94   *Entretien Bruge avec Bizard, 15 Novembre 1995* (Bruge Collection, Box 26); *Lettre de Ulpat à Bruge, 29 Décembre 1995* (Bruge Collection, Box 29).

95   *Lettre de Ménage à Bruge, 3 Octobre 1995* (Bruge Collection, Box 28).

96   Lê, *[From Dong Quan to Dien Bien Phu]*, 336–337.

97   *ibid.*, 337; Bruge, *Les hommes*, 435.

98   Langlais, "La dernière nuit de DBP"; *Lettre de Ménage à Bruge, 30 Mai 1995* (Bruge Collection, Box 28).

99   Fall, *Hell*, 382.

100   *Lettre de Lepage à Bruge, 3 Juillet 1995* (Bruge Collection, Box 27).

101   Bruge, *Les hommes*, 436; Langlais, "La dernière nuit de DBP."

102   Lê, *[From Dong Quan to Dien Bien Phu]*, 337–338.

103   Fall, *Hell*, 392–393; Windrow, *Last Valley*, 609.

104   Bruge, *Les hommes*, 427; *Lettre de Tréhiou à Bruge 10 Octobre 1995* and *Lettre de Morel à Bruge, 26 Octobre 1995* (both in Bruge Collection, Box 29).

105   Mengelle, *des chars et des hommes*, 297.

106   Nguyễn, *[History of Division 316]*, 125–126.

107   *ibid.*, 126–127; Langlais, "La dernière nuit de DBP"; Mengelle, *des chars et des hommes*, 299.

108   Langlais, "La dernière nuit de DBP"; *Lettre de Tréhiou à la famille Dupire, 16 Octobre 1954* (Bruge Collection, Box 29); Fall, *Hell*, 387.

109   Lê, *[From Dong Quan to Dien Bien Phu]*, 341.

110   *Lettre de Lecour-Grandmaison à Bruge, 30 Janvier 1998.*

111   Giáp, *Rendezvous*, 373.

112   *[A Few Memories]*, 168.

113   Fall, *Hell*, 388.

114   Pierre Langlais, *Dien Bien Phu* (Paris: Editions France-Empire, 1963), *227.*

115   Thanh, *vu d'en face*, 228.

116   Fall, *Hell*, 392.

117   Thánh, *[History of Regiment 209]*, 127; Lê, *[From Dong Quan to Dien Bien Phu]*, 343.

118   I/2 REI, *JMO pour la période du 1er Mars 1954 au 7 Mai 1954*, 17.

119   Thánh, *[History of Regiment 209]*, 127; Lê, *[From Dong Quan to Dien Bien Phu]*, 343.

120   Giáp, *Rendezvous*, 375.

121   Pierre Rocolle, *Pourquoi Dien Bien Phu?* (Paris: Flammarion, 1968), 540.

122   Fall, *Hell*, 394–396

123   *ibid.*, 398; Windrow, *Last Valley*, 609.

124   Giáp, *Rendezvous*, 377.

125   Fall, *Hell*, 399; Windrow, *Last Valley*, 611.

126   Lê, *[From Dong Quan to Dien Bien Phu]*, 344–345; Thánh, *[History of Regiment 209]*, 128.

127   *Phone conversation Michel Sleurs and Luc Olivier, 26 October 2017.*

128   *Lettre de Nicod à Bruge, 27 Novembre 1997* and *Conférence du Capitaine Nicod à Marrakech le 15 avril 1955* (both in Bruge Collection, Box 28).

129   Giáp, *Rendezvous*, 378.

130 For example, *Contribution to the History of Dien Phu – Vietnamese Studies #3* (Hanoi: Foreign Languages Publishing House, 1965), 205–206.

131 Rocolle, *Pourquoi*, 538.

132 Windrow, *Last Valley*, 611–613; Fall, *Hell*, 402–408.

133 Windrow, *Last Valley*, 615.

134 *ibid.*

135 *ibid.*

136 Fall, *Hell*, 402; Thánh, *[History of Regiment 209]*, 128.

137 Lê, *[From Dong Quan to Dien Bien Phu]*, 345; Giáp, *Rendezvous*, 378.

138 Giáp, *Rendezvous*, 379.

139 *JMO du C.R. Isabelle*, 7.

140 Wieme, *JMO du Groupement Wieme*, 125–126; *Mémoire du Cdt Robert Lacote, novembre 1973* (1KT585, SHD); *JMO du C.R. Isabelle*, 7.

141 Phạm, *[History of Division 304]*, 167.

142 Wieme, *JMO du Groupement Wieme*, 126–127; Fall, *Hell*, 413–414.

143 *Lettre de Surbier à Bruge, 13 septembre 1997* (Bruge Collection, Box 28).

144 Wieme, *JMO du Groupement Wieme*, 127.

145 Windrow, *Last Valley*, 618.

146 Mengelle, *des chars et des hommes*, 313–316.

147 Phạm, *[History of Division 304]*, 167.

148 Wieme, *JMO du Groupement Wieme*, 129.

149 *ibid.*, 128–129; *Lettre de Michot à Bruge, 2 janvier 1998* (Bruge Collection, Box 28).

150 *ibid.*, 128–131.

Chapter 9

1 Martin Windrow, *The Last Valley: Dien Bien Phu and the French Defeat in Vietnam* (Cambridge, MA: Da Capo Press, 2004), 627–629.

2 Pierre Rocolle, *Pourquoi Dien Bien Phu?* (Paris: Flammarion, 1968), 548–549; Bohemia Interactive, *Dien bien phu 1954–2004: 50 years anniversary*, https://forums.bistudio.com/forums/topic/34966-dien-bien-phu-1954-2004-50-years-anniversary/ (accessed October 31, 2017).

3 Windrow, *Last Valley*, 622–623.

4 *ibid.*, 637–647; Bernard B. Fall, *Hell in a Very Small Place: The Siege of Dien Bien Phu* (New York & Philadelphia: Lippincott, 1967), 437–442.

5 Jules Roy, *La Bataille de Dien Bien Phu* (Paris: Rene Julliard, 1963), 572–573.

6 Văn Cẩn Phan, *Lịch sử Bộ Tổng tham mưu trong kháng chiến chống Pháp 1945–1954 [History of the General Staff in the Resistance War against the French 1945–1954]* (Hanoi: People's Army Publishing House, 1999), 799.

7 Ministry of Defense, General Logistics Department, *Công tác bảo đảm hậu cần trong chiến dịch Điện Biên Phủ: bài học kinh nghiệm và thực tiễn [Rear Services Support Operations During the Điện Biên Phủ Campaign: Lessons from Experience and Practice]* (Hanoi: People's Army Publishing House, 2004), 30, 161, 227.

8   Gia Đức Phạm et al., *Điện Biên Phủ, Mốc Vàng Thời Đại [Điện Biên Phủ: Landmark of the Golden Era]*, (Hanoi: People's Army Publishing House, 2004), 402.

9   Fredrik Logevall, *Embers of War: The Fall of an Empire and the Making of America's Vietnam* (New York: Random House, 2013), 549–616.

10   Windrow, *Last Valley*, 631–632.

11   Pierre Langlais, *Dien Bien Phu* (Paris: Éditions France-Empire, 1963), 256.

12   Quoted in Fall, *Hell*, 453.

13   Guy Vaillant, *Rapport du Colonel Vaillant sur l'artillerie dans la bataille de Dien Bien Phu*, 12 Octobre, 1954 (1K233, SHD), Annexe IV.

14   Henri Navarre, *Agonie de l'Indochine (1954–1954)* (Paris: Libraire Plon, 1958), 220.

15   Fall, *Hell*, 127.

16   Readers familiar with Jules Roy's *Battle of Điện Biên Phủ* (1966) may not be aware that the original *La Bataille de Điện Biên Phủ* from which it was abridged is twice as long, and contains masses of text, data, and documents that were excluded from the English-language edition.

17   Forces Terrestres Navales et Aériennes en Indochine, État-Major Interarmées et des Forces Terrestres, 1e Bureau, *Fiche: Aspect financier de l'opération de ĐIỆN BIÊN PHỦ, 1955* (10H1177, SHD), I Armement.

18   Fall, *Hell*, 451.

19   Navarre, *Agonie*, 220; Roy, *La Bataille*, 619.

20   Fall, *Hell*, 128, says 30,000 105mm shells and 100,000 of other calibers, but on page .451 Fall puts total shell consumption at 103,000. A transposition error for 130,000?

21   Commandement des Forces Terrestres du Nord Vietnam, Direction du Matériel, Section Munitions, *Nᵒ11/MU: État des munitions posées ou parachutées au profit du G.O.N.O. pendant les périodes du*, no date (CDHLE).

22   Fall, *Hell*, 451, 473 fn 2; Võ Nguyên Giáp, Hữu Mai and Lady Borton, *Dien Bien Phu: Rendezvous with History* (Hanoi, Thế Giới Publishers, 2004), 353.

23   Fall, *Hell*, 451; Ivan Cadeau, *Điện Biên Phủ: 13 mars – 7 mai* (Paris: Editions Tallardier, 2013), 188 fn13.

24   Guy Vaillant, *Rapport du Colonel Vaillant sur l'artillerie dans la bataille de Dien Bien Phu, 12 Octobre, 1954* (1K233, SHD), Annexe IV.

25   Windrow, *Last Valley*, 475.

26   Noam Chomsky and Howard Zinn, eds., *The Senator Gravel Edition – The Pentagon Papers: The Defense Department History of United States Decisionmaking in Vietnam, Volume I* (Boston: Beacon Press, 1972), 461–462.

27   *[Rear Services]*, 167.

28   Langlais, *Dien Bien Phu*, 149–150.

29   Logevall, *Embers of War*, 307–309.

30   Jacques Favreau & Nicolas Dufour, *Nasan: La Victoire Oubliée (1952–1953), Base Aéroterrestre au Tonkin* (Paris: Economica, 1999); Paul Gaujac, ed., *Histoire des Parachutistes Français, Volume II* (Paris: SPL, 1975), 362 Map.

31   Fall, *Hell*, 455.

32   *ibid.*

33   Windrow, *Last Valley*, 556–562.

34   Philippe Gras, *L'armée de l'air en Indochine: (1945–1954); l'impossible mission* (Paris, L'Harmattan, 2002), 559.

35   *ibid.*, 561.

36   Guy Vaillant, *Rapport du Colonel Vaillant sur l'artillerie dans la bataille de Dien Bien Phu*, 12 Octobre, 1954 (1K233, SHD), Annexe V.

Appendices

1   FTNV, 1ᵉ Bureau, *Effectifs présents à Dien Bien Phu à la date du 10 mars 1954* (10H1157, SHD).

2   Commandement des Forces Terrestres du Nord Vietnam, Direction du Matériel, Section Munitions, *N°11/MU: État des munitions posées ou parachutes au profit du G.O.N.O. pendant les périodes du, no date* (CDHLE).

3   Philippe Gras, *L'armée de l'air en Indochine: (1945-1954; l'impossible mission* (Paris, L'Harmattan, 2002), 540.

4   Forces Terrestres Navales et Aériennes en Indochine, État-Major Interarmées et des Forces Terrestres, 1e Bureau, *Fiche: Aspect financier de l'opération de ĐIỆN BIÊN PHỦ, 1955* (10H1177, SHD), I Armement.

INDEX

References to maps are in **bold**.